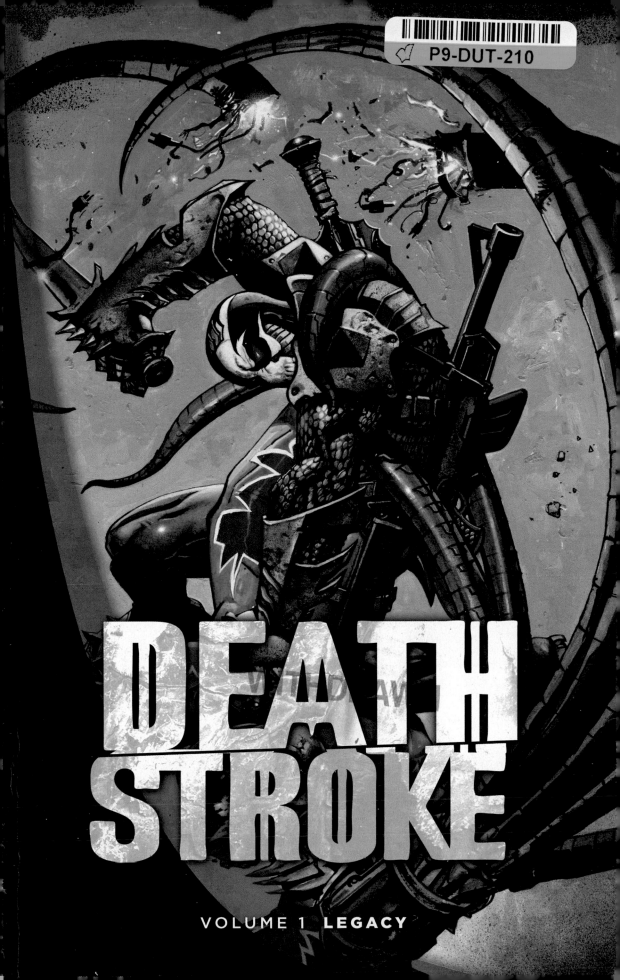

DEATH
STROKE

VOLUME 1 LEGACY

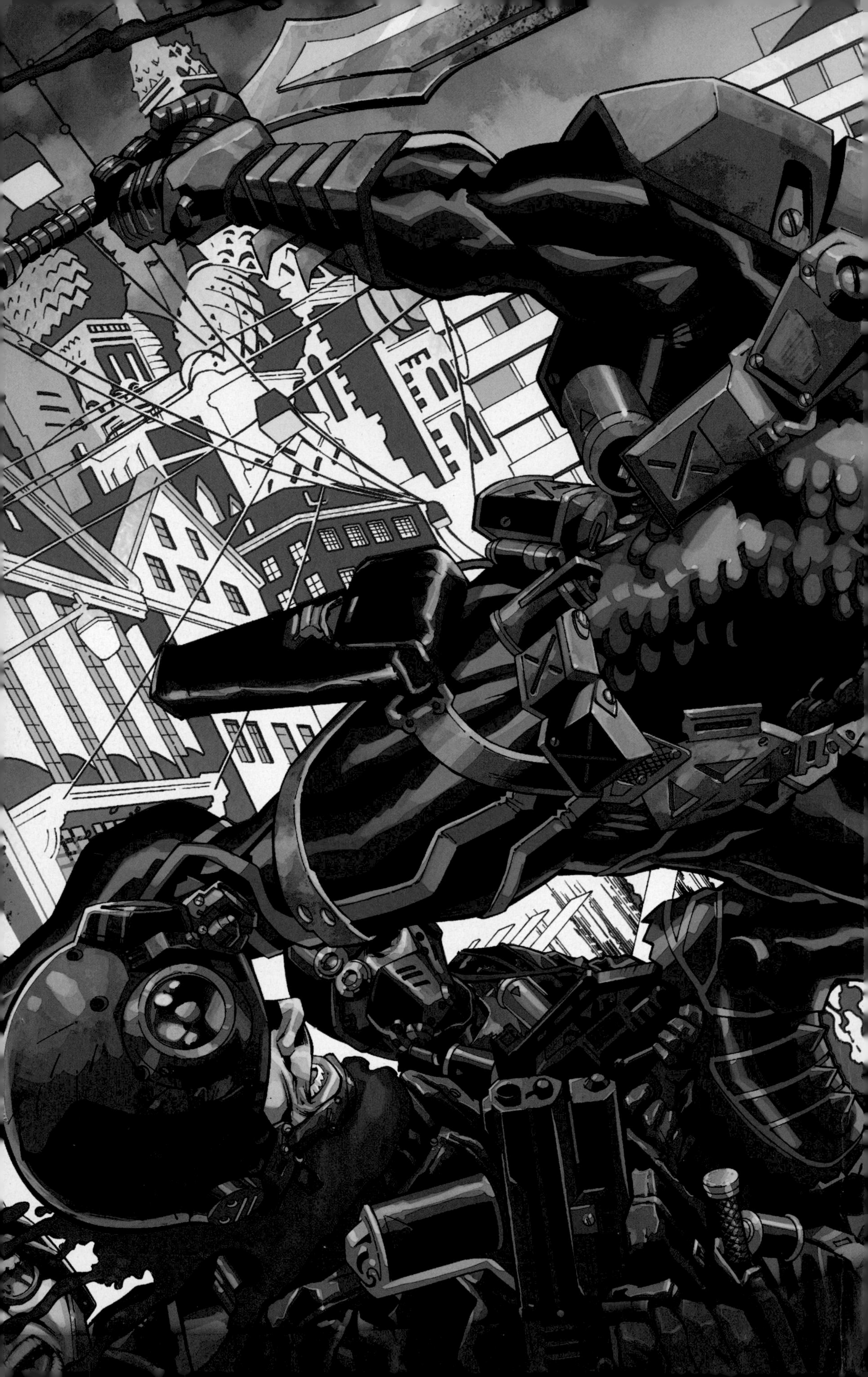

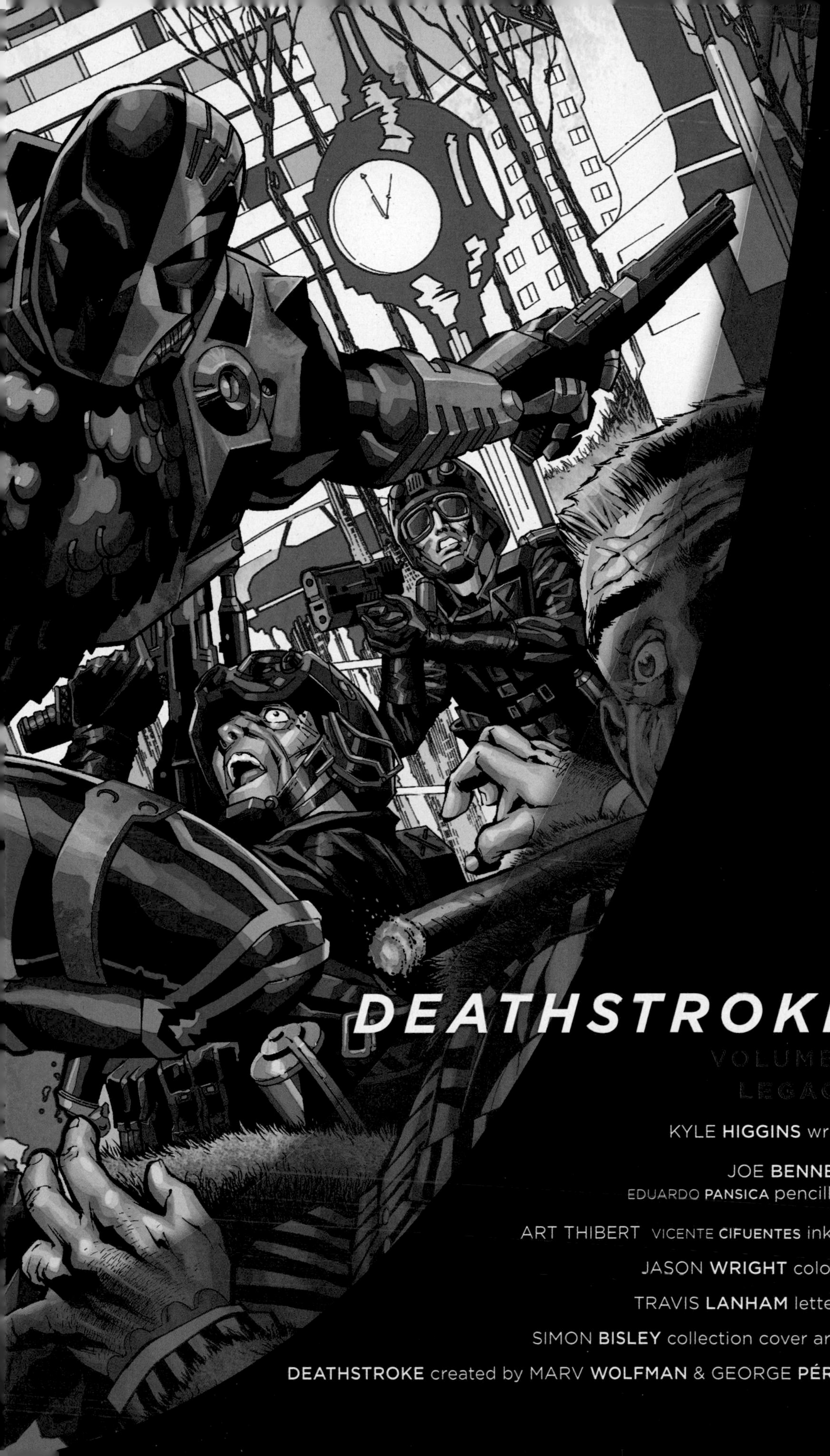

DEATHSTROKE

VOLUME 1
LEGACY

KYLE **HIGGINS** writer

JOE **BENNETT**
EDUARDO **PANSICA** pencillers

ART THIBERT VICENTE **CIFUENTES** inkers

JASON **WRIGHT** colorist

TRAVIS **LANHAM** letterer

SIMON **BISLEY** collection cover artist

DEATHSTROKE created by MARV **WOLFMAN** & GEORGE **PÉREZ**

RACHEL GLUCKSTERN BRIAN SMITH Editors – Original Series RICKEY PURDIN Assistant Editor – Original Series ROBIN WILDMAN Editor
ROBBIN BROSTERMAN Design Director – Books ROBBIE BIEDERMAN Publication Design

BOB HARRAS Senior VP – Editor-in-Chief, DC Comics

DIANE NELSON President DAN DIDIO and JIM LEE Co-Publishers GEOFF JOHNS Chief Creative Officer
AMIT DESAI Senior VP – Marketing & Franchise Management
AMY GENKINS Senior VP – Business and Legal Affairs NAIRI GARDINER Senior VP – Finance
JEFF BOISON VP – Publishing Planning MARK CHIARELLO VP – Art Direction and Design
JOHN CUNNINGHAM VP – Marketing TERRI CUNNINGHAM VP – Editorial Administration LARRY GANEM VP – Talent Relations & Services
ALISON GILL Senior VP – Manufacturing and Operations HANK KANALZ Senior VP – Vertigo and Integrated Publishing
JAY KOGAN VP – Business and Legal Affairs, Publishing JACK MAHAN VP – Business Affairs, Talent
NICK NAPOLITANO VP – Manufacturing Administration SUE POHJA VP – Book Sales FRED RUIZ VP – Manufacturing Operations
COURTNEY SIMMONS Senior VP – Publicity BOB WAYNE Senior VP – Sales

DEATHSTROKE VOLUME 1: LEGACY

DC Comics, 4000 Warner Blvd., Burbank, CA 91522
A Warner Bros. Entertainment Company.
Printed by Solisco Printers, Scott, QC, Canada. 9/23/15. Fifth Printing.
ISBN: 978-1-4012-3481-2

Library of Congress Cataloging-in-Publication Data

Higgins, Kyle, 1985-
Deathstroke volume 1 : legacy / Kyle Higgins, Joe Bennett, Art Thibert.
p. cm.
"Originally published in single magazine form in DEATHSTROKE 1-8."
ISBN 978-1-4012-3481-2
I. Bennett, Joe. II. Thibert, Art. III. Title. IV. Title: Legacy.
PN6728.D363H54 2012
741.5'973–dc23

2012015217

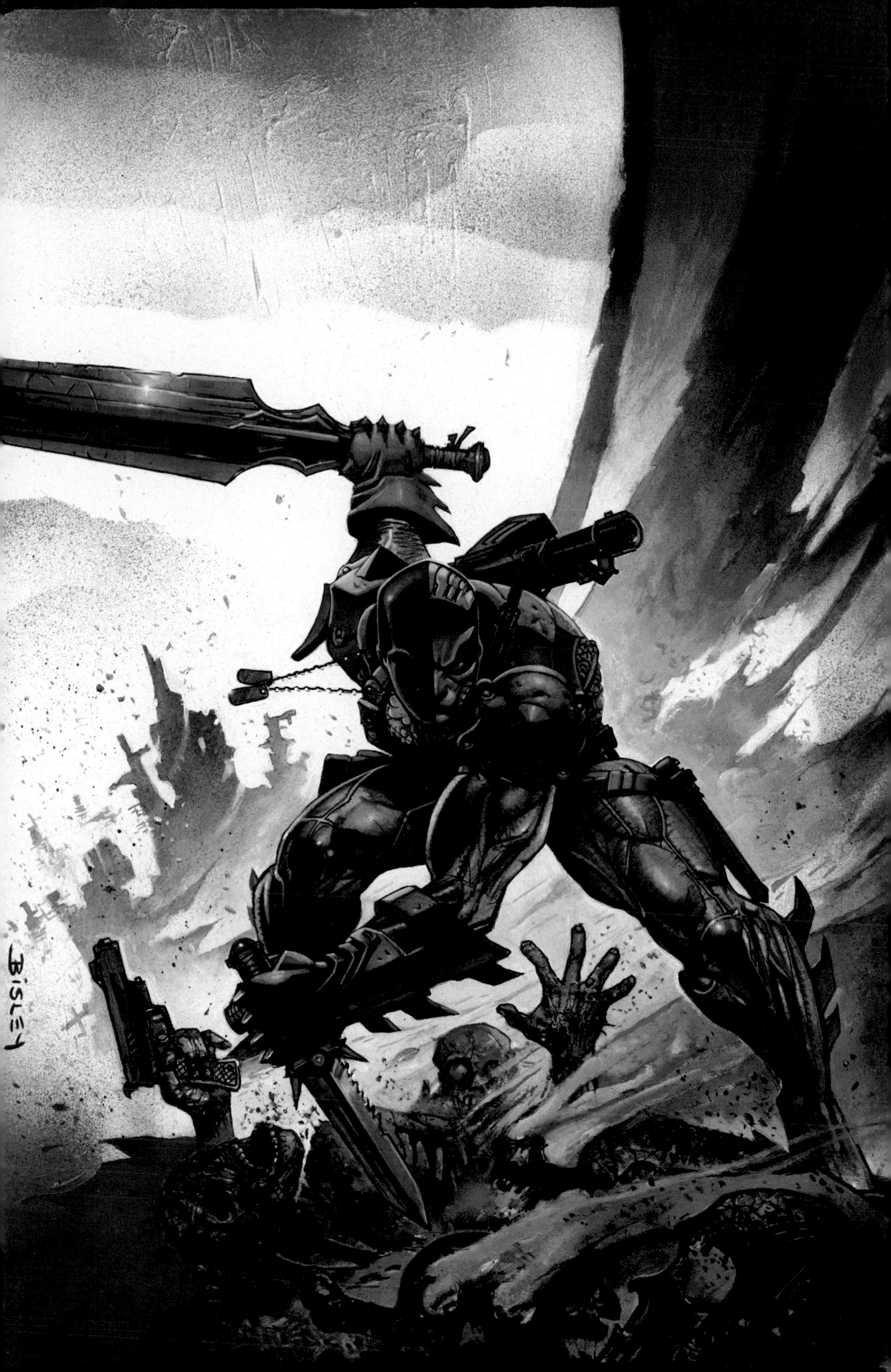
BISLEY

BACK TO BASICS

KYLE HIGGINS writer **JOE BENNETT** penciller **ART THIBERT** inker cover by **SIMON BISLEY**

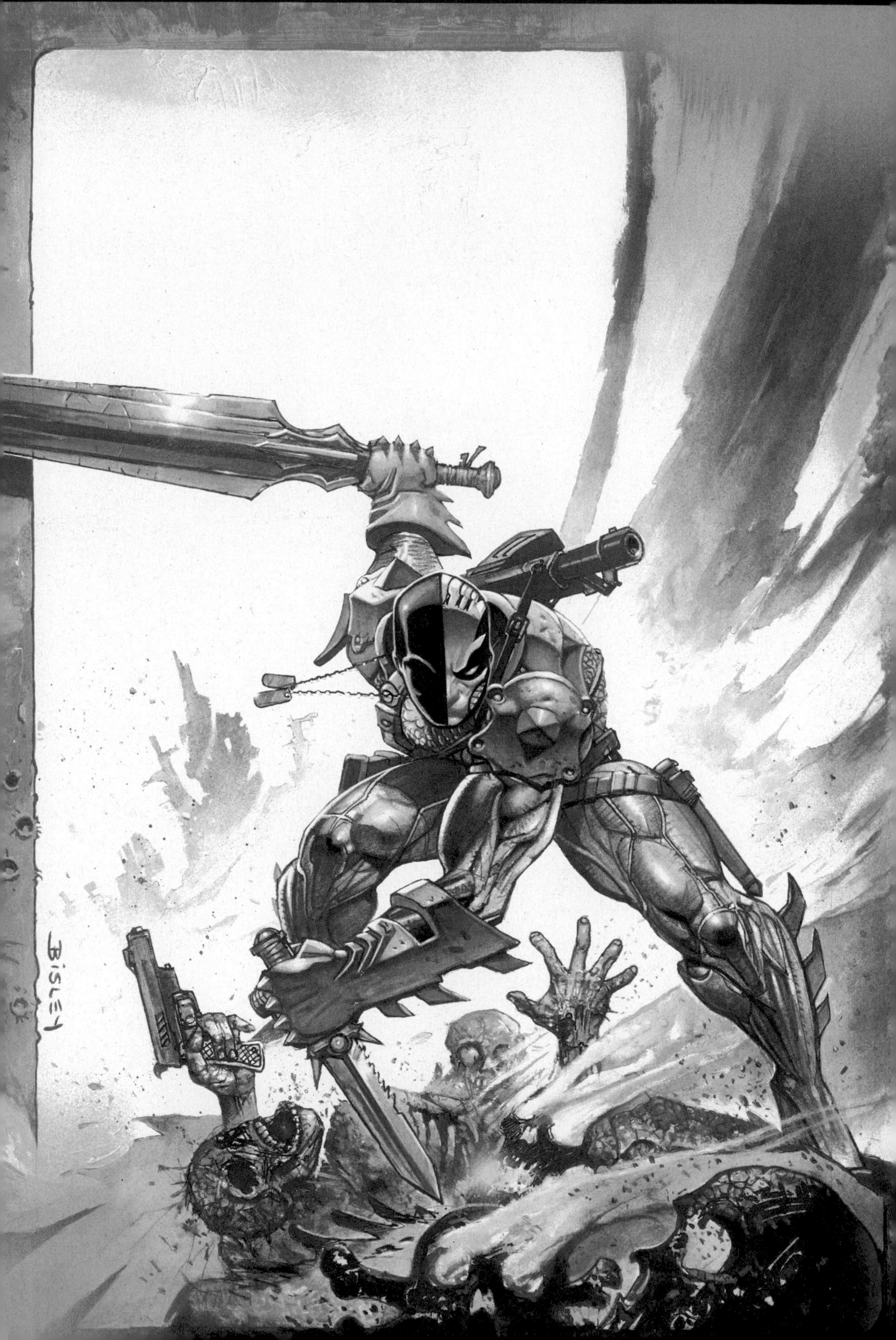

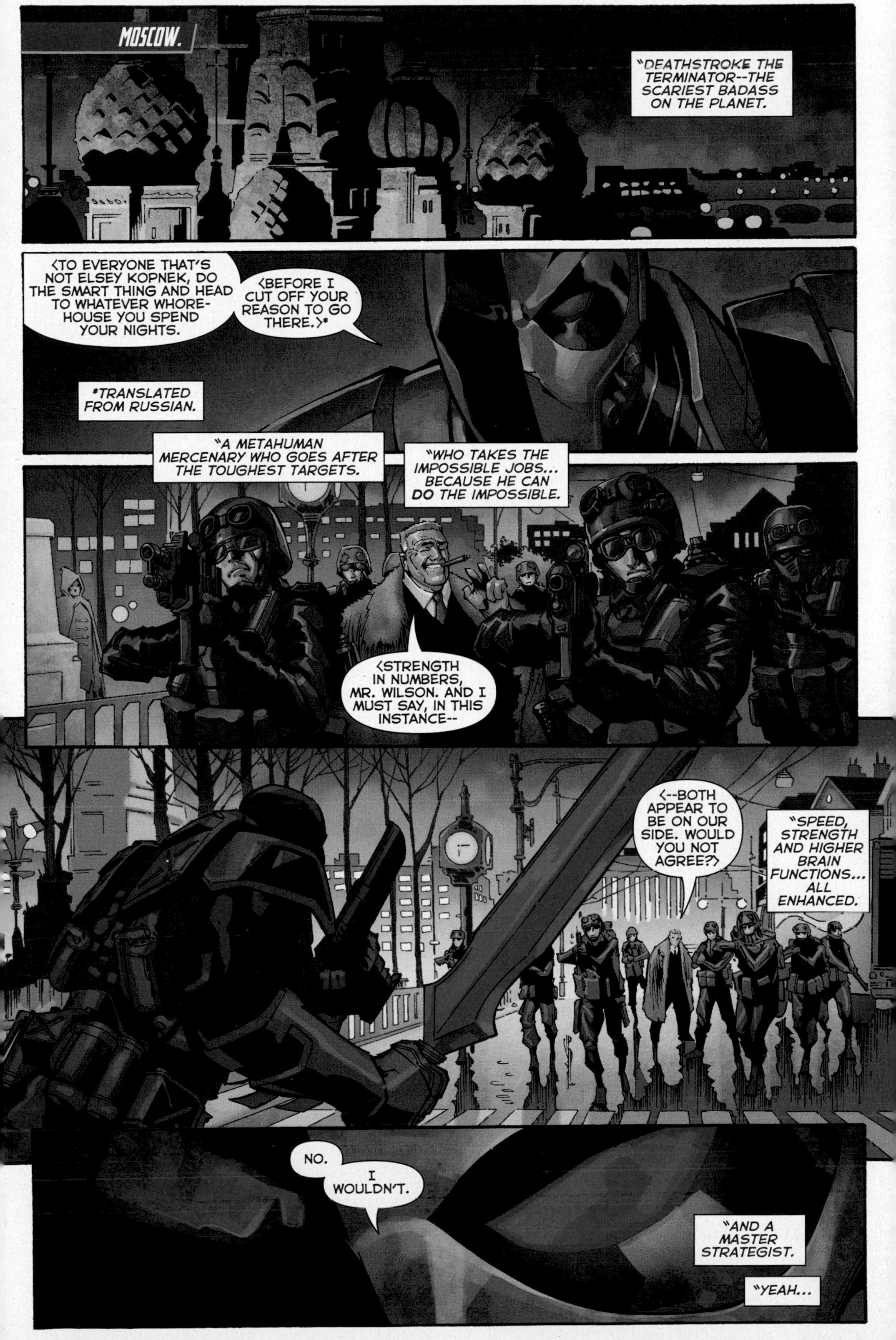
MOSCOW.
"DEATHSTROKE THE TERMINATOR--THE SCARIEST BADASS ON THE PLANET.
<TO EVERYONE THAT'S NOT ELSEY KOPNEK, DO THE SMART THING AND HEAD TO WHATEVER WHORE-HOUSE YOU SPEND YOUR NIGHTS.
<BEFORE I CUT OFF YOUR REASON TO GO THERE.>*
*TRANSLATED FROM RUSSIAN.
"A METAHUMAN MERCENARY WHO GOES AFTER THE TOUGHEST TARGETS.
"WHO TAKES THE IMPOSSIBLE JOBS... BECAUSE HE CAN DO THE IMPOSSIBLE.
<STRENGTH IN NUMBERS, MR. WILSON. AND I MUST SAY, IN THIS INSTANCE--
<--BOTH APPEAR TO BE ON OUR SIDE. WOULD YOU NOT AGREE?>
"SPEED, STRENGTH AND HIGHER BRAIN FUNCTIONS... ALL ENHANCED.
NO.
I WOULDN'T.
"AND A MASTER STRATEGIST.
"YEAH...

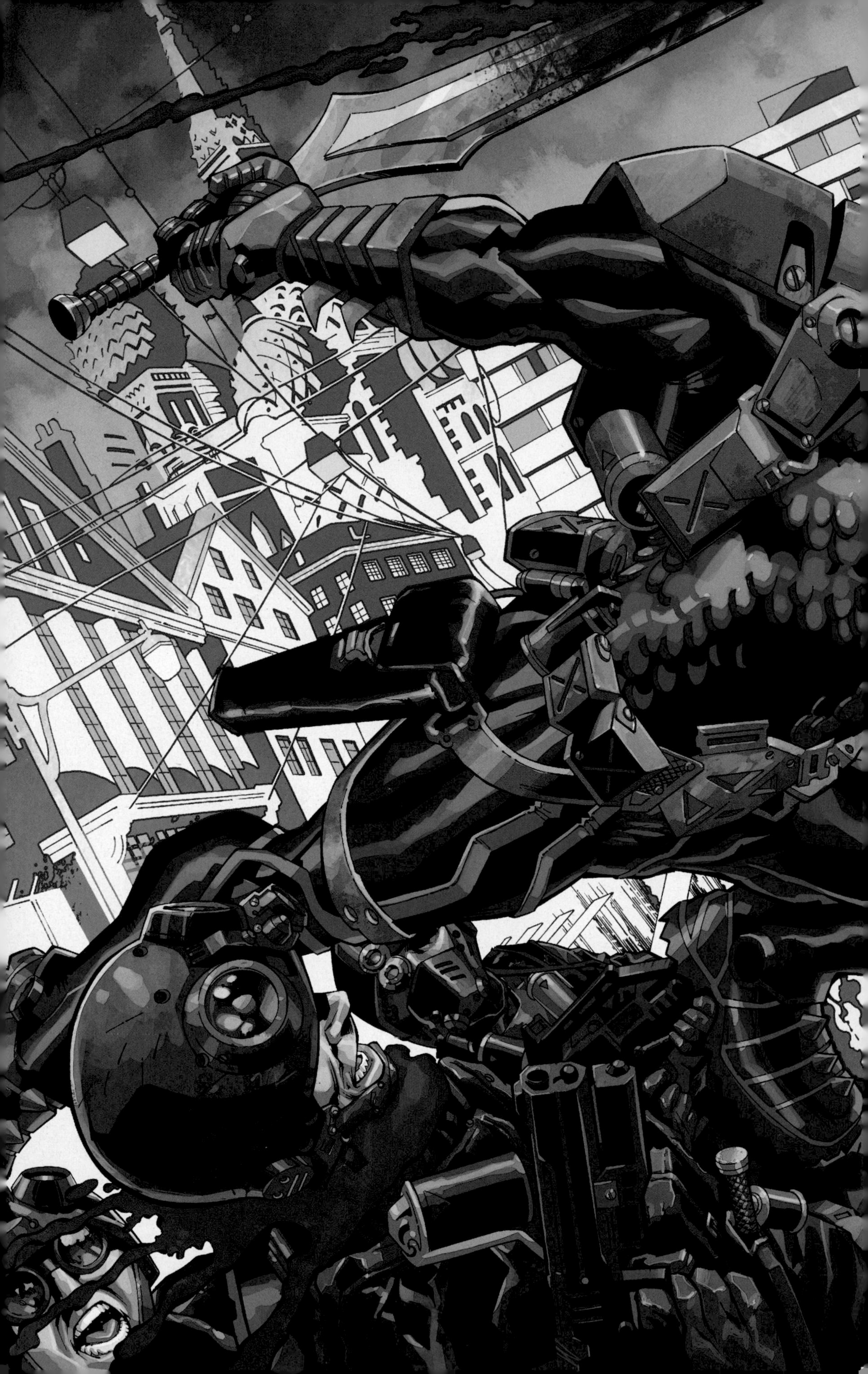

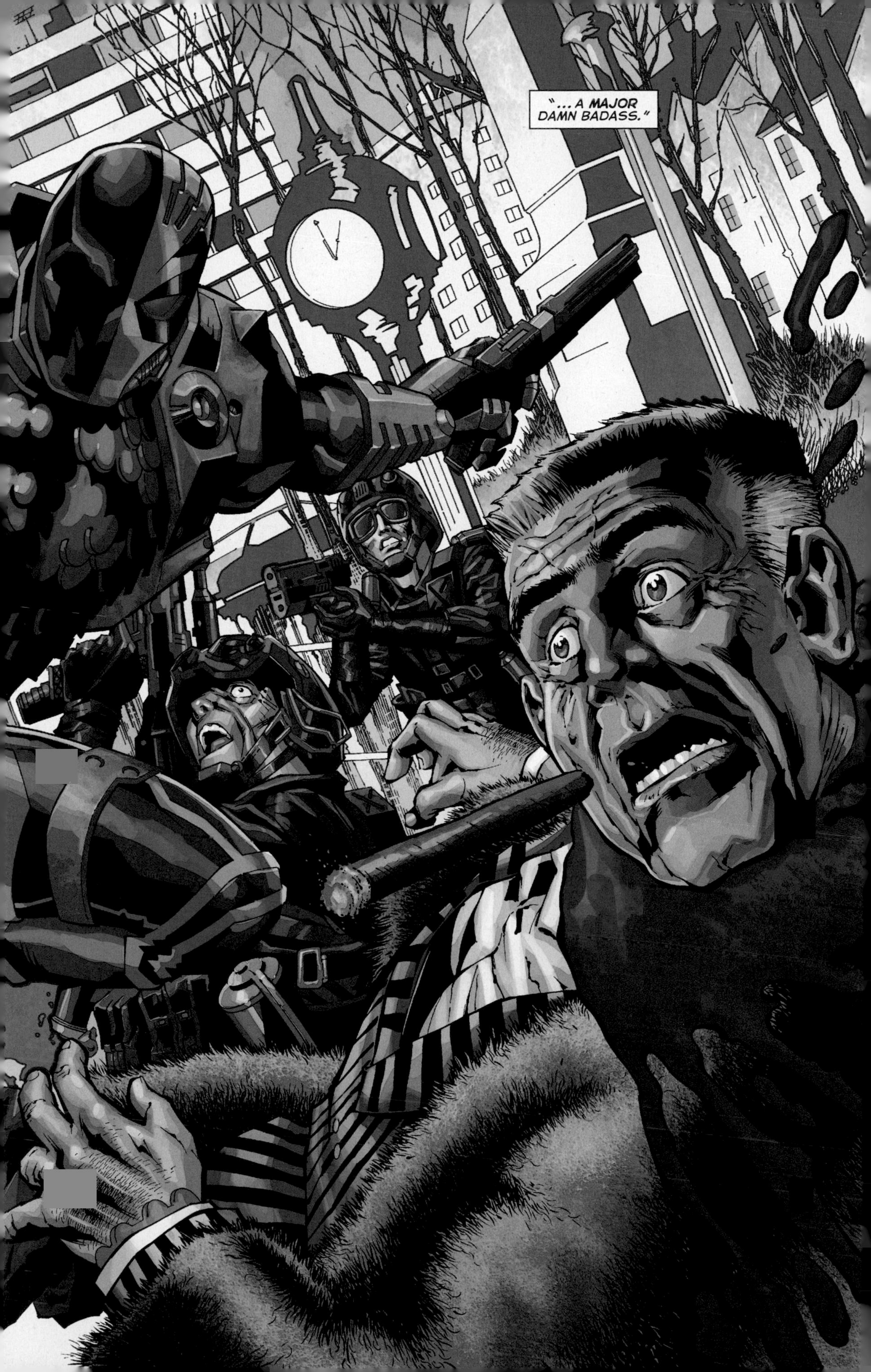
"... A MAJOR DAMN BADASS."

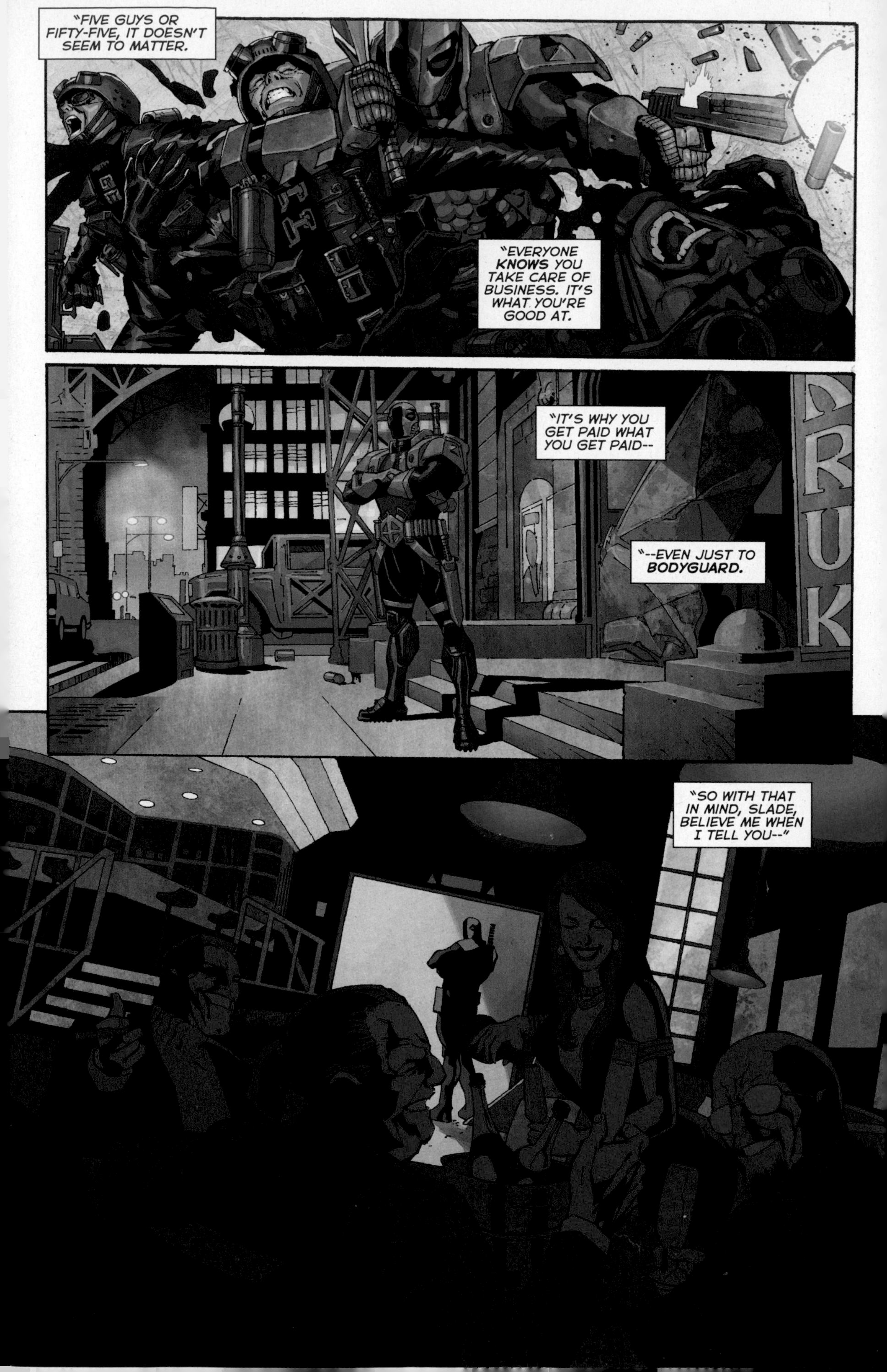
"FIVE GUYS OR FIFTY-FIVE, IT DOESN'T SEEM TO MATTER.
"EVERYONE **KNOWS** YOU TAKE CARE OF BUSINESS. IT'S WHAT YOU'RE GOOD AT.
"IT'S WHY YOU GET PAID WHAT YOU GET PAID--
"--EVEN JUST TO **BODYGUARD.**
DRUK
"SO WITH THAT IN MIND, SLADE, BELIEVE ME WHEN I TELL YOU--"

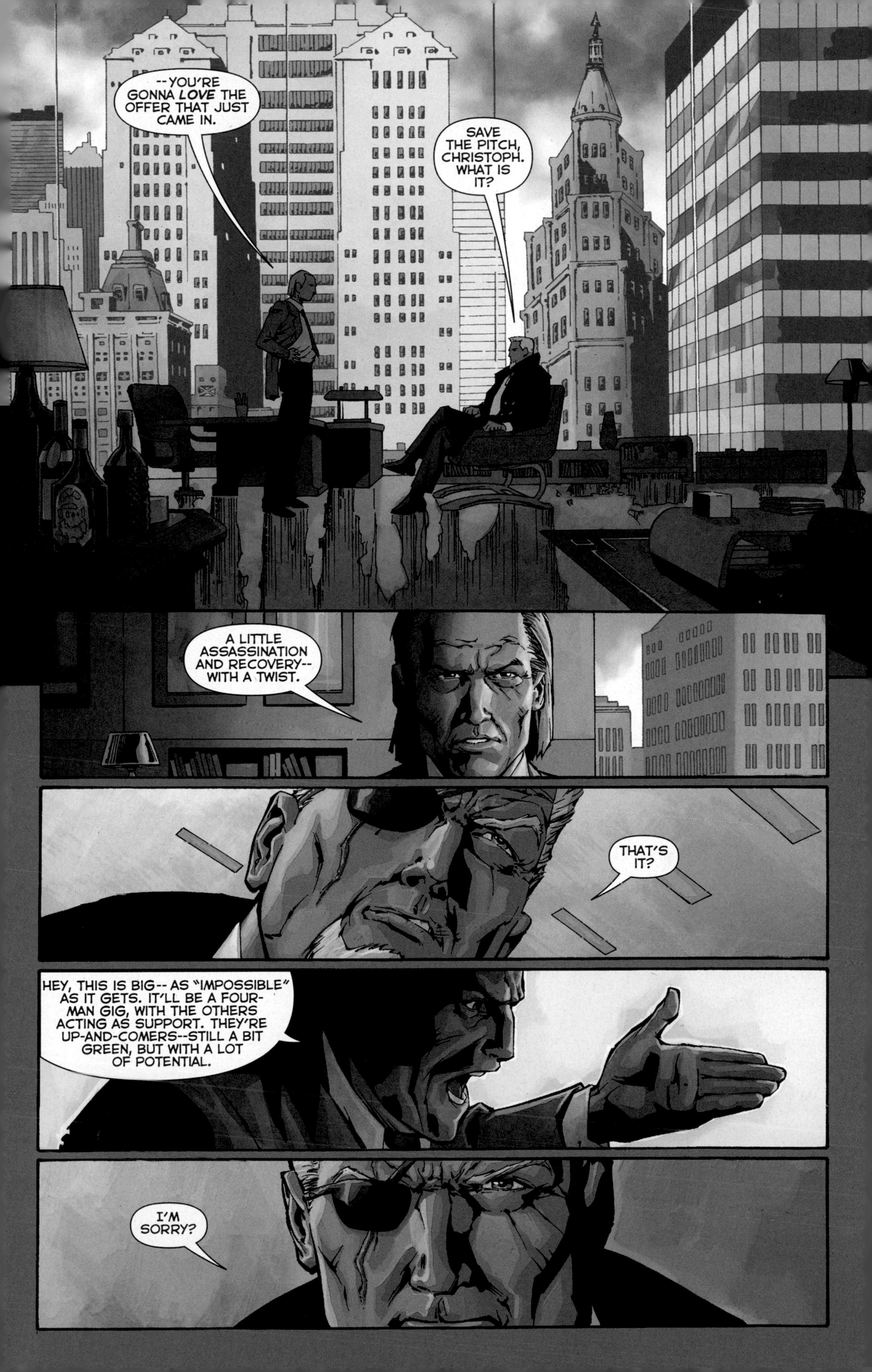
--YOU'RE GONNA *LOVE* THE OFFER THAT JUST CAME IN.
SAVE THE PITCH, CHRISTOPH. WHAT IS IT?
A LITTLE ASSASSINATION AND RECOVERY-- WITH A TWIST.
THAT'S IT?
HEY, THIS IS BIG-- AS "IMPOSSIBLE" AS IT GETS. IT'LL BE A FOUR-MAN GIG, WITH THE OTHERS ACTING AS SUPPORT. THEY'RE UP-AND-COMERS--STILL A BIT GREEN, BUT WITH A LOT OF POTENTIAL.
I'M SORRY?

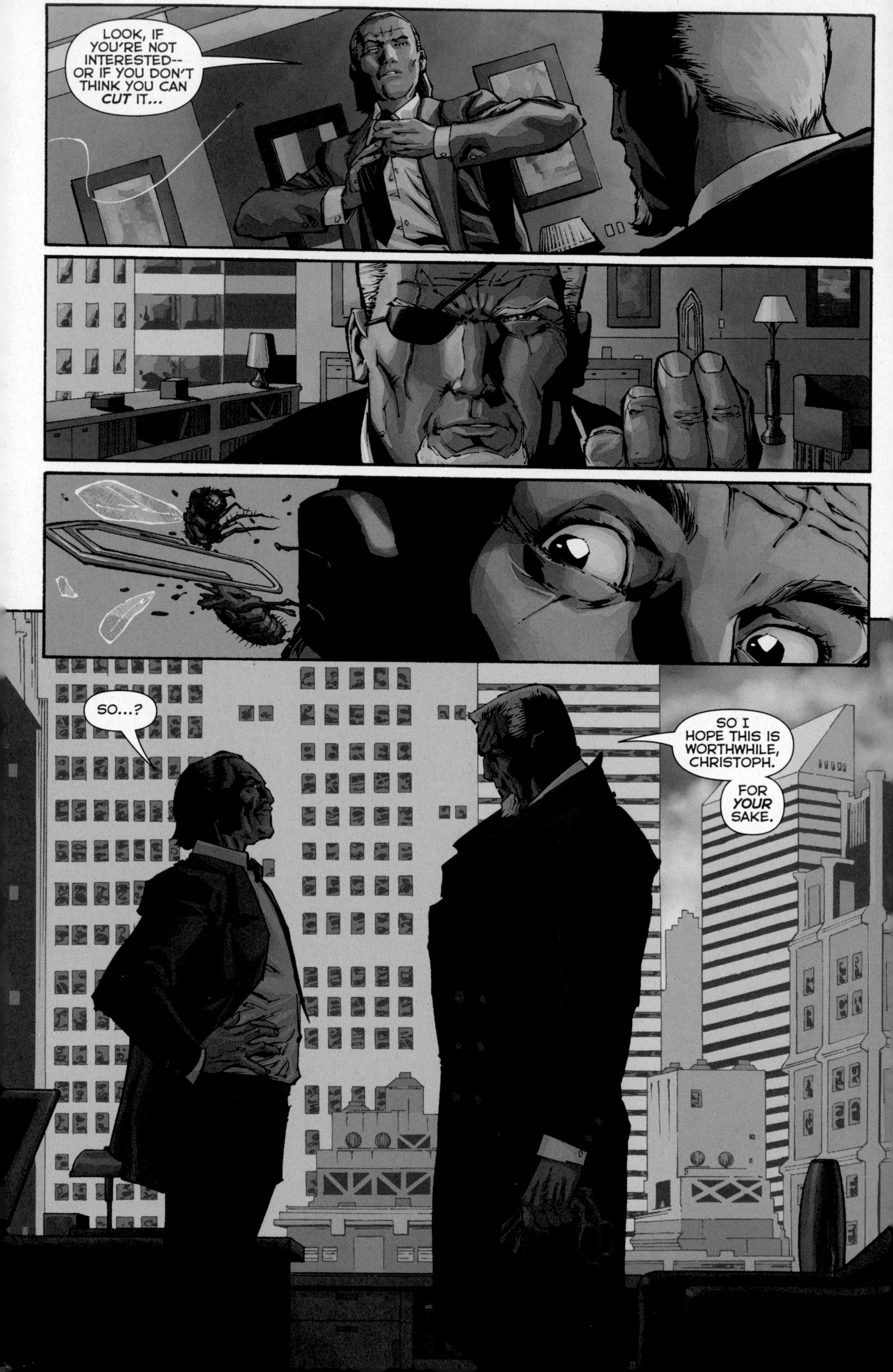
LOOK, IF YOU'RE NOT INTERESTED-- OR IF YOU DON'T THINK YOU CAN CUT IT...
SO...?
SO I HOPE THIS IS WORTHWHILE, CHRISTOPH.
FOR YOUR SAKE.

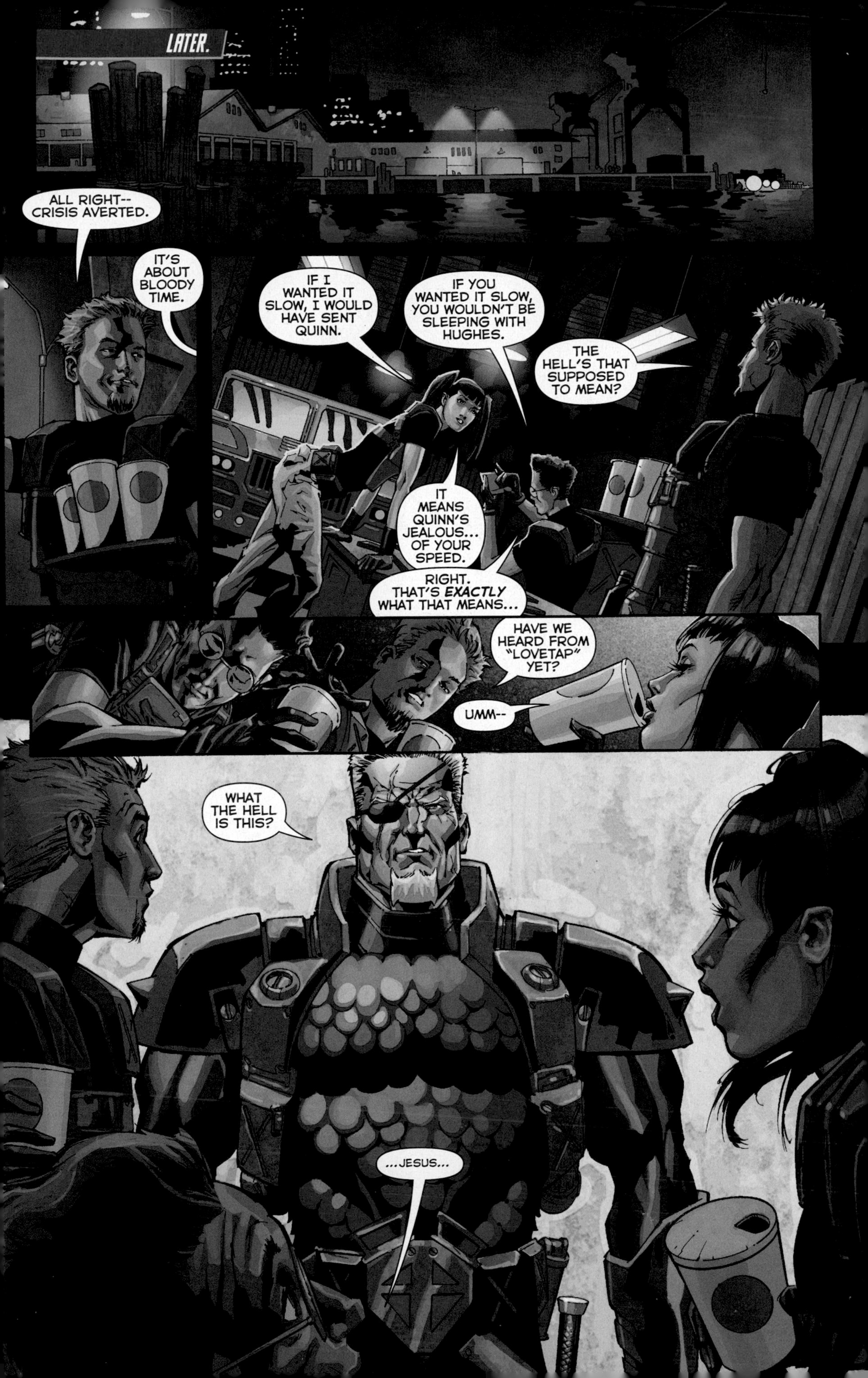
LATER.
ALL RIGHT-- CRISIS AVERTED.
IT'S ABOUT BLOODY TIME.
IF I WANTED IT SLOW, I WOULD HAVE SENT QUINN.
IF YOU WANTED IT SLOW, YOU WOULDN'T BE SLEEPING WITH HUGHES.
THE HELL'S THAT SUPPOSED TO MEAN?
IT MEANS QUINN'S JEALOUS... OF YOUR SPEED.
RIGHT. THAT'S *EXACTLY* WHAT THAT MEANS...
HAVE WE HEARD FROM "LOVETAP" YET?
UMM--
WHAT THE HELL IS THIS?
...JESUS...

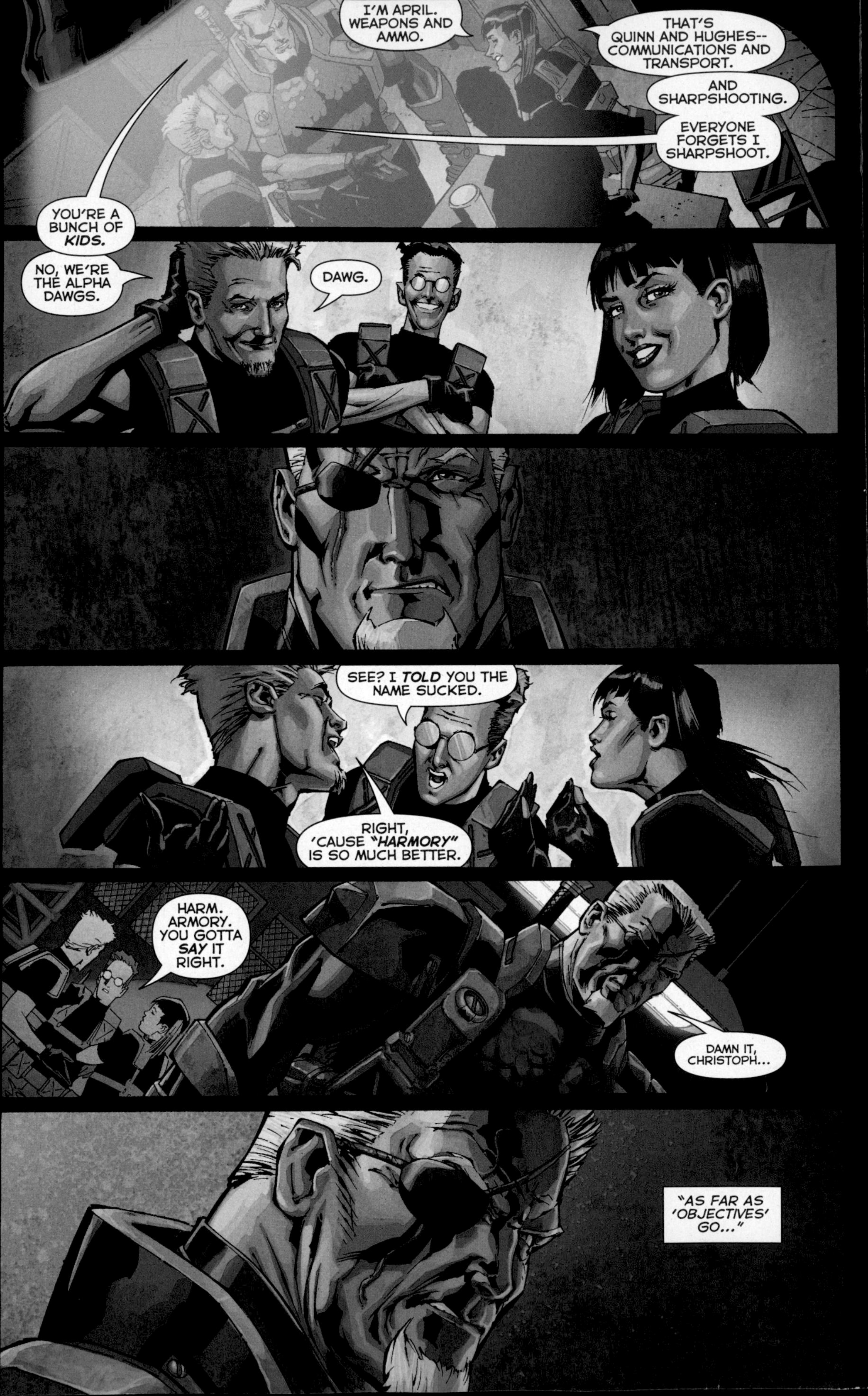
I'M APRIL. WEAPONS AND AMMO.
THAT'S QUINN AND HUGHES-- COMMUNICATIONS AND TRANSPORT.
AND SHARPSHOOTING.
EVERYONE FORGETS I SHARPSHOOT.
YOU'RE A BUNCH OF KIDS.
NO, WE'RE THE ALPHA DAWGS.
DAWG.
SEE? I TOLD YOU THE NAME SUCKED.
RIGHT, 'CAUSE "HARMORY" IS SO MUCH BETTER.
HARM. ARMORY. YOU GOTTA SAY IT RIGHT.
DAMN IT, CHRISTOPH...
"AS FAR AS 'OBJECTIVES' GO..."

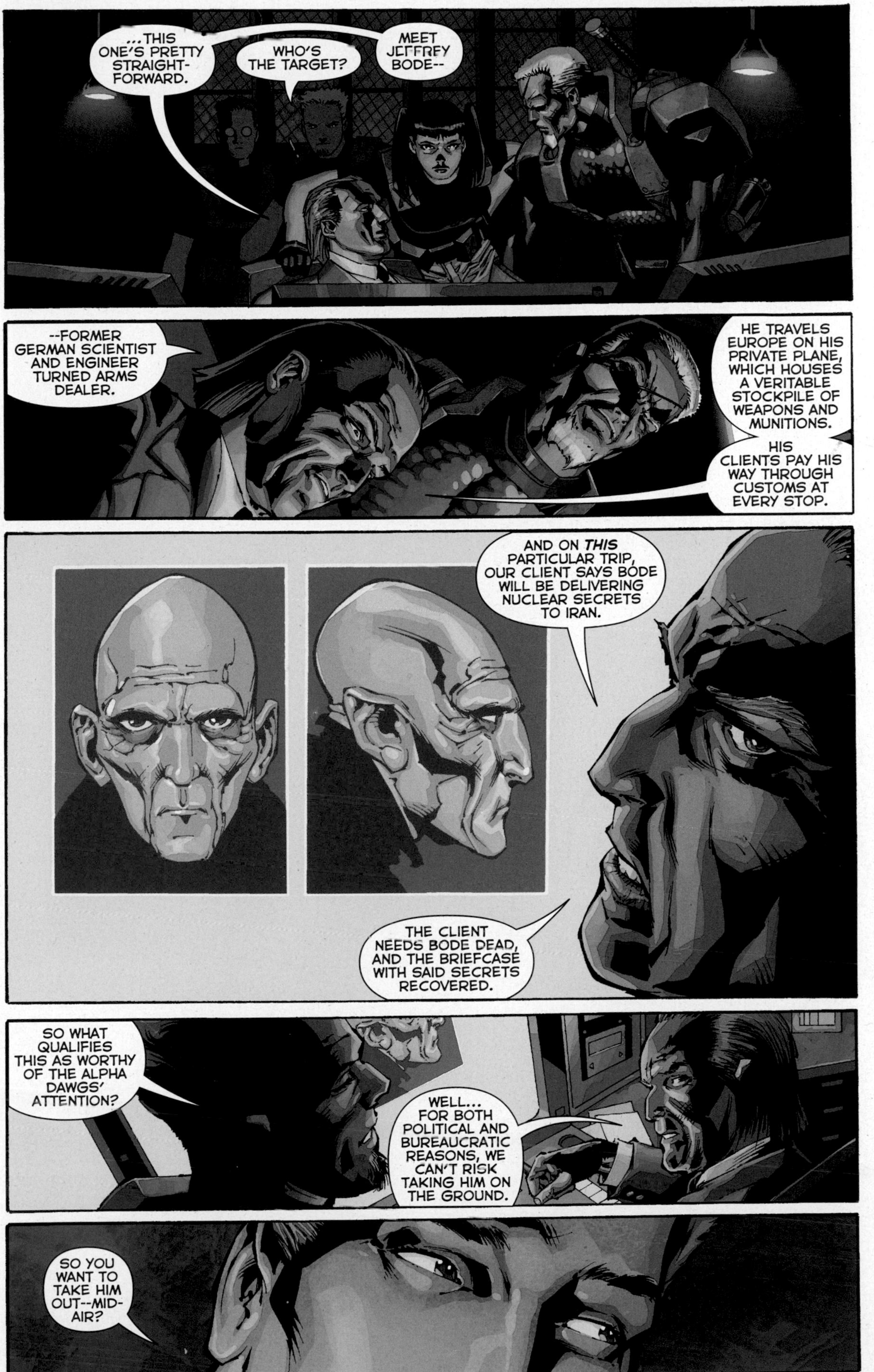
...THIS ONE'S PRETTY STRAIGHT-FORWARD.
WHO'S THE TARGET?
MEET JEFFREY BODE--
--FORMER GERMAN SCIENTIST AND ENGINEER TURNED ARMS DEALER.
HE TRAVELS EUROPE ON HIS PRIVATE PLANE, WHICH HOUSES A VERITABLE STOCKPILE OF WEAPONS AND MUNITIONS.
HIS CLIENTS PAY HIS WAY THROUGH CUSTOMS AT EVERY STOP.
AND ON THIS PARTICULAR TRIP, OUR CLIENT SAYS BODE WILL BE DELIVERING NUCLEAR SECRETS TO IRAN.
THE CLIENT NEEDS BODE DEAD, AND THE BRIEFCASE WITH SAID SECRETS RECOVERED.
SO WHAT QUALIFIES THIS AS WORTHY OF THE ALPHA DAWGS' ATTENTION?
WELL... FOR BOTH POLITICAL AND BUREAUCRATIC REASONS, WE CAN'T RISK TAKING HIM ON THE GROUND.
SO YOU WANT TO TAKE HIM OUT--MID-AIR?

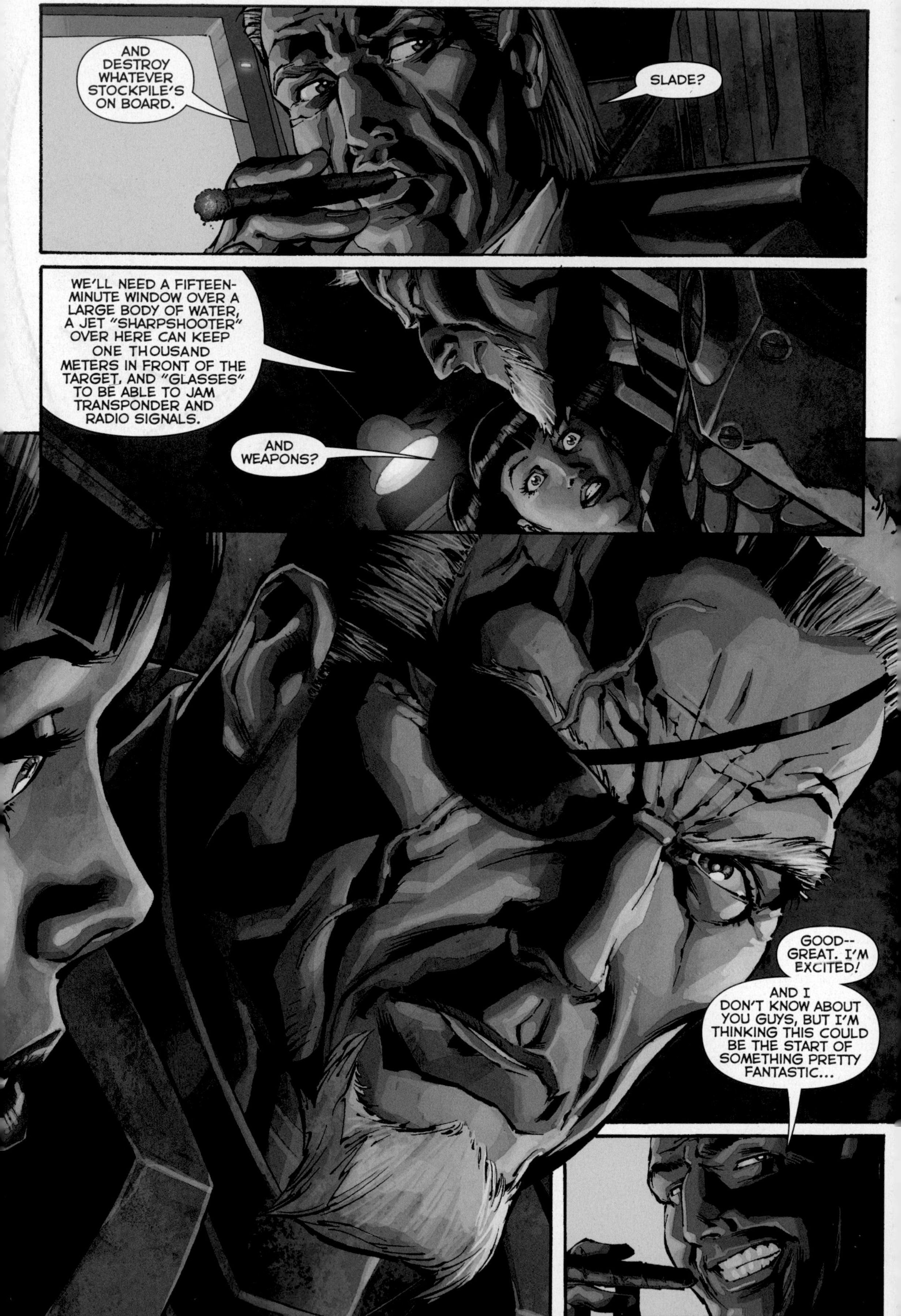
AND DESTROY WHATEVER STOCKPILE'S ON BOARD.
SLADE?
WE'LL NEED A FIFTEEN-MINUTE WINDOW OVER A LARGE BODY OF WATER, A JET "SHARPSHOOTER" OVER HERE CAN KEEP ONE THOUSAND METERS IN FRONT OF THE TARGET, AND "GLASSES" TO BE ABLE TO JAM TRANSPONDER AND RADIO SIGNALS.
AND WEAPONS?
GOOD--GREAT. I'M EXCITED!
AND I DON'T KNOW ABOUT YOU GUYS, BUT I'M THINKING THIS COULD BE THE START OF SOMETHING PRETTY FANTASTIC...

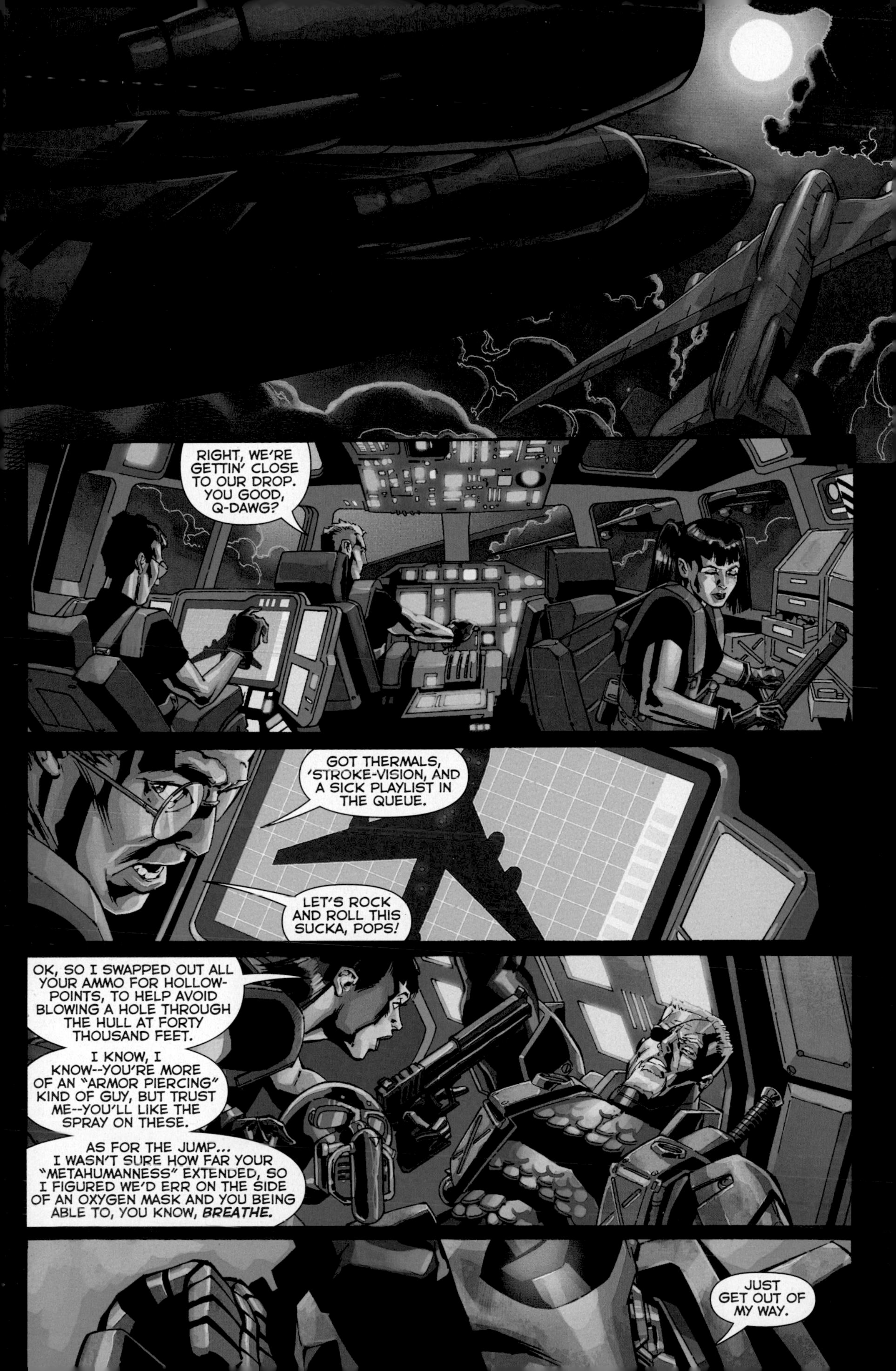
RIGHT, WE'RE GETTIN' CLOSE TO OUR DROP. YOU GOOD, Q-DAWG?
GOT THERMALS, 'STROKE-VISION, AND A SICK PLAYLIST IN THE QUEUE.
LET'S ROCK AND ROLL THIS SUCKA, POPS!
OK, SO I SWAPPED OUT ALL YOUR AMMO FOR HOLLOW-POINTS, TO HELP AVOID BLOWING A HOLE THROUGH THE HULL AT FORTY THOUSAND FEET.
I KNOW, I KNOW--YOU'RE MORE OF AN "ARMOR PIERCING" KIND OF GUY, BUT TRUST ME--YOU'LL LIKE THE SPRAY ON THESE.
AS FOR THE JUMP... I WASN'T SURE HOW FAR YOUR "METAHUMANNESS" EXTENDED, SO I FIGURED WE'D ERR ON THE SIDE OF AN OXYGEN MASK AND YOU BEING ABLE TO, YOU KNOW, *BREATHE.*
JUST GET OUT OF MY WAY.

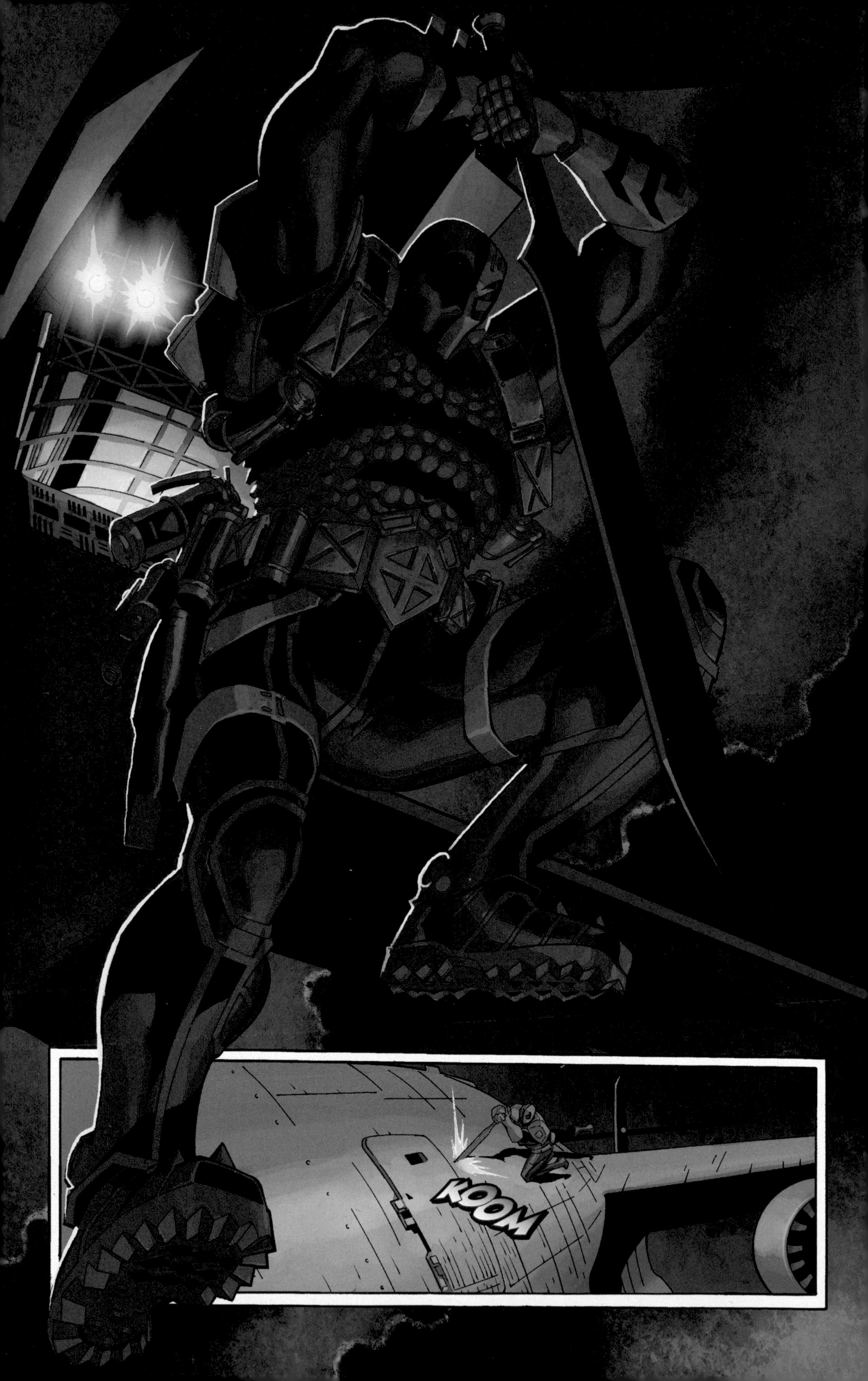
KOOM

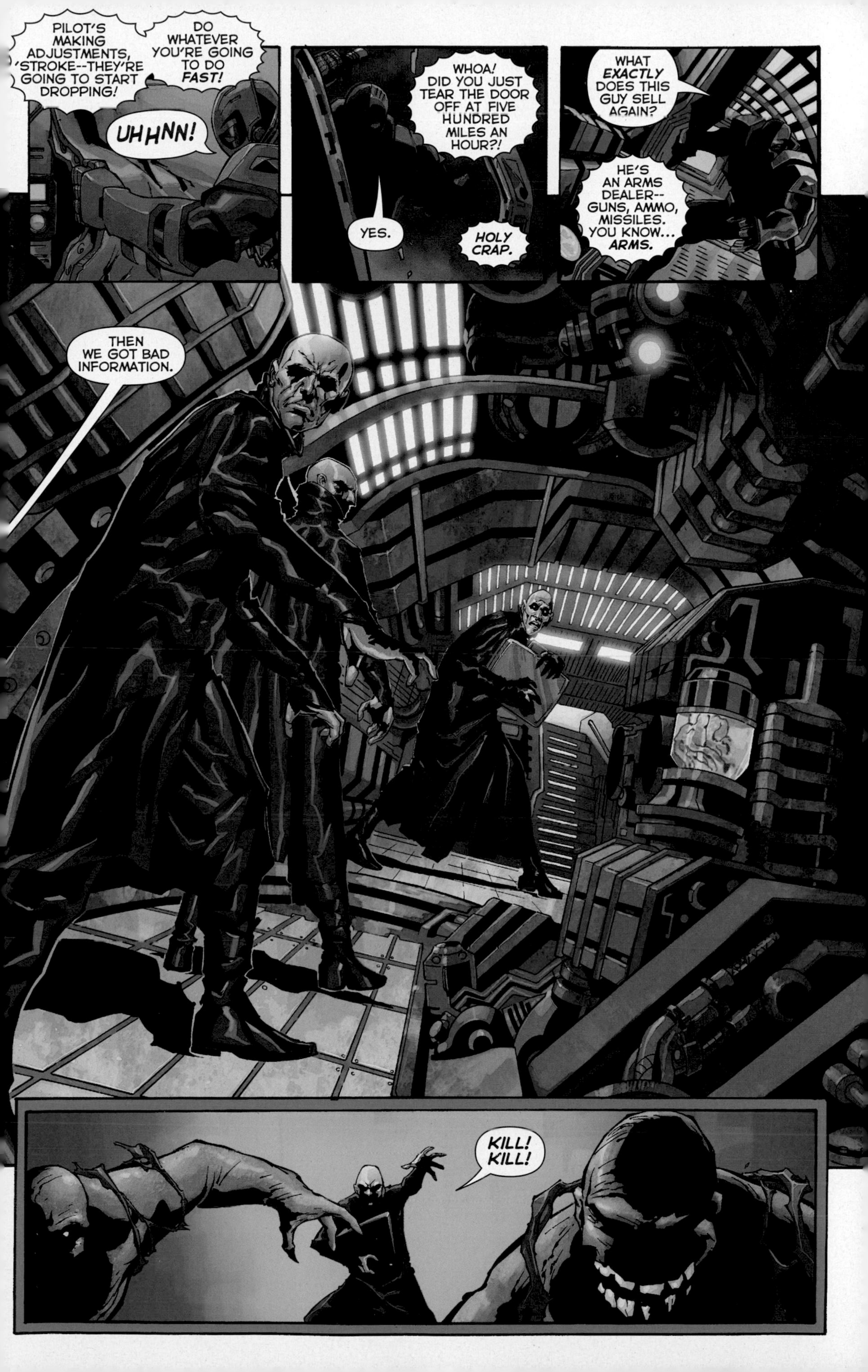
PILOT'S MAKING ADJUSTMENTS, 'STROKE--THEY'RE GOING TO START DROPPING!
DO WHATEVER YOU'RE GOING TO DO *FAST!*
UHHNN!
WHOA! DID YOU JUST TEAR THE DOOR OFF AT FIVE HUNDRED MILES AN HOUR?!
YES.
HOLY CRAP.
WHAT *EXACTLY* DOES THIS GUY SELL AGAIN?
HE'S AN ARMS DEALER--GUNS, AMMO, MISSILES. YOU KNOW... *ARMS.*
THEN WE GOT BAD INFORMATION.
KILL! KILL!

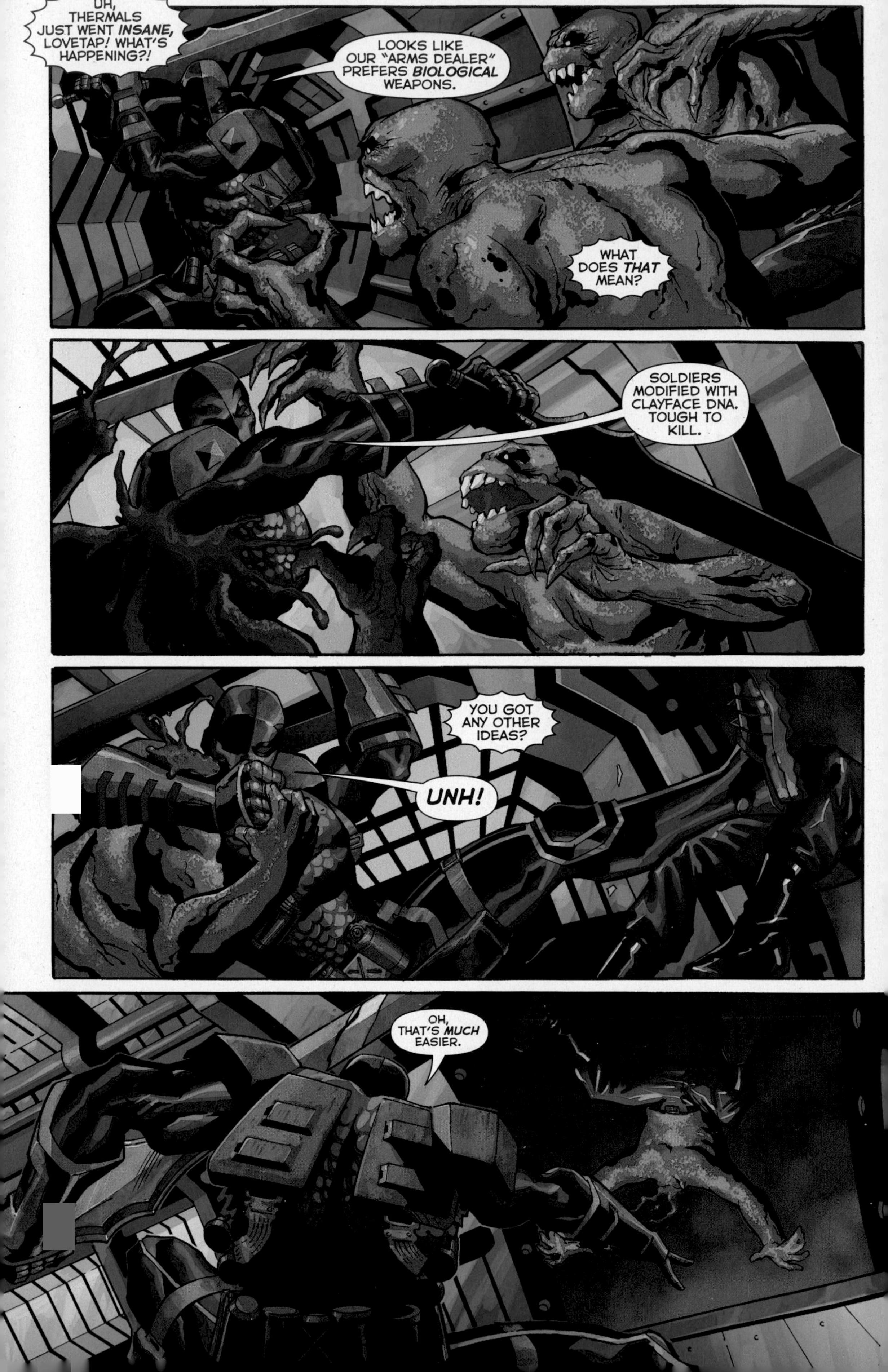
UH, THERMALS JUST WENT *INSANE,* LOVETAP! WHAT'S HAPPENING?!
LOOKS LIKE OUR "ARMS DEALER" PREFERS *BIOLOGICAL* WEAPONS.
WHAT DOES *THAT* MEAN?
SOLDIERS MODIFIED WITH CLAYFACE DNA. TOUGH TO KILL.
YOU GOT ANY OTHER IDEAS?
UNH!
OH, THAT'S *MUCH* EASIER.

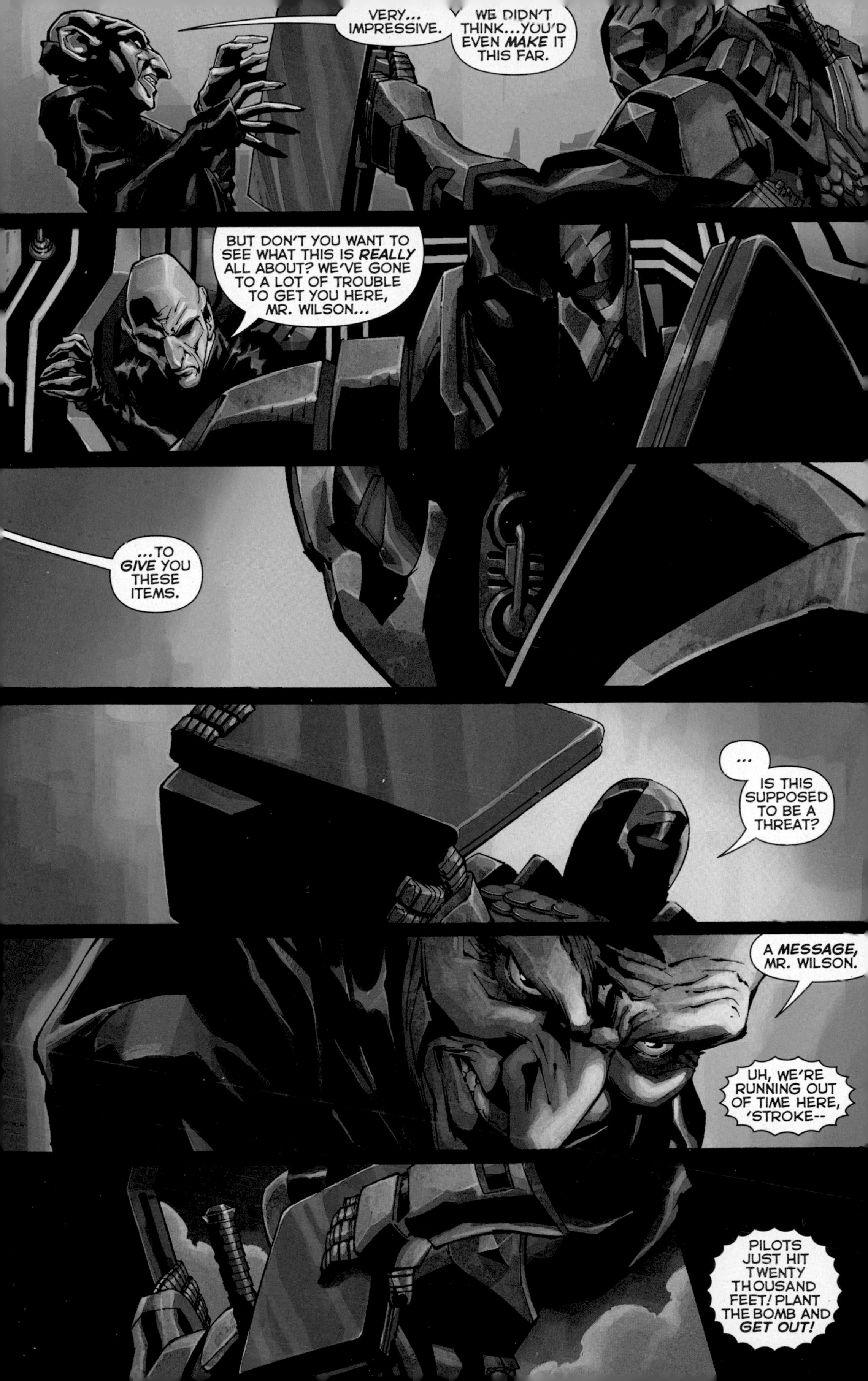
VERY... IMPRESSIVE.
WE DIDN'T THINK...YOU'D EVEN MAKE IT THIS FAR.
BUT DON'T YOU WANT TO SEE WHAT THIS IS REALLY ALL ABOUT? WE'VE GONE TO A LOT OF TROUBLE TO GET YOU HERE, MR. WILSON...
...TO GIVE YOU THESE ITEMS.
...
IS THIS SUPPOSED TO BE A THREAT?
A MESSAGE, MR. WILSON.
UH, WE'RE RUNNING OUT OF TIME HERE, 'STROKE--
PILOTS JUST HIT TWENTY THOUSAND FEET! PLANT THE BOMB AND GET OUT!

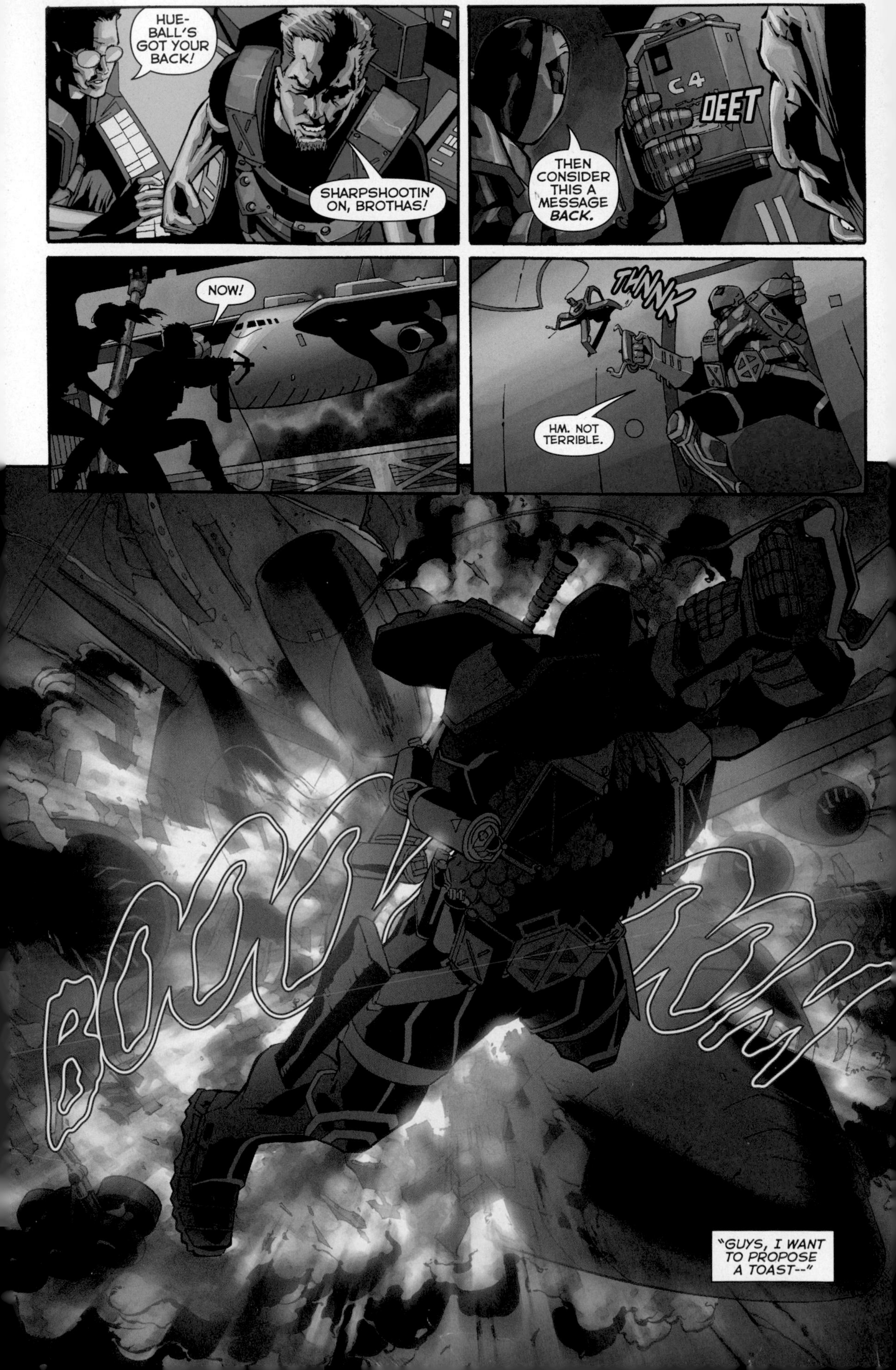
HUE-BALL'S GOT YOUR BACK!
SHARPSHOOTIN' ON, BROTHAS!
C4
DEET
THEN CONSIDER THIS A MESSAGE BACK.
NOW!
THNNK
HM. NOT TERRIBLE.
BOOM
"GUYS, I WANT TO PROPOSE A TOAST--"

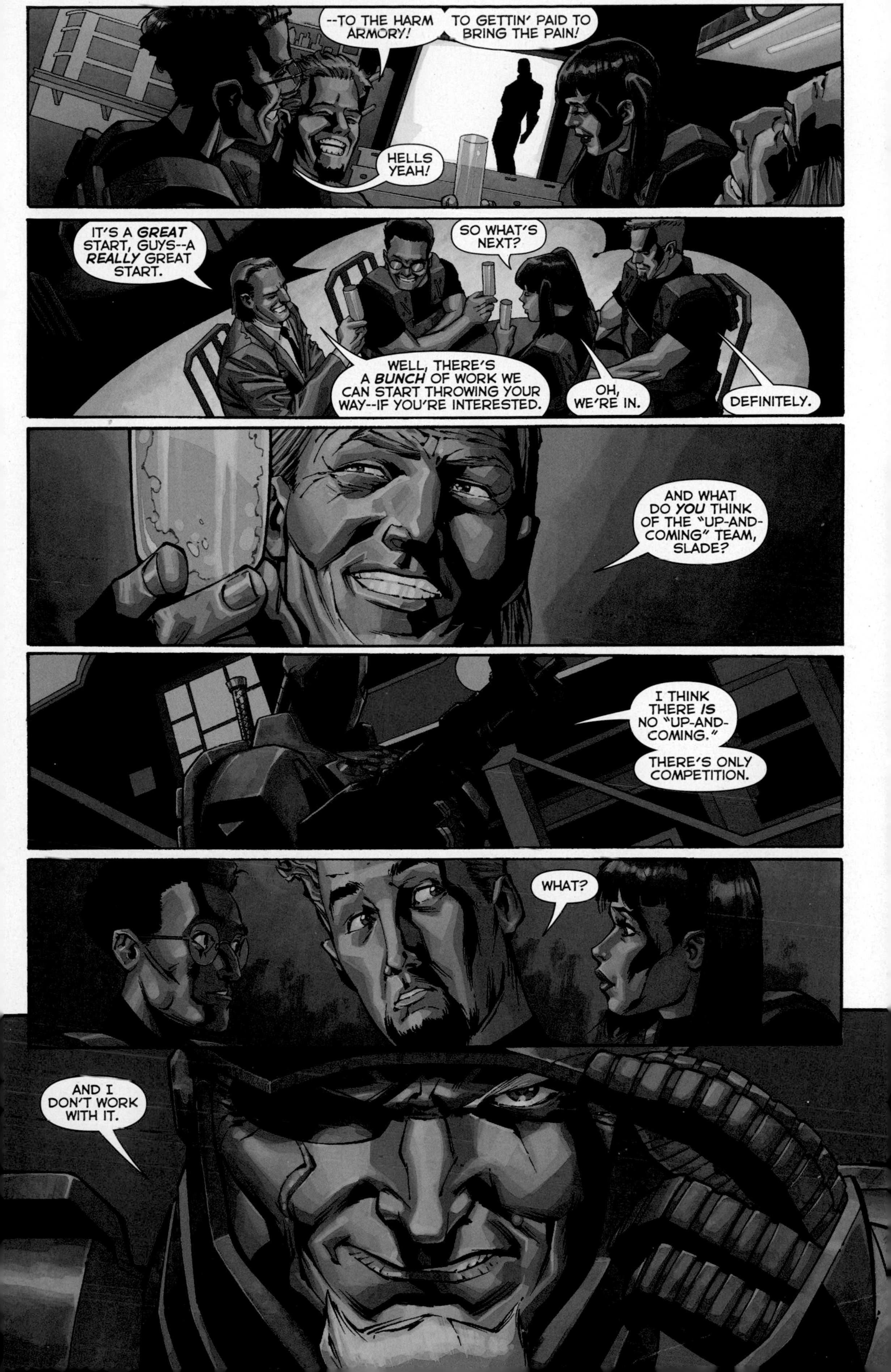
--TO THE HARM ARMORY!
TO GETTIN' PAID TO BRING THE PAIN!
HELLS YEAH!
IT'S A *GREAT* START, GUYS--A *REALLY* GREAT START.
SO WHAT'S NEXT?
WELL, THERE'S A *BUNCH* OF WORK WE CAN START THROWING YOUR WAY--IF YOU'RE INTERESTED.
OH, WE'RE IN.
DEFINITELY.
AND WHAT DO *YOU* THINK OF THE "UP-AND-COMING" TEAM, SLADE?
I THINK THERE *IS* NO "UP-AND-COMING."
THERE'S ONLY COMPETITION.
WHAT?
AND I DON'T WORK WITH IT.

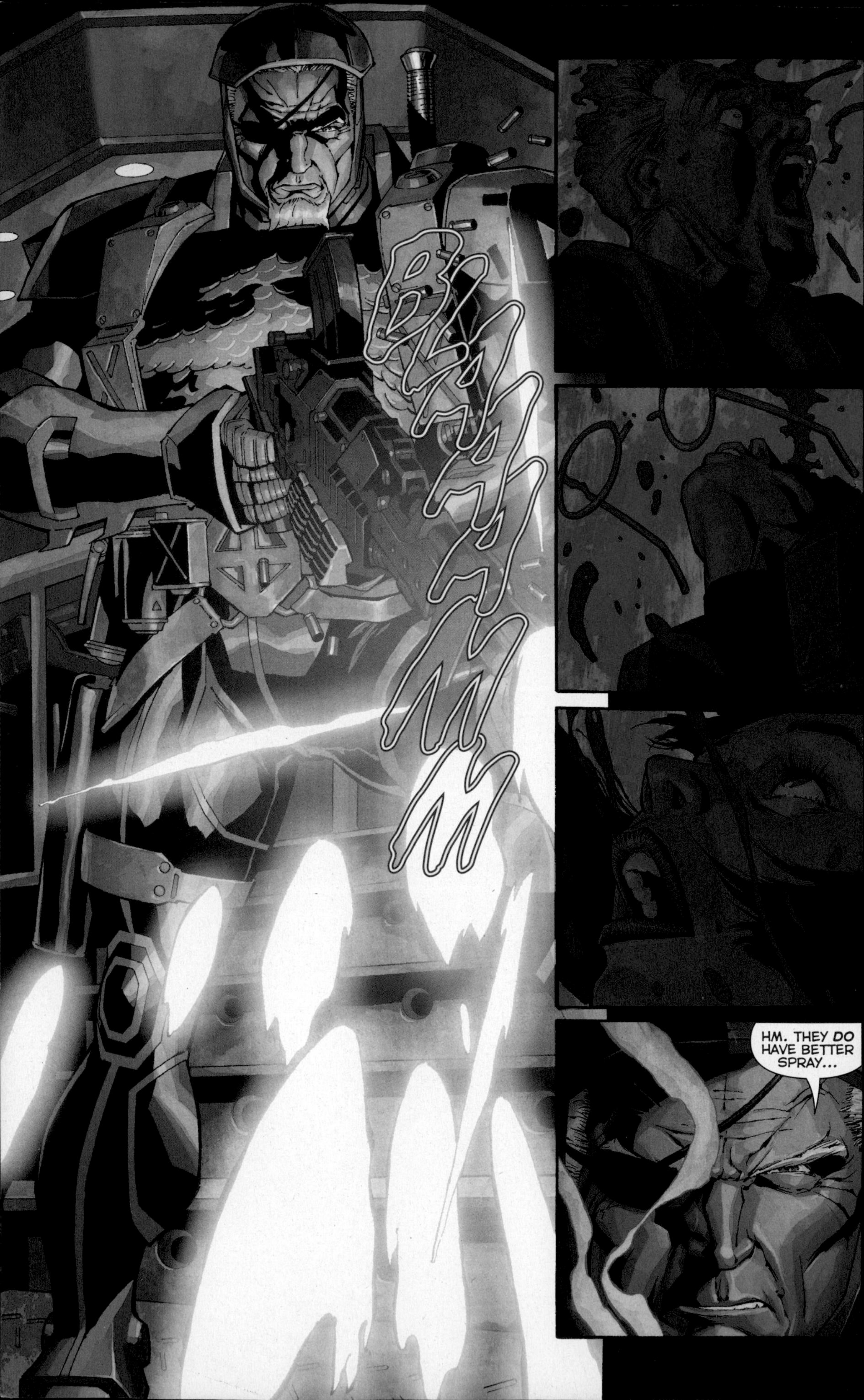
HM. THEY *DO* HAVE BETTER SPRAY...

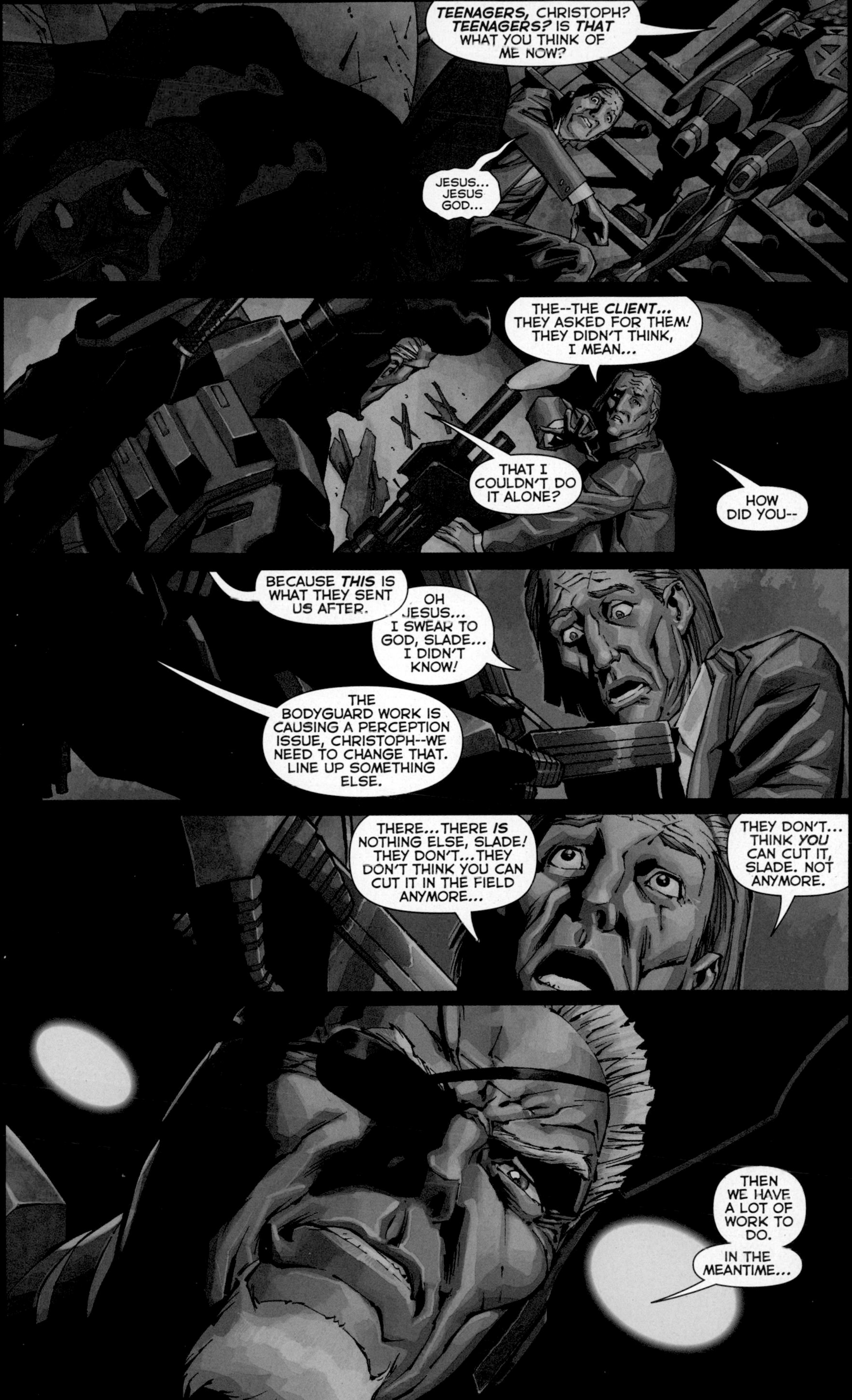
TEENAGERS, CHRISTOPH? TEENAGERS? IS THAT WHAT YOU THINK OF ME NOW?
JESUS... JESUS GOD...
THE--THE CLIENT... THEY ASKED FOR THEM! THEY DIDN'T THINK, I MEAN...
THAT I COULDN'T DO IT ALONE?
HOW DID YOU--
BECAUSE THIS IS WHAT THEY SENT US AFTER.
OH JESUS... I SWEAR TO GOD, SLADE... I DIDN'T KNOW!
THE BODYGUARD WORK IS CAUSING A PERCEPTION ISSUE, CHRISTOPH--WE NEED TO CHANGE THAT. LINE UP SOMETHING ELSE.
THERE... THERE IS NOTHING ELSE, SLADE! THEY DON'T... THEY DON'T THINK YOU CAN CUT IT IN THE FIELD ANYMORE...
THEY DON'T... THINK YOU CAN CUT IT, SLADE. NOT ANYMORE.
THEN WE HAVE A LOT OF WORK TO DO.
IN THE MEANTIME...

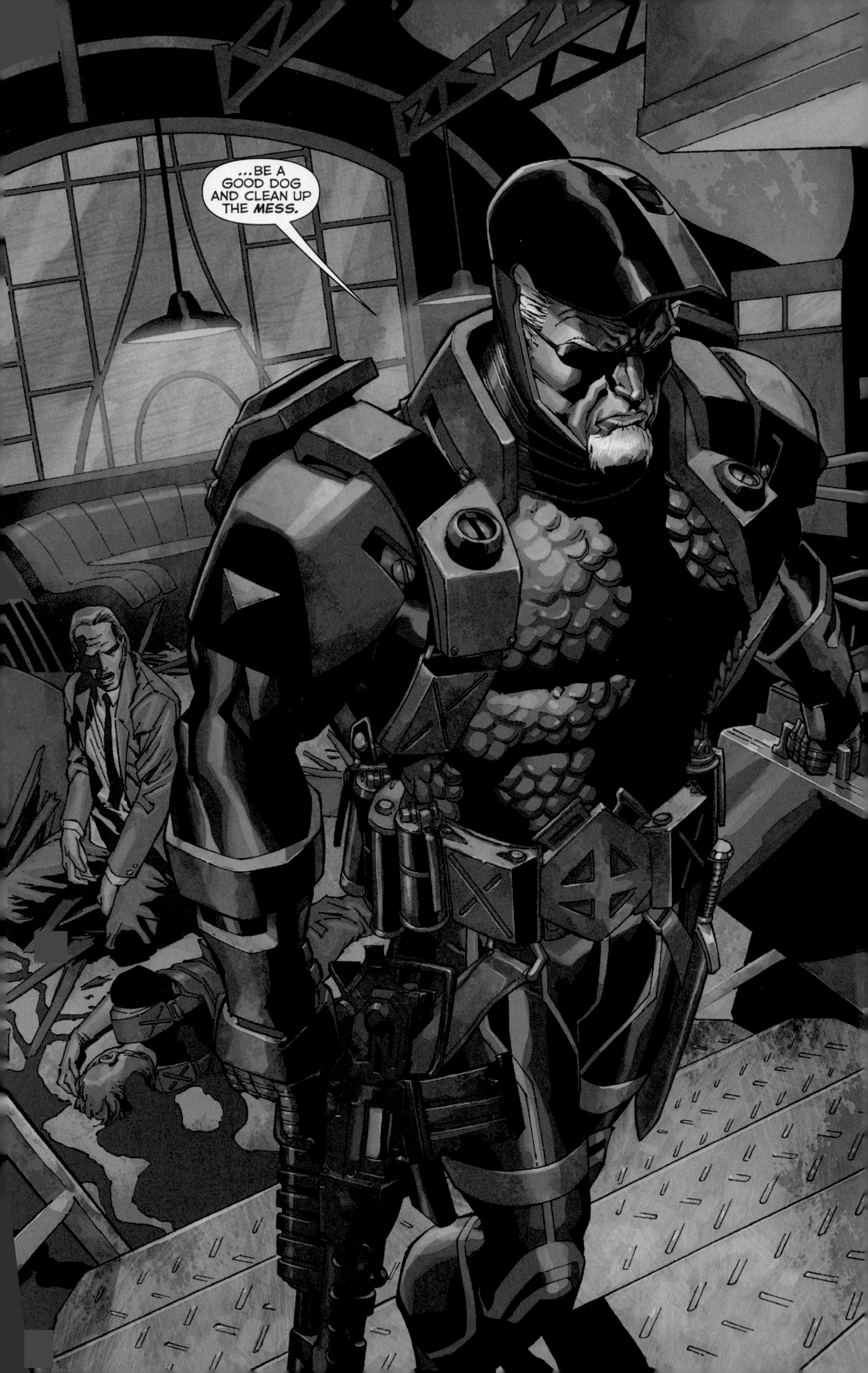
...BE A GOOD DOG AND CLEAN UP THE MESS.

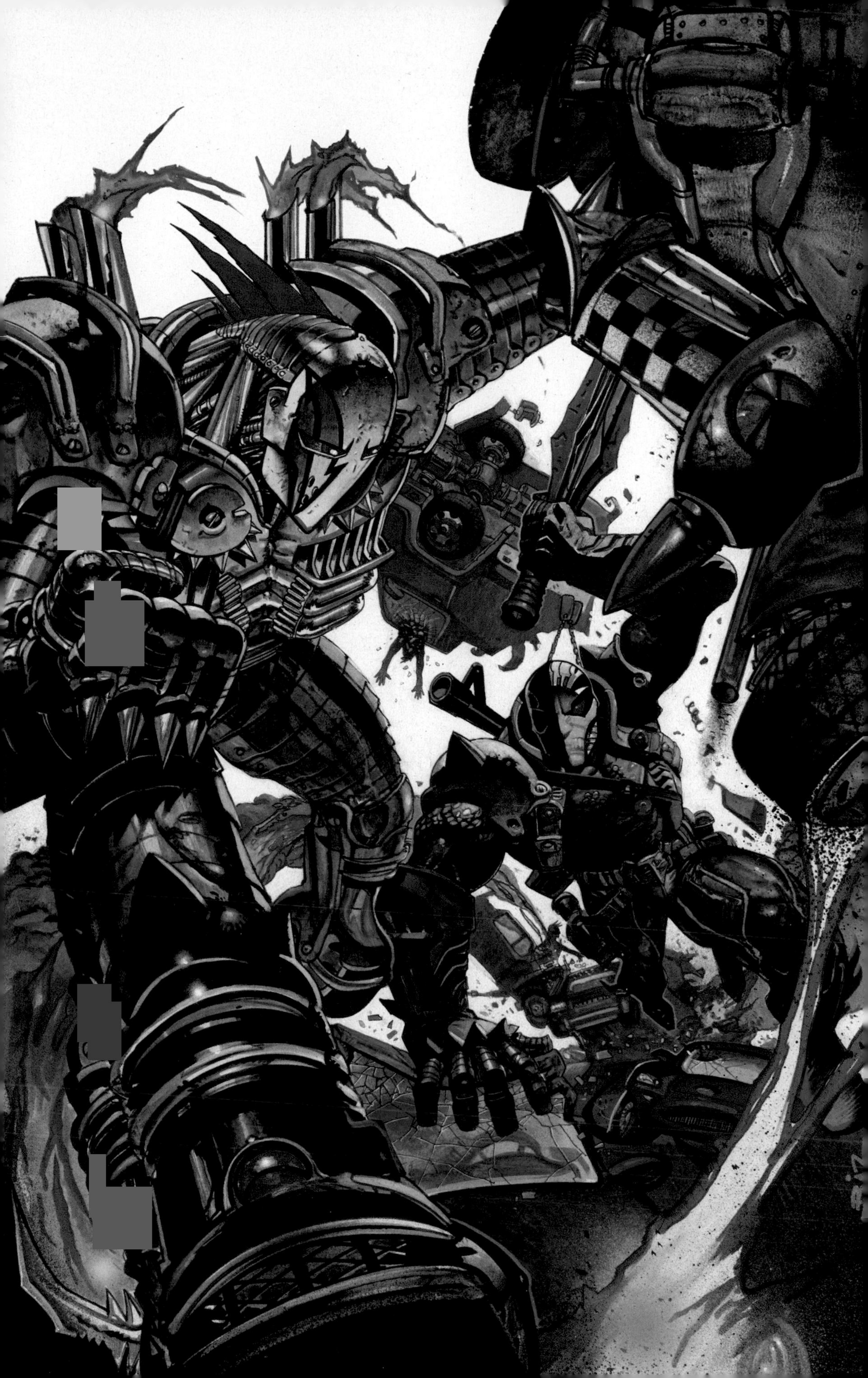

THE CARPOCALYPSE

KYLE HIGGINS writer **JOE BENNETT** penciller **ART THIBERT** inker cover by **SIMON BISLEY**

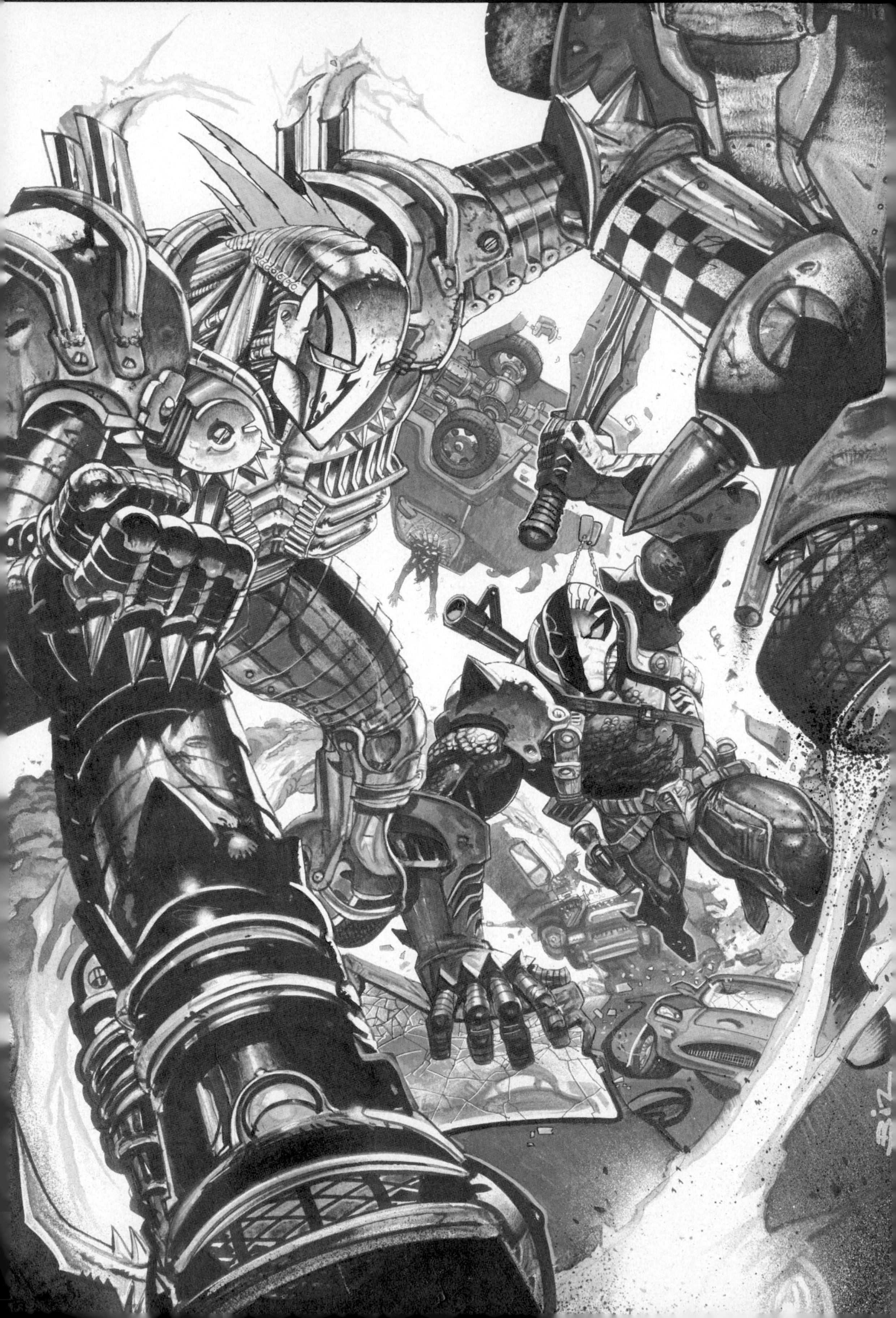
BIZ

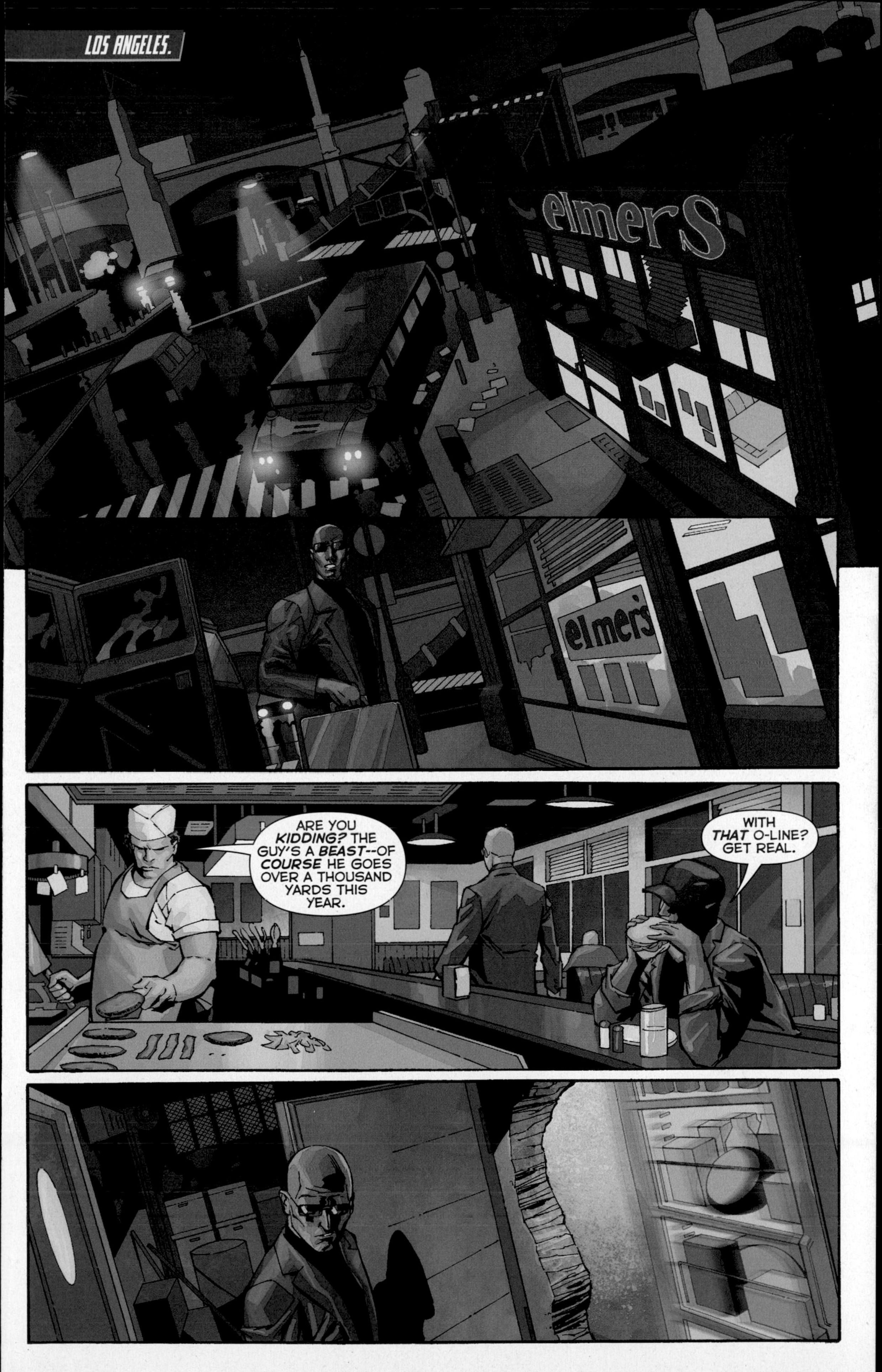
LOS ANGELES.
elmer's
elmer's
ARE YOU KIDDING? THE GUY'S A BEAST--OF COURSE HE GOES OVER A THOUSAND YARDS THIS YEAR.
WITH THAT O-LINE? GET REAL.

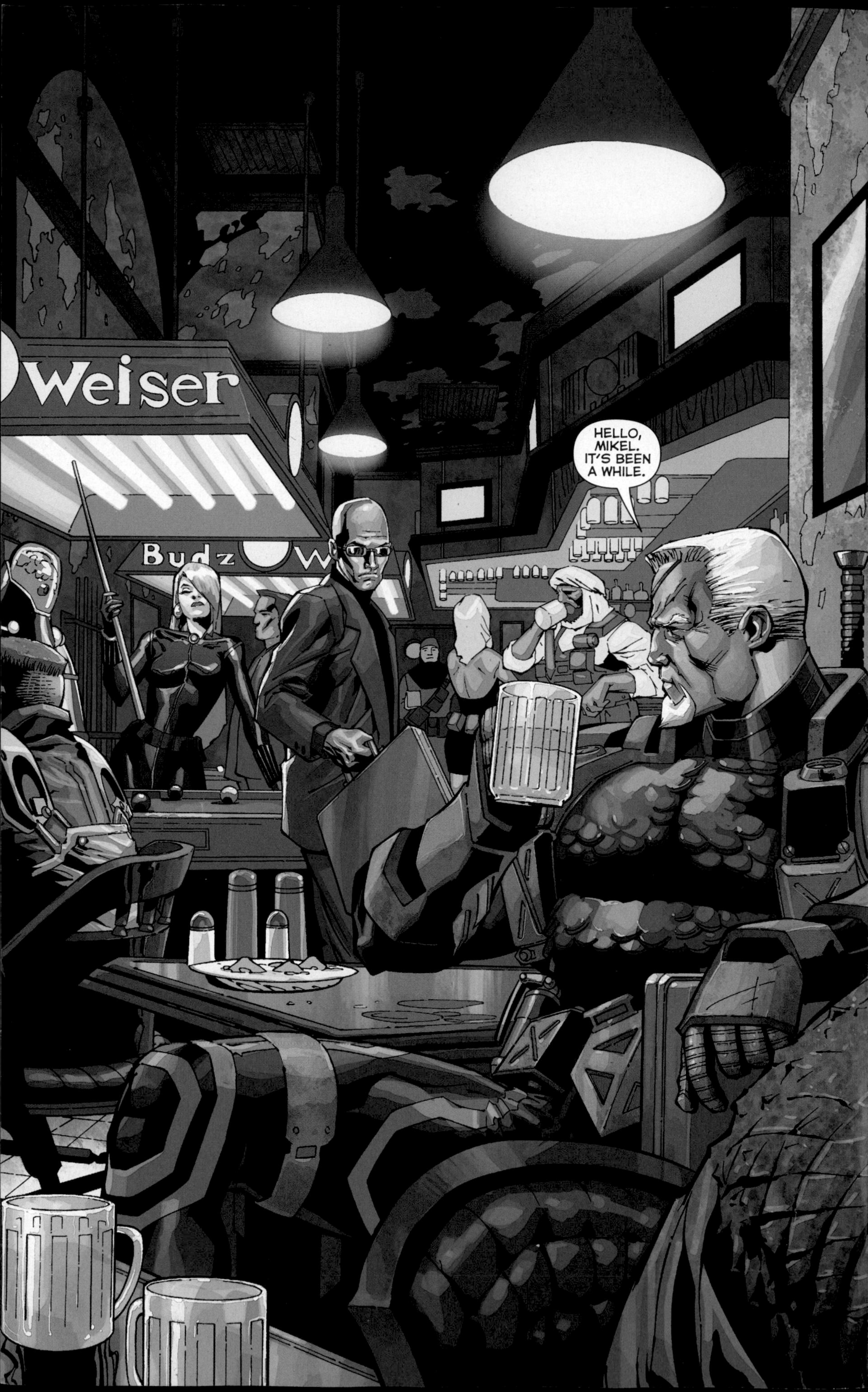
Weiser
Budz
HELLO, MIKEL. IT'S BEEN A WHILE.

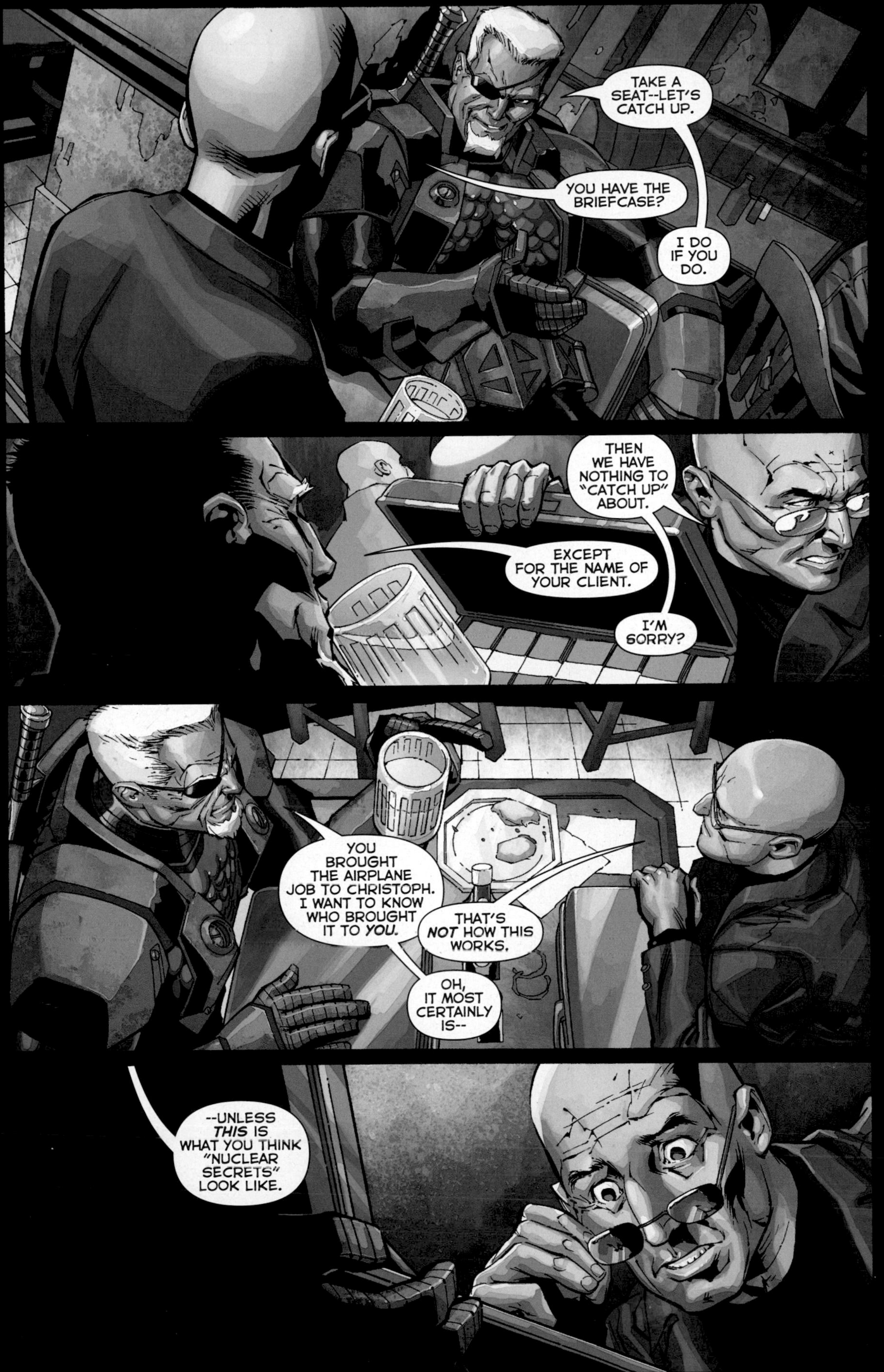
TAKE A SEAT--LET'S CATCH UP.
YOU HAVE THE BRIEFCASE?
I DO IF YOU DO.
THEN WE HAVE NOTHING TO "CATCH UP" ABOUT.
EXCEPT FOR THE NAME OF YOUR CLIENT.
I'M SORRY?
YOU BROUGHT THE AIRPLANE JOB TO CHRISTOPH. I WANT TO KNOW WHO BROUGHT IT TO *YOU.*
THAT'S *NOT* HOW THIS WORKS.
OH, IT MOST CERTAINLY IS--
--UNLESS *THIS* IS WHAT YOU THINK "NUCLEAR SECRETS" LOOK LIKE.

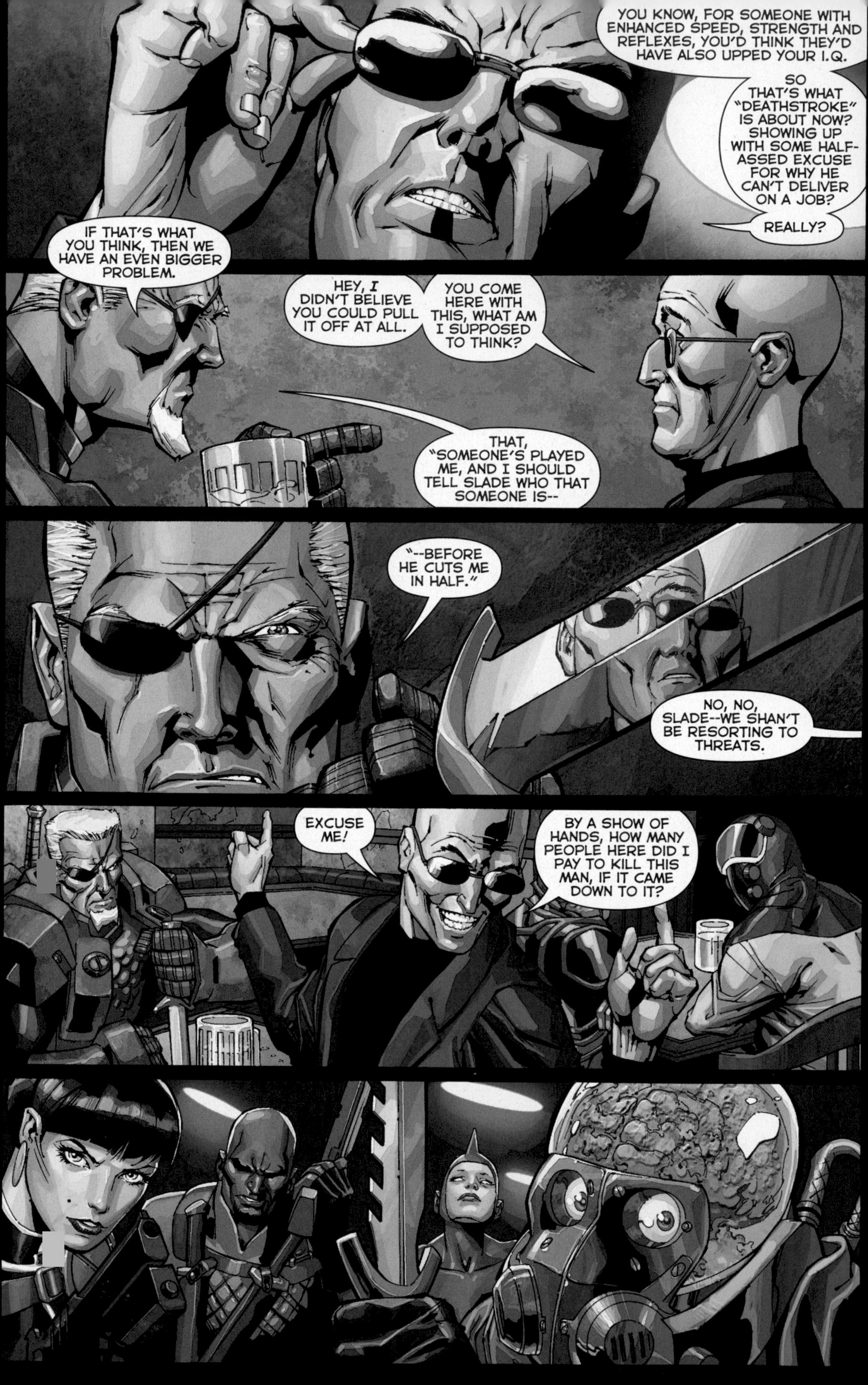

YOU KNOW, FOR SOMEONE WITH ENHANCED SPEED, STRENGTH AND REFLEXES, YOU'D THINK THEY'D HAVE ALSO UPPED YOUR I.Q.
SO THAT'S WHAT "DEATHSTROKE" IS ABOUT NOW? SHOWING UP WITH SOME HALF-ASSED EXCUSE FOR WHY HE CAN'T DELIVER ON A JOB?
REALLY?
IF THAT'S WHAT YOU THINK, THEN WE HAVE AN EVEN BIGGER PROBLEM.
YOU COME HERE WITH THIS, WHAT AM I SUPPOSED TO THINK?
HEY, *I* DIDN'T BELIEVE YOU COULD PULL IT OFF AT ALL.
THAT, "SOMEONE'S PLAYED ME, AND I SHOULD TELL SLADE WHO THAT SOMEONE IS--
"--BEFORE HE CUTS ME IN HALF."
NO, NO, SLADE--WE SHAN'T BE RESORTING TO THREATS.
EXCUSE *ME!*
BY A SHOW OF HANDS, HOW MANY PEOPLE HERE DID I PAY TO KILL THIS MAN, IF IT CAME DOWN TO IT?

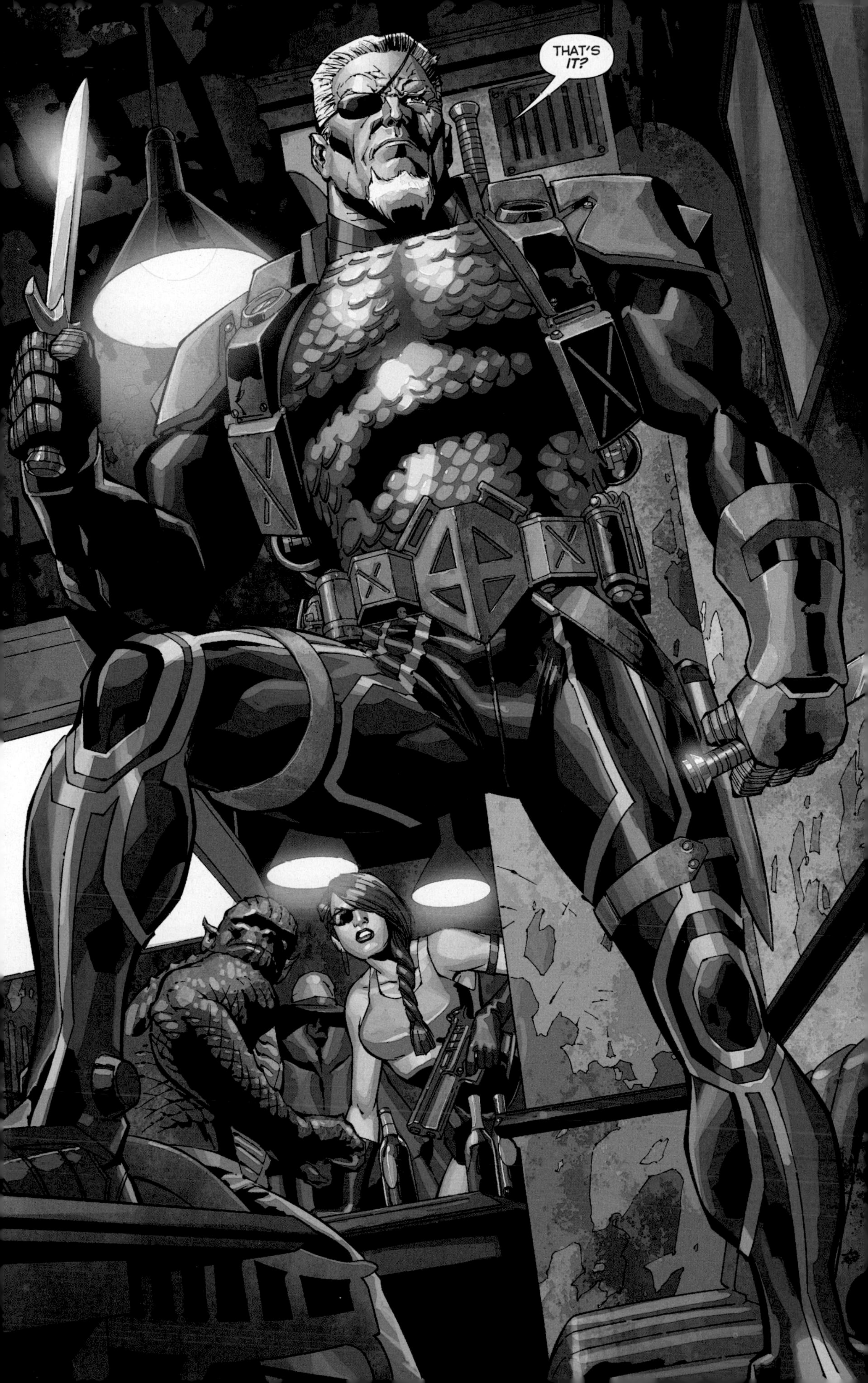
THAT'S IT?

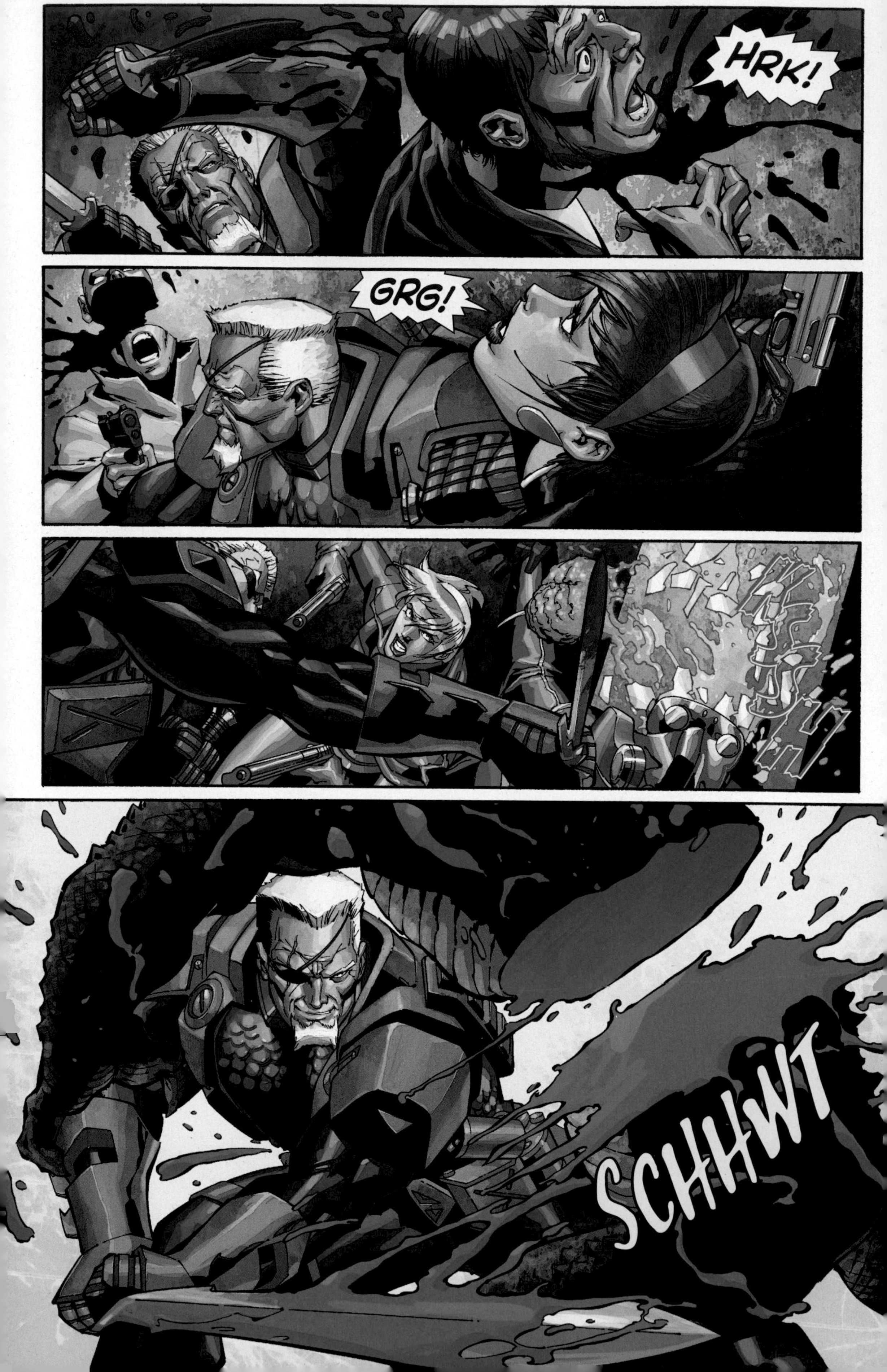
HRK!
GRG!
SCHHWT

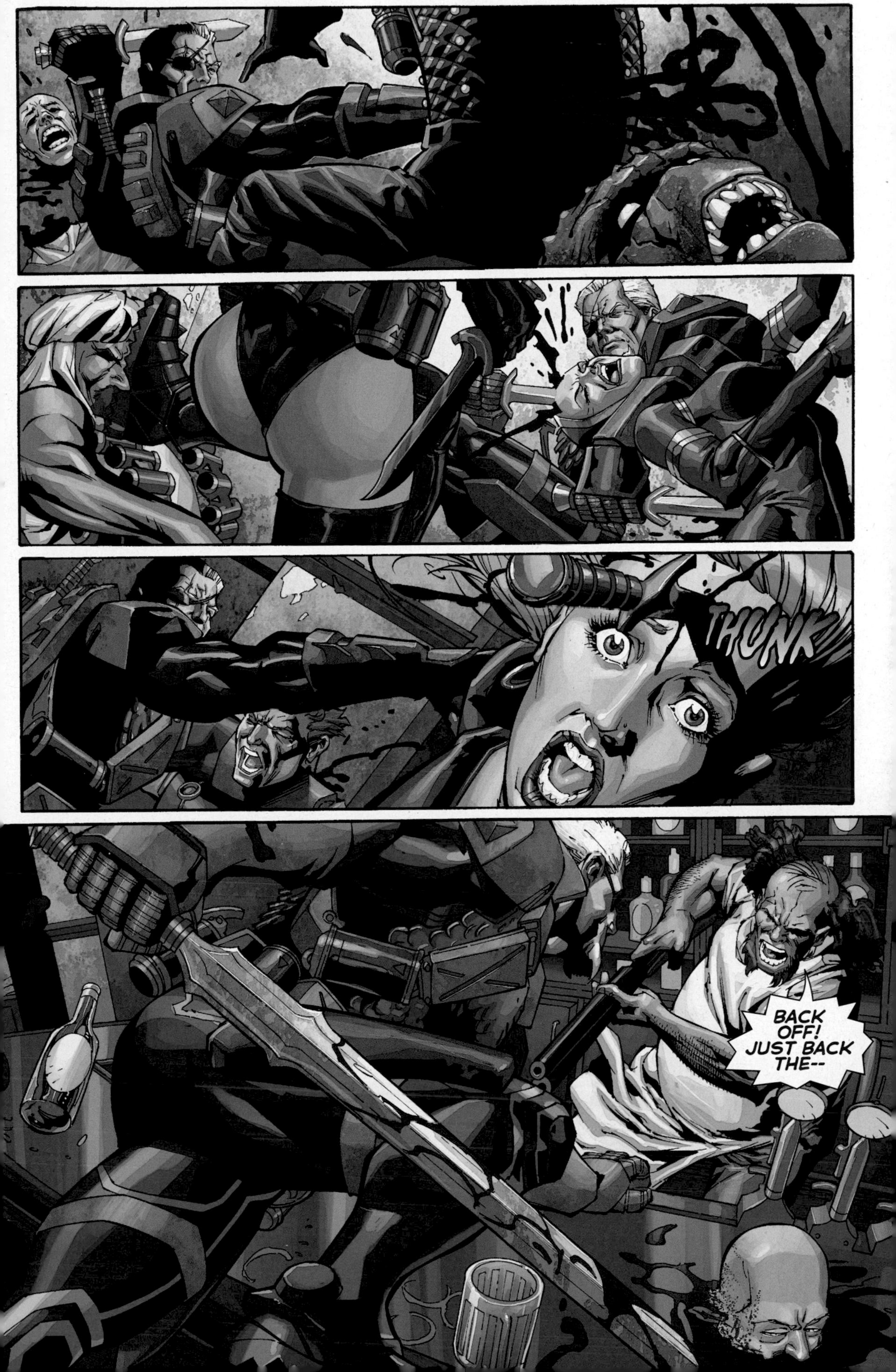
THUNK
BACK OFF! JUST BACK THE--

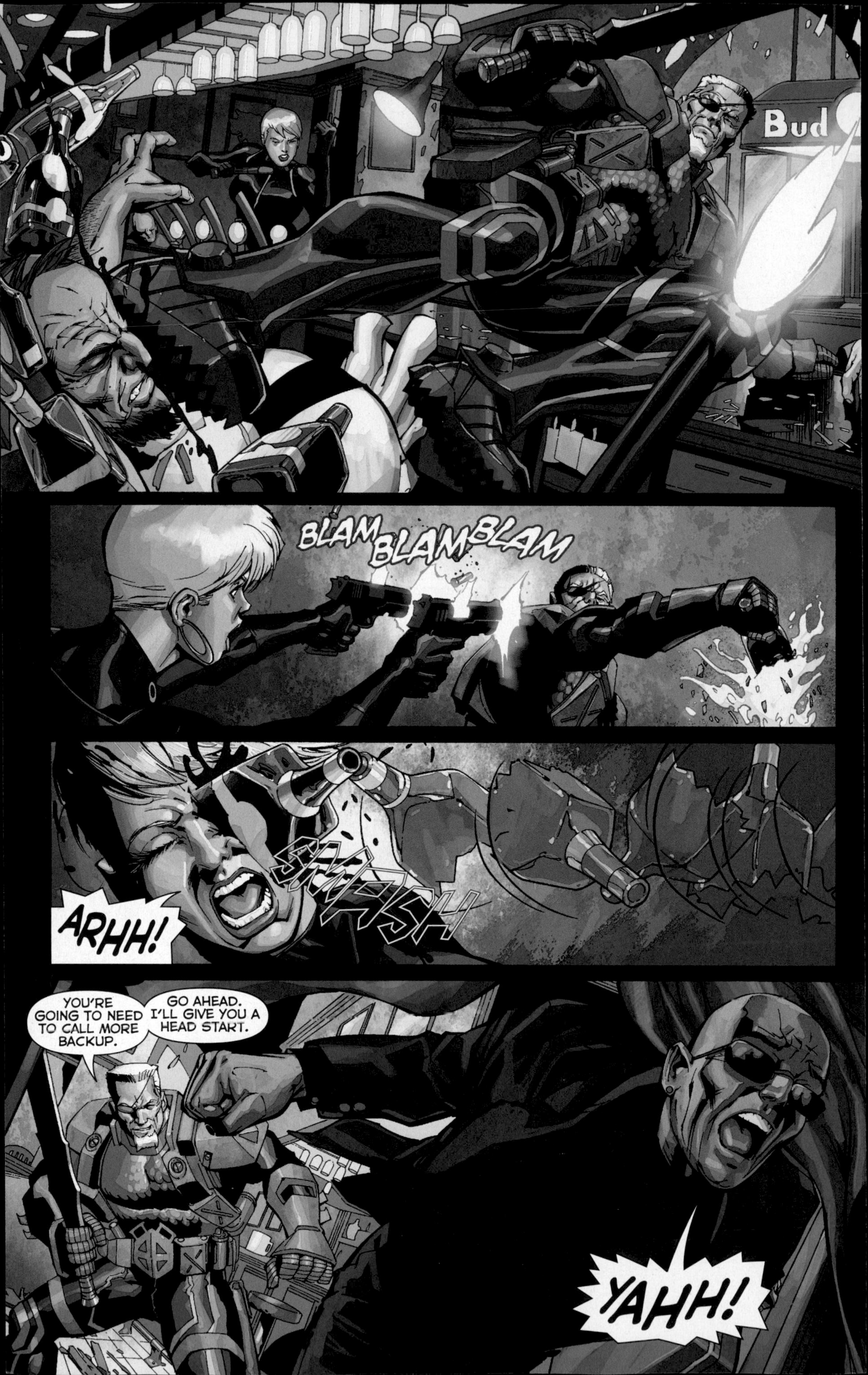
Bud
BLAM BLAM BLAM
SMASH
ARHH!
YOU'RE GOING TO NEED TO CALL MORE BACKUP.
GO AHEAD. I'LL GIVE YOU A HEAD START.
YAHH!

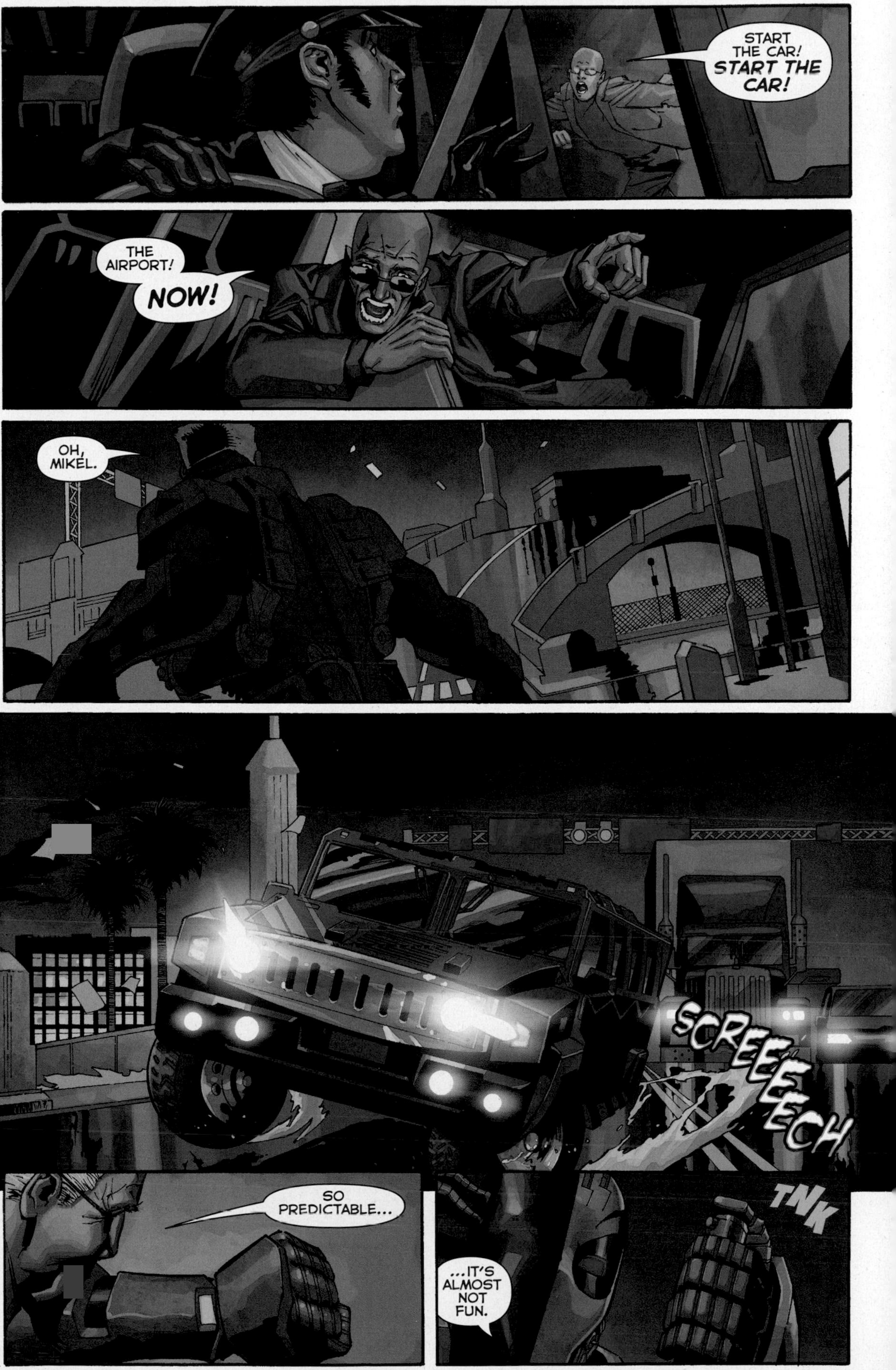
START THE CAR! START THE CAR!
THE AIRPORT!
NOW!
OH, MIKEL.
SCREEEEECH
SO PREDICTABLE...
TNK
...IT'S ALMOST NOT FUN.

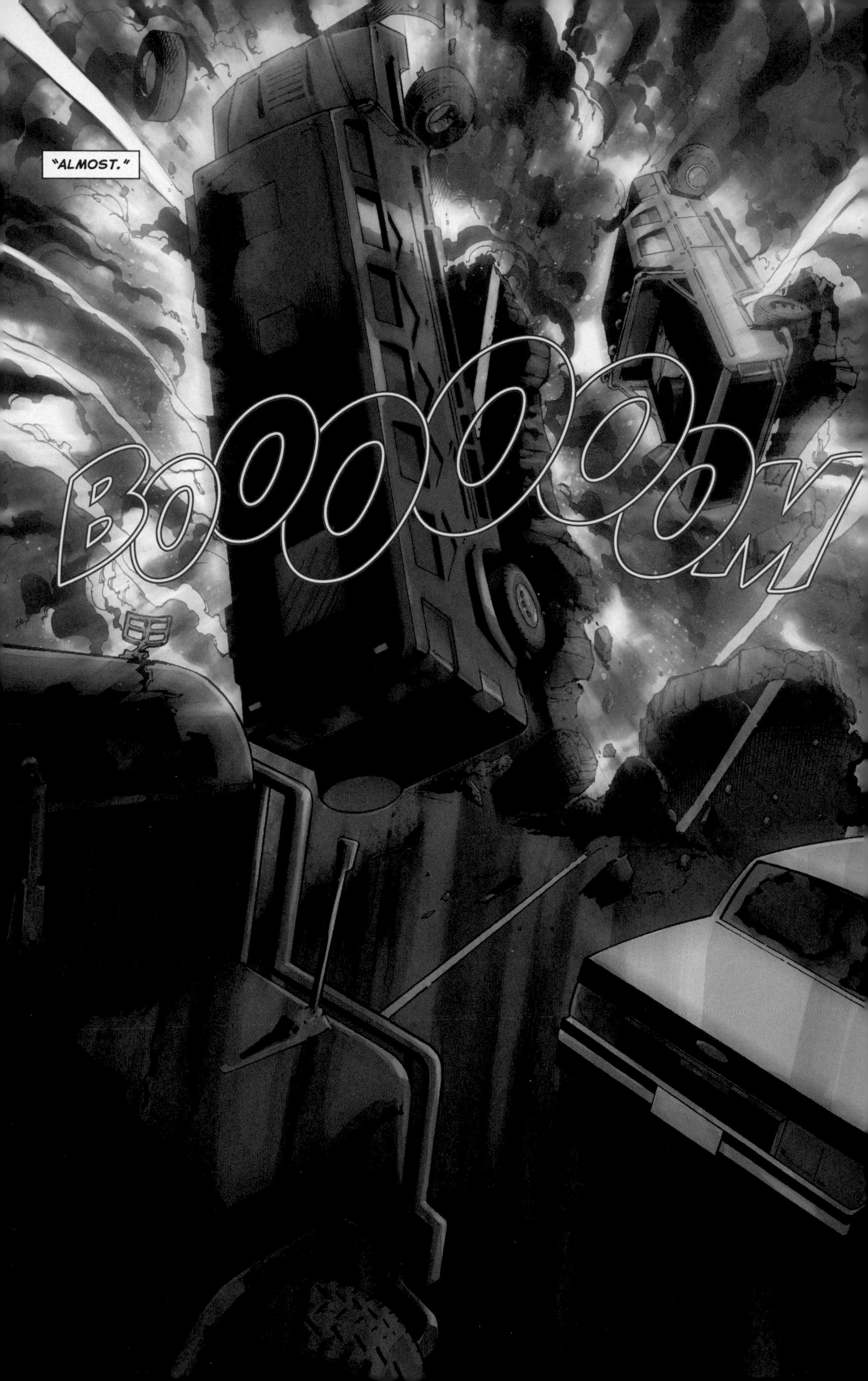
"ALMOST."
BOOOOOOOM

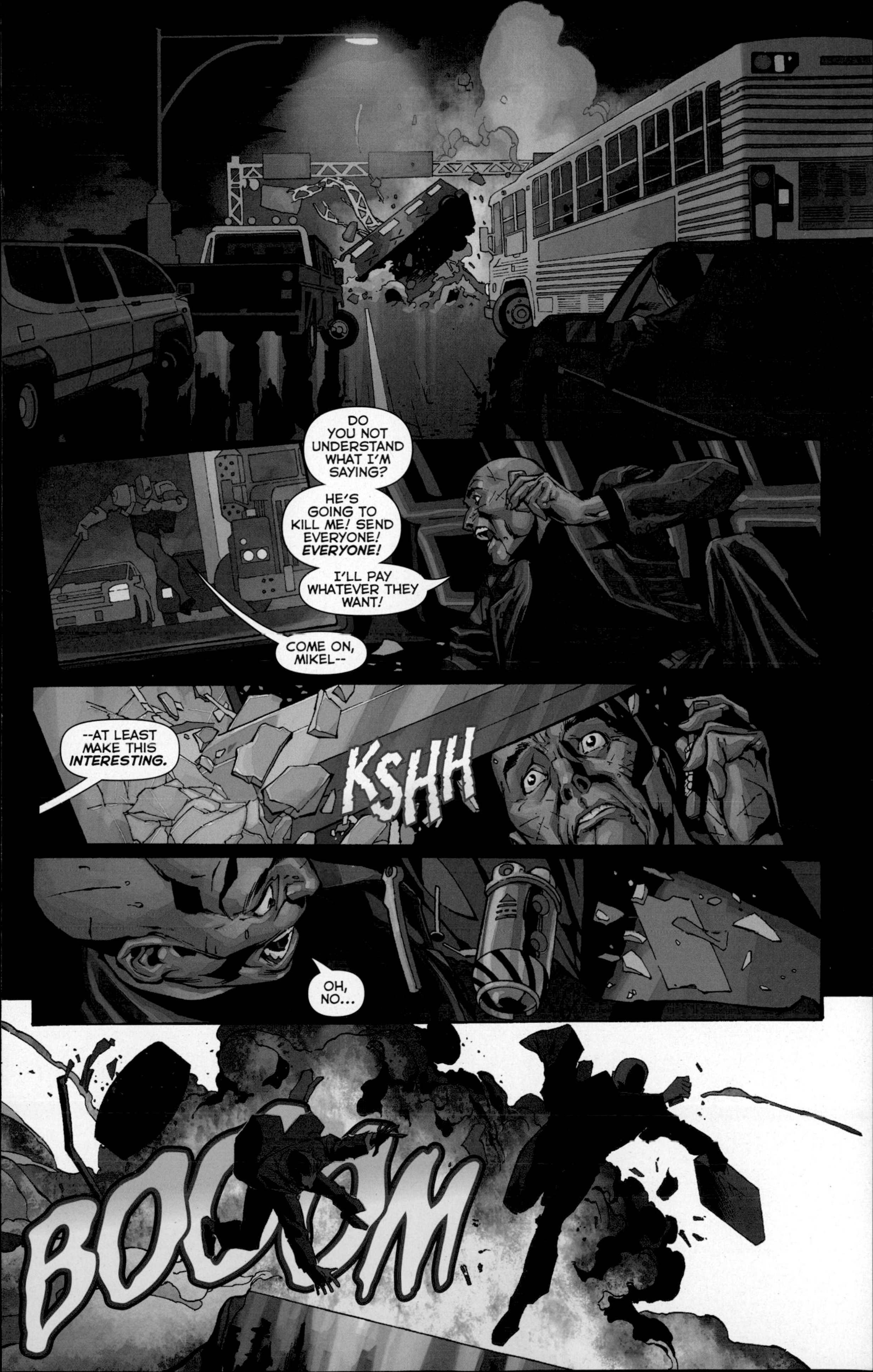

DO YOU NOT UNDERSTAND WHAT I'M SAYING?
HE'S GOING TO KILL ME! SEND EVERYONE! *EVERYONE!*
I'LL PAY WHATEVER THEY WANT!
COME ON, MIKEL--
--AT LEAST MAKE THIS *INTERESTING.*
KSHH
OH, NO...
BOOOM

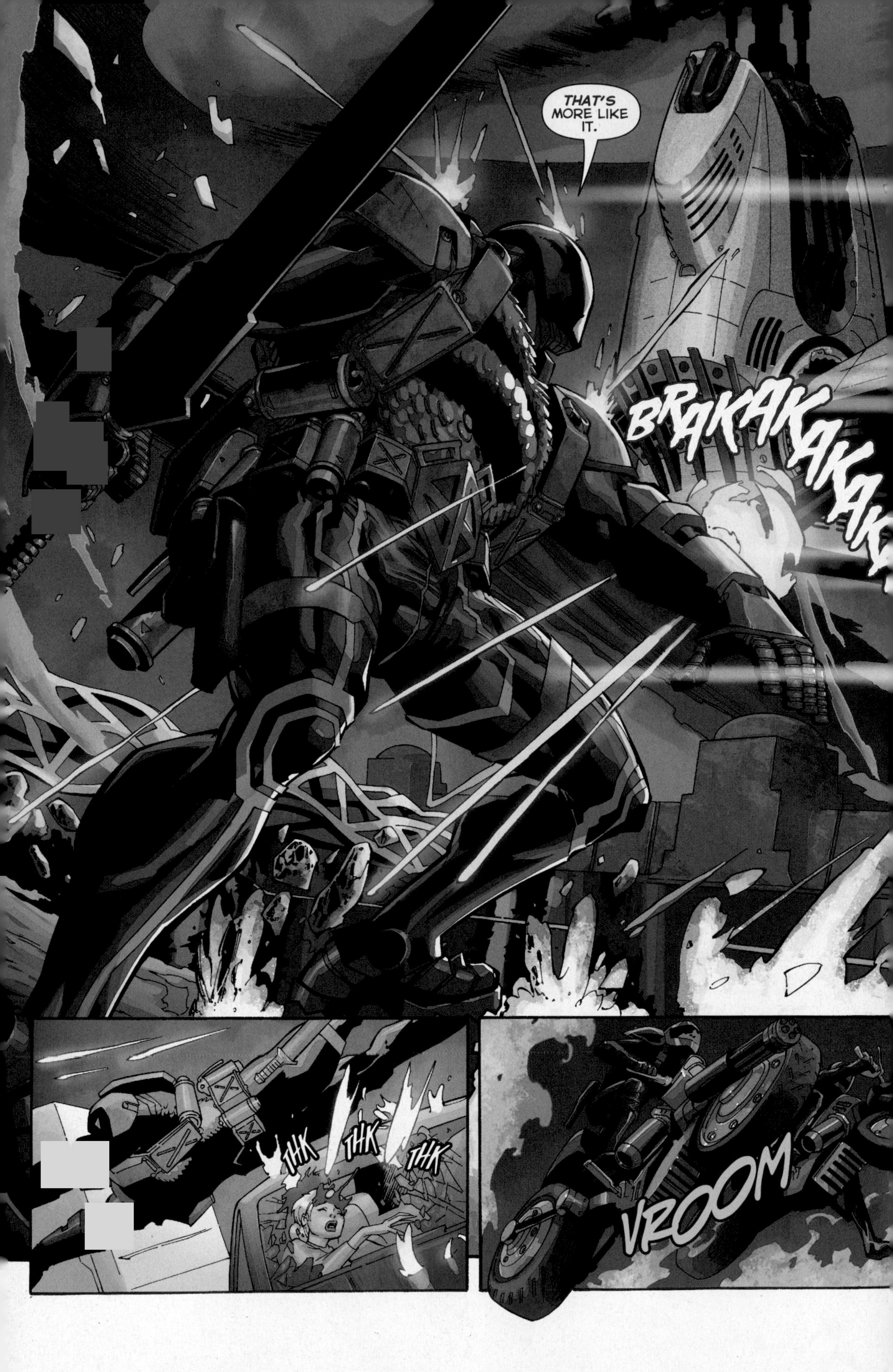
THAT'S MORE LIKE IT.
BRAKAKAKAK
THK
THK
THK
VROOM

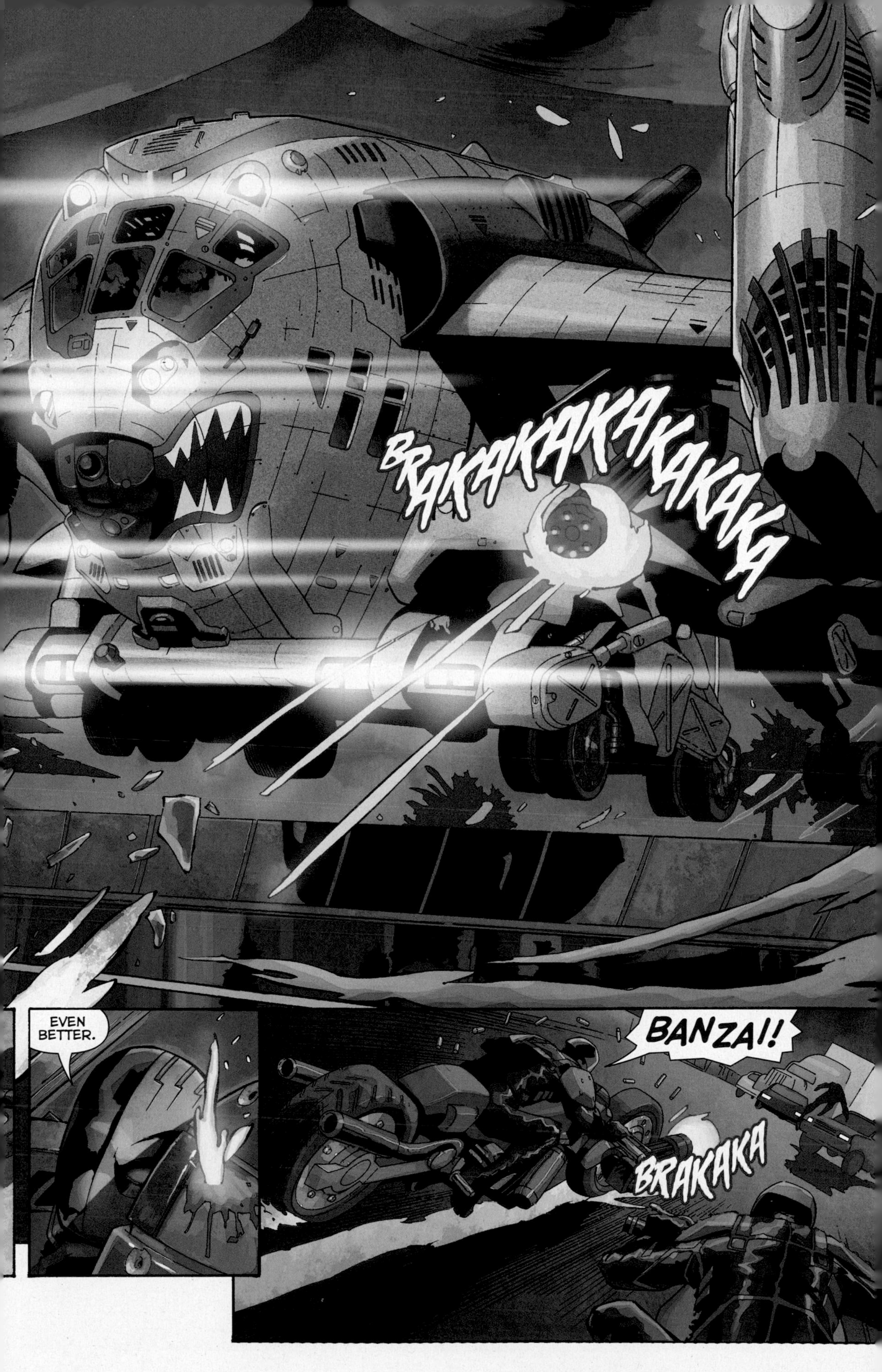
BRAKAKAKAKAKAKAKA
EVEN BETTER.
BANZAI!!
BRAKAKA

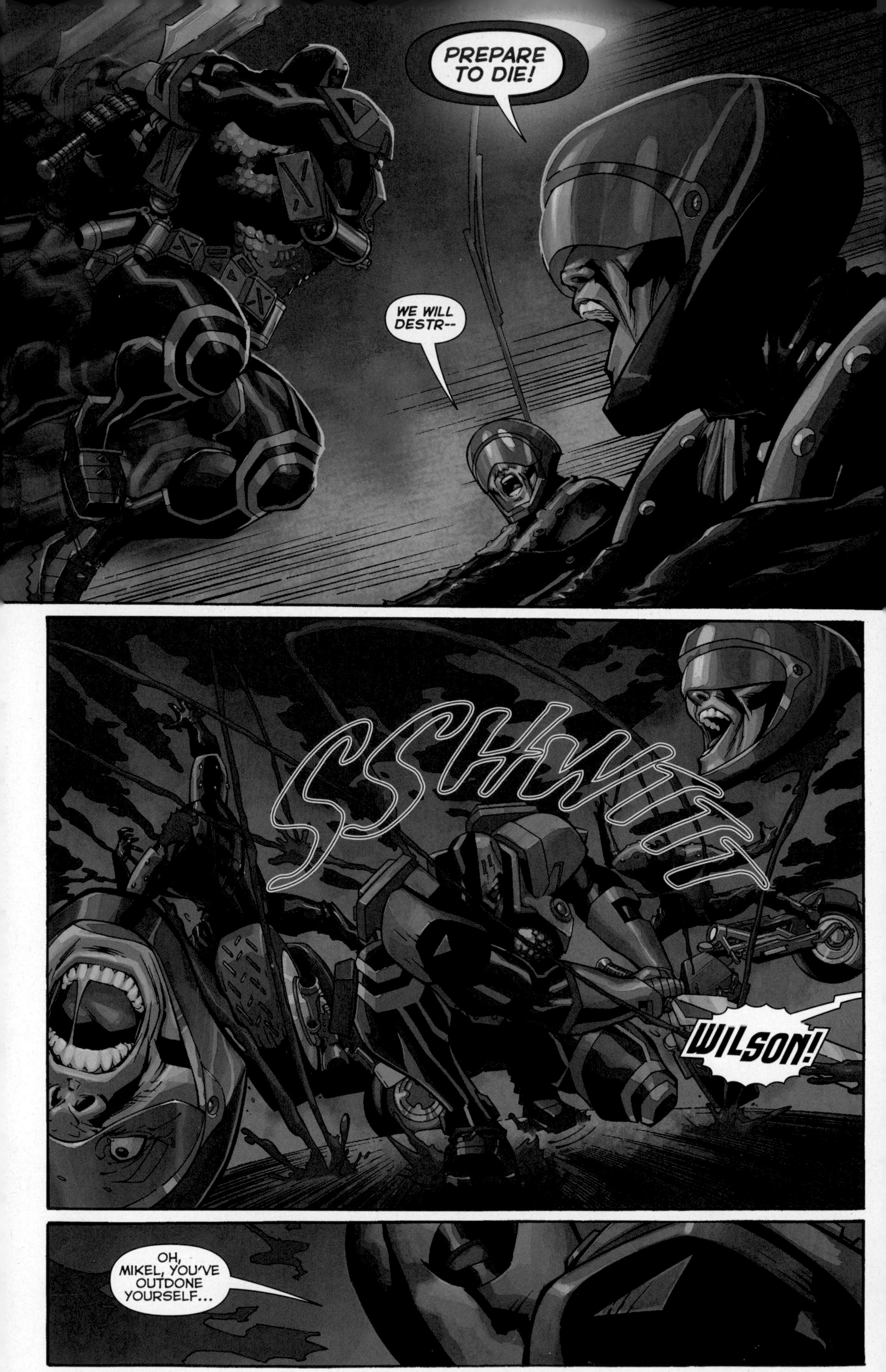
PREPARE TO DIE!
WE WILL DESTR--
SCHWIIT
WILSON!
OH, MIKEL, YOU'VE OUTDONE YOURSELF...

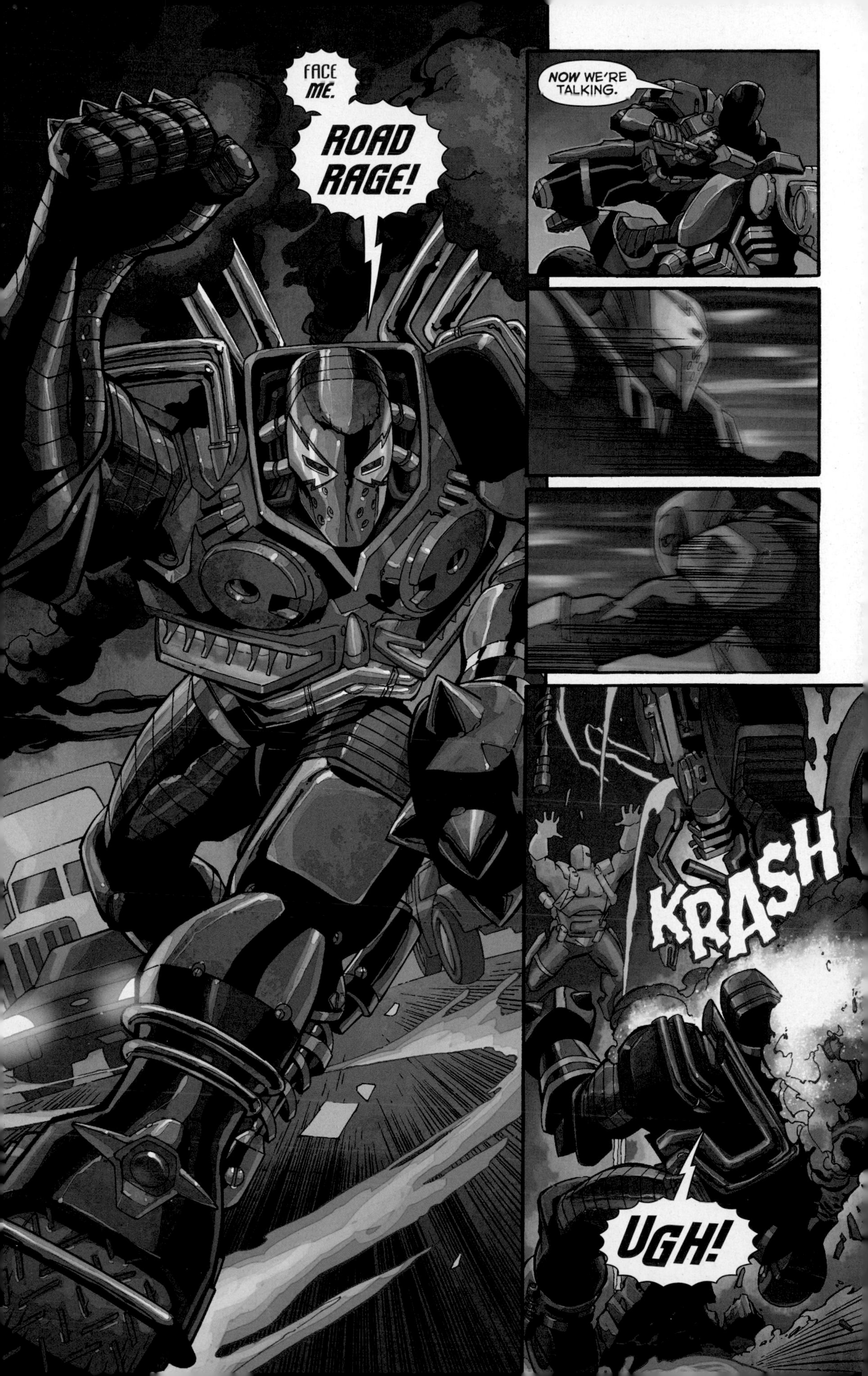
FACE ME.
ROAD RAGE!
NOW WE'RE TALKING.
KRASH
UGH!

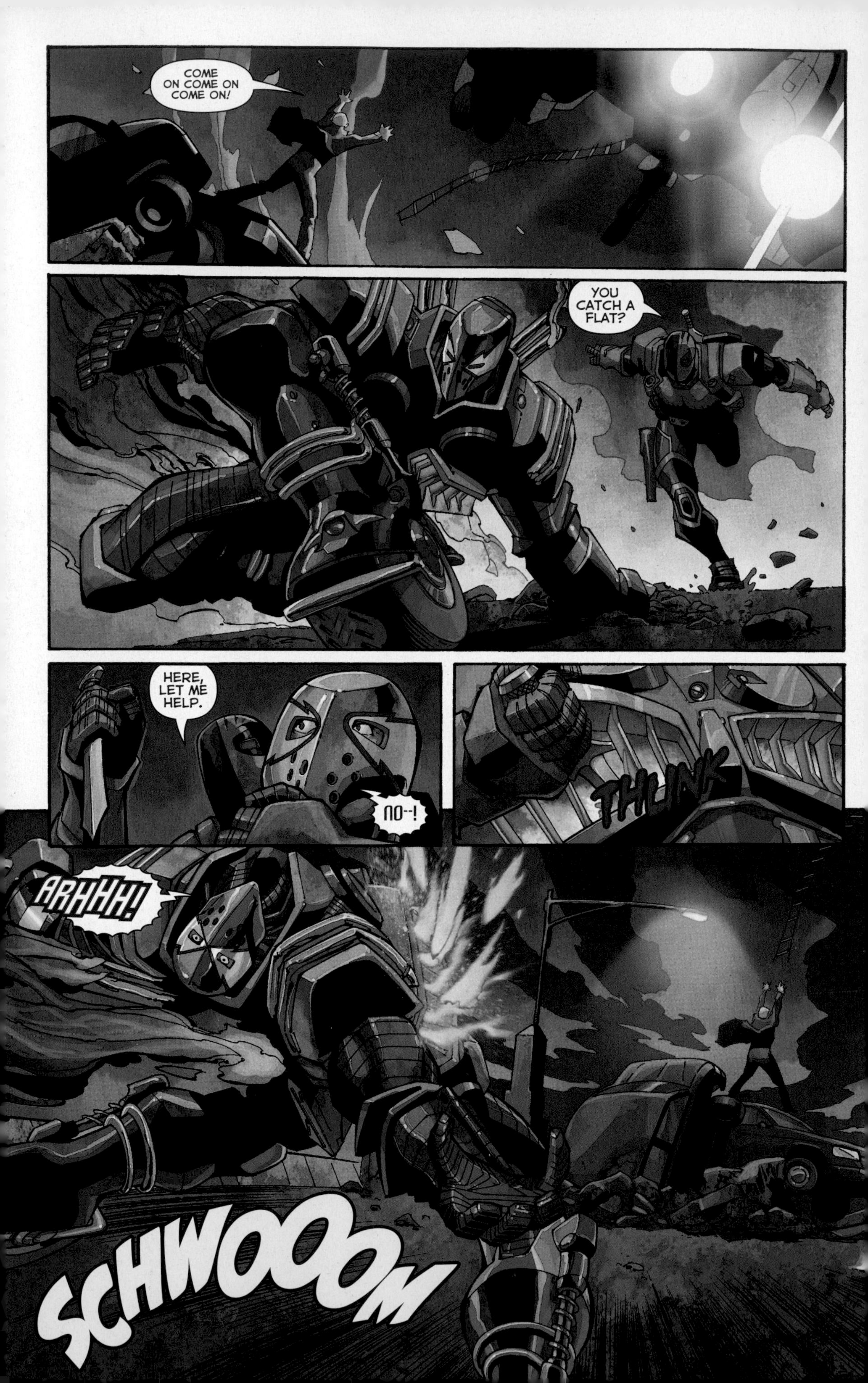

COME ON COME ON COME ON!
YOU CATCH A FLAT?
HERE, LET ME HELP.
NO--!
THUNK
ARHHH!
SCHWOOOM

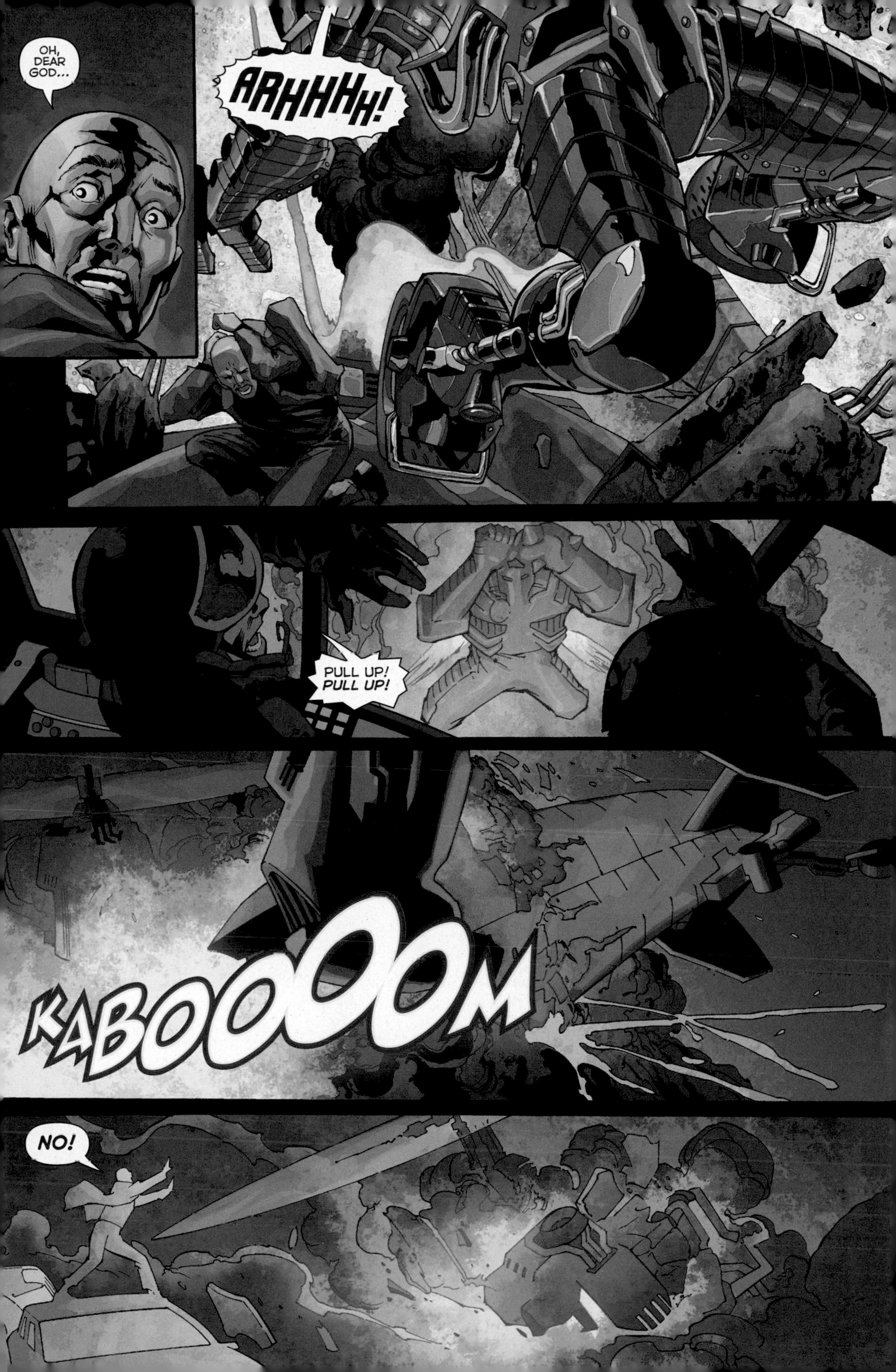
OH, DEAR GOD...
ARHHHH!
PULL UP! PULL UP!
KABOOOOM
NO!

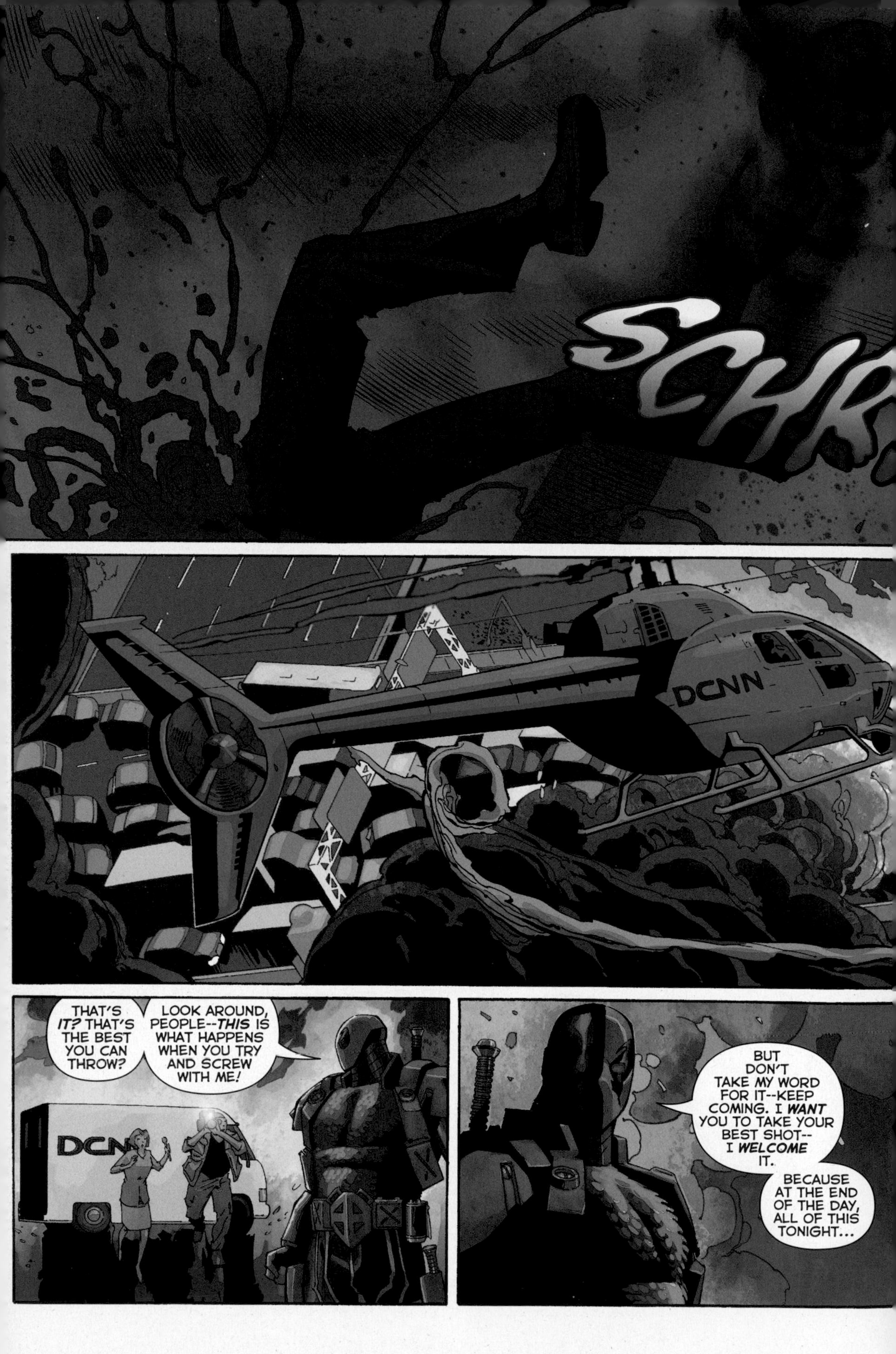
SCHK
DCNN
THAT'S IT? THAT'S THE BEST YOU CAN THROW?
LOOK AROUND, PEOPLE--THIS IS WHAT HAPPENS WHEN YOU TRY AND SCREW WITH ME!
DCN
BUT DON'T TAKE MY WORD FOR IT--KEEP COMING. I WANT YOU TO TAKE YOUR BEST SHOT-- I WELCOME IT.
BECAUSE AT THE END OF THE DAY, ALL OF THIS TONIGHT...

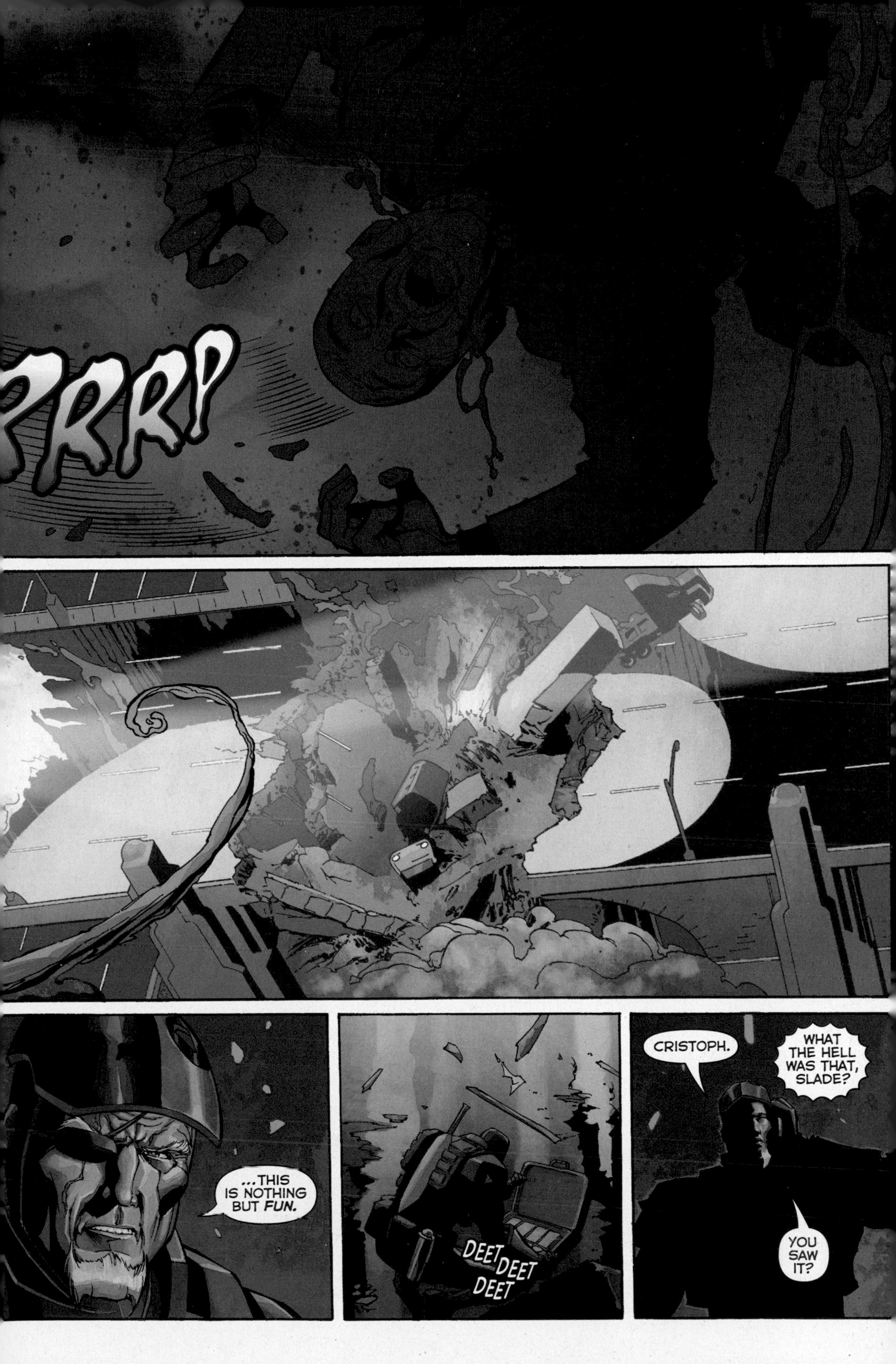
RRRP
...THIS IS NOTHING BUT FUN.
DEET DEET DEET
CRISTOPH.
WHAT THE HELL WAS THAT, SLADE?
YOU SAW IT?

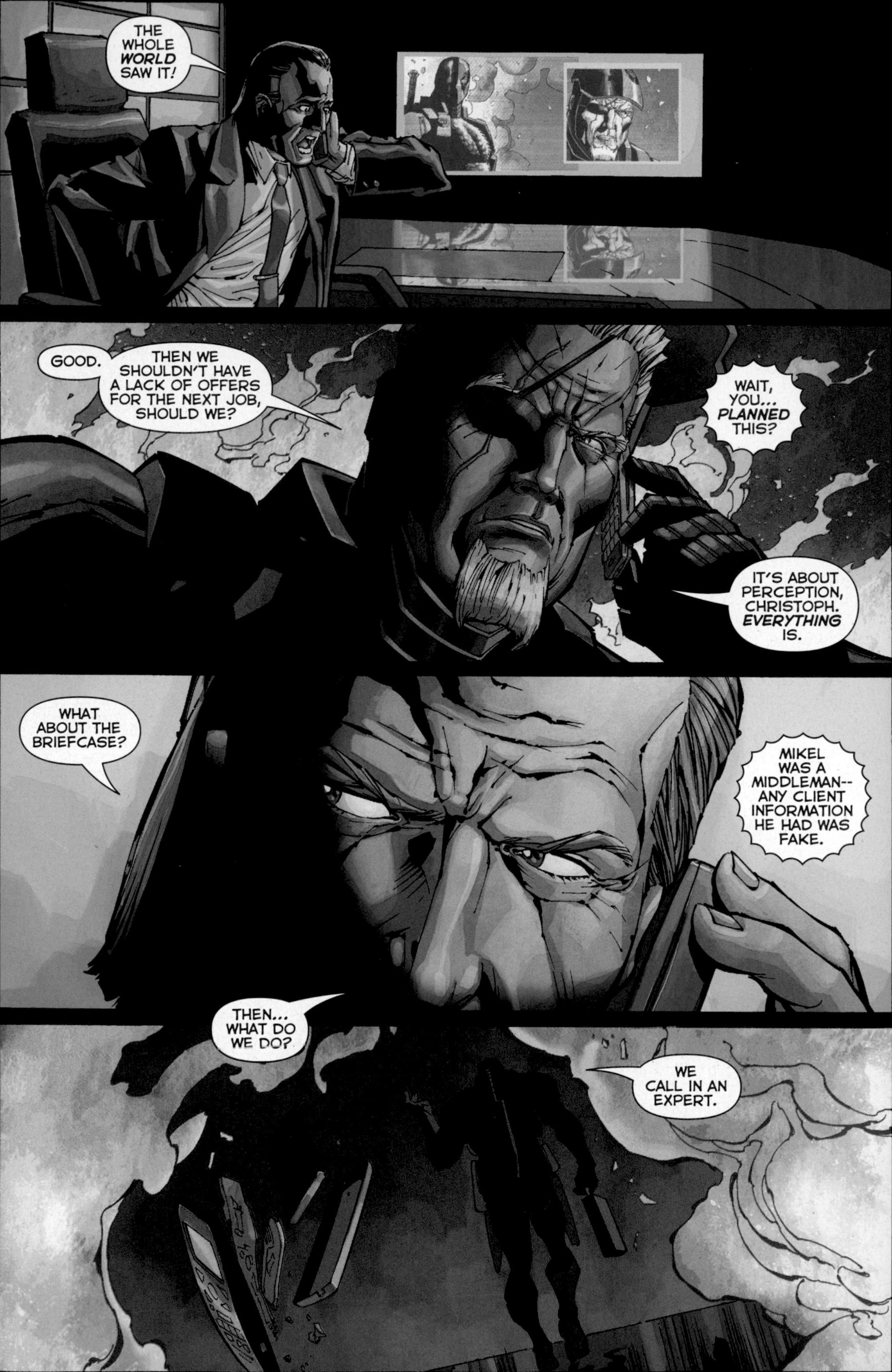
THE WHOLE WORLD SAW IT!
GOOD.
THEN WE SHOULDN'T HAVE A LACK OF OFFERS FOR THE NEXT JOB, SHOULD WE?
WAIT, YOU... PLANNED THIS?
IT'S ABOUT PERCEPTION, CHRISTOPH. EVERYTHING IS.
WHAT ABOUT THE BRIEFCASE?
MIKEL WAS A MIDDLEMAN-- ANY CLIENT INFORMATION HE HAD WAS FAKE.
THEN... WHAT DO WE DO?
WE CALL IN AN EXPERT.

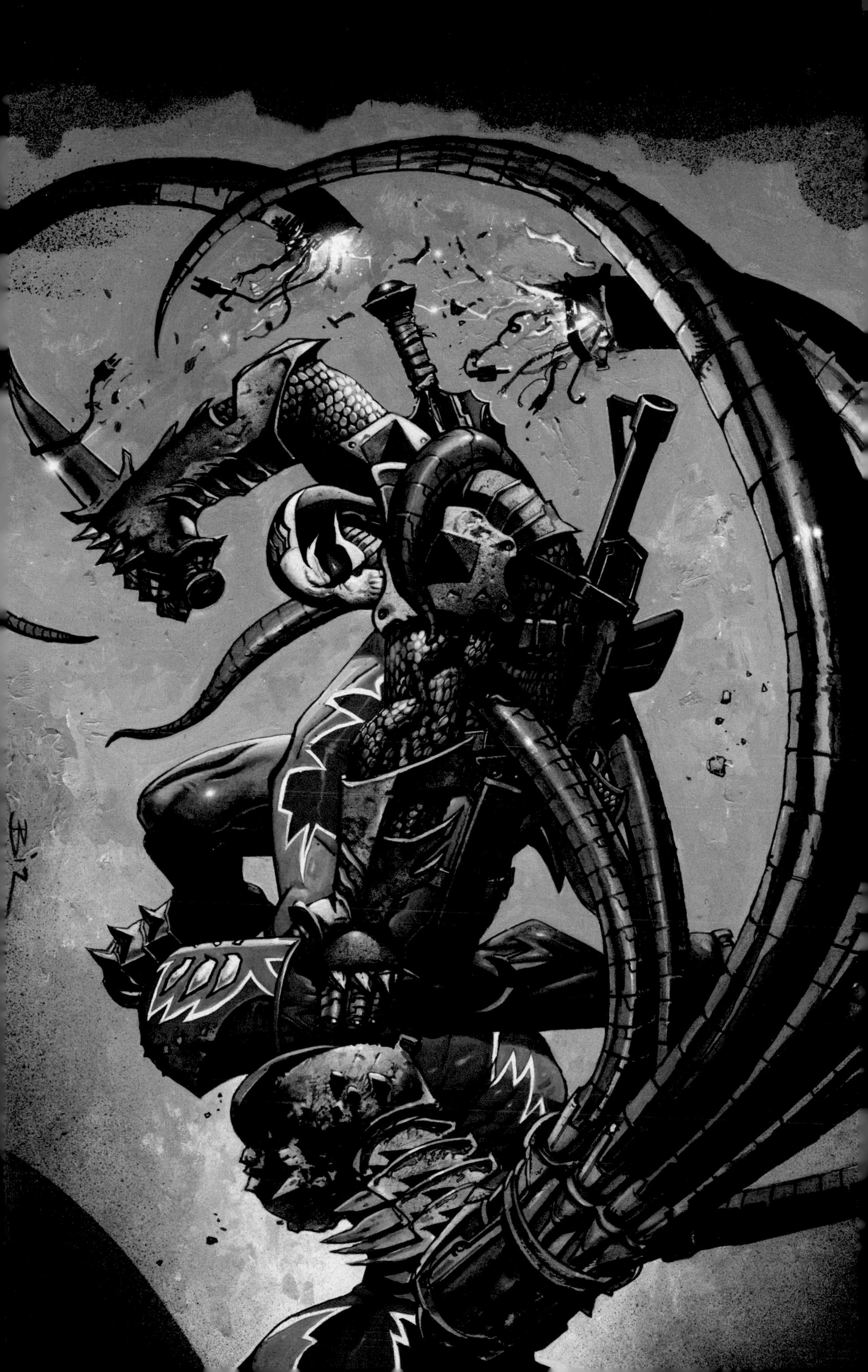

LEGACY

KYLE HIGGINS writer **JOE BENNETT** penciller **ART THIBERT** inker cover by **SIMON BISLEY**

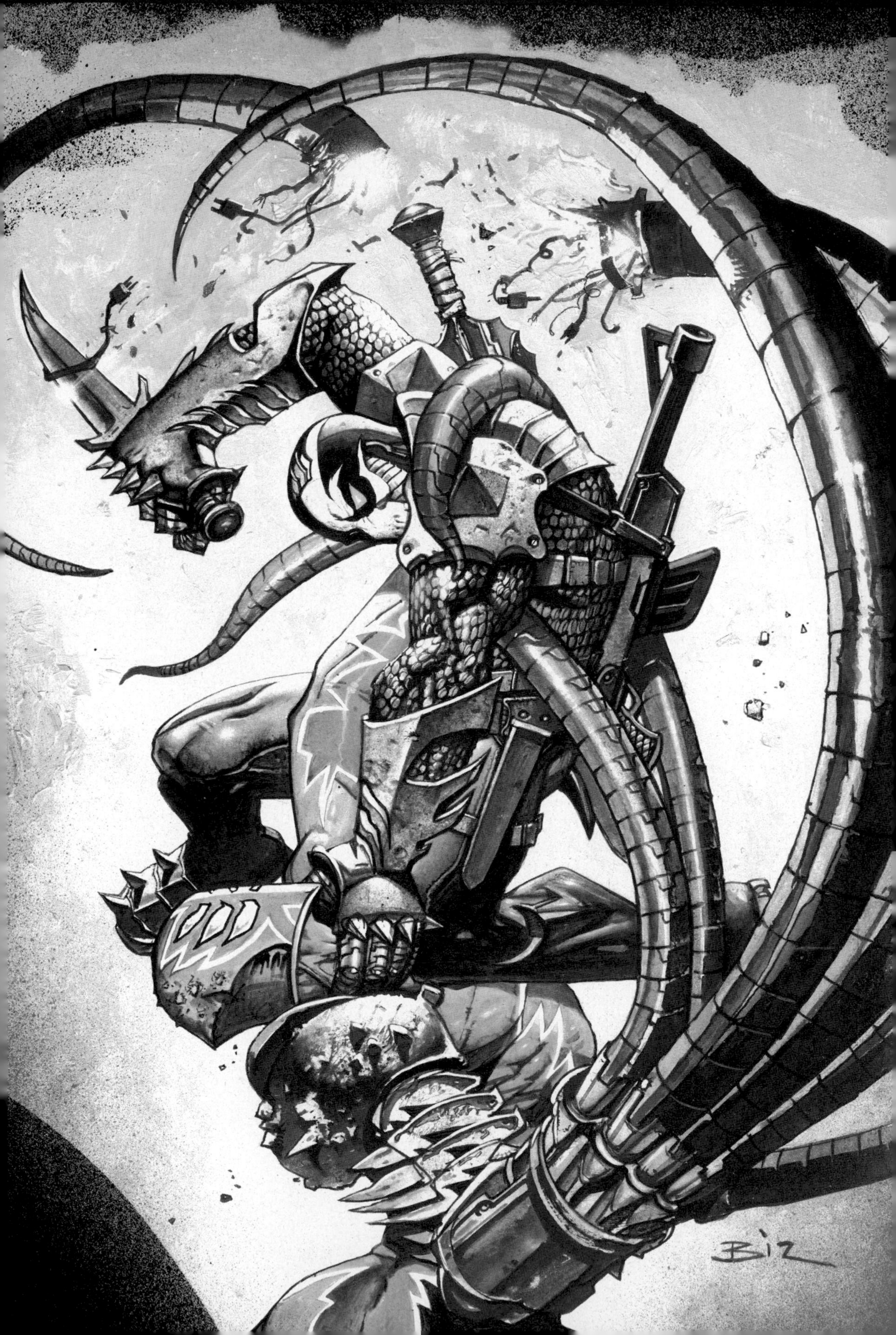
BIZ

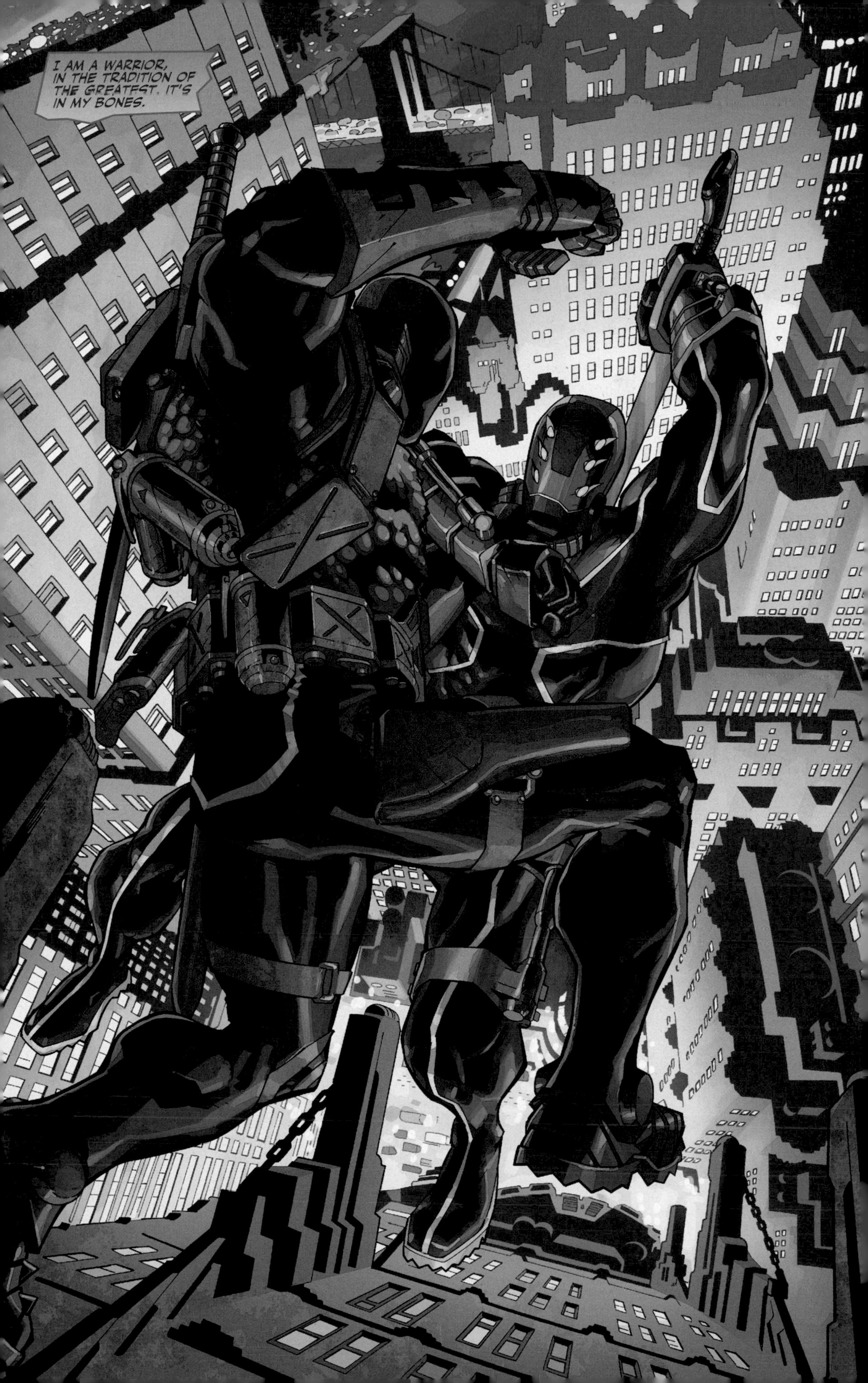
I AM A WARRIOR, IN THE TRADITION OF THE GREATEST. IT'S IN MY BONES.

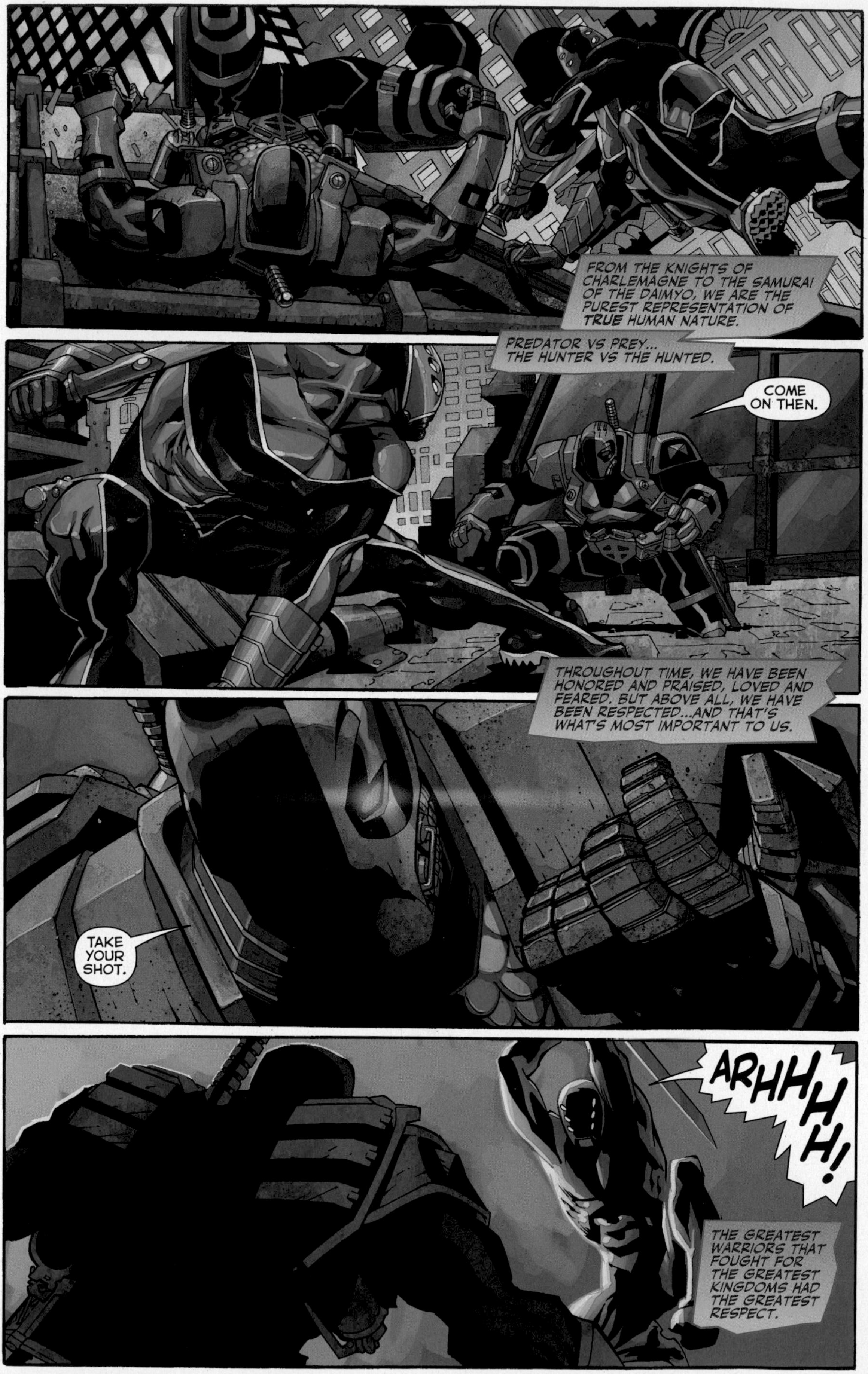
FROM THE KNIGHTS OF CHARLEMAGNE TO THE SAMURAI OF THE DAIMYO, WE ARE THE PUREST REPRESENTATION OF TRUE HUMAN NATURE.
PREDATOR VS PREY... THE HUNTER VS THE HUNTED.
COME ON THEN.
THROUGHOUT TIME, WE HAVE BEEN HONORED AND PRAISED, LOVED AND FEARED. BUT ABOVE ALL, WE HAVE BEEN RESPECTED...AND THAT'S WHAT'S MOST IMPORTANT TO US.
TAKE YOUR SHOT.
ARHHHHH!
THE GREATEST WARRIORS THAT FOUGHT FOR THE GREATEST KINGDOMS HAD THE GREATEST RESPECT.

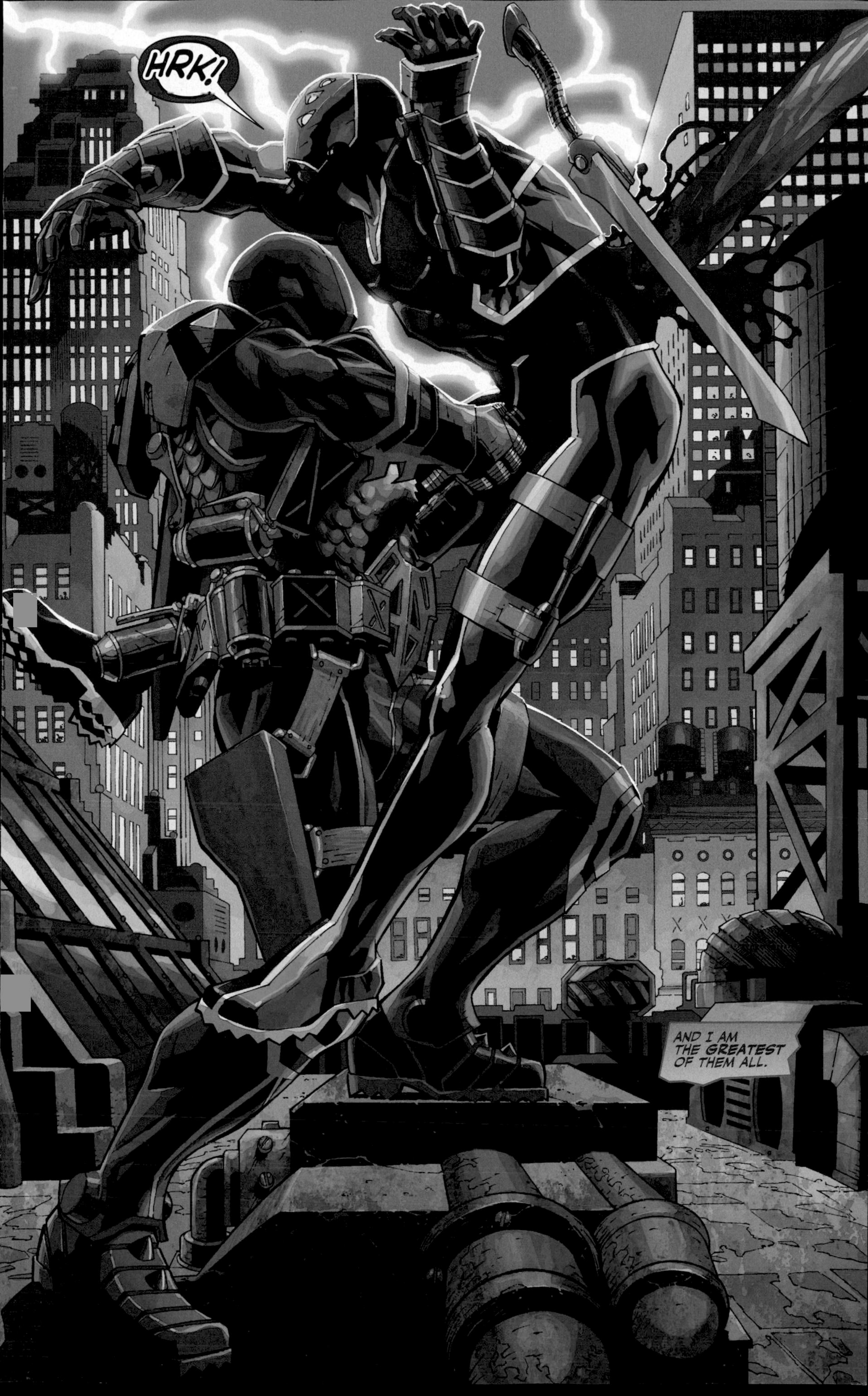
HRK!
AND I AM THE GREATEST OF THEM ALL.

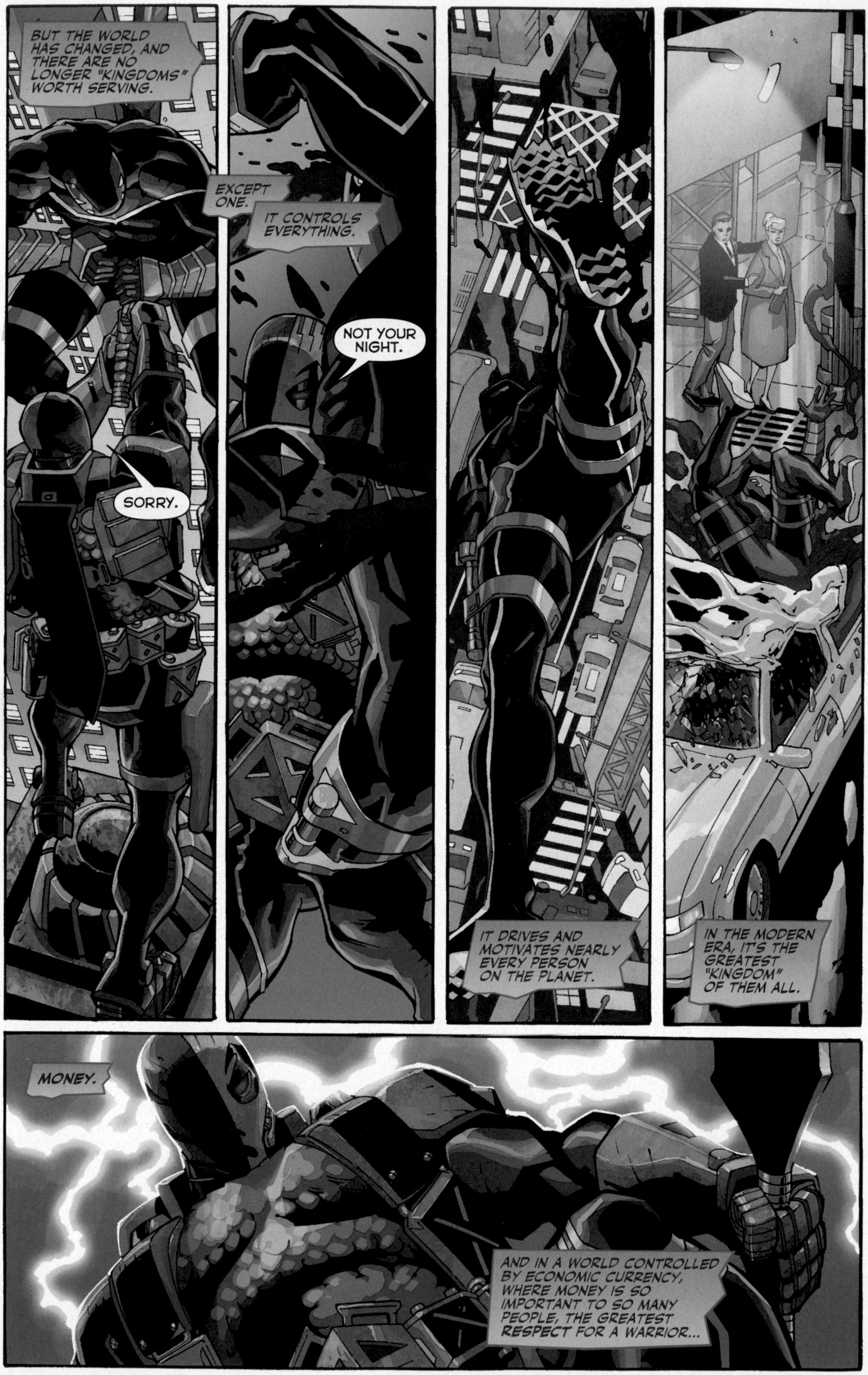
BUT THE WORLD HAS CHANGED, AND THERE ARE NO LONGER "KINGDOMS" WORTH SERVING.
SORRY.
EXCEPT ONE.
IT CONTROLS EVERYTHING.
NOT YOUR NIGHT.
IT DRIVES AND MOTIVATES NEARLY EVERY PERSON ON THE PLANET.
IN THE MODERN ERA, IT'S THE GREATEST "KINGDOM" OF THEM ALL.
MONEY.
AND IN A WORLD CONTROLLED BY ECONOMIC CURRENCY, WHERE MONEY IS SO IMPORTANT TO SO MANY PEOPLE, THE GREATEST RESPECT FOR A WARRIOR...

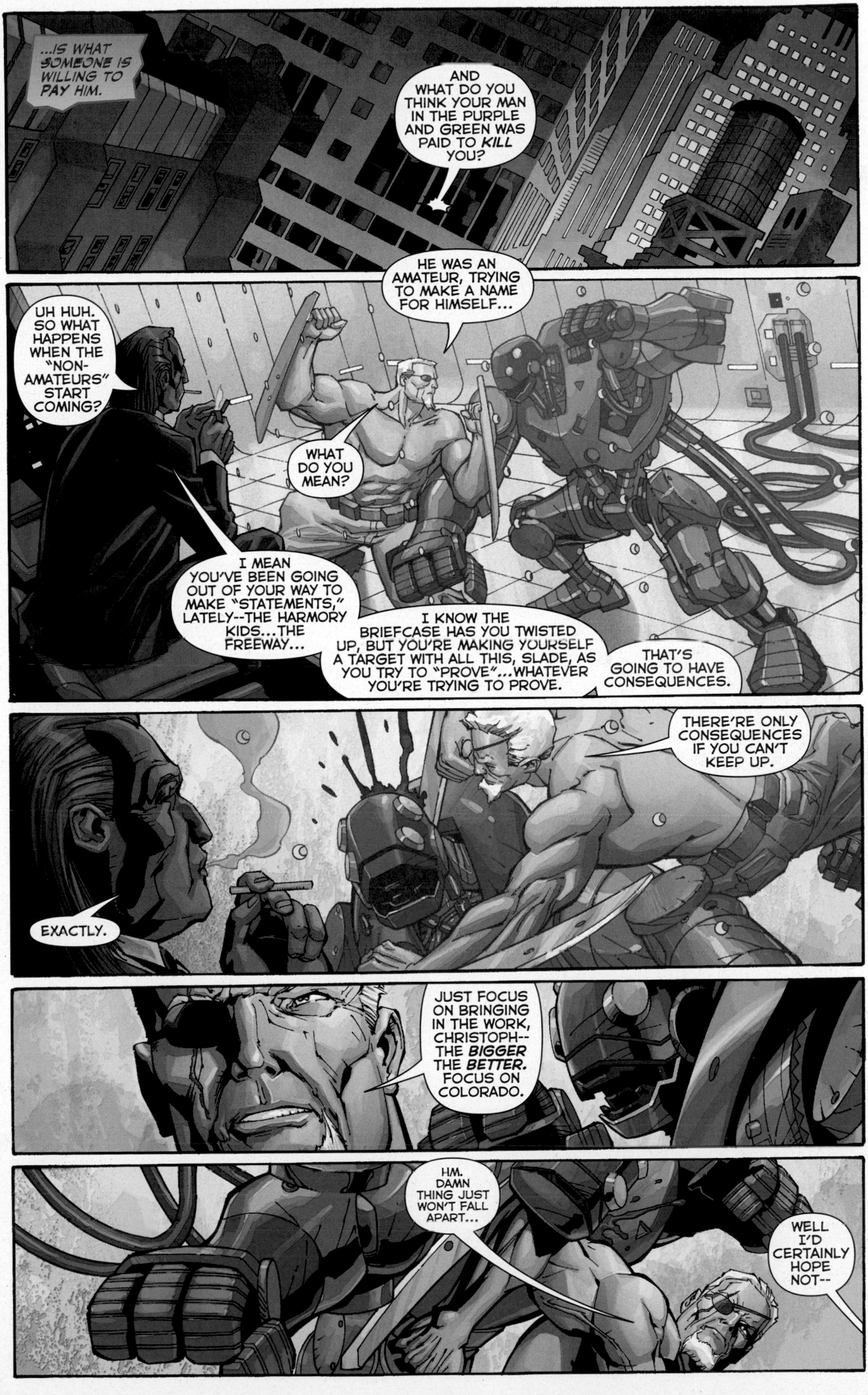
...IS WHAT SOMEONE IS WILLING TO PAY HIM.
AND WHAT DO YOU THINK YOUR MAN IN THE PURPLE AND GREEN WAS PAID TO KILL YOU?
HE WAS AN AMATEUR, TRYING TO MAKE A NAME FOR HIMSELF...
UH HUH. SO WHAT HAPPENS WHEN THE "NON-AMATEURS" START COMING?
WHAT DO YOU MEAN?
I MEAN YOU'VE BEEN GOING OUT OF YOUR WAY TO MAKE "STATEMENTS," LATELY--THE HARMORY KIDS...THE FREEWAY...
I KNOW THE BRIEFCASE HAS YOU TWISTED UP, BUT YOU'RE MAKING YOURSELF A TARGET WITH ALL THIS, SLADE, AS YOU TRY TO "PROVE"...WHATEVER YOU'RE TRYING TO PROVE.
THAT'S GOING TO HAVE CONSEQUENCES.
THERE'RE ONLY CONSEQUENCES IF YOU CAN'T KEEP UP.
EXACTLY.
JUST FOCUS ON BRINGING IN THE WORK, CHRISTOPH-- THE BIGGER THE BETTER. FOCUS ON COLORADO.
HM. DAMN THING JUST WON'T FALL APART...
WELL I'D CERTAINLY HOPE NOT--

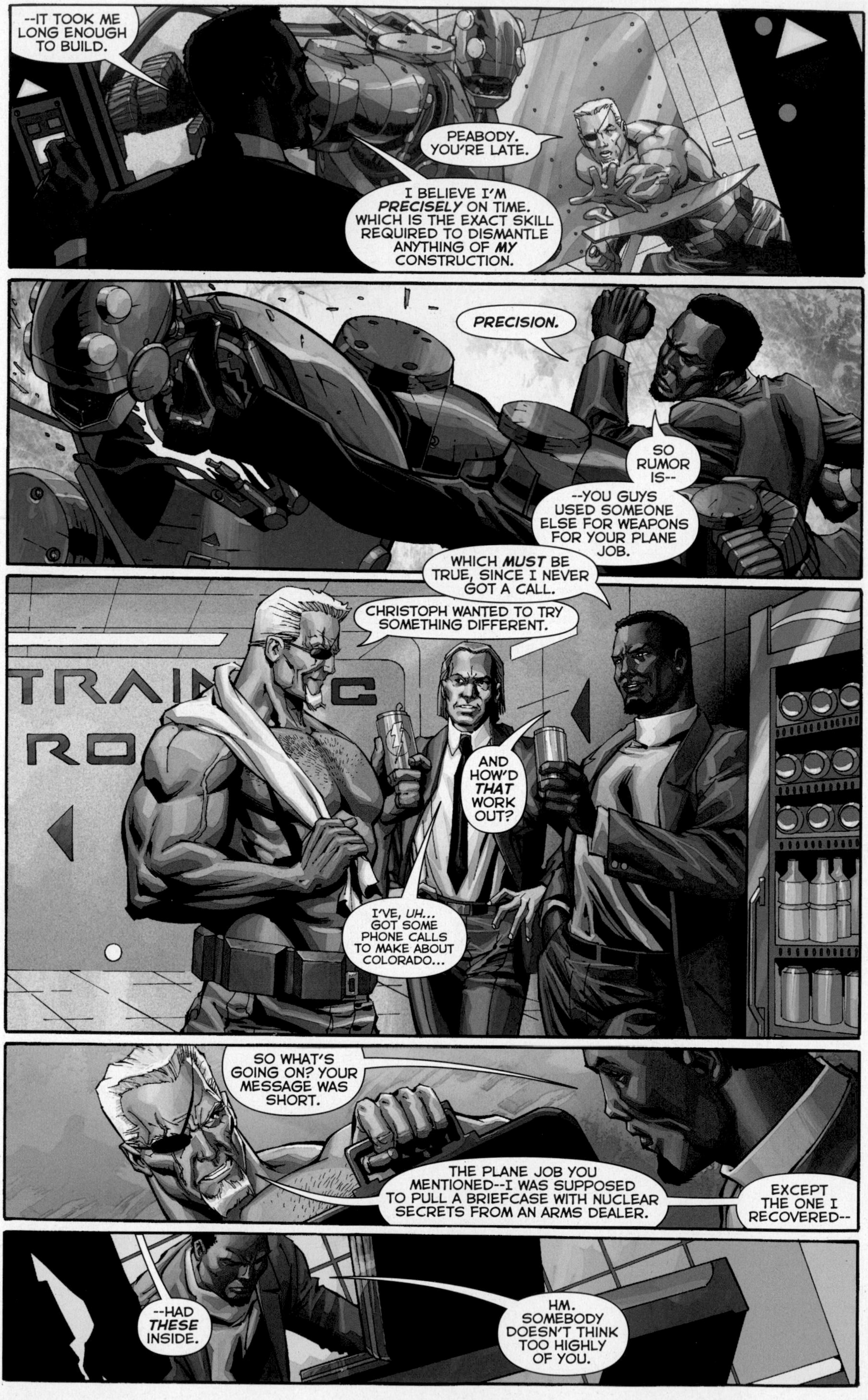
--IT TOOK ME LONG ENOUGH TO BUILD.
PEABODY. YOU'RE LATE.
I BELIEVE I'M *PRECISELY* ON TIME. WHICH IS THE EXACT SKILL REQUIRED TO DISMANTLE ANYTHING OF *MY* CONSTRUCTION.
PRECISION.
SO RUMOR IS--
--YOU GUYS USED SOMEONE ELSE FOR WEAPONS FOR YOUR PLANE JOB.
WHICH *MUST* BE TRUE, SINCE I NEVER GOT A CALL.
CHRISTOPH WANTED TO TRY SOMETHING DIFFERENT.
AND HOW'D *THAT* WORK OUT?
I'VE, *UH*... GOT SOME PHONE CALLS TO MAKE ABOUT COLORADO...
SO WHAT'S GOING ON? YOUR MESSAGE WAS SHORT.
THE PLANE JOB YOU MENTIONED--I WAS SUPPOSED TO PULL A BRIEFCASE WITH NUCLEAR SECRETS FROM AN ARMS DEALER.
EXCEPT THE ONE I RECOVERED--
--HAD *THESE* INSIDE.
HM. SOMEBODY DOESN'T THINK TOO HIGHLY OF YOU.

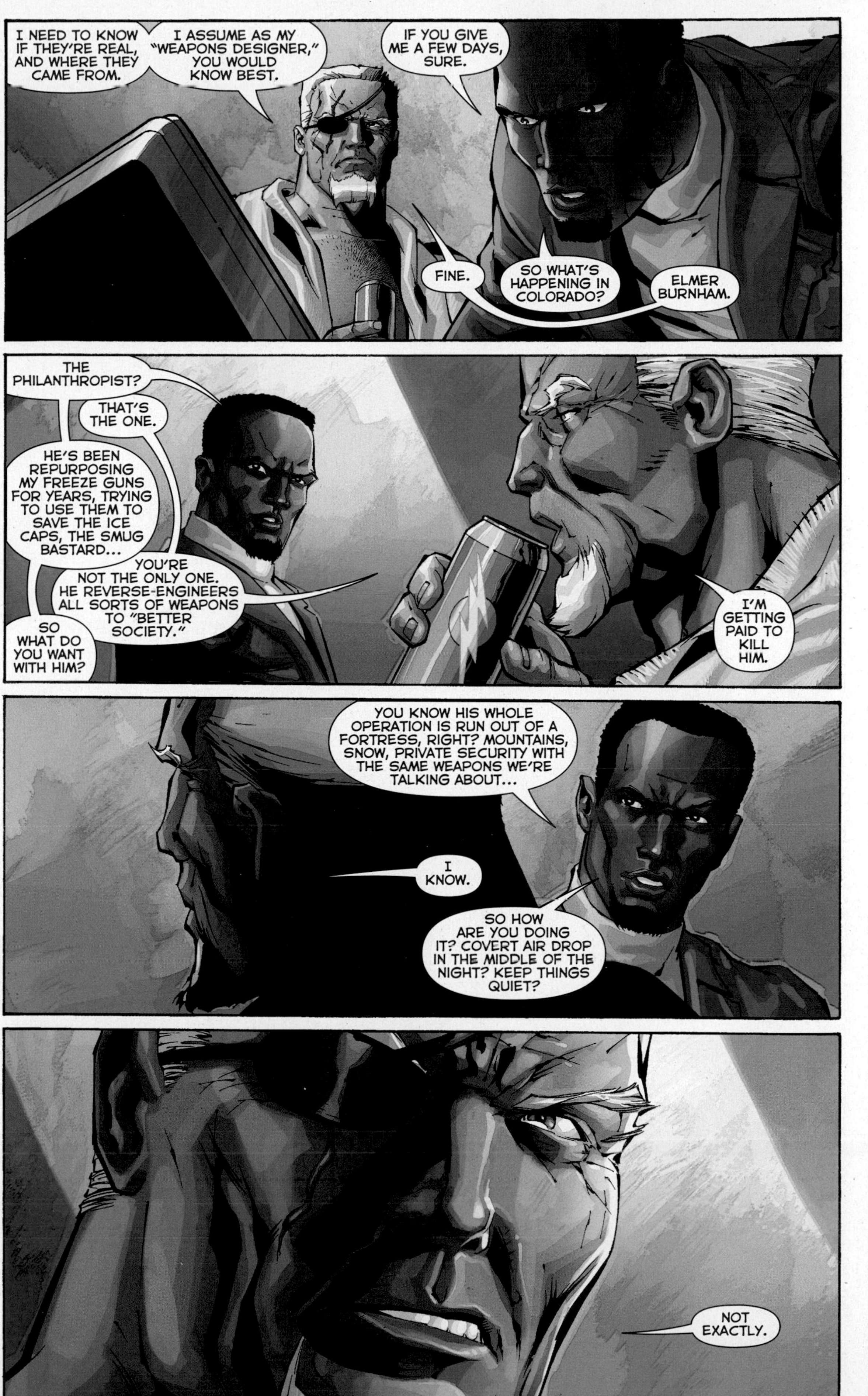
I NEED TO KNOW IF THEY'RE REAL, AND WHERE THEY CAME FROM.
I ASSUME AS MY "WEAPONS DESIGNER," YOU WOULD KNOW BEST.
IF YOU GIVE ME A FEW DAYS, SURE.
FINE.
SO WHAT'S HAPPENING IN COLORADO?
ELMER BURNHAM.
THE PHILANTHROPIST?
THAT'S THE ONE.
HE'S BEEN REPURPOSING MY FREEZE GUNS FOR YEARS, TRYING TO USE THEM TO SAVE THE ICE CAPS, THE SMUG BASTARD...
YOU'RE NOT THE ONLY ONE. HE REVERSE-ENGINEERS ALL SORTS OF WEAPONS TO "BETTER SOCIETY."
SO WHAT DO YOU WANT WITH HIM?
I'M GETTING PAID TO KILL HIM.
YOU KNOW HIS WHOLE OPERATION IS RUN OUT OF A FORTRESS, RIGHT? MOUNTAINS, SNOW, PRIVATE SECURITY WITH THE SAME WEAPONS WE'RE TALKING ABOUT...
I KNOW.
SO HOW ARE YOU DOING IT? COVERT AIR DROP IN THE MIDDLE OF THE NIGHT? KEEP THINGS QUIET?
NOT EXACTLY.

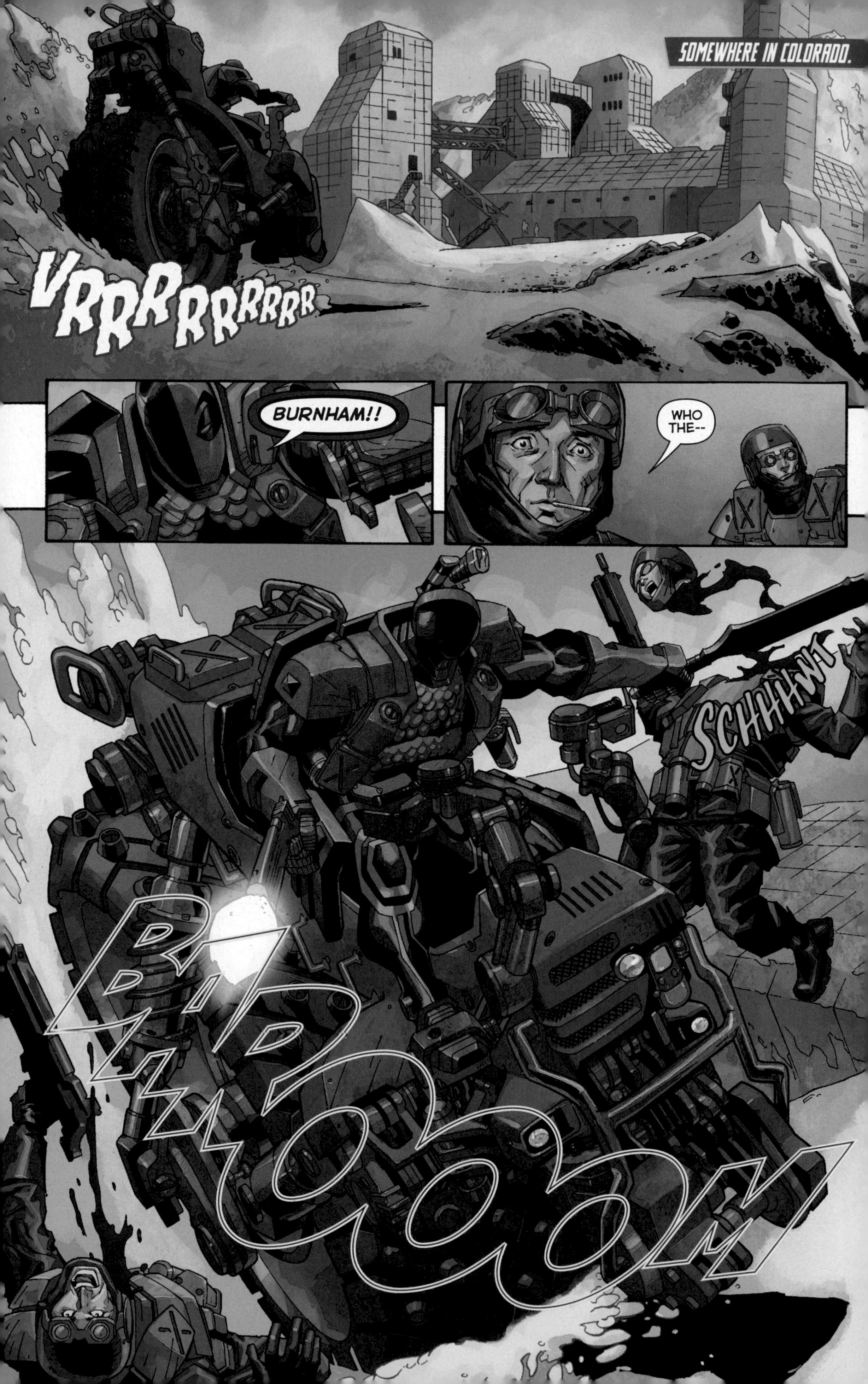
SOMEWHERE IN COLORADO.
VRRRRRRRRR
BURNHAM!!
WHO THE--
SCHHHWT
BRRZAKOOOM

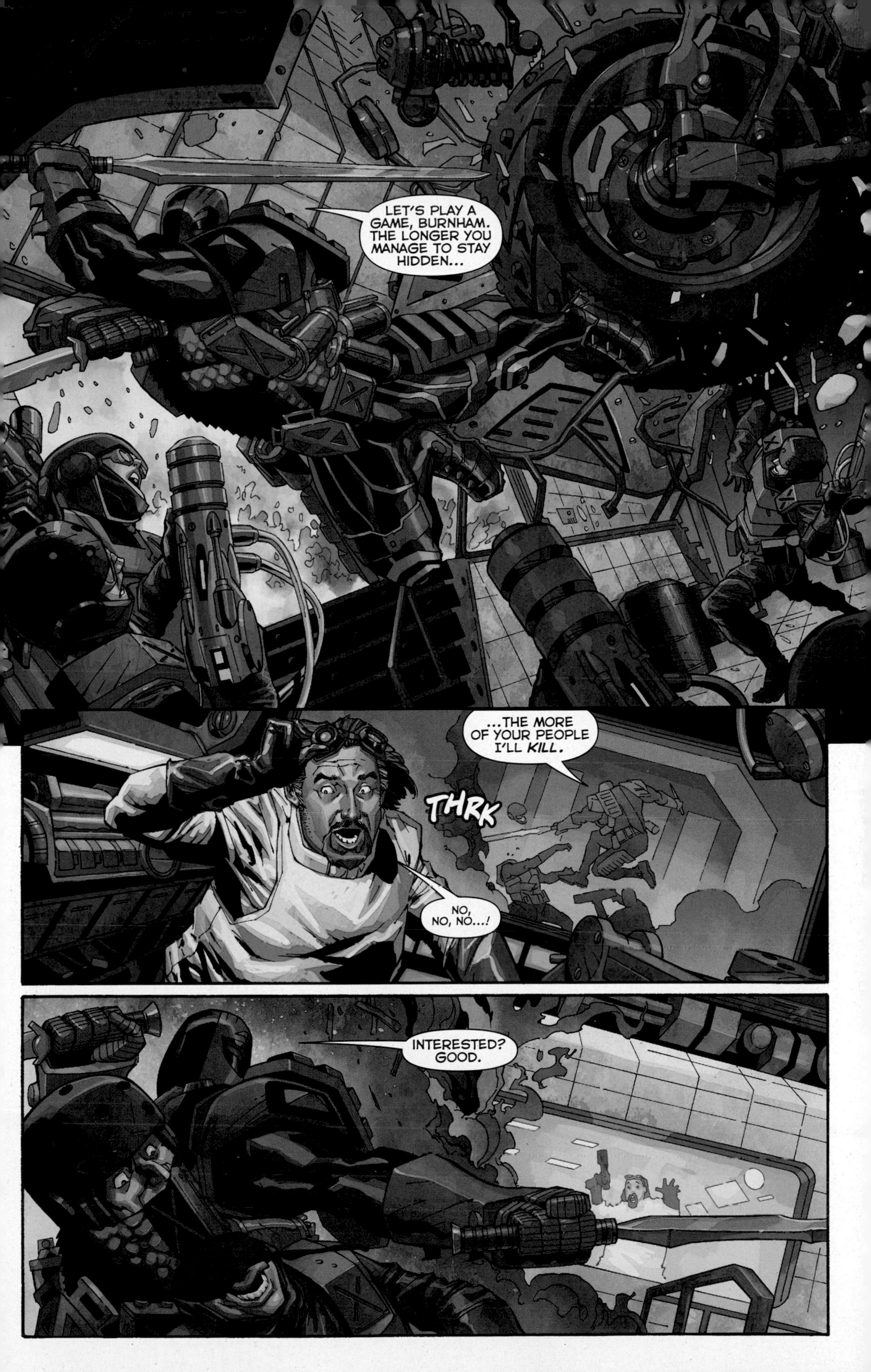
LET'S PLAY A GAME, BURNHAM. THE LONGER YOU MANAGE TO STAY HIDDEN...
...THE MORE OF YOUR PEOPLE I'LL KILL.
THRK
NO, NO, NO...!
INTERESTED? GOOD.

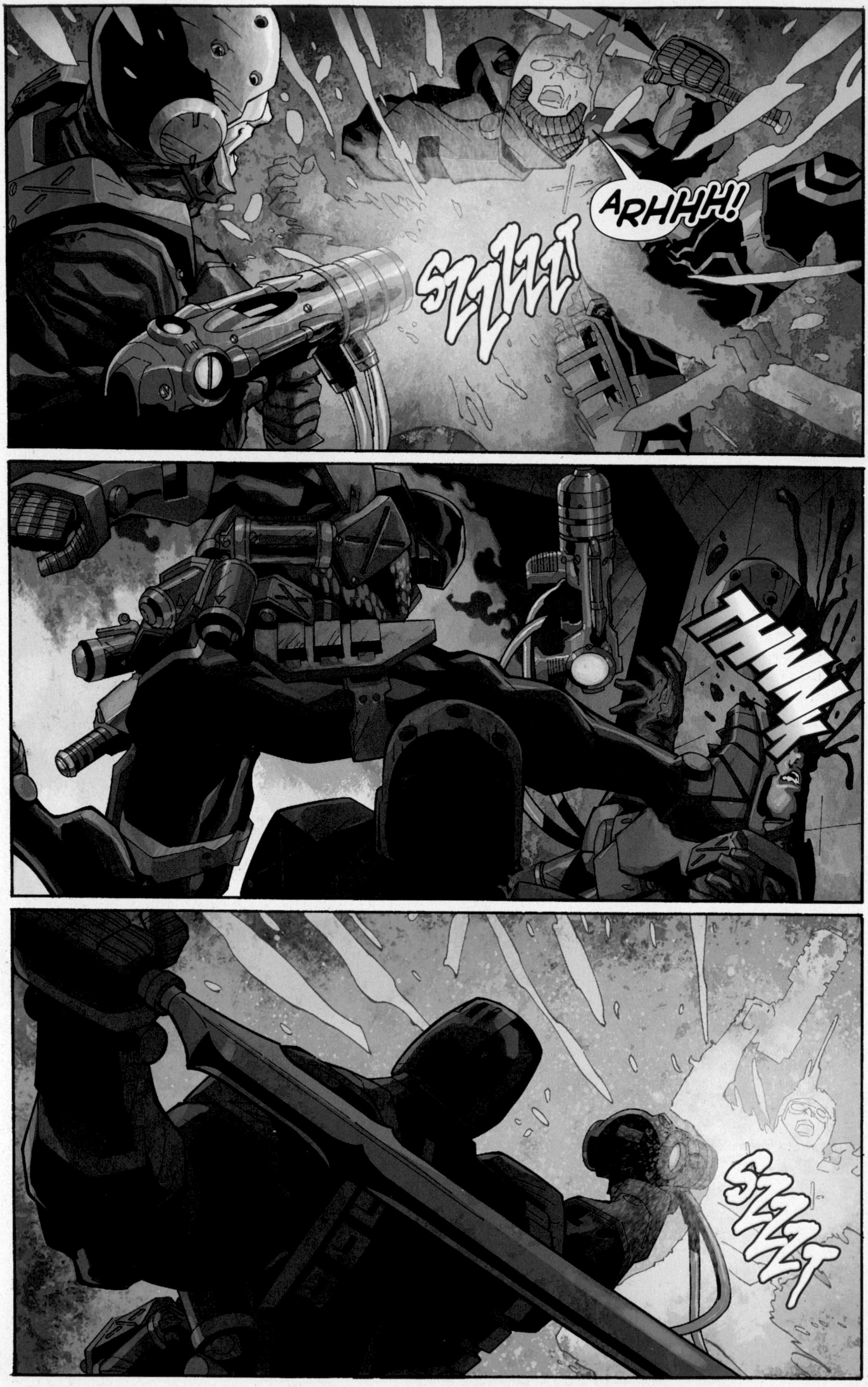
ARHHH!
SZZZZZT
THWNK
SZZZT

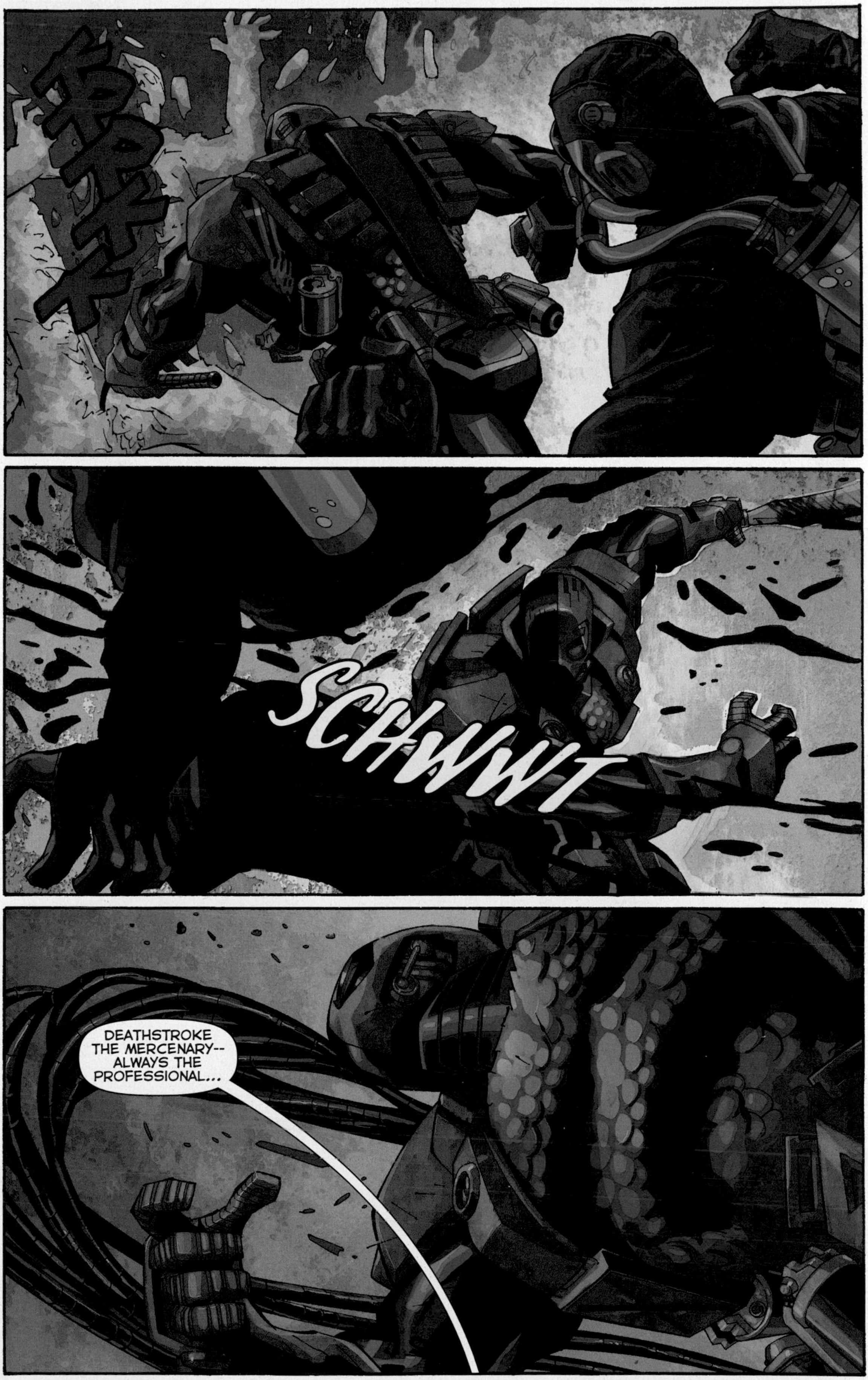
KRRKK
SCHWWT
DEATHSTROKE THE MERCENARY-- ALWAYS THE PROFESSIONAL...

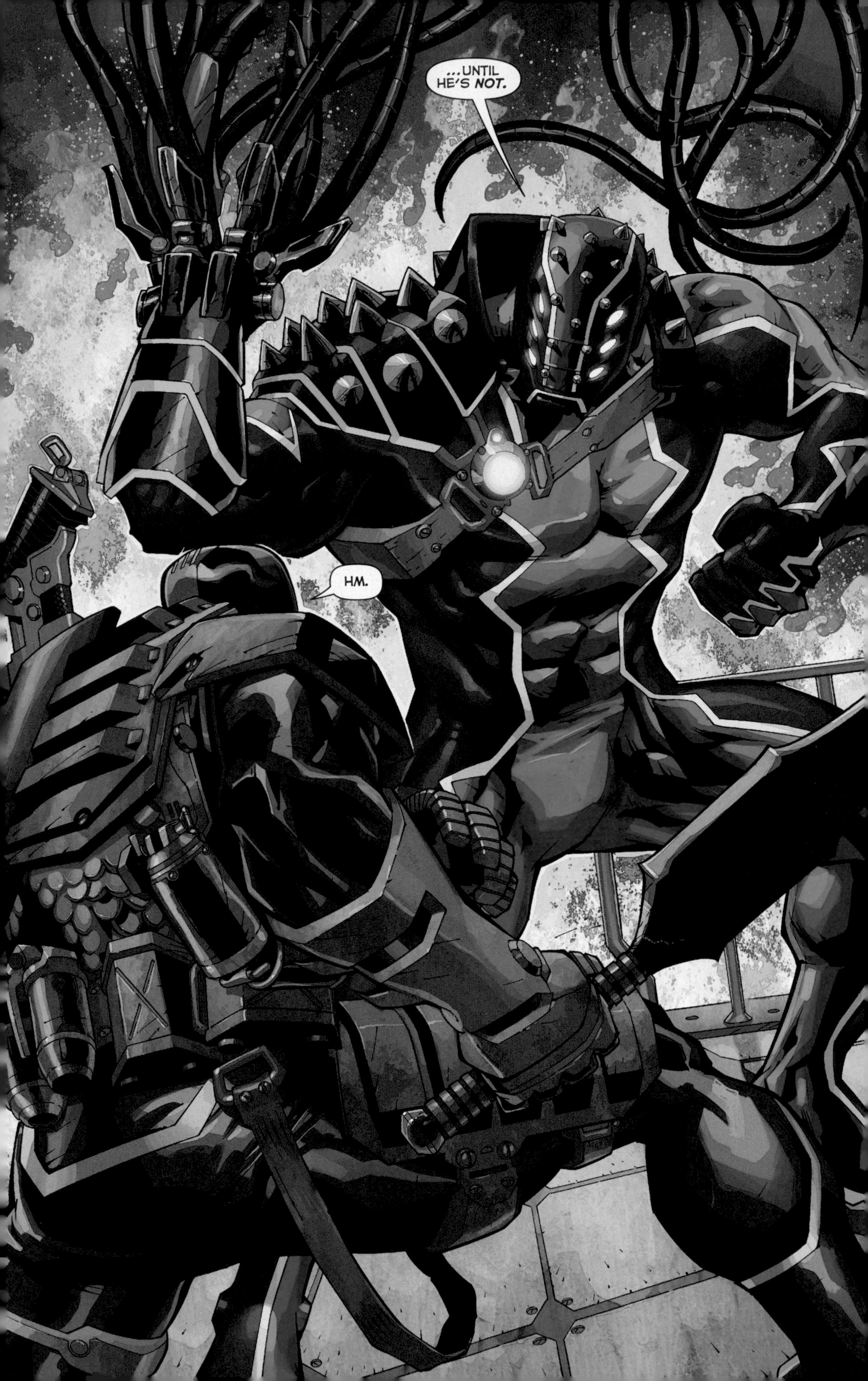
...UNTIL HE'S NOT.
HM.

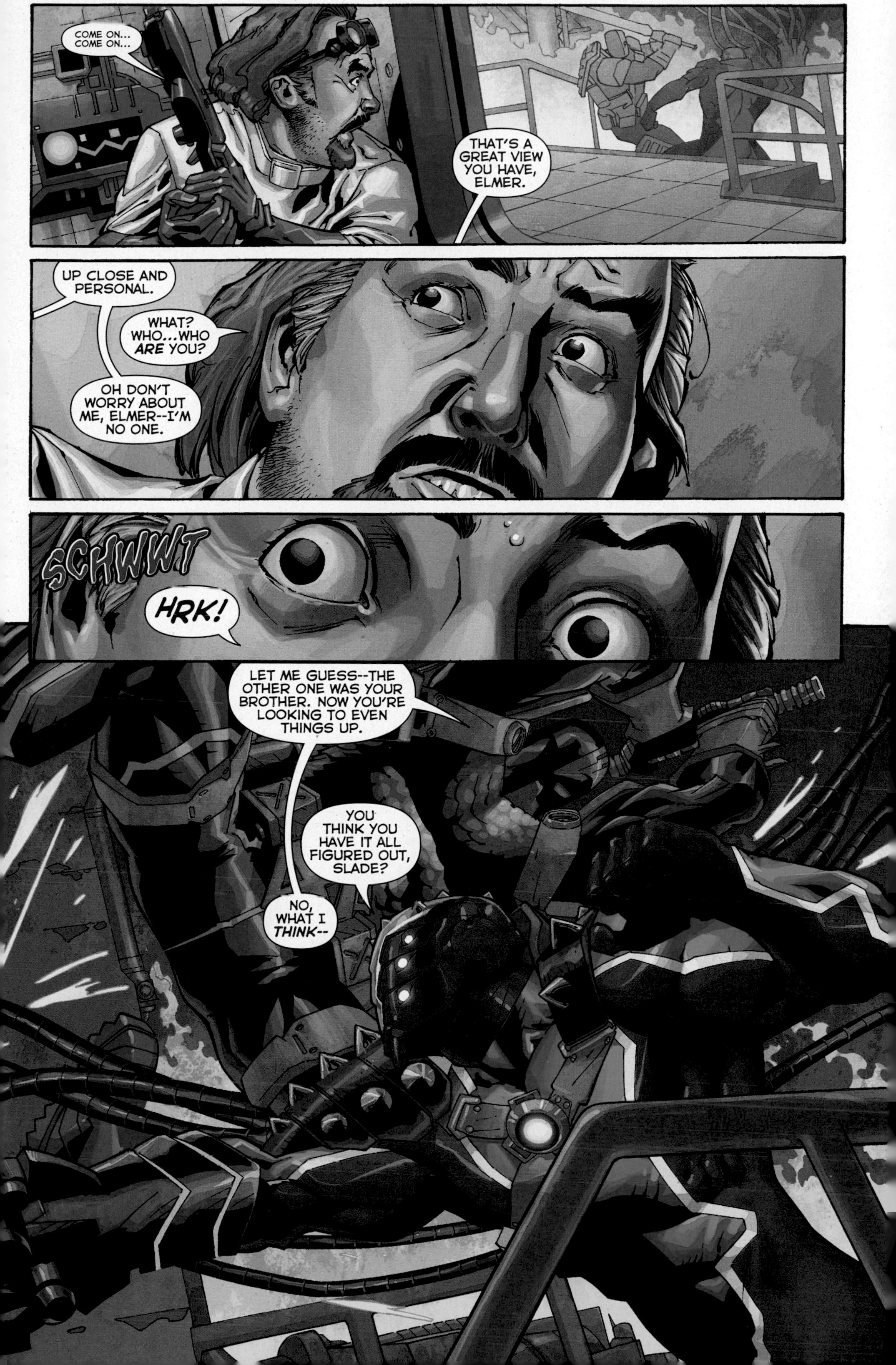
COME ON... COME ON...
THAT'S A GREAT VIEW YOU HAVE, ELMER.
UP CLOSE AND PERSONAL.
WHAT? WHO...WHO *ARE* YOU?
OH DON'T WORRY ABOUT ME, ELMER--I'M NO ONE.
SCHWWT
HRK!
LET ME GUESS--THE OTHER ONE WAS YOUR BROTHER. NOW YOU'RE LOOKING TO EVEN THINGS UP.
YOU THINK YOU HAVE IT ALL FIGURED OUT, SLADE?
NO, WHAT I *THINK*--

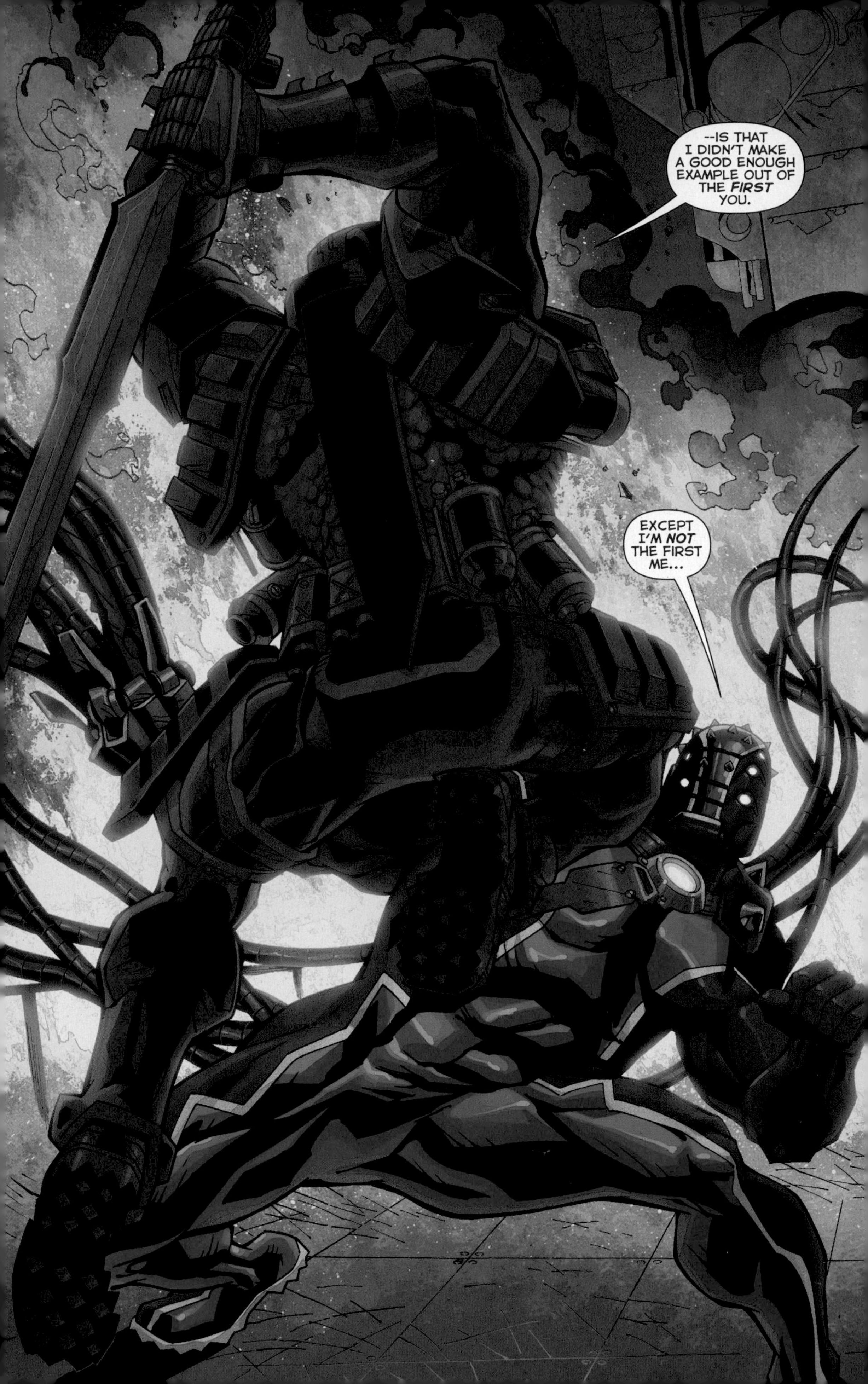

--IS THAT I DIDN'T MAKE A GOOD ENOUGH EXAMPLE OUT OF THE *FIRST* YOU.
EXCEPT I'M *NOT* THE FIRST ME...

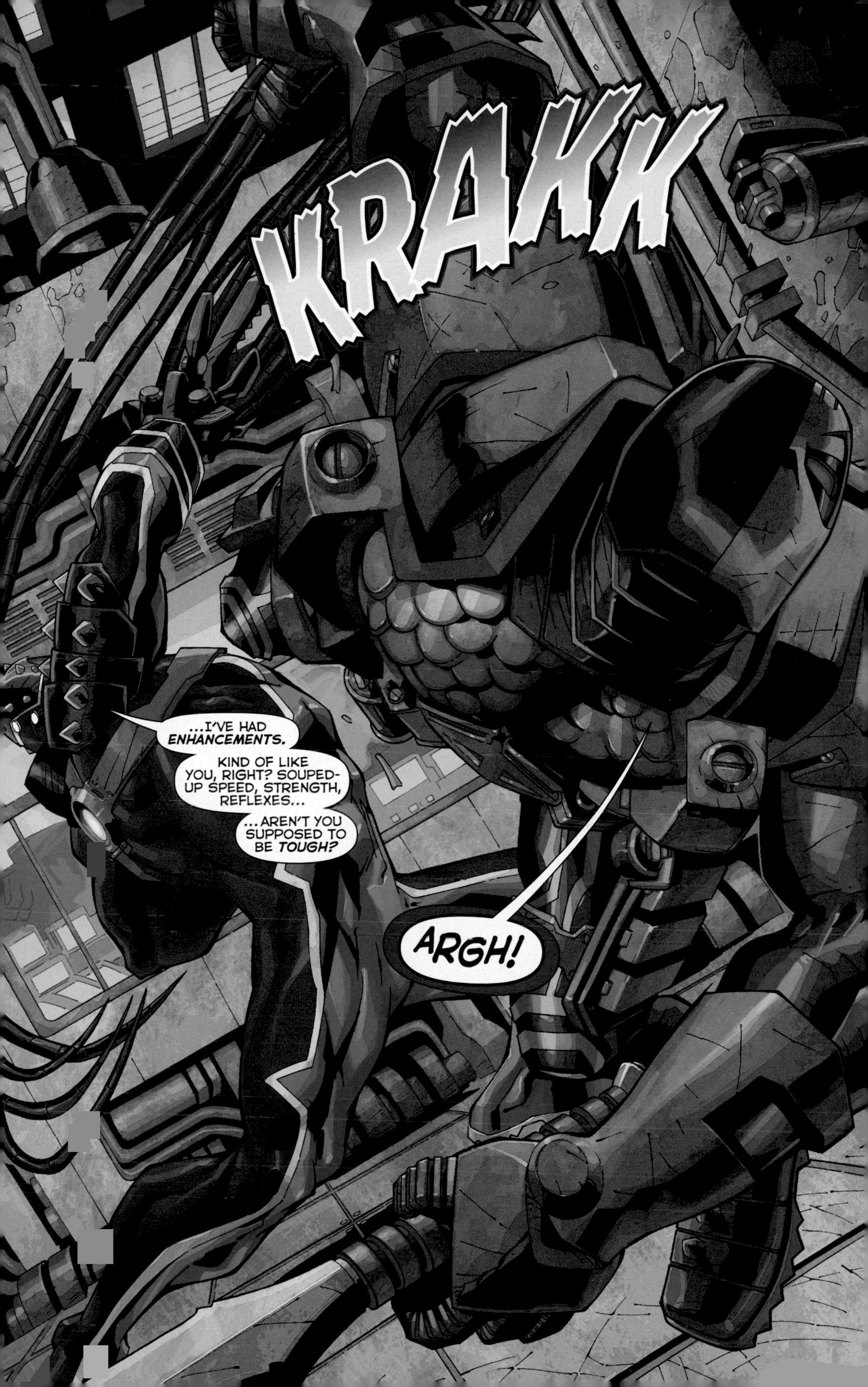
KRAKK
...I'VE HAD ENHANCEMENTS.
KIND OF LIKE YOU, RIGHT? SOUPED-UP SPEED, STRENGTH, REFLEXES...
...AREN'T YOU SUPPOSED TO BE TOUGH?
ARGH!

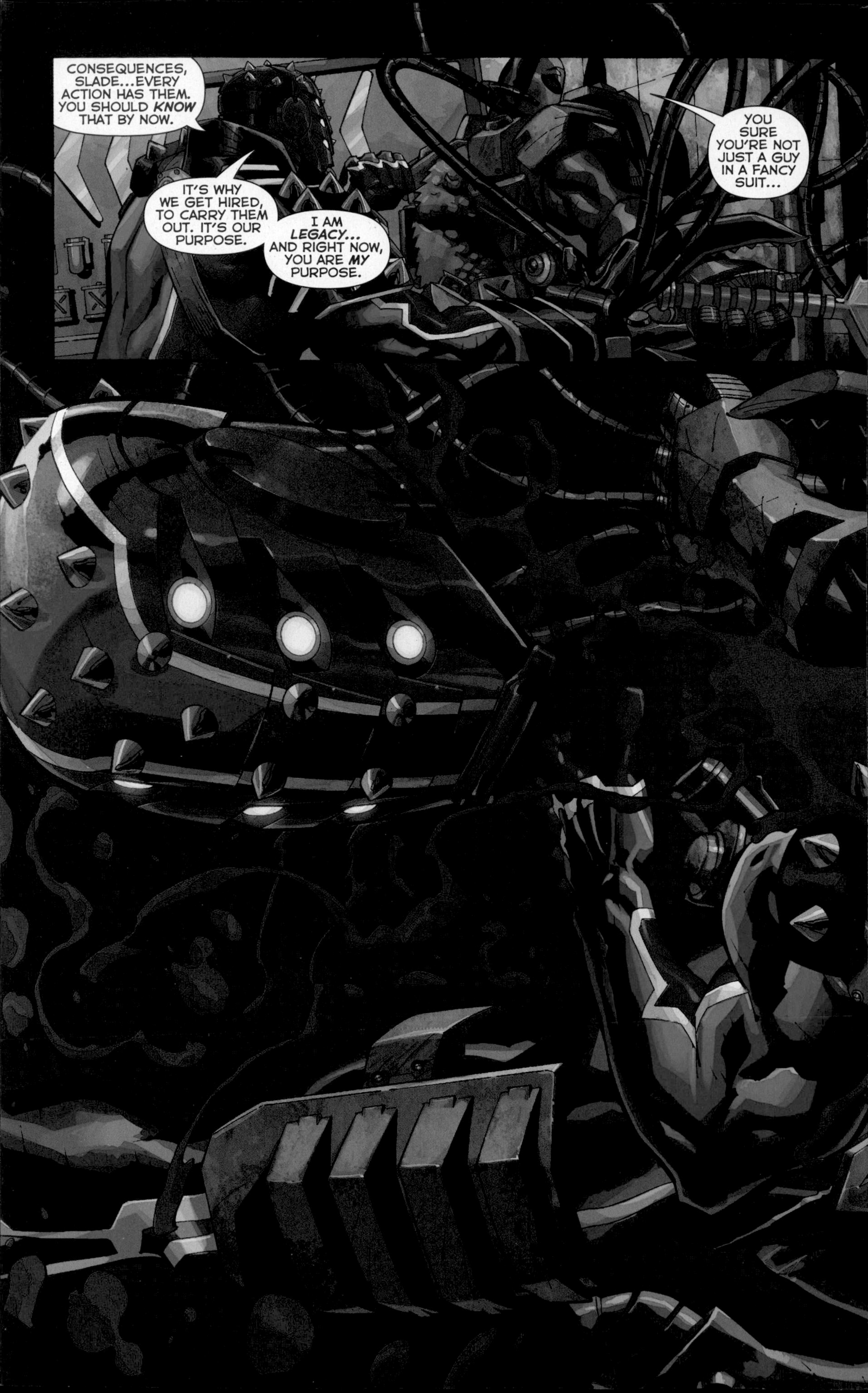
CONSEQUENCES, SLADE...EVERY ACTION HAS THEM. YOU SHOULD *KNOW* THAT BY NOW.
IT'S WHY WE GET HIRED, TO CARRY THEM OUT. IT'S OUR PURPOSE.
I AM *LEGACY...* AND RIGHT NOW, YOU ARE *MY* PURPOSE.
YOU SURE YOU'RE NOT JUST A GUY IN A FANCY SUIT...

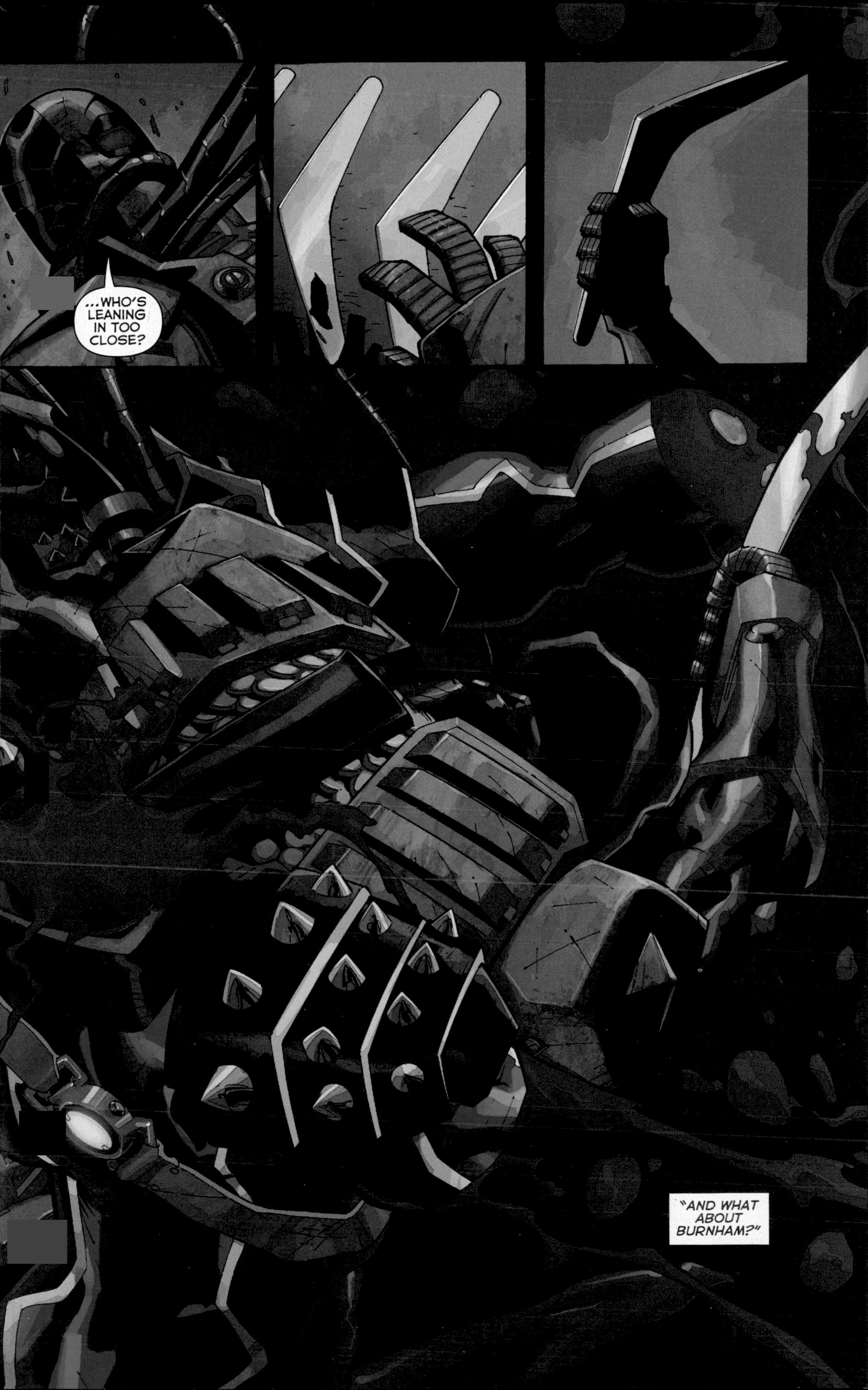
...WHO'S LEANING IN TOO CLOSE?
"AND WHAT ABOUT BURNHAM?"

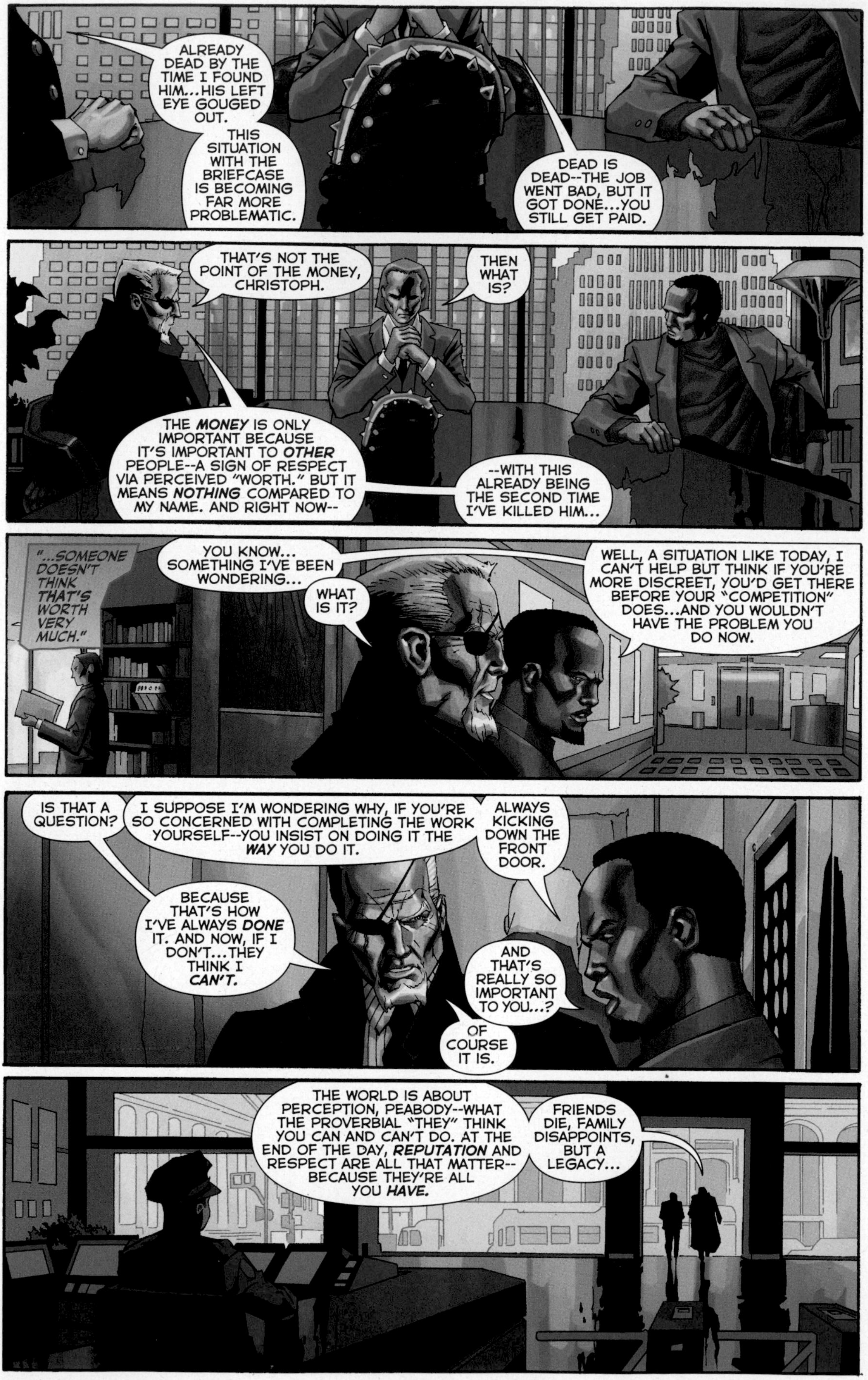
ALREADY DEAD BY THE TIME I FOUND HIM...HIS LEFT EYE GOUGED OUT.
THIS SITUATION WITH THE BRIEFCASE IS BECOMING FAR MORE PROBLEMATIC.
DEAD IS DEAD--THE JOB WENT BAD, BUT IT GOT DONE...YOU STILL GET PAID.
THAT'S NOT THE POINT OF THE MONEY, CHRISTOPH.
THEN WHAT IS?
THE MONEY IS ONLY IMPORTANT BECAUSE IT'S IMPORTANT TO OTHER PEOPLE--A SIGN OF RESPECT VIA PERCEIVED "WORTH." BUT IT MEANS NOTHING COMPARED TO MY NAME. AND RIGHT NOW--
--WITH THIS ALREADY BEING THE SECOND TIME I'VE KILLED HIM...
"...SOMEONE DOESN'T THINK THAT'S WORTH VERY MUCH."
YOU KNOW... SOMETHING I'VE BEEN WONDERING...
WHAT IS IT?
WELL, A SITUATION LIKE TODAY, I CAN'T HELP BUT THINK IF YOU'RE MORE DISCREET, YOU'D GET THERE BEFORE YOUR "COMPETITION" DOES...AND YOU WOULDN'T HAVE THE PROBLEM YOU DO NOW.
IS THAT A QUESTION?
I SUPPOSE I'M WONDERING WHY, IF YOU'RE SO CONCERNED WITH COMPLETING THE WORK YOURSELF--YOU INSIST ON DOING IT THE WAY YOU DO IT.
ALWAYS KICKING DOWN THE FRONT DOOR.
BECAUSE THAT'S HOW I'VE ALWAYS DONE IT. AND NOW, IF I DON'T...THEY THINK I CAN'T.
AND THAT'S REALLY SO IMPORTANT TO YOU...?
OF COURSE IT IS.
THE WORLD IS ABOUT PERCEPTION, PEABODY--WHAT THE PROVERBIAL "THEY" THINK YOU CAN AND CAN'T DO. AT THE END OF THE DAY, REPUTATION AND RESPECT ARE ALL THAT MATTER--BECAUSE THEY'RE ALL YOU HAVE.
FRIENDS DIE, FAMILY DISAPPOINTS, BUT A LEGACY...

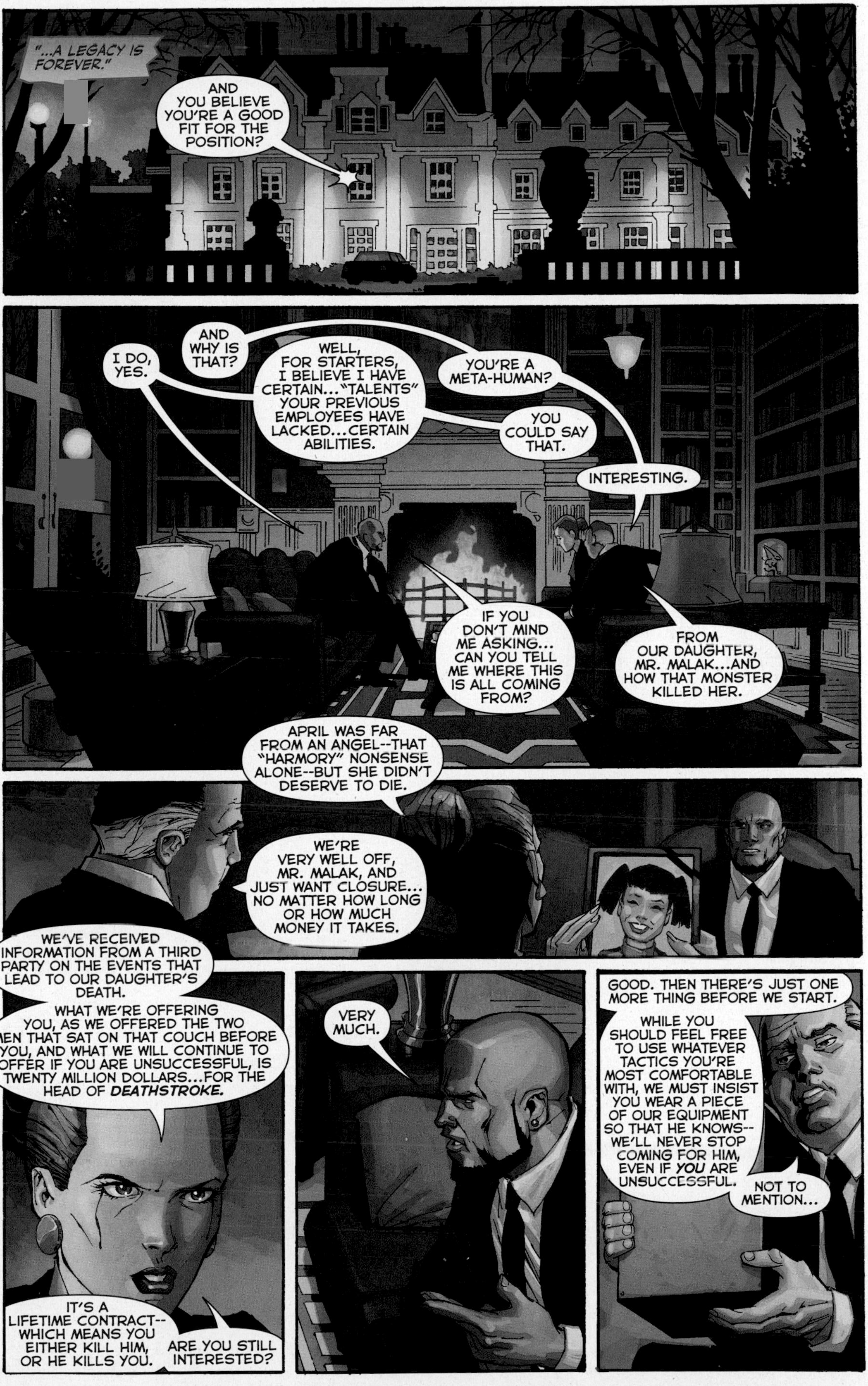
"...A LEGACY IS FOREVER."
AND YOU BELIEVE YOU'RE A GOOD FIT FOR THE POSITION?
I DO, YES.
AND WHY IS THAT?
WELL, FOR STARTERS, I BELIEVE I HAVE CERTAIN... "TALENTS" YOUR PREVIOUS EMPLOYEES HAVE LACKED...CERTAIN ABILITIES.
YOU'RE A META-HUMAN?
YOU COULD SAY THAT.
INTERESTING.
IF YOU DON'T MIND ME ASKING... CAN YOU TELL ME WHERE THIS IS ALL COMING FROM?
FROM OUR DAUGHTER, MR. MALAK...AND HOW THAT MONSTER KILLED HER.
APRIL WAS FAR FROM AN ANGEL--THAT "HARMORY" NONSENSE ALONE--BUT SHE DIDN'T DESERVE TO DIE.
WE'RE VERY WELL OFF, MR. MALAK, AND JUST WANT CLOSURE... NO MATTER HOW LONG OR HOW MUCH MONEY IT TAKES.
WE'VE RECEIVED INFORMATION FROM A THIRD PARTY ON THE EVENTS THAT LEAD TO OUR DAUGHTER'S DEATH.
WHAT WE'RE OFFERING YOU, AS WE OFFERED THE TWO MEN THAT SAT ON THAT COUCH BEFORE YOU, AND WHAT WE WILL CONTINUE TO OFFER IF YOU ARE UNSUCCESSFUL, IS TWENTY MILLION DOLLARS...FOR THE HEAD OF *DEATHSTROKE.*
IT'S A LIFETIME CONTRACT-- WHICH MEANS YOU EITHER KILL HIM, OR HE KILLS YOU.
ARE YOU STILL INTERESTED?
VERY MUCH.
GOOD. THEN THERE'S JUST ONE MORE THING BEFORE WE START.
WHILE YOU SHOULD FEEL FREE TO USE WHATEVER TACTICS YOU'RE MOST COMFORTABLE WITH, WE MUST INSIST YOU WEAR A PIECE OF OUR EQUIPMENT SO THAT HE KNOWS-- WE'LL NEVER STOP COMING FOR HIM, EVEN IF *YOU* ARE UNSUCCESSFUL.
NOT TO MENTION...

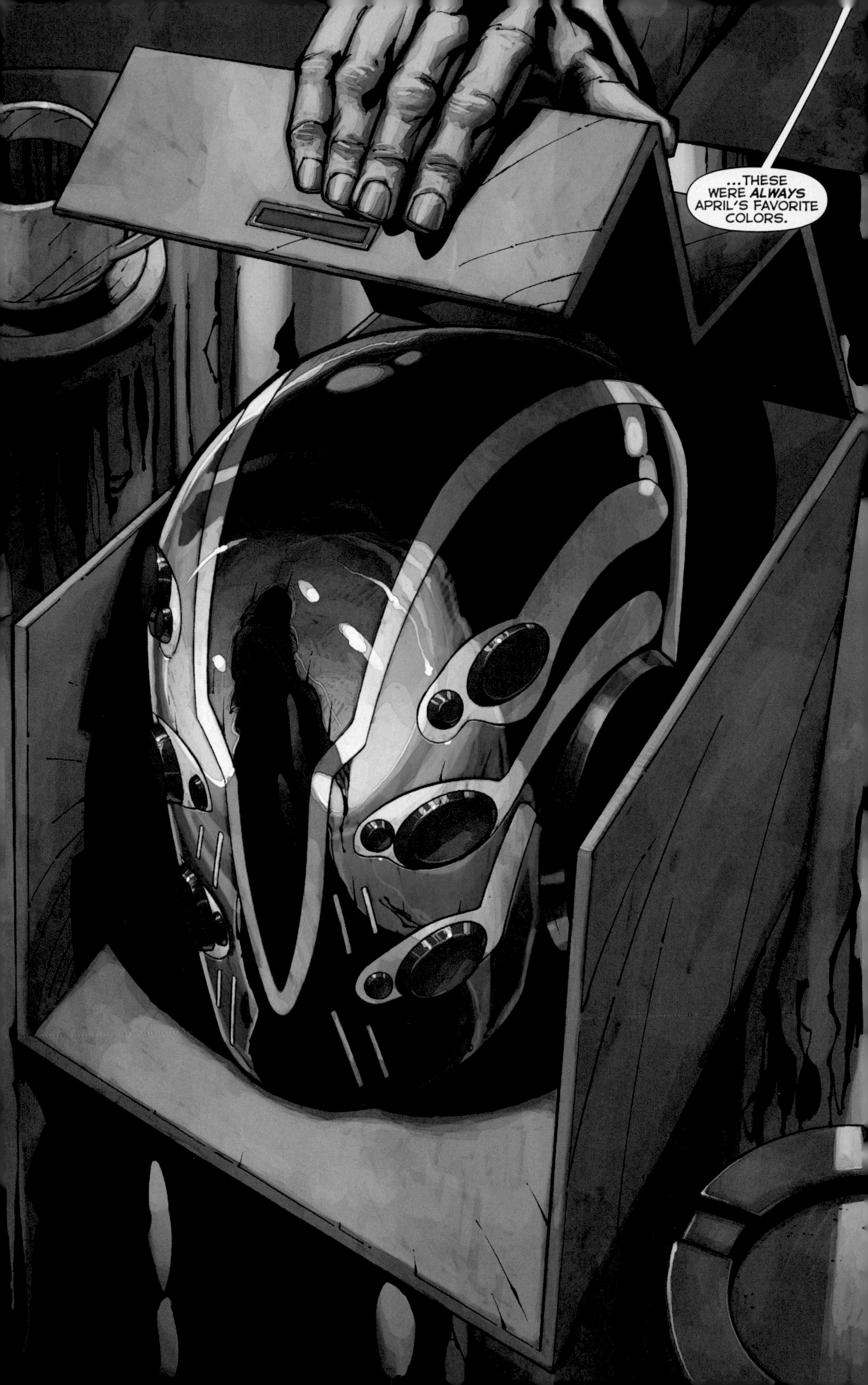
...THESE WERE ALWAYS APRIL'S FAVORITE COLORS.

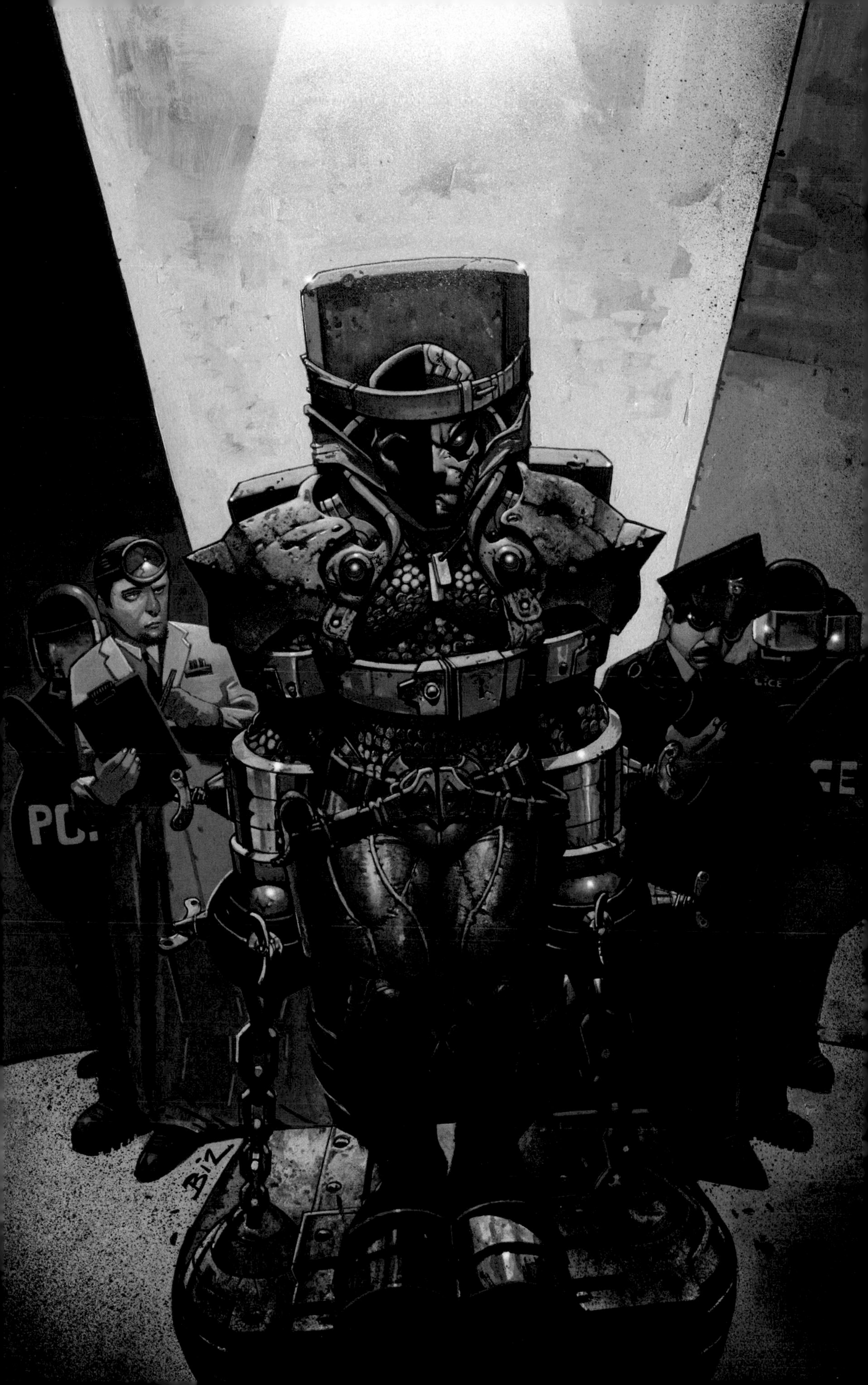

TIME'S UP

KYLE HIGGINS writer **JOE BENNETT** penciller **ART THIBERT** inker cover by **SIMON BISLEY**

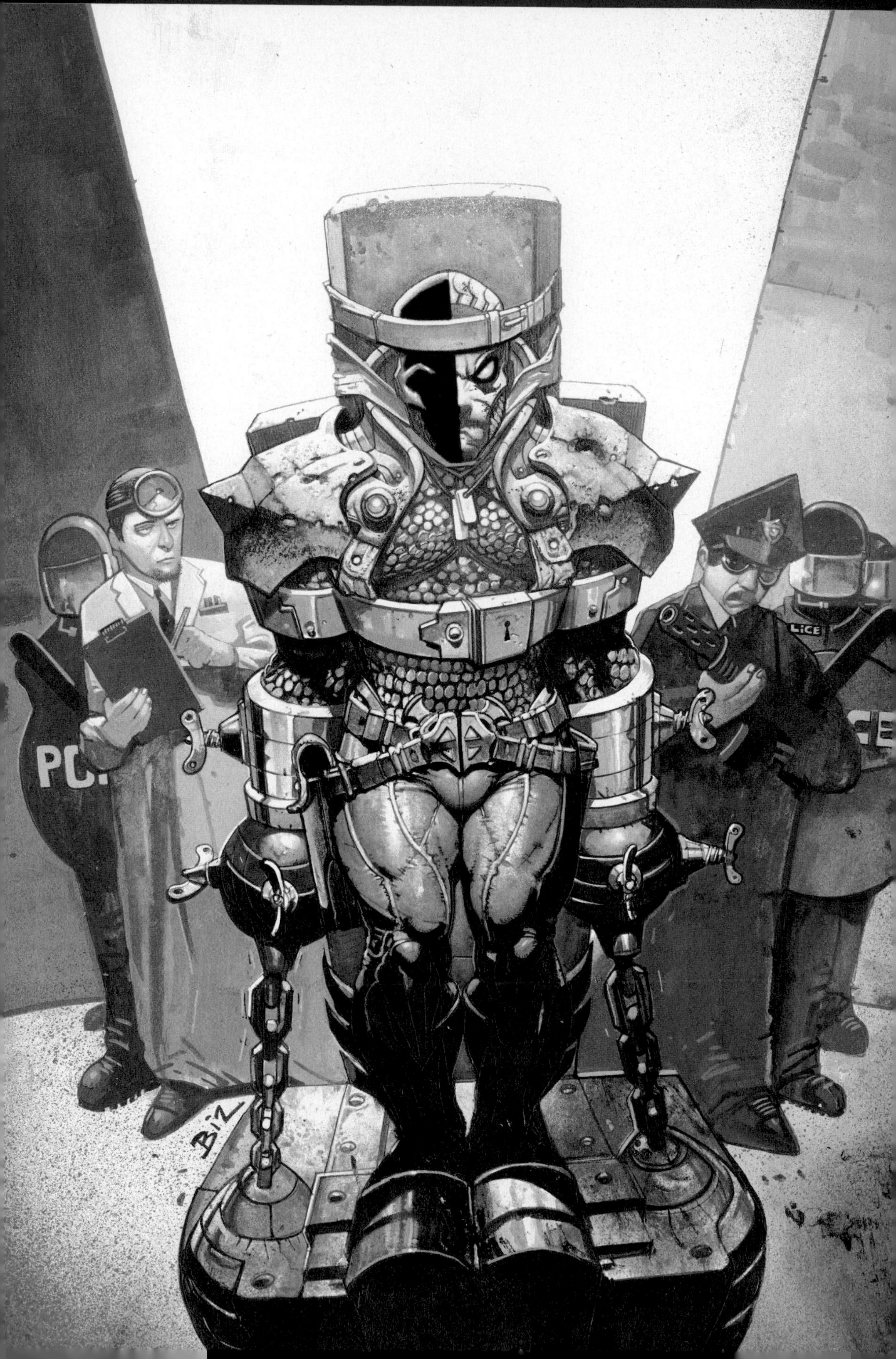

POL
LICE
CE
BIZ

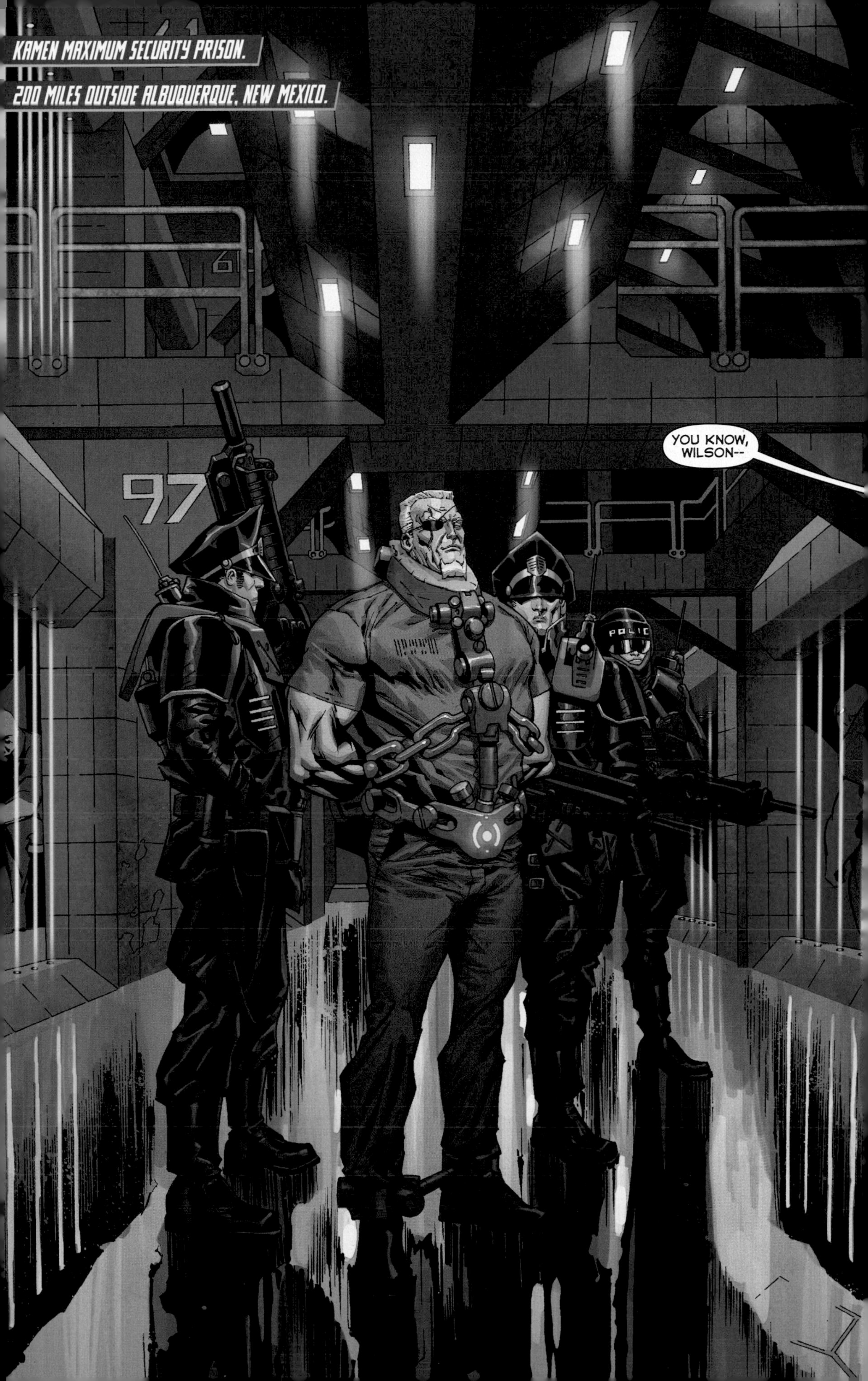

KAMEN MAXIMUM SECURITY PRISON.
200 MILES OUTSIDE ALBUQUERQUE, NEW MEXICO.
97
YOU KNOW, WILSON--

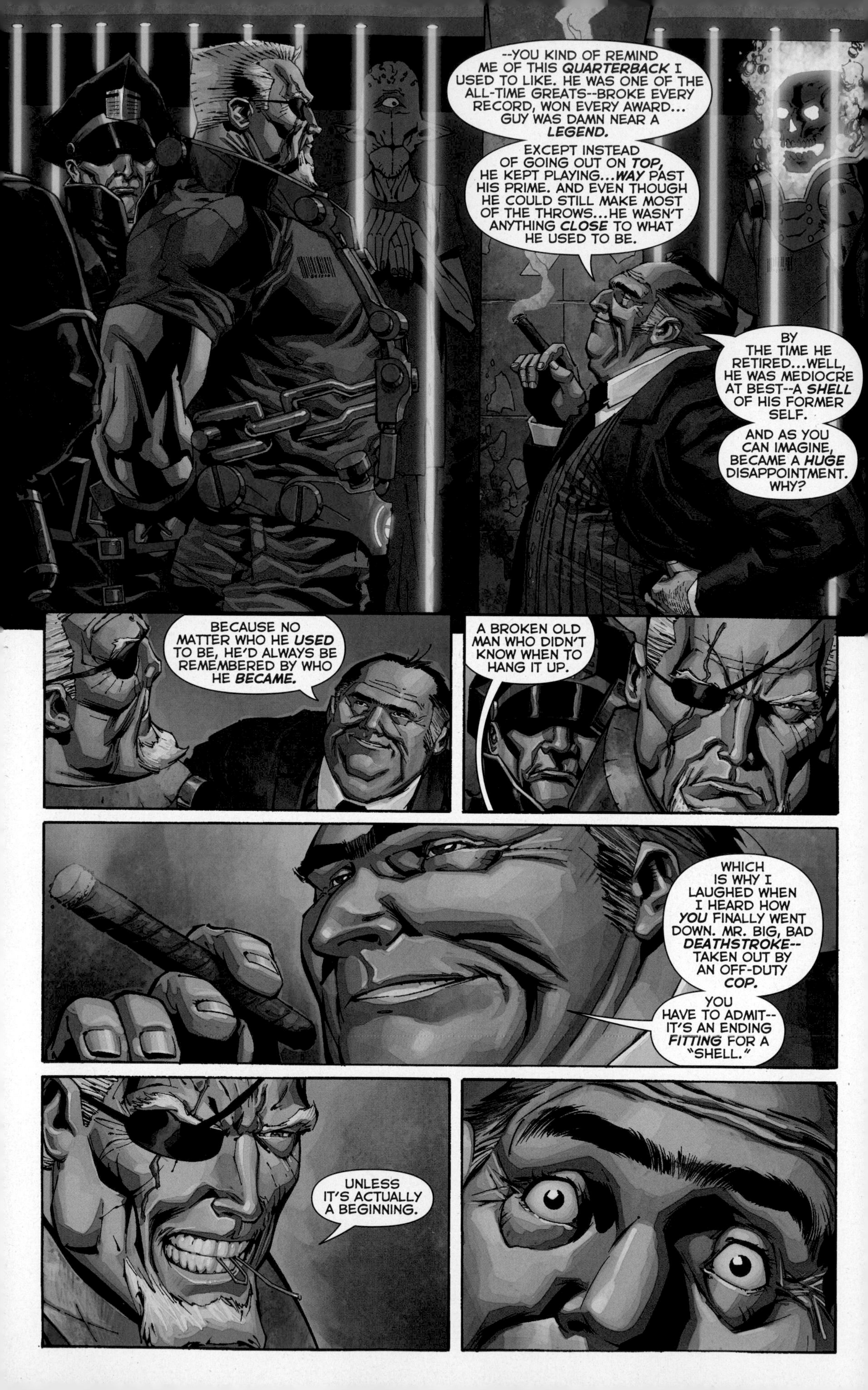
--YOU KIND OF REMIND ME OF THIS QUARTERBACK I USED TO LIKE. HE WAS ONE OF THE ALL-TIME GREATS--BROKE EVERY RECORD, WON EVERY AWARD... GUY WAS DAMN NEAR A LEGEND.
EXCEPT INSTEAD OF GOING OUT ON TOP, HE KEPT PLAYING...WAY PAST HIS PRIME. AND EVEN THOUGH HE COULD STILL MAKE MOST OF THE THROWS...HE WASN'T ANYTHING CLOSE TO WHAT HE USED TO BE.
BY THE TIME HE RETIRED...WELL, HE WAS MEDIOCRE AT BEST--A SHELL OF HIS FORMER SELF.
AND AS YOU CAN IMAGINE, BECAME A HUGE DISAPPOINTMENT. WHY?
BECAUSE NO MATTER WHO HE USED TO BE, HE'D ALWAYS BE REMEMBERED BY WHO HE BECAME.
A BROKEN OLD MAN WHO DIDN'T KNOW WHEN TO HANG IT UP.
WHICH IS WHY I LAUGHED WHEN I HEARD HOW YOU FINALLY WENT DOWN. MR. BIG, BAD DEATHSTROKE--TAKEN OUT BY AN OFF-DUTY COP.
YOU HAVE TO ADMIT--IT'S AN ENDING FITTING FOR A "SHELL."
UNLESS IT'S ACTUALLY A BEGINNING.

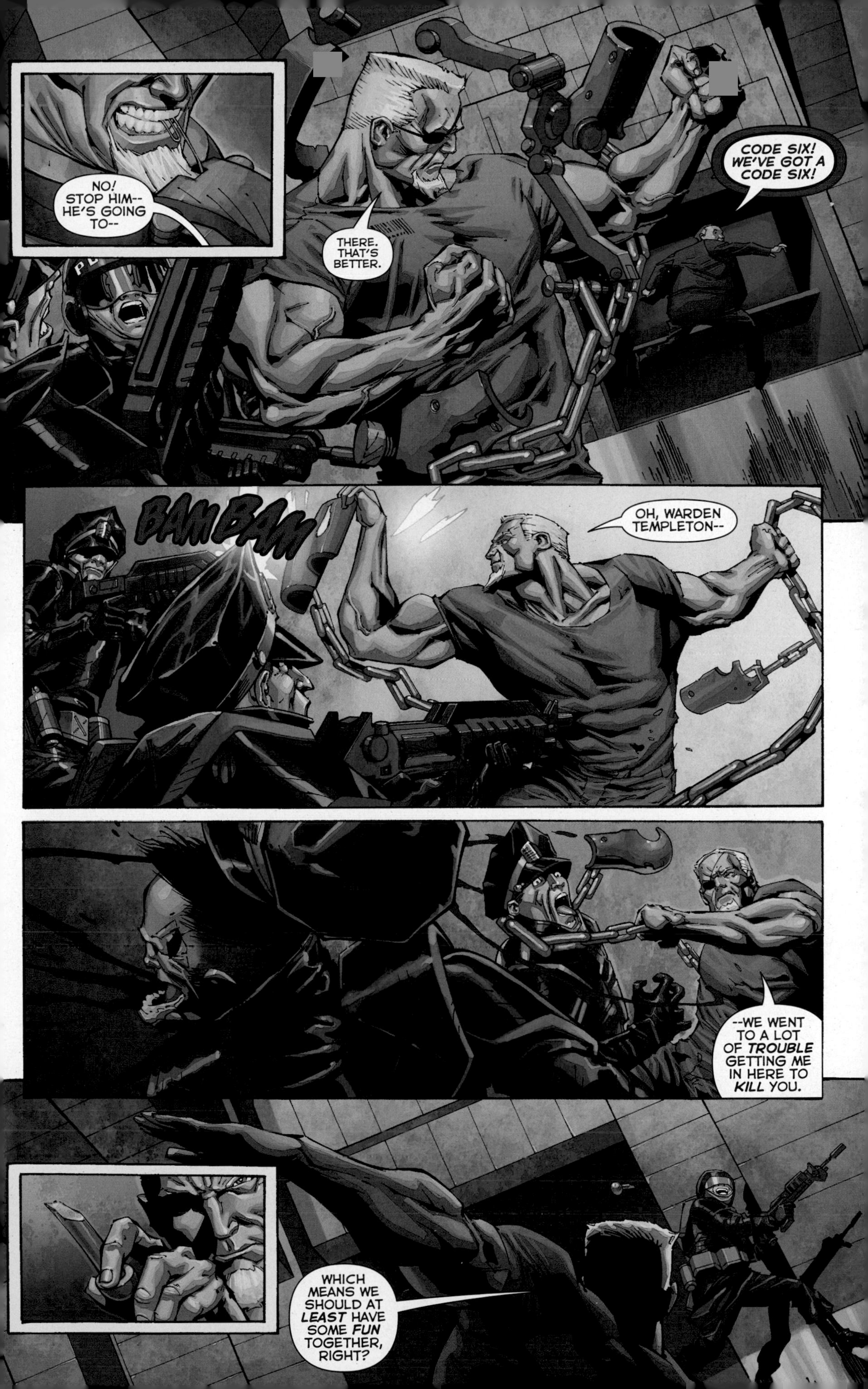
NO! STOP HIM-- HE'S GOING TO--
THERE. THAT'S BETTER.
CODE SIX! WE'VE GOT A CODE SIX!
BAM BAM
OH, WARDEN TEMPLETON--
--WE WENT TO A LOT OF TROUBLE GETTING ME IN HERE TO KILL YOU.
WHICH MEANS WE SHOULD AT LEAST HAVE SOME FUN TOGETHER, RIGHT?

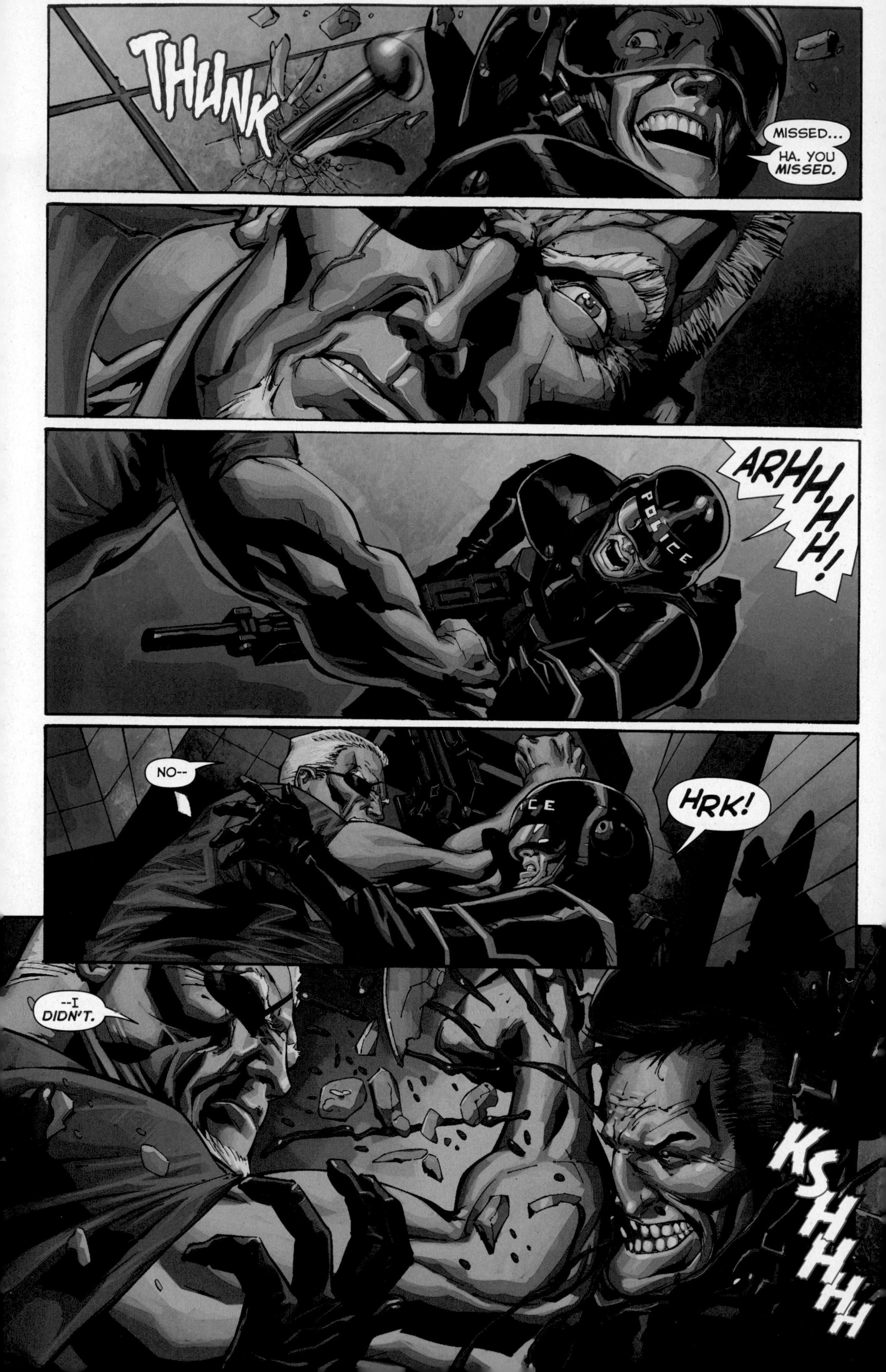
THUNK
MISSED...
HA. YOU MISSED.
ARHHHH!
NO--
HRK!
--I DIDN'T.
KSHHHH

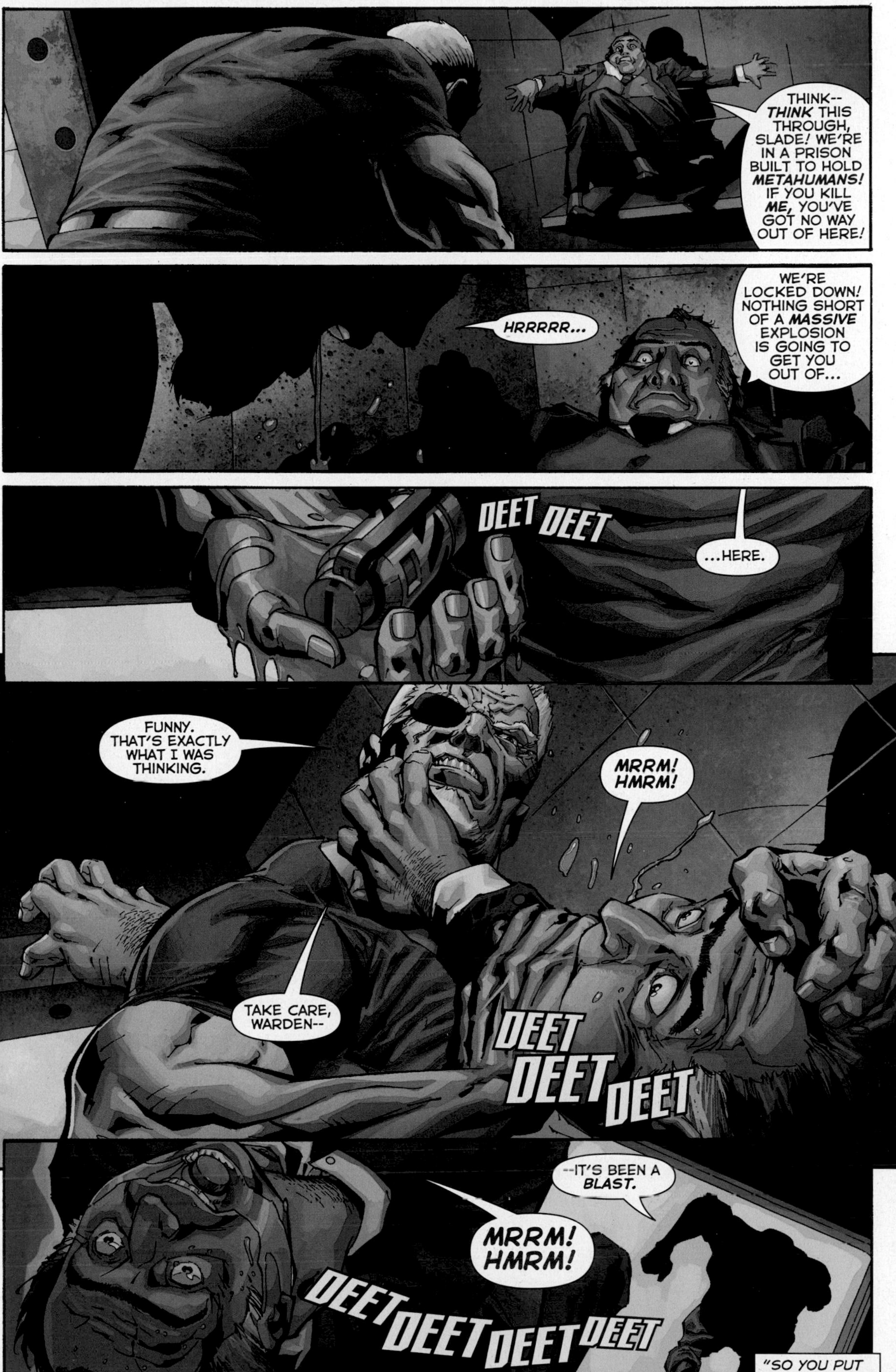
THINK-- THINK THIS THROUGH, SLADE! WE'RE IN A PRISON BUILT TO HOLD METAHUMANS! IF YOU KILL ME, YOU'VE GOT NO WAY OUT OF HERE!
HRRRRR...
WE'RE LOCKED DOWN! NOTHING SHORT OF A MASSIVE EXPLOSION IS GOING TO GET YOU OUT OF...
DEET DEET
...HERE.
FUNNY. THAT'S EXACTLY WHAT I WAS THINKING.
MRRM! HMRM!
TAKE CARE, WARDEN--
DEET DEET DEET
--IT'S BEEN A BLAST.
MRRM! HMRM!
DEET DEET DEET DEET
"SO YOU PUT THE BOMB IN HIS MOUTH..."

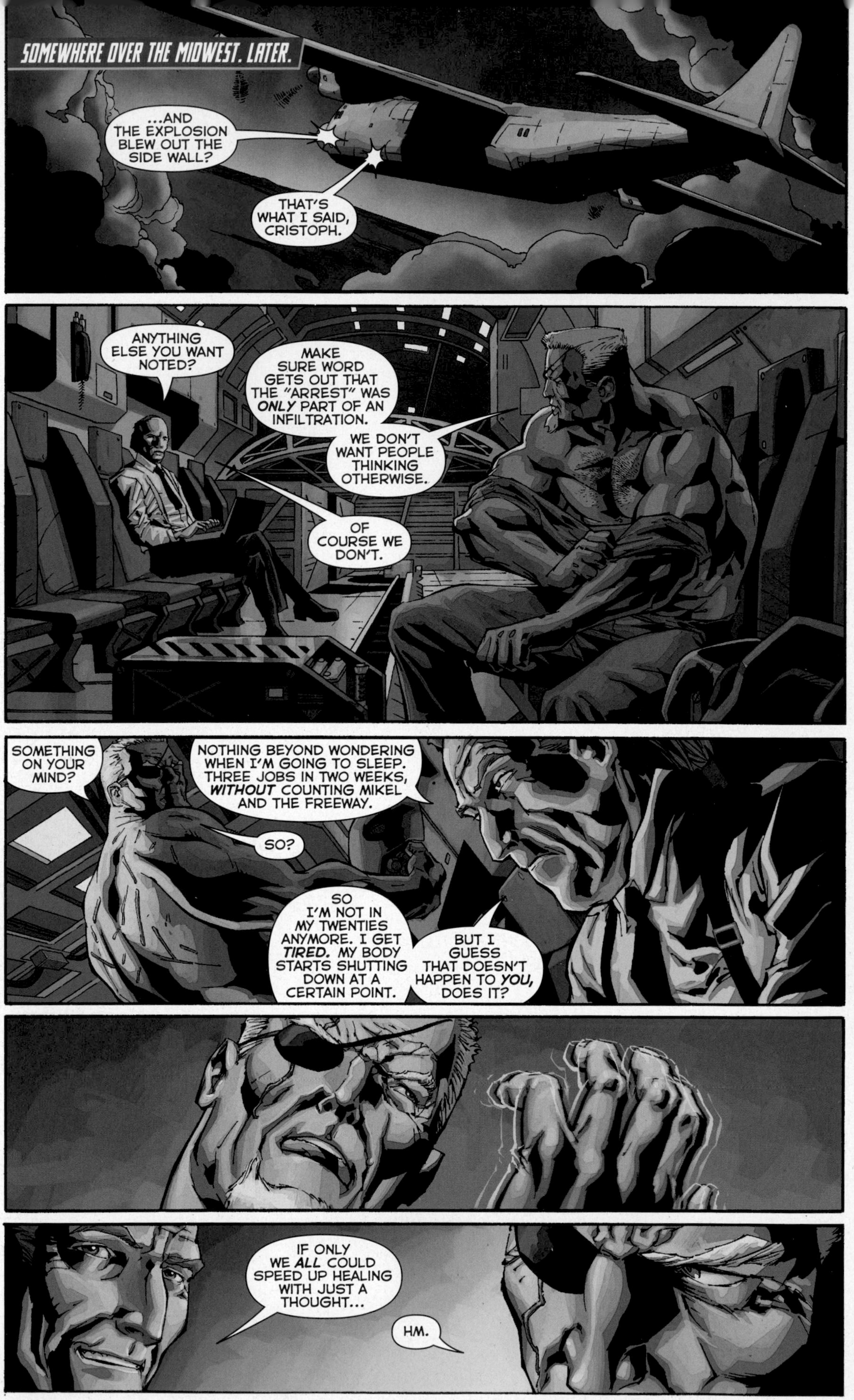
SOMEWHERE OVER THE MIDWEST. LATER.
...AND THE EXPLOSION BLEW OUT THE SIDE WALL?
THAT'S WHAT I SAID, CRISTOPH.
ANYTHING ELSE YOU WANT NOTED?
MAKE SURE WORD GETS OUT THAT THE "ARREST" WAS ONLY PART OF AN INFILTRATION.
WE DON'T WANT PEOPLE THINKING OTHERWISE.
OF COURSE WE DON'T.
SOMETHING ON YOUR MIND?
NOTHING BEYOND WONDERING WHEN I'M GOING TO SLEEP. THREE JOBS IN TWO WEEKS, WITHOUT COUNTING MIKEL AND THE FREEWAY.
SO?
SO I'M NOT IN MY TWENTIES ANYMORE. I GET TIRED. MY BODY STARTS SHUTTING DOWN AT A CERTAIN POINT.
BUT I GUESS THAT DOESN'T HAPPEN TO YOU, DOES IT?
IF ONLY WE ALL COULD SPEED UP HEALING WITH JUST A THOUGHT...
HM.

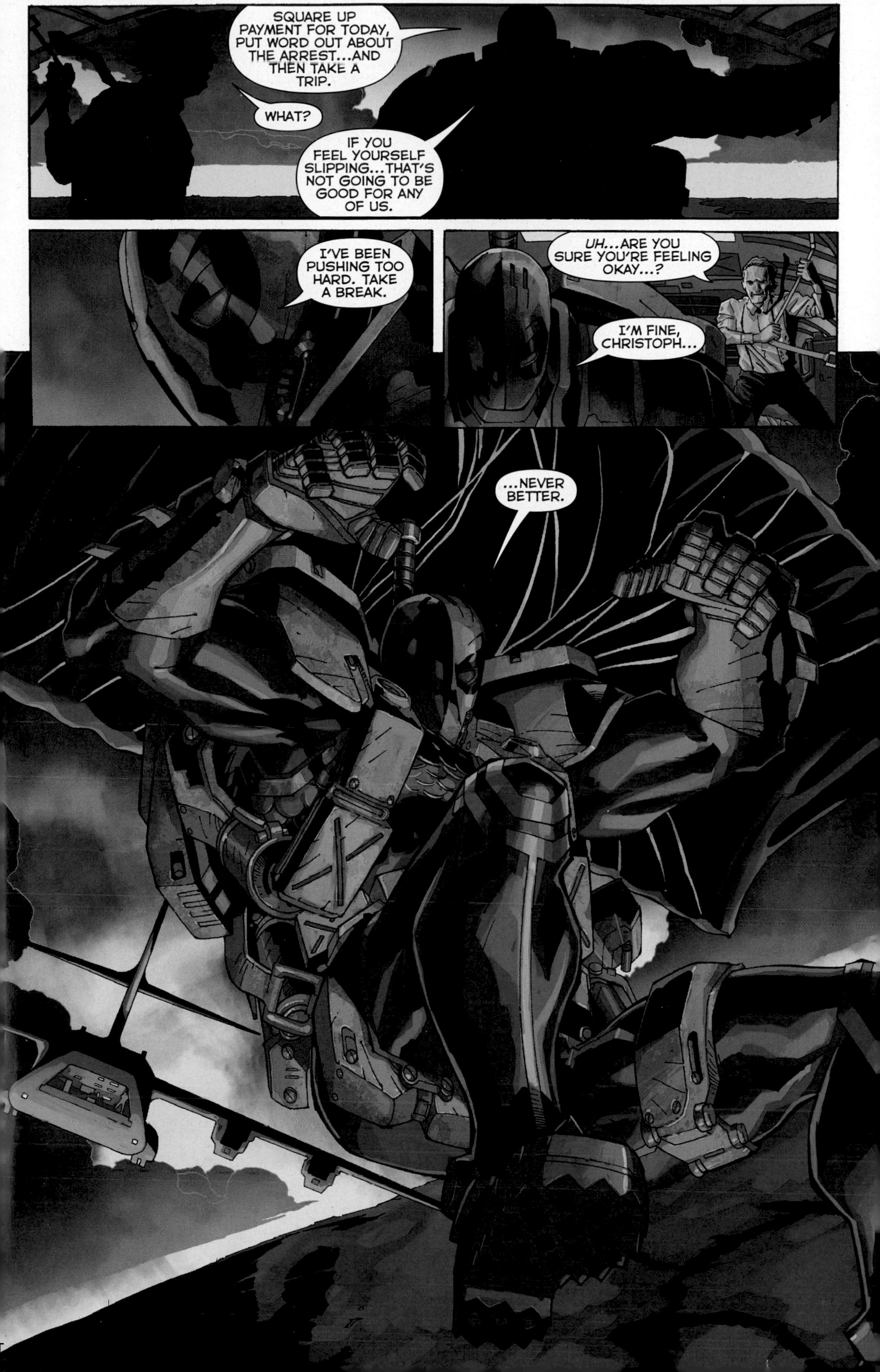
SQUARE UP PAYMENT FOR TODAY, PUT WORD OUT ABOUT THE ARREST...AND THEN TAKE A TRIP.
WHAT?
IF YOU FEEL YOURSELF SLIPPING...THAT'S NOT GOING TO BE GOOD FOR ANY OF US.
I'VE BEEN PUSHING TOO HARD. TAKE A BREAK.
UH...ARE YOU SURE YOU'RE FEELING OKAY...?
I'M FINE, CHRISTOPH...
...NEVER BETTER.

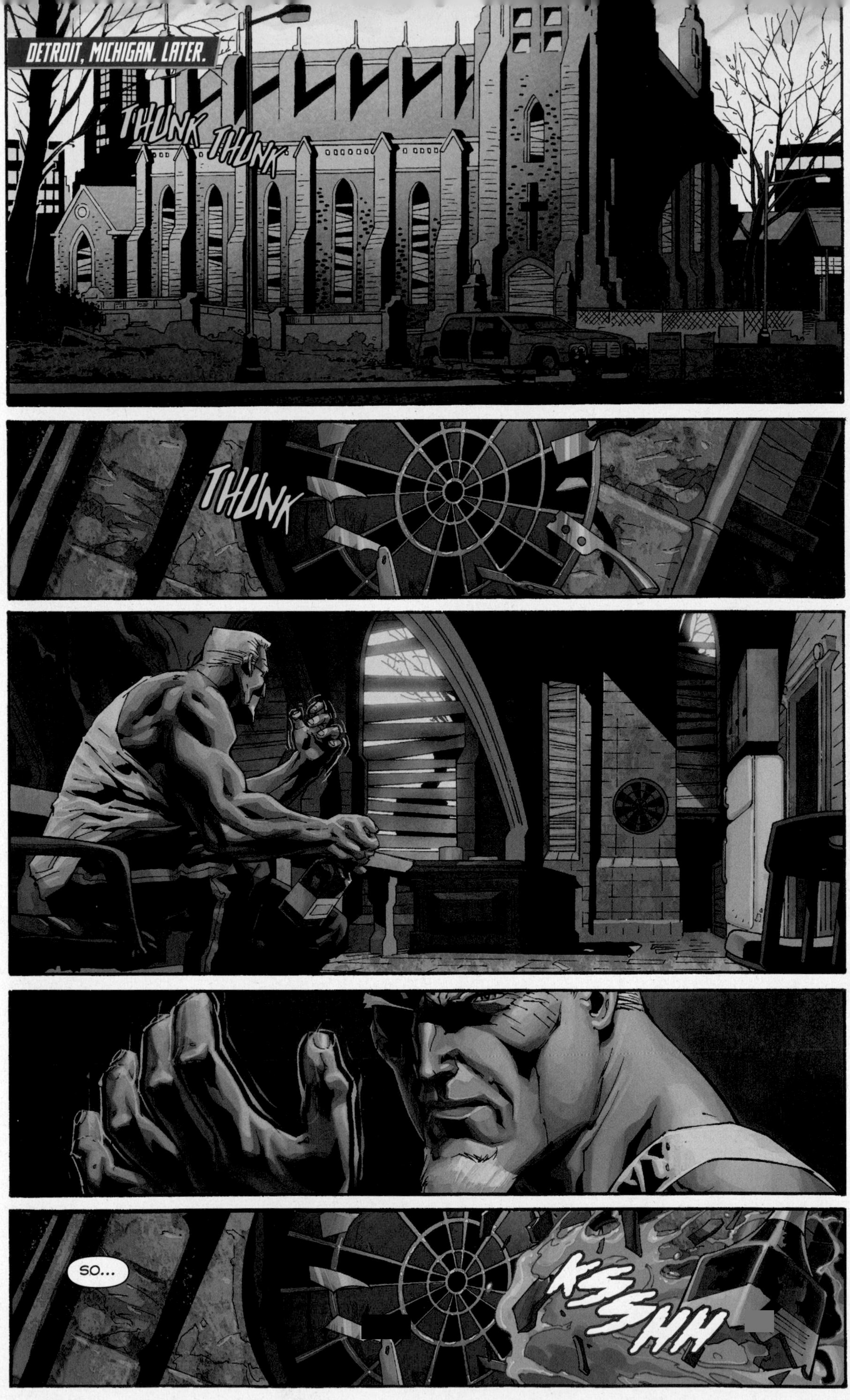
DETROIT, MICHIGAN. LATER.
THUNK THUNK
THUNK
SO...
KSSHH

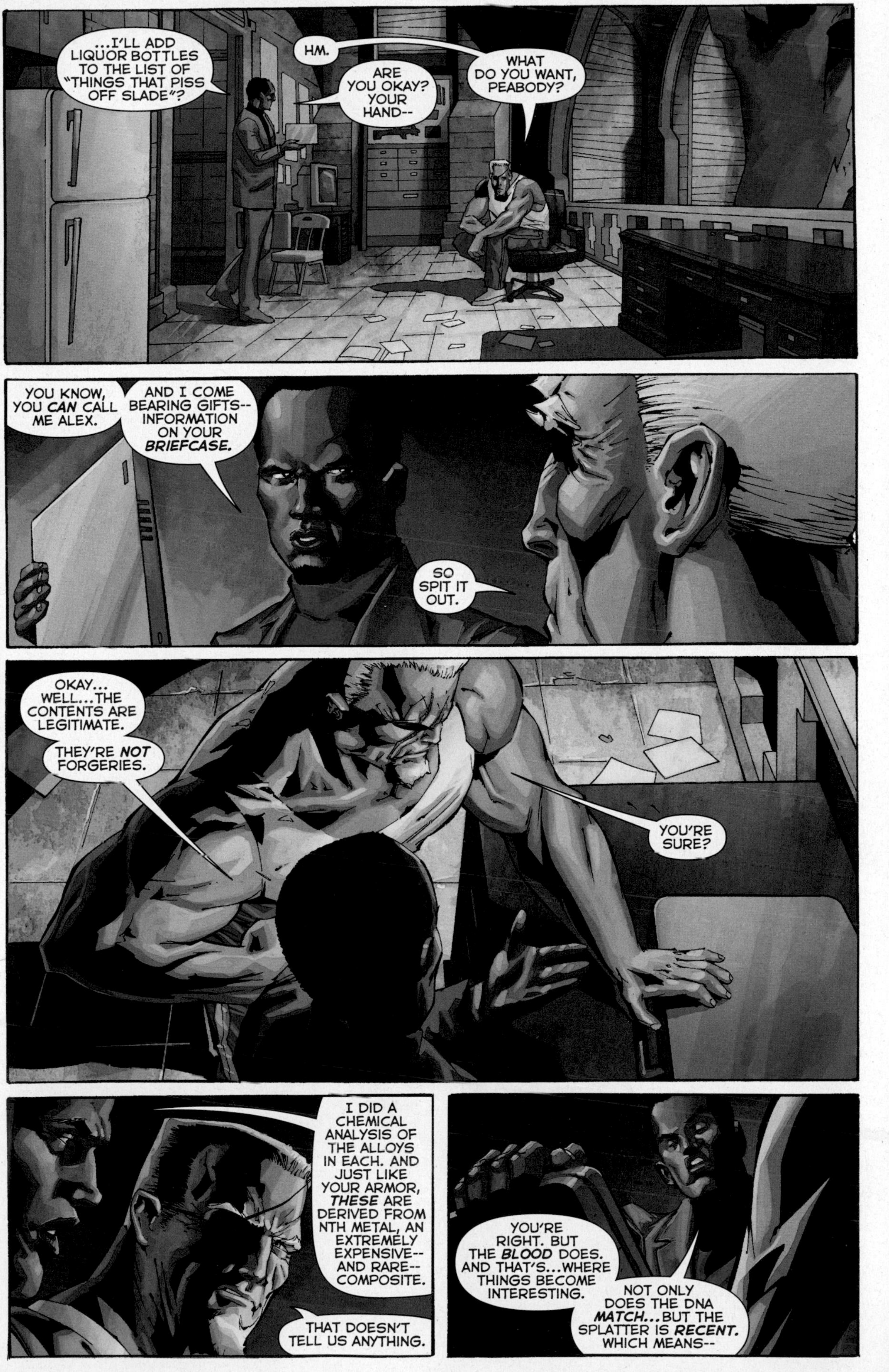
...I'LL ADD LIQUOR BOTTLES TO THE LIST OF "THINGS THAT PISS OFF SLADE"?
HM.
ARE YOU OKAY? YOUR HAND--
WHAT DO YOU WANT, PEABODY?
YOU KNOW, YOU CAN CALL ME ALEX.
AND I COME BEARING GIFTS-- INFORMATION ON YOUR BRIEFCASE.
SO SPIT IT OUT.
OKAY... WELL...THE CONTENTS ARE LEGITIMATE.
THEY'RE NOT FORGERIES.
YOU'RE SURE?
I DID A CHEMICAL ANALYSIS OF THE ALLOYS IN EACH. AND JUST LIKE YOUR ARMOR, THESE ARE DERIVED FROM NTH METAL, AN EXTREMELY EXPENSIVE-- AND RARE-- COMPOSITE.
THAT DOESN'T TELL US ANYTHING.
YOU'RE RIGHT. BUT THE BLOOD DOES. AND THAT'S...WHERE THINGS BECOME INTERESTING.
NOT ONLY DOES THE DNA MATCH...BUT THE SPLATTER IS RECENT. WHICH MEANS--

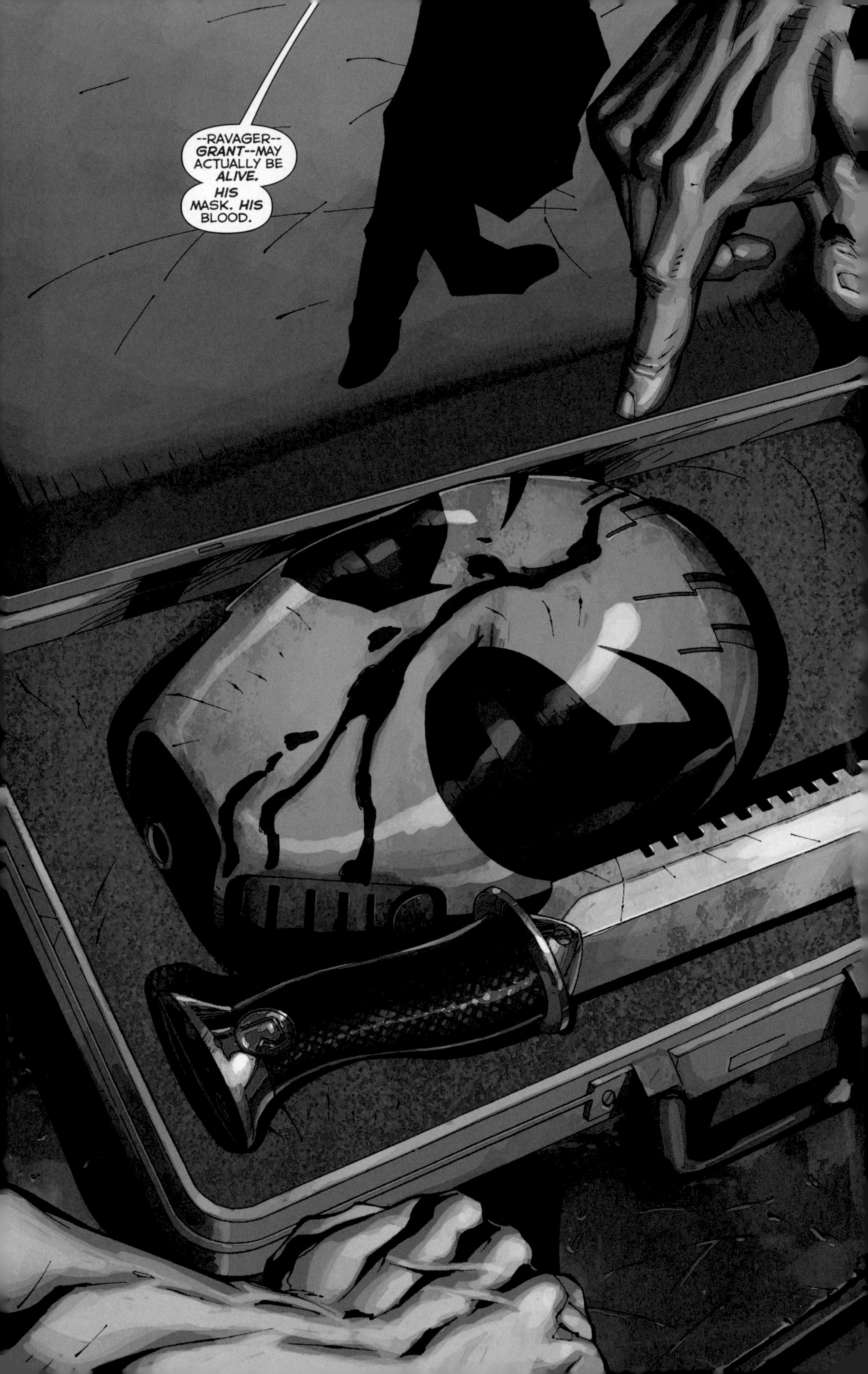
--RAVAGER--GRANT--MAY ACTUALLY BE ALIVE.
HIS MASK. HIS BLOOD.

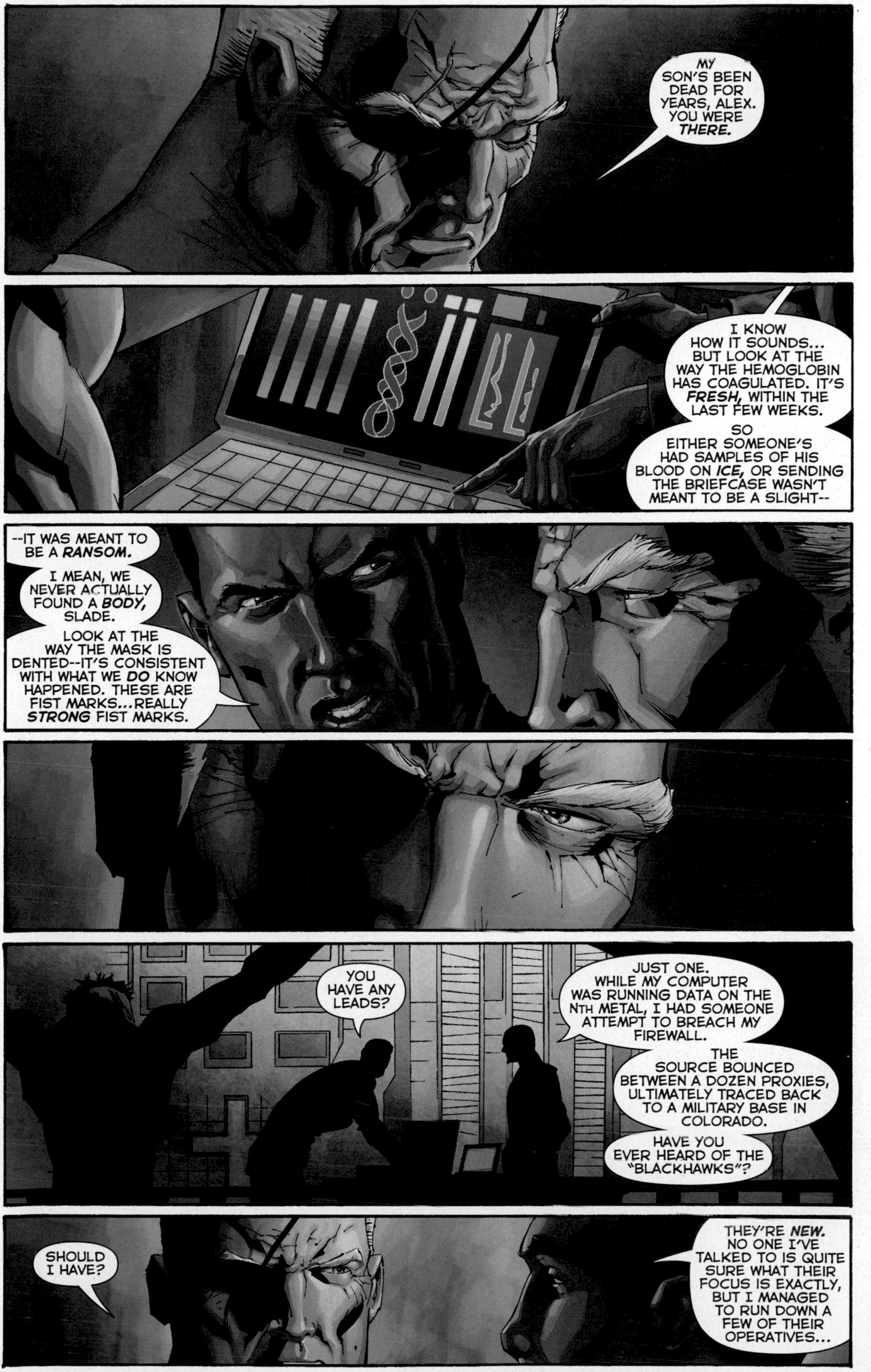
MY SON'S BEEN DEAD FOR YEARS, ALEX. YOU WERE THERE.
I KNOW HOW IT SOUNDS... BUT LOOK AT THE WAY THE HEMOGLOBIN HAS COAGULATED. IT'S FRESH, WITHIN THE LAST FEW WEEKS.
SO EITHER SOMEONE'S HAD SAMPLES OF HIS BLOOD ON ICE, OR SENDING THE BRIEFCASE WASN'T MEANT TO BE A SLIGHT--
--IT WAS MEANT TO BE A RANSOM.
I MEAN, WE NEVER ACTUALLY FOUND A BODY, SLADE.
LOOK AT THE WAY THE MASK IS DENTED--IT'S CONSISTENT WITH WHAT WE DO KNOW HAPPENED. THESE ARE FIST MARKS...REALLY STRONG FIST MARKS.
YOU HAVE ANY LEADS?
JUST ONE. WHILE MY COMPUTER WAS RUNNING DATA ON THE NTH METAL, I HAD SOMEONE ATTEMPT TO BREACH MY FIREWALL.
THE SOURCE BOUNCED BETWEEN A DOZEN PROXIES, ULTIMATELY TRACED BACK TO A MILITARY BASE IN COLORADO.
HAVE YOU EVER HEARD OF THE "BLACKHAWKS"?
SHOULD I HAVE?
THEY'RE NEW. NO ONE I'VE TALKED TO IS QUITE SURE WHAT THEIR FOCUS IS EXACTLY, BUT I MANAGED TO RUN DOWN A FEW OF THEIR OPERATIVES...

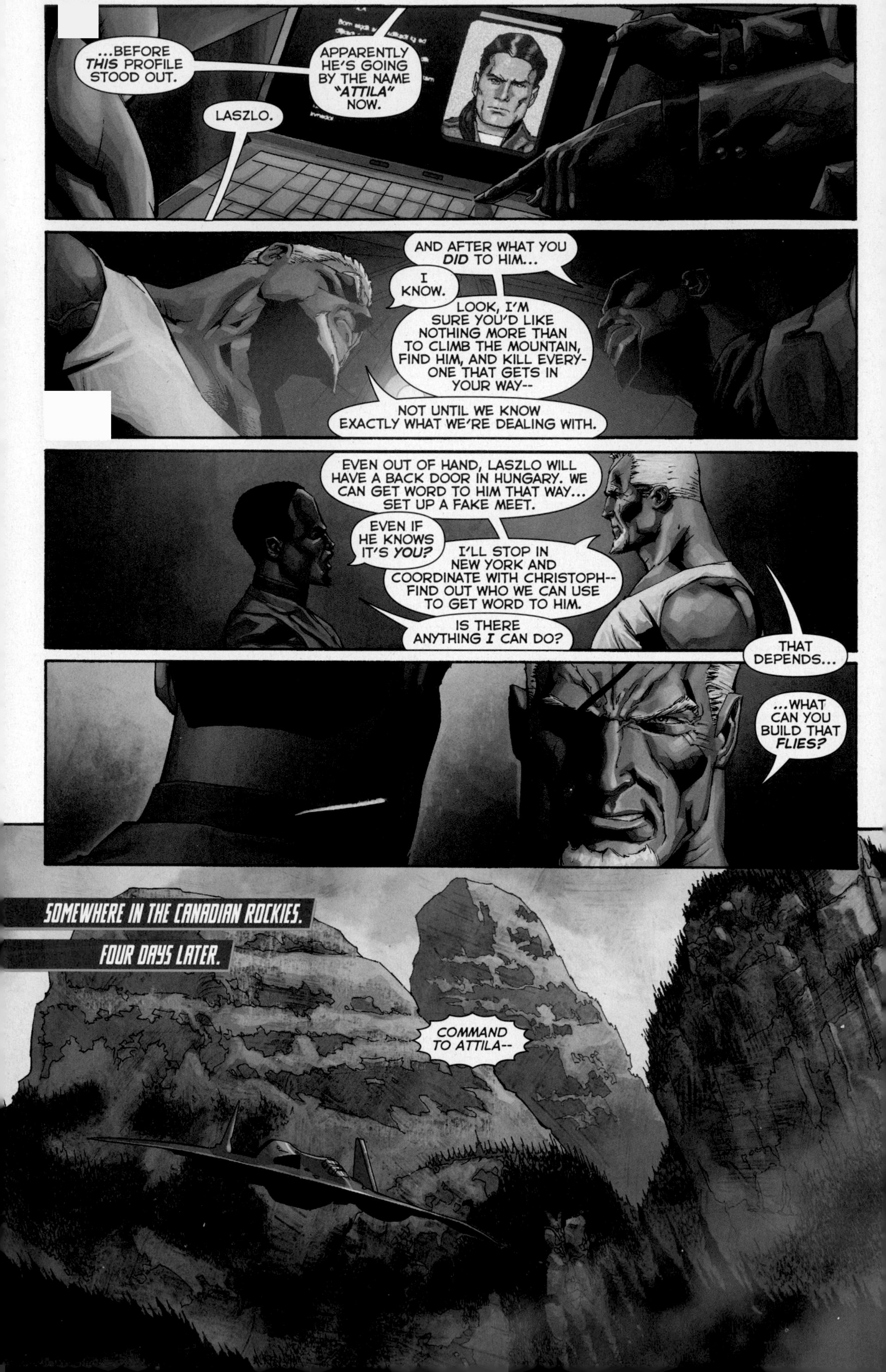
...BEFORE THIS PROFILE STOOD OUT.
APPARENTLY HE'S GOING BY THE NAME "ATTILA" NOW.
LASZLO.
AND AFTER WHAT YOU DID TO HIM...
I KNOW.
LOOK, I'M SURE YOU'D LIKE NOTHING MORE THAN TO CLIMB THE MOUNTAIN, FIND HIM, AND KILL EVERY-ONE THAT GETS IN YOUR WAY--
NOT UNTIL WE KNOW EXACTLY WHAT WE'RE DEALING WITH.
EVEN OUT OF HAND, LASZLO WILL HAVE A BACK DOOR IN HUNGARY. WE CAN GET WORD TO HIM THAT WAY... SET UP A FAKE MEET.
EVEN IF HE KNOWS IT'S YOU?
I'LL STOP IN NEW YORK AND COORDINATE WITH CHRISTOPH-- FIND OUT WHO WE CAN USE TO GET WORD TO HIM.
IS THERE ANYTHING I CAN DO?
THAT DEPENDS...
...WHAT CAN YOU BUILD THAT FLIES?
SOMEWHERE IN THE CANADIAN ROCKIES.
FOUR DAYS LATER.
COMMAND TO ATTILA--

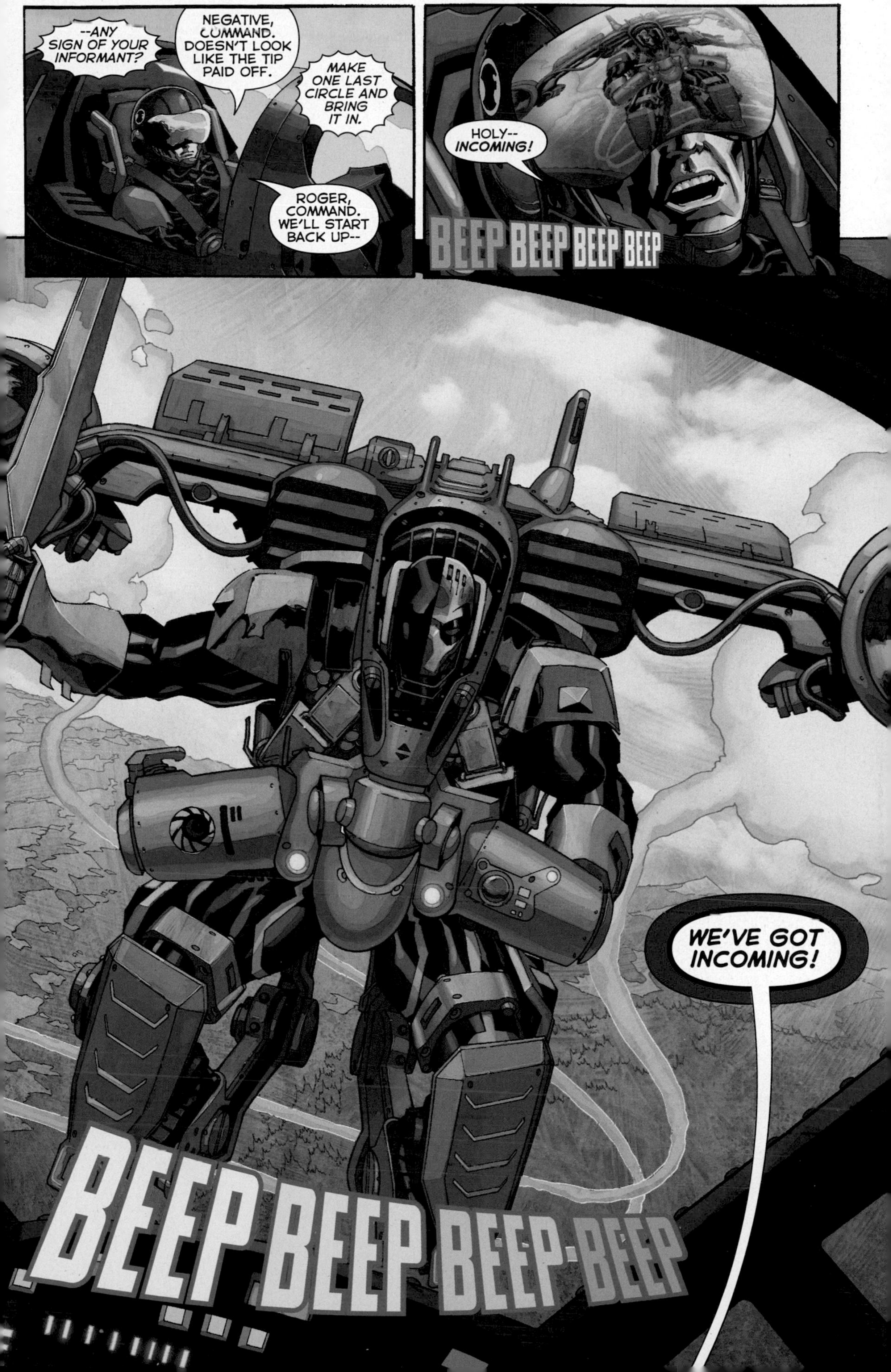
--ANY SIGN OF YOUR INFORMANT?
NEGATIVE, COMMAND. DOESN'T LOOK LIKE THE TIP PAID OFF.
MAKE ONE LAST CIRCLE AND BRING IT IN.
ROGER, COMMAND. WE'LL START BACK UP--
HOLY-- INCOMING!
BEEP BEEP BEEP BEEP
WE'VE GOT INCOMING!
BEEP BEEP BEEP BEEP

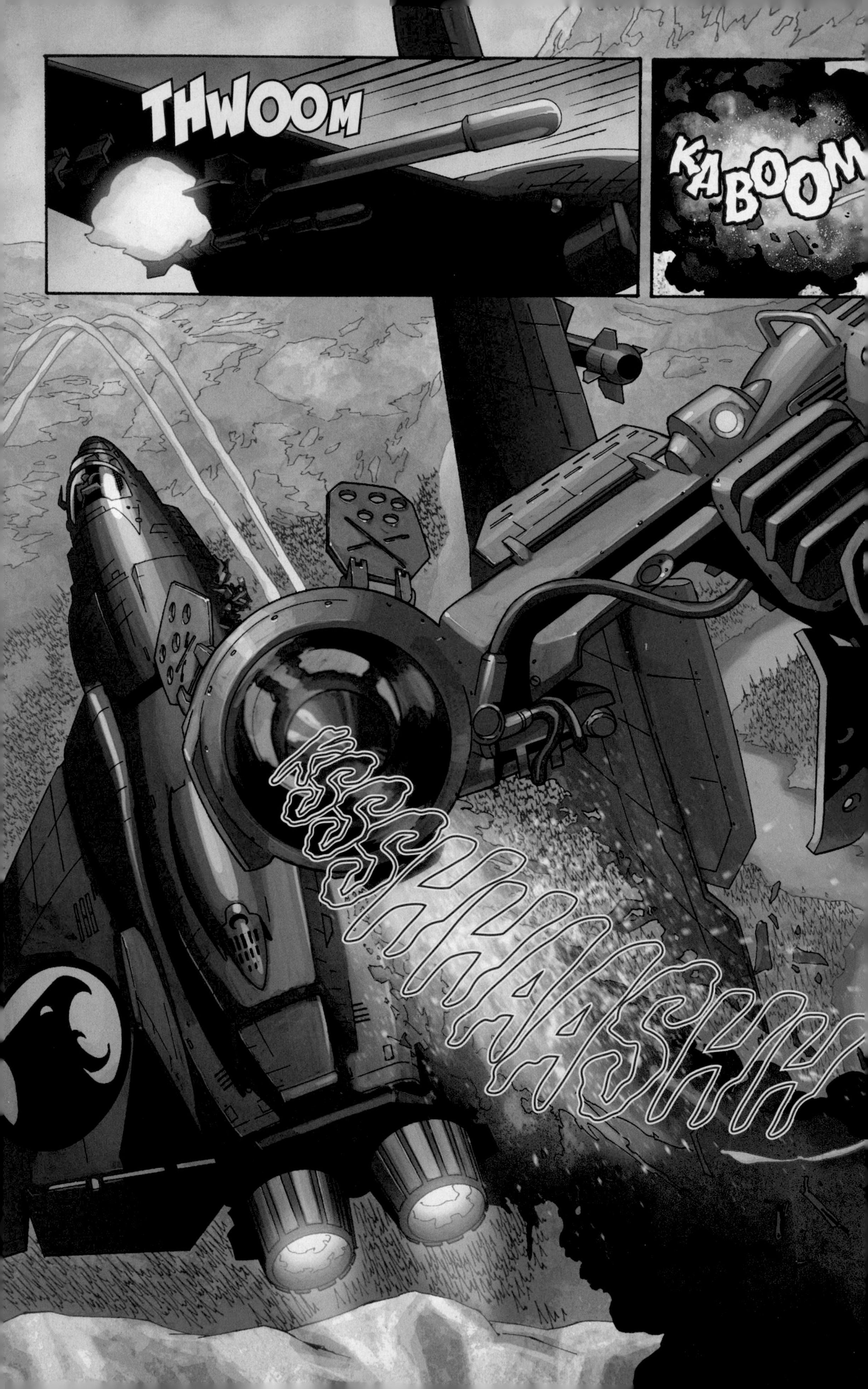
THWOOM
KABOOM

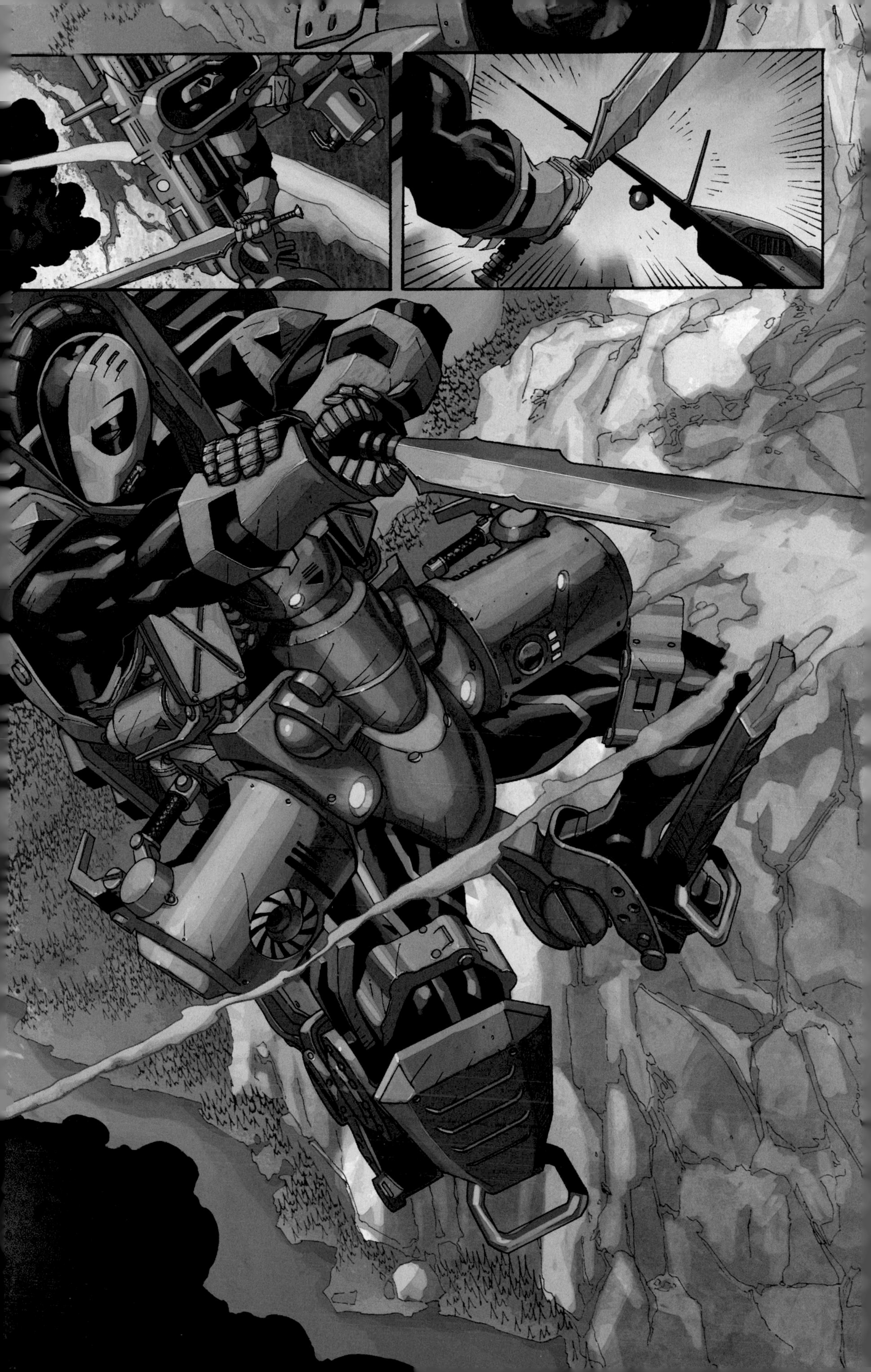

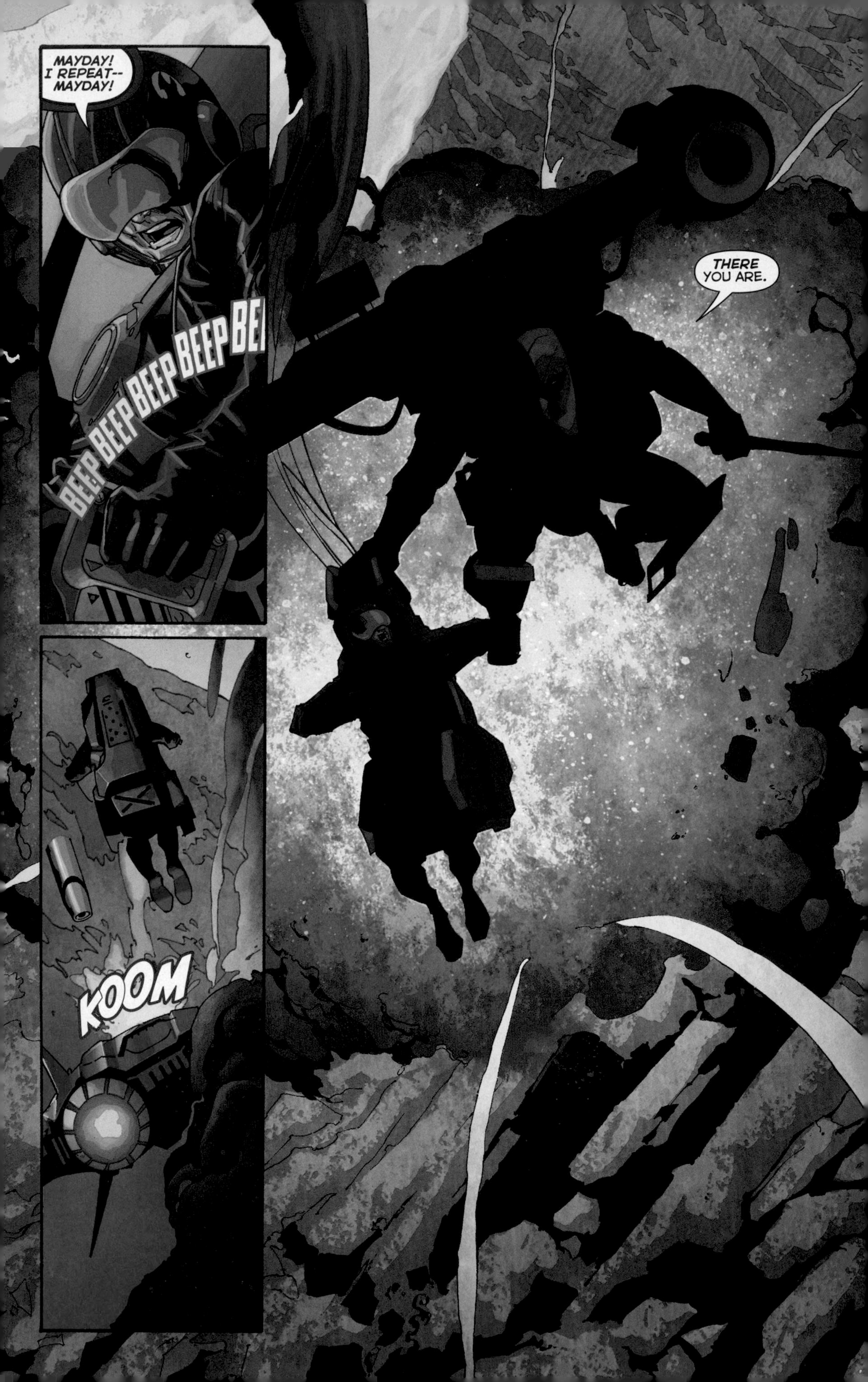
MAYDAY! I REPEAT-- MAYDAY!
BEEP BEEP BEEP BEEP BE
KOOM
THERE YOU ARE.

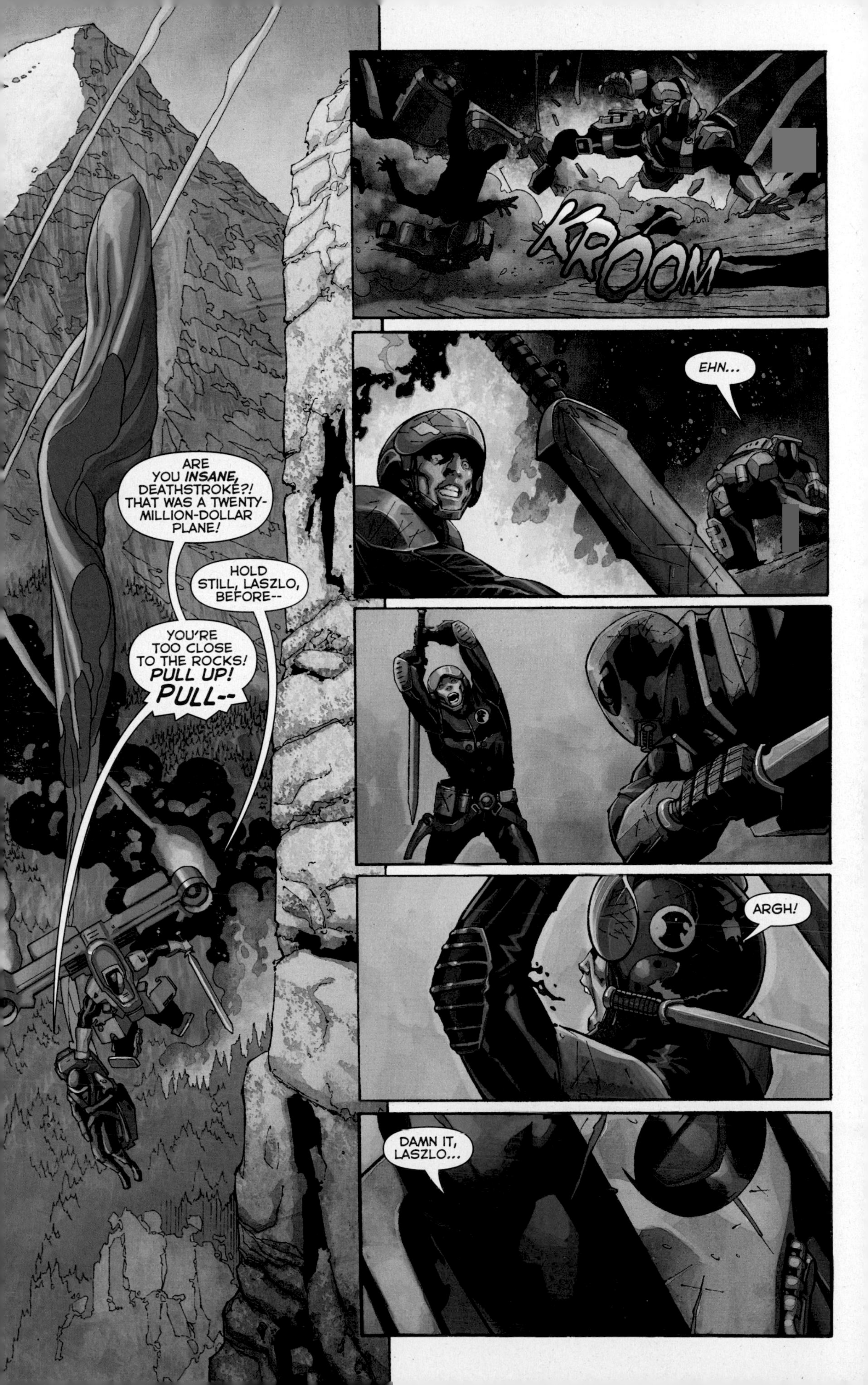
ARE YOU INSANE, DEATHSTROKE?! THAT WAS A TWENTY-MILLION-DOLLAR PLANE!
HOLD STILL, LASZLO, BEFORE--
YOU'RE TOO CLOSE TO THE ROCKS! PULL UP! PULL--
KROOM
EHN...
ARGH!
DAMN IT, LASZLO...

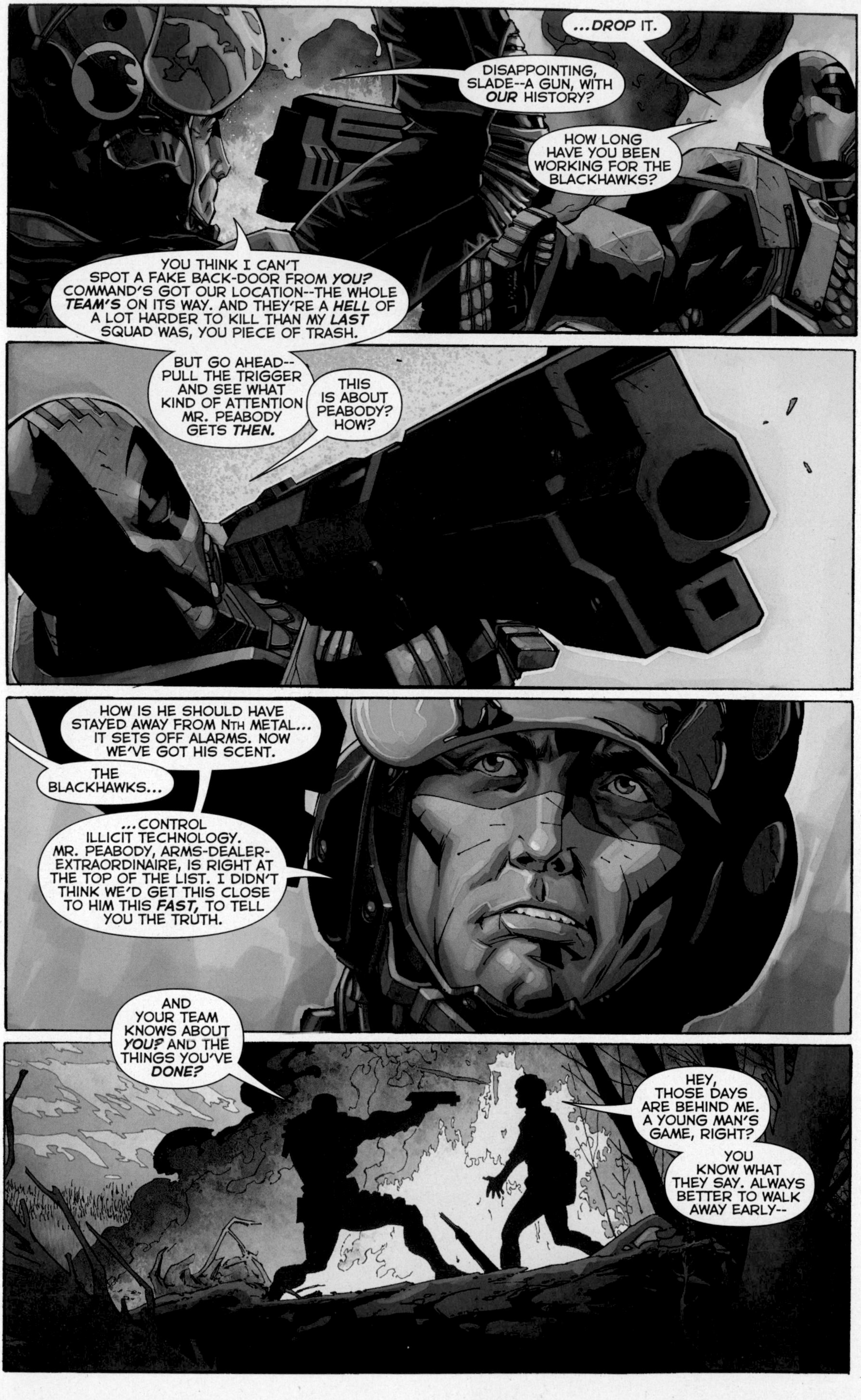
...DROP IT.
DISAPPOINTING, SLADE--A GUN, WITH OUR HISTORY?
HOW LONG HAVE YOU BEEN WORKING FOR THE BLACKHAWKS?
YOU THINK I CAN'T SPOT A FAKE BACK-DOOR FROM YOU? COMMAND'S GOT OUR LOCATION--THE WHOLE TEAM'S ON ITS WAY. AND THEY'RE A HELL OF A LOT HARDER TO KILL THAN MY LAST SQUAD WAS, YOU PIECE OF TRASH.
BUT GO AHEAD--PULL THE TRIGGER AND SEE WHAT KIND OF ATTENTION MR. PEABODY GETS THEN.
THIS IS ABOUT PEABODY? HOW?
HOW IS HE SHOULD HAVE STAYED AWAY FROM NTH METAL... IT SETS OFF ALARMS. NOW WE'VE GOT HIS SCENT.
THE BLACKHAWKS...
...CONTROL ILLICIT TECHNOLOGY. MR. PEABODY, ARMS-DEALER-EXTRAORDINAIRE, IS RIGHT AT THE TOP OF THE LIST. I DIDN'T THINK WE'D GET THIS CLOSE TO HIM THIS FAST, TO TELL YOU THE TRUTH.
AND YOUR TEAM KNOWS ABOUT YOU? AND THE THINGS YOU'VE DONE?
HEY, THOSE DAYS ARE BEHIND ME. A YOUNG MAN'S GAME, RIGHT?
YOU KNOW WHAT THEY SAY. ALWAYS BETTER TO WALK AWAY EARLY--

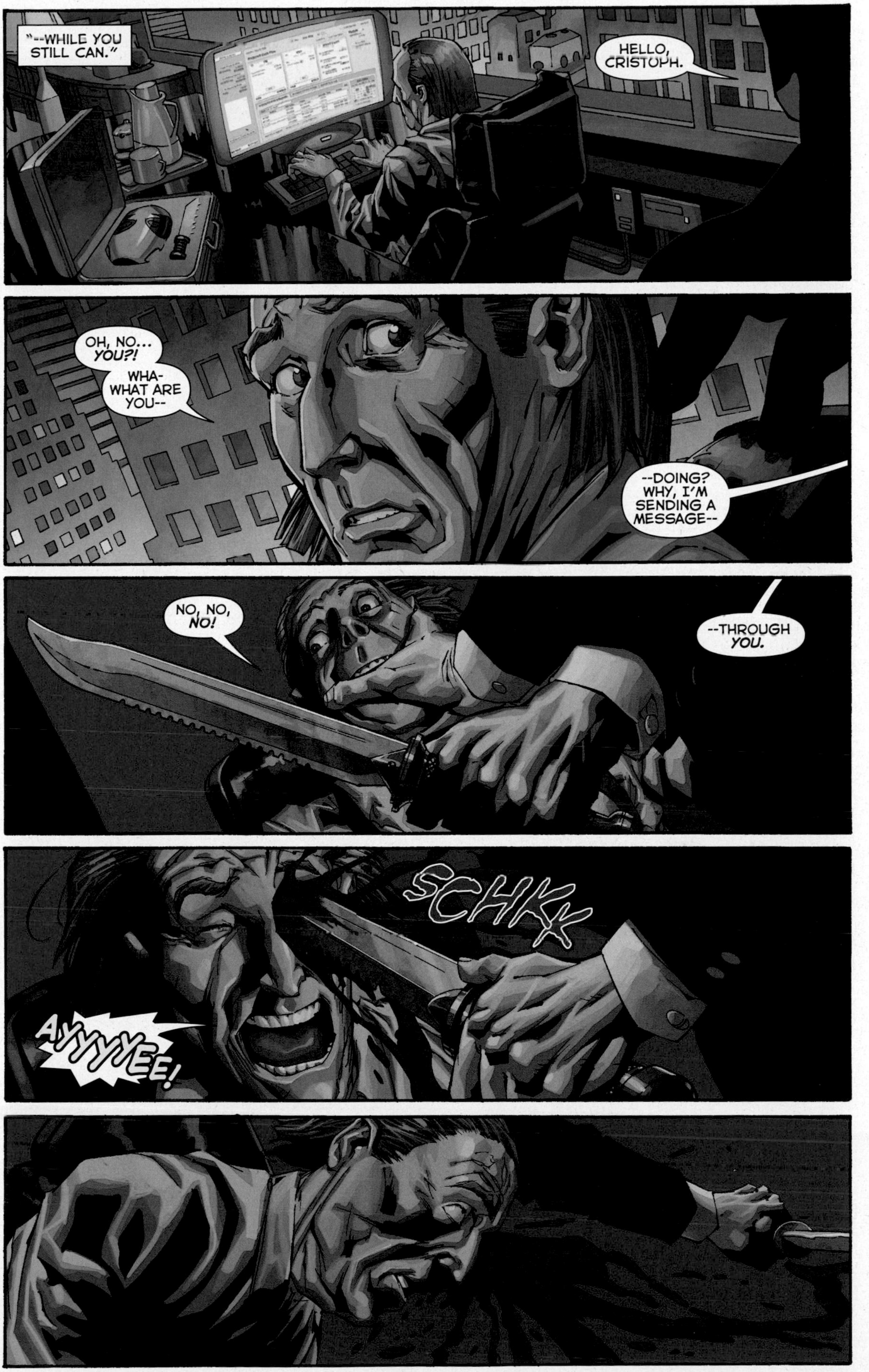
"--WHILE YOU STILL CAN."
HELLO, CRISTOPH.
OH, NO... YOU?!
WHA- WHAT ARE YOU--
--DOING? WHY, I'M SENDING A MESSAGE--
NO, NO, NO!
--THROUGH YOU.
SCHKK
AYYYYEE!

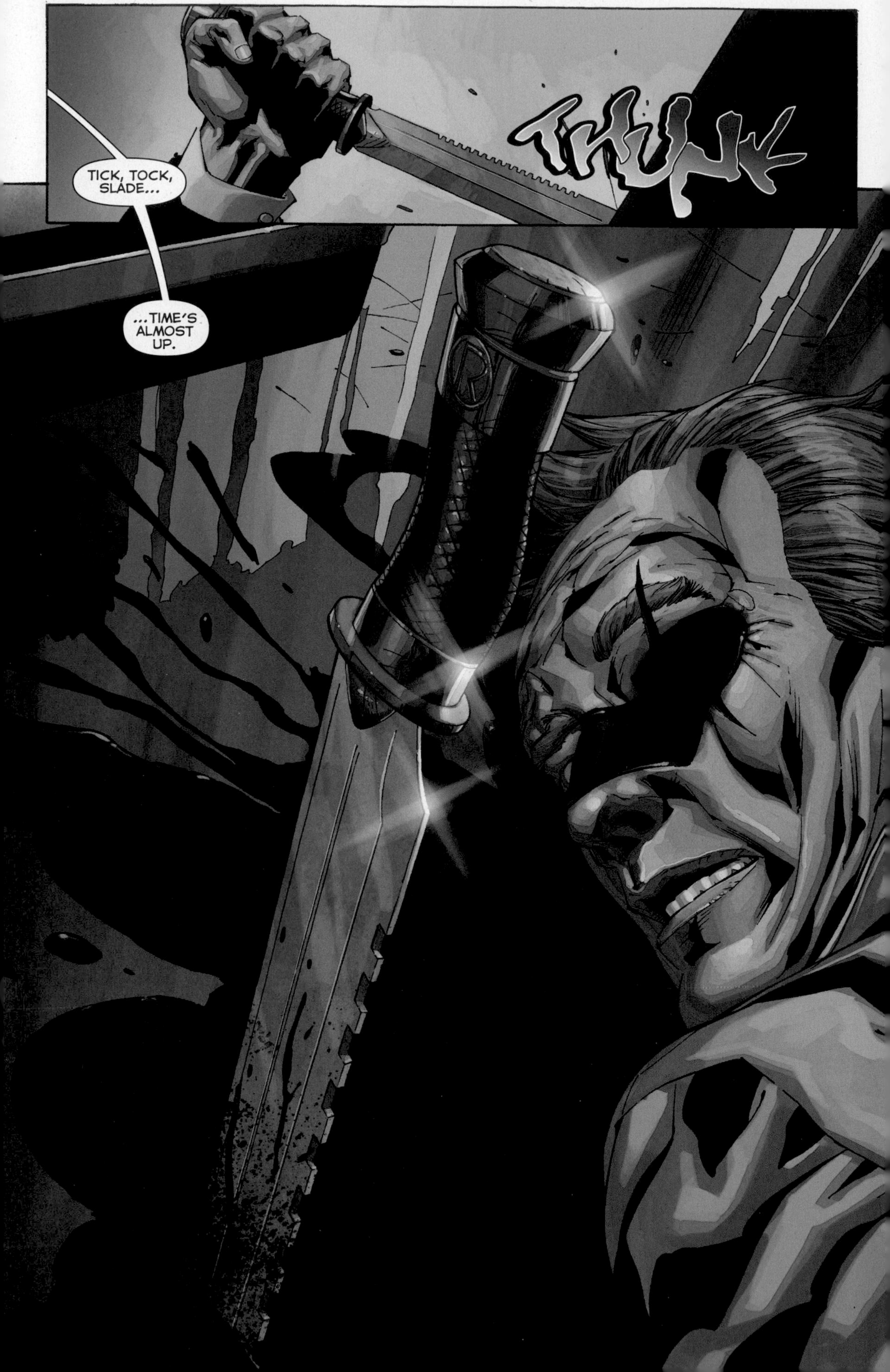
THUNK
TICK, TOCK, SLADE...
...TIME'S ALMOST UP.

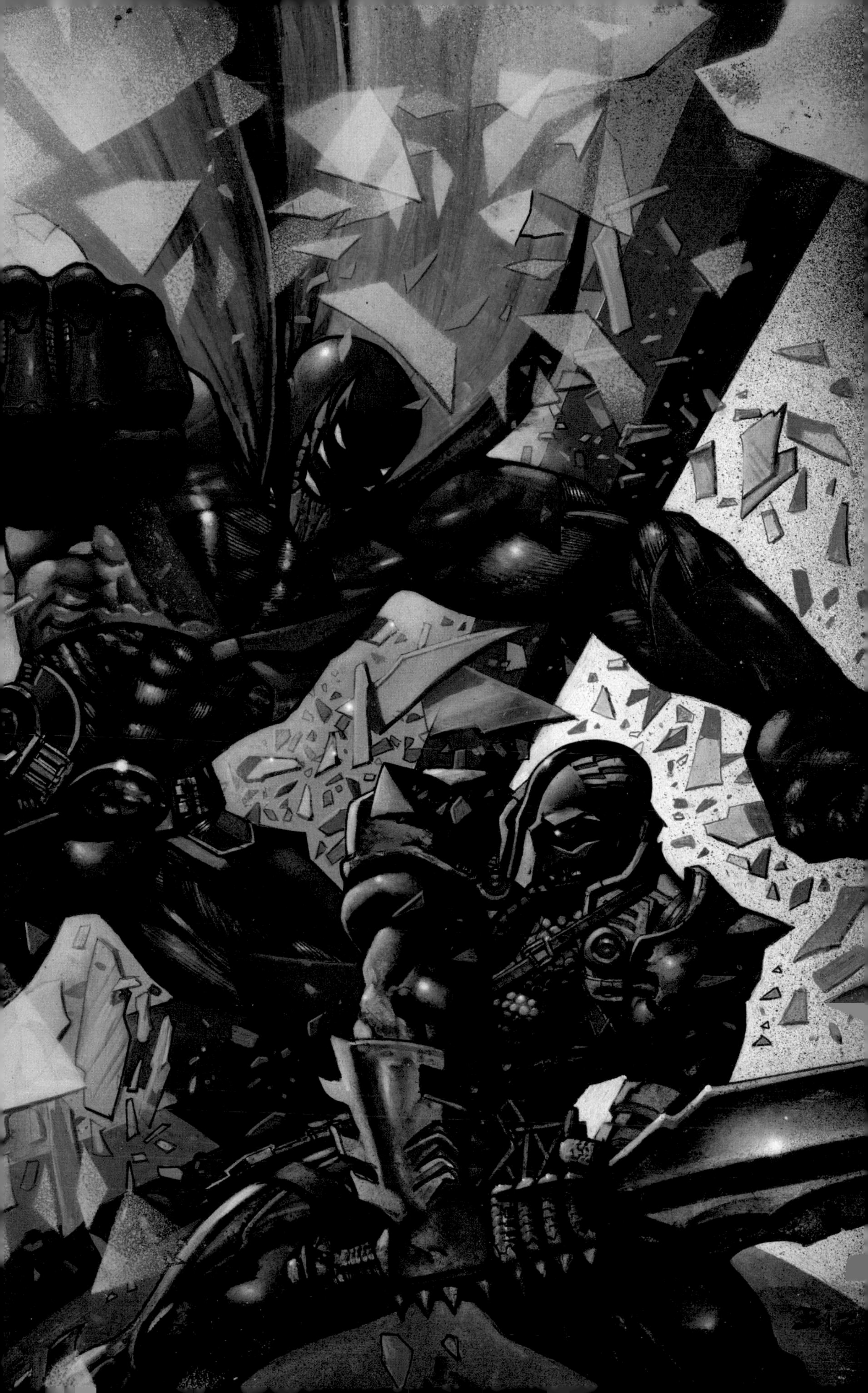

BLOWBACK

KYLE HIGGINS writer **JOE BENNETT** penciller **ART THIBERT** inker cover by **SIMON BISLEY**

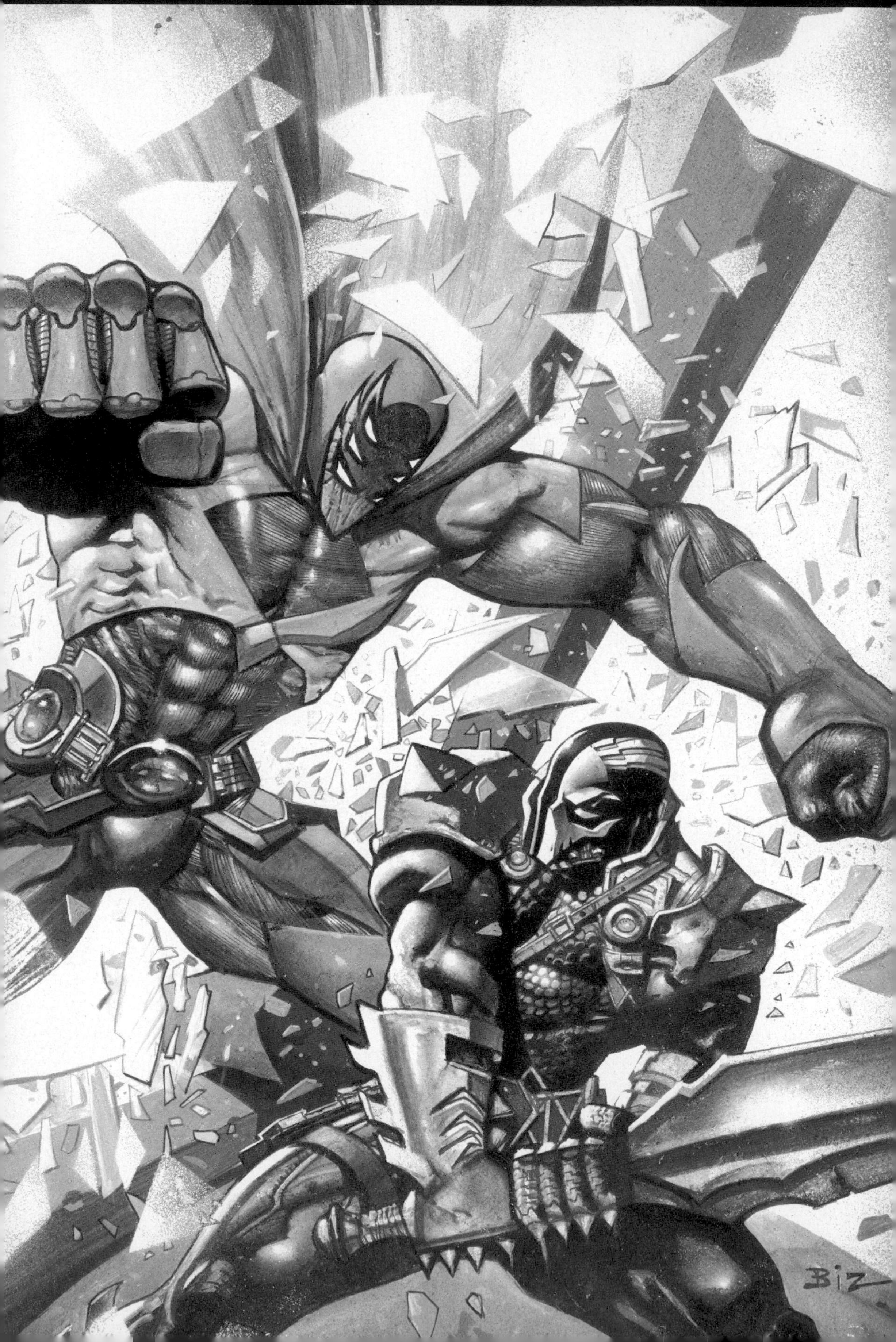
BIZ

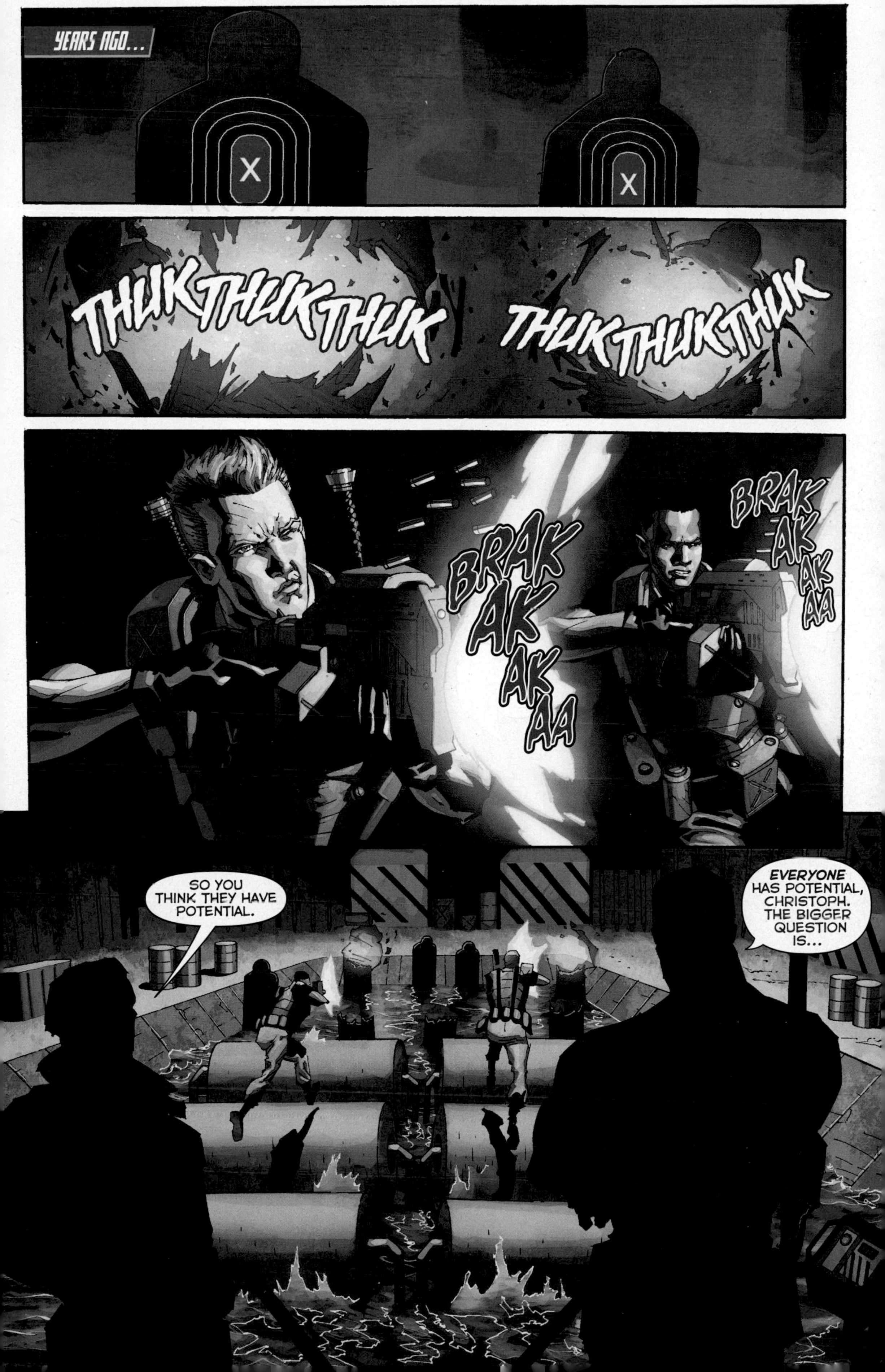
YEARS AGO...
X
X
THUKTHUKTHUK
THUKTHUKTHUK
BRAK AK AK AA
BRAK AK AK AA
SO YOU THINK THEY HAVE POTENTIAL.
EVERYONE HAS POTENTIAL, CHRISTOPH. THE BIGGER QUESTION IS...

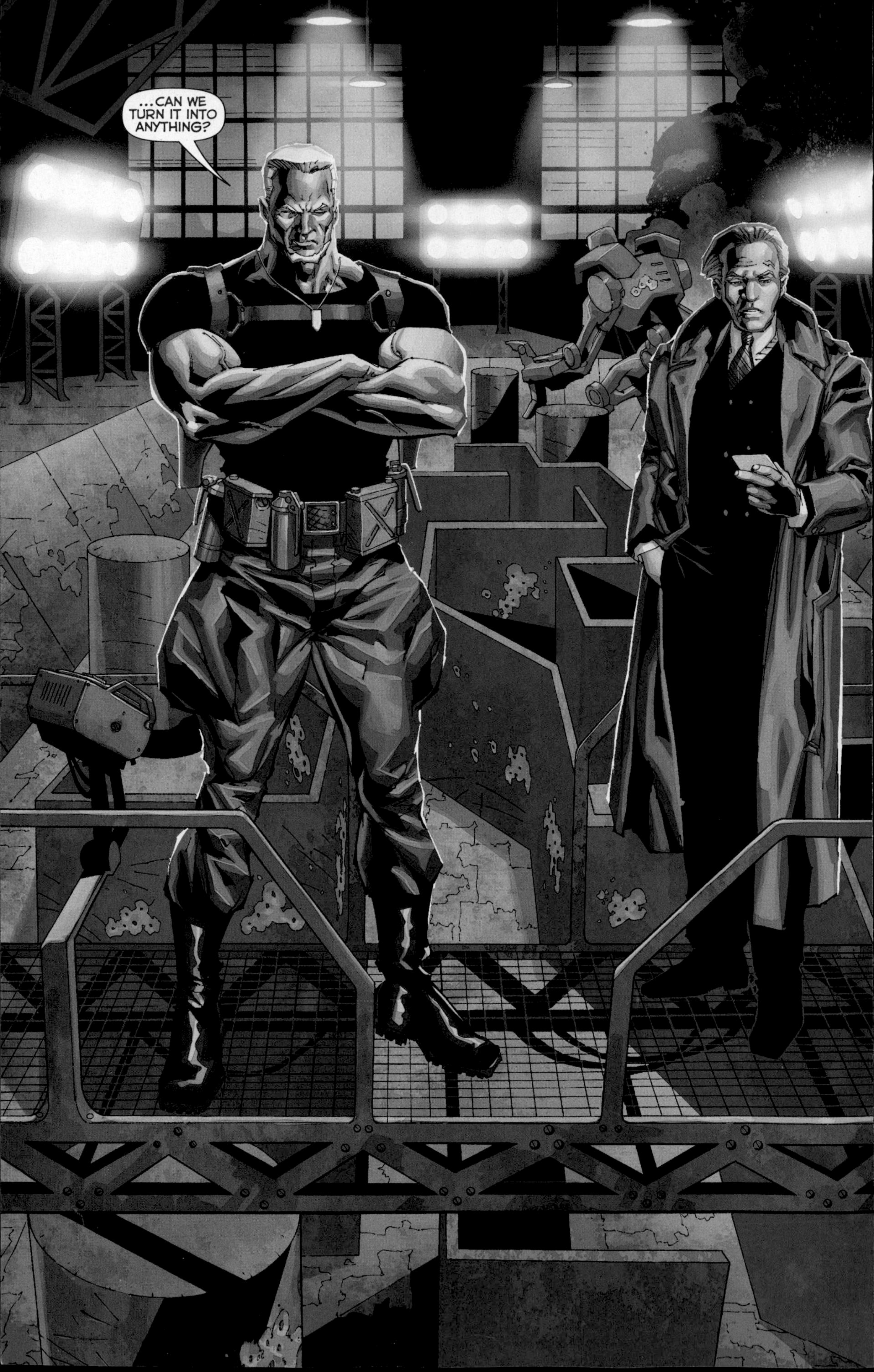
...CAN WE TURN IT INTO ANYTHING?

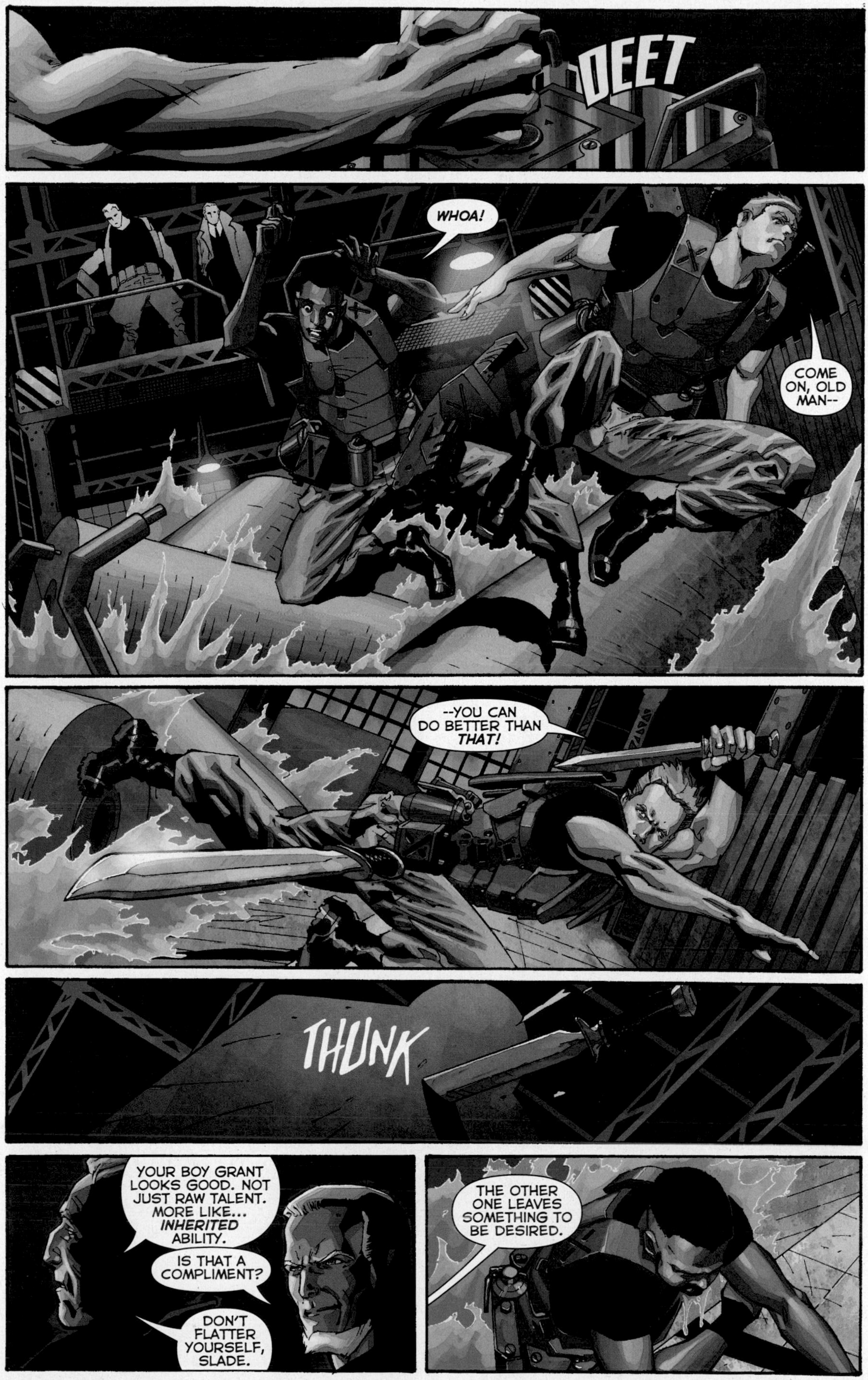
DEET
WHOA!
COME ON, OLD MAN--
--YOU CAN DO BETTER THAN *THAT!*
THUNK
YOUR BOY GRANT LOOKS GOOD. NOT JUST RAW TALENT. MORE LIKE... *INHERITED* ABILITY.
IS THAT A COMPLIMENT?
DON'T FLATTER YOURSELF, SLADE.
THE OTHER ONE LEAVES SOMETHING TO BE DESIRED.

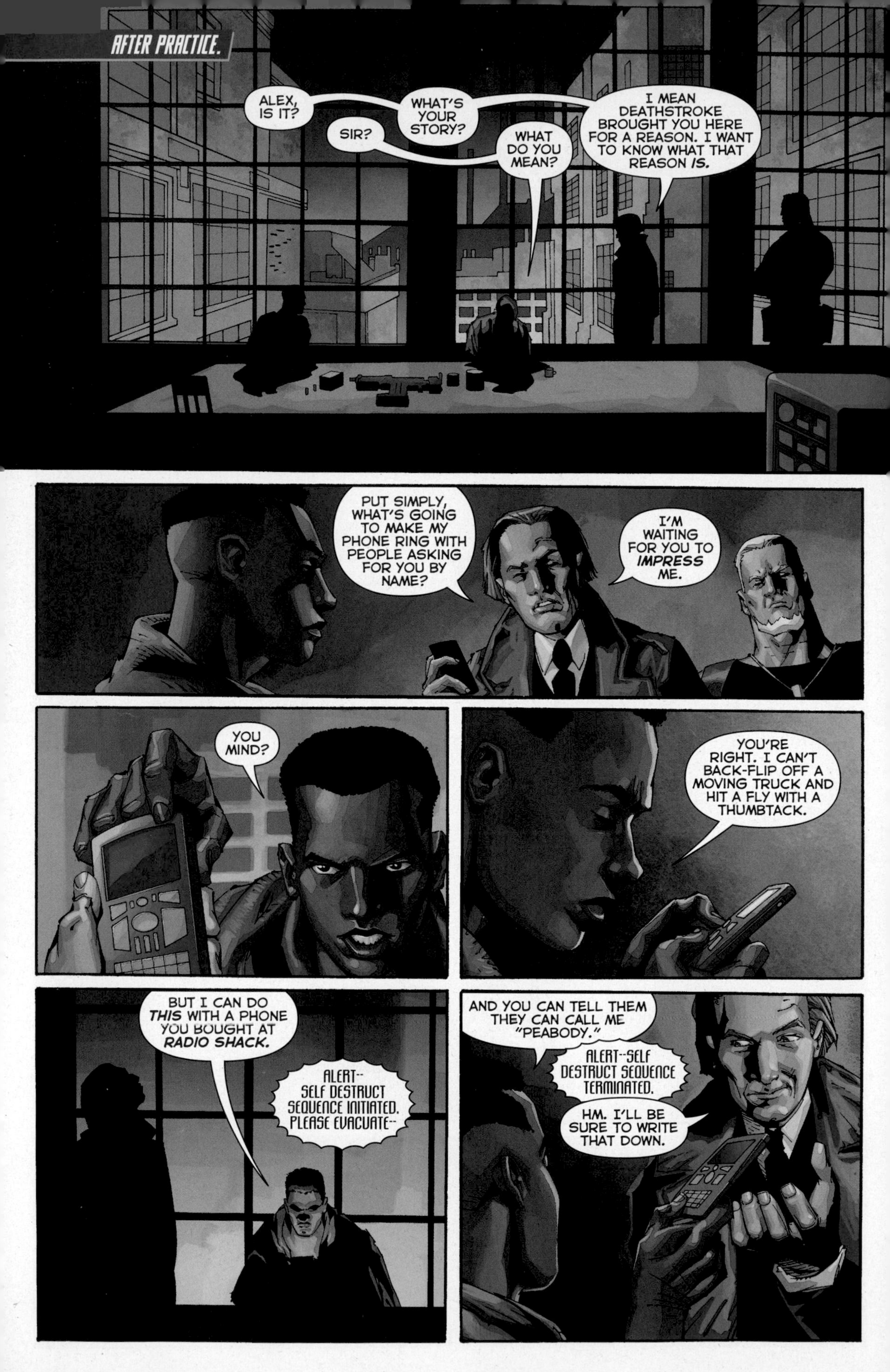
AFTER PRACTICE.
ALEX, IS IT?
WHAT'S YOUR STORY?
SIR?
WHAT DO YOU MEAN?
I MEAN DEATHSTROKE BROUGHT YOU HERE FOR A REASON. I WANT TO KNOW WHAT THAT REASON IS.
PUT SIMPLY, WHAT'S GOING TO MAKE MY PHONE RING WITH PEOPLE ASKING FOR YOU BY NAME?
I'M WAITING FOR YOU TO IMPRESS ME.
YOU MIND?
YOU'RE RIGHT. I CAN'T BACK-FLIP OFF A MOVING TRUCK AND HIT A FLY WITH A THUMBTACK.
BUT I CAN DO THIS WITH A PHONE YOU BOUGHT AT RADIO SHACK.
ALERT-- SELF DESTRUCT SEQUENCE INITIATED. PLEASE EVACUATE--
AND YOU CAN TELL THEM THEY CAN CALL ME "PEABODY."
ALERT--SELF DESTRUCT SEQUENCE TERMINATED.
HM. I'LL BE SURE TO WRITE THAT DOWN.

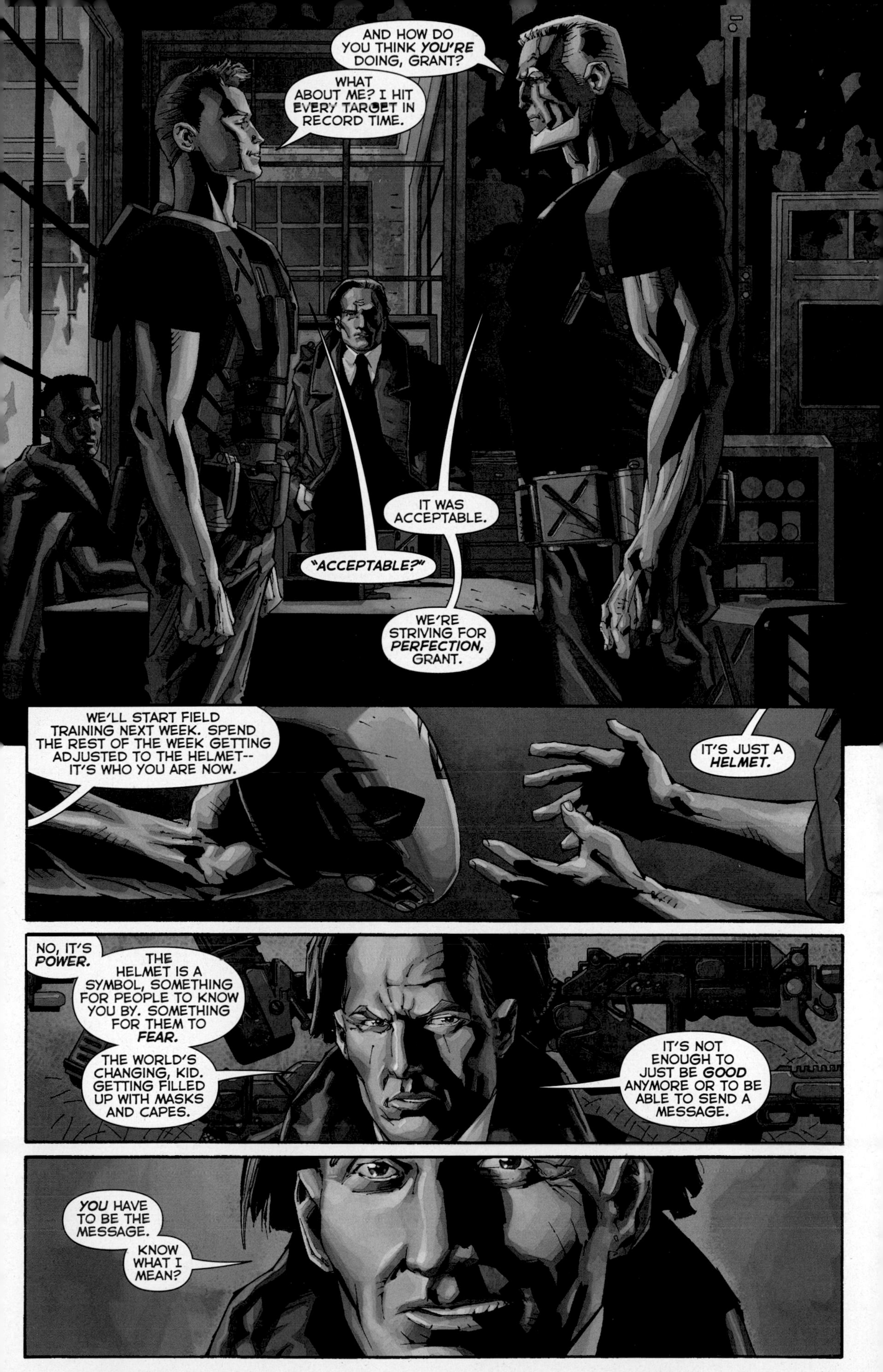

AND HOW DO YOU THINK *YOU'RE* DOING, GRANT?
WHAT ABOUT ME? I HIT EVERY TARGET IN RECORD TIME.
IT WAS ACCEPTABLE.
"ACCEPTABLE?"
WE'RE STRIVING FOR *PERFECTION,* GRANT.
WE'LL START FIELD TRAINING NEXT WEEK. SPEND THE REST OF THE WEEK GETTING ADJUSTED TO THE HELMET-- IT'S WHO YOU ARE NOW.
IT'S JUST A *HELMET.*
NO, IT'S *POWER.*
THE HELMET IS A SYMBOL, SOMETHING FOR PEOPLE TO KNOW YOU BY. SOMETHING FOR THEM TO *FEAR.*
THE WORLD'S CHANGING, KID. GETTING FILLED UP WITH MASKS AND CAPES.
IT'S NOT ENOUGH TO JUST BE *GOOD* ANYMORE OR TO BE ABLE TO SEND A MESSAGE.
YOU HAVE TO BE THE MESSAGE.
KNOW WHAT I MEAN?

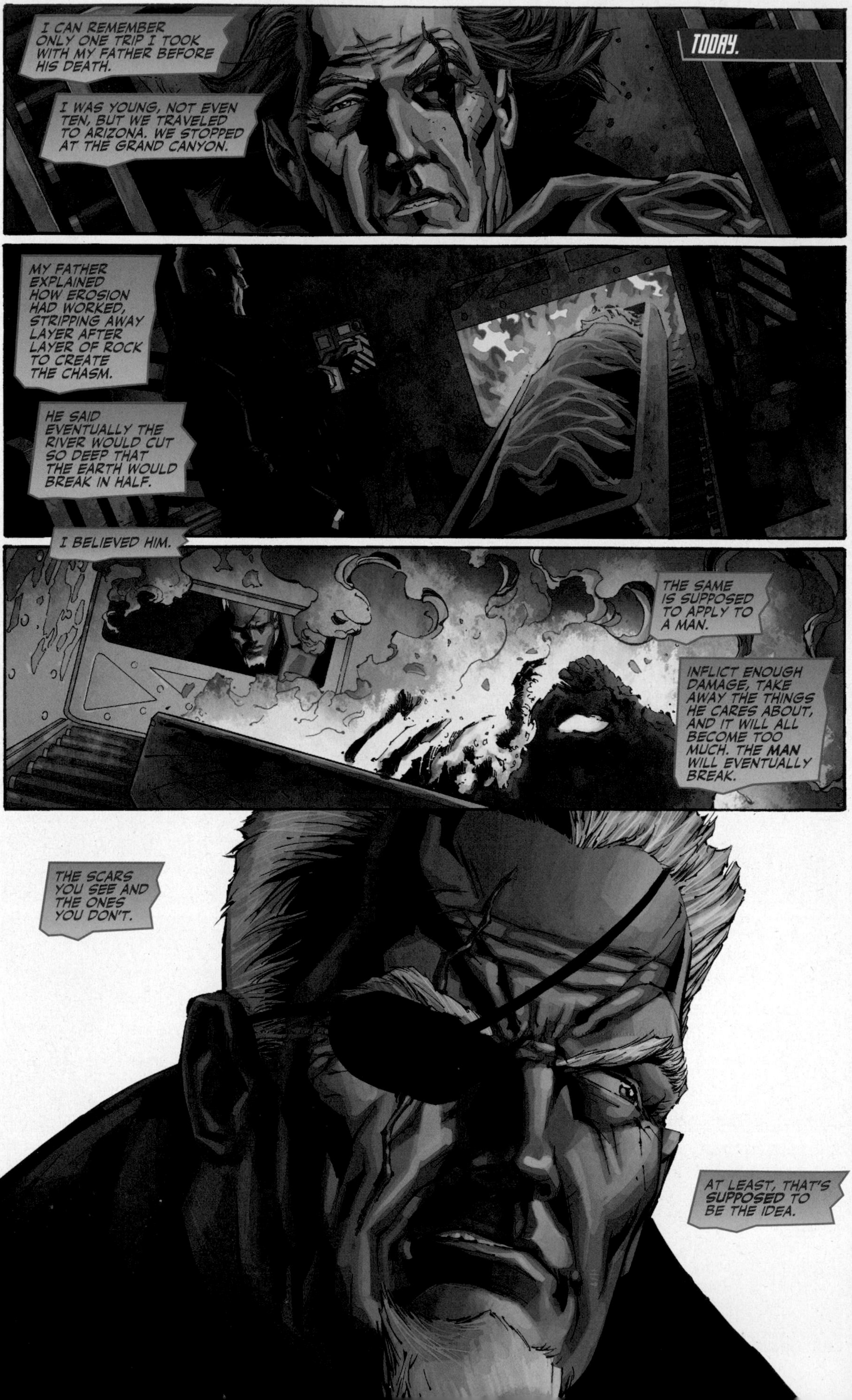

I CAN REMEMBER ONLY ONE TRIP I TOOK WITH MY FATHER BEFORE HIS DEATH.
TODAY.
I WAS YOUNG, NOT EVEN TEN, BUT WE TRAVELED TO ARIZONA. WE STOPPED AT THE GRAND CANYON.
MY FATHER EXPLAINED HOW EROSION HAD WORKED, STRIPPING AWAY LAYER AFTER LAYER OF ROCK TO CREATE THE CHASM.
HE SAID EVENTUALLY THE RIVER WOULD CUT SO DEEP THAT THE EARTH WOULD BREAK IN HALF.
I BELIEVED HIM.
THE SAME IS SUPPOSED TO APPLY TO A MAN.
INFLICT ENOUGH DAMAGE, TAKE AWAY THE THINGS HE CARES ABOUT, AND IT WILL ALL BECOME TOO MUCH. THE MAN WILL EVENTUALLY BREAK.
THE SCARS YOU SEE AND THE ONES YOU DON'T.
AT LEAST, THAT'S SUPPOSED TO BE THE IDEA.

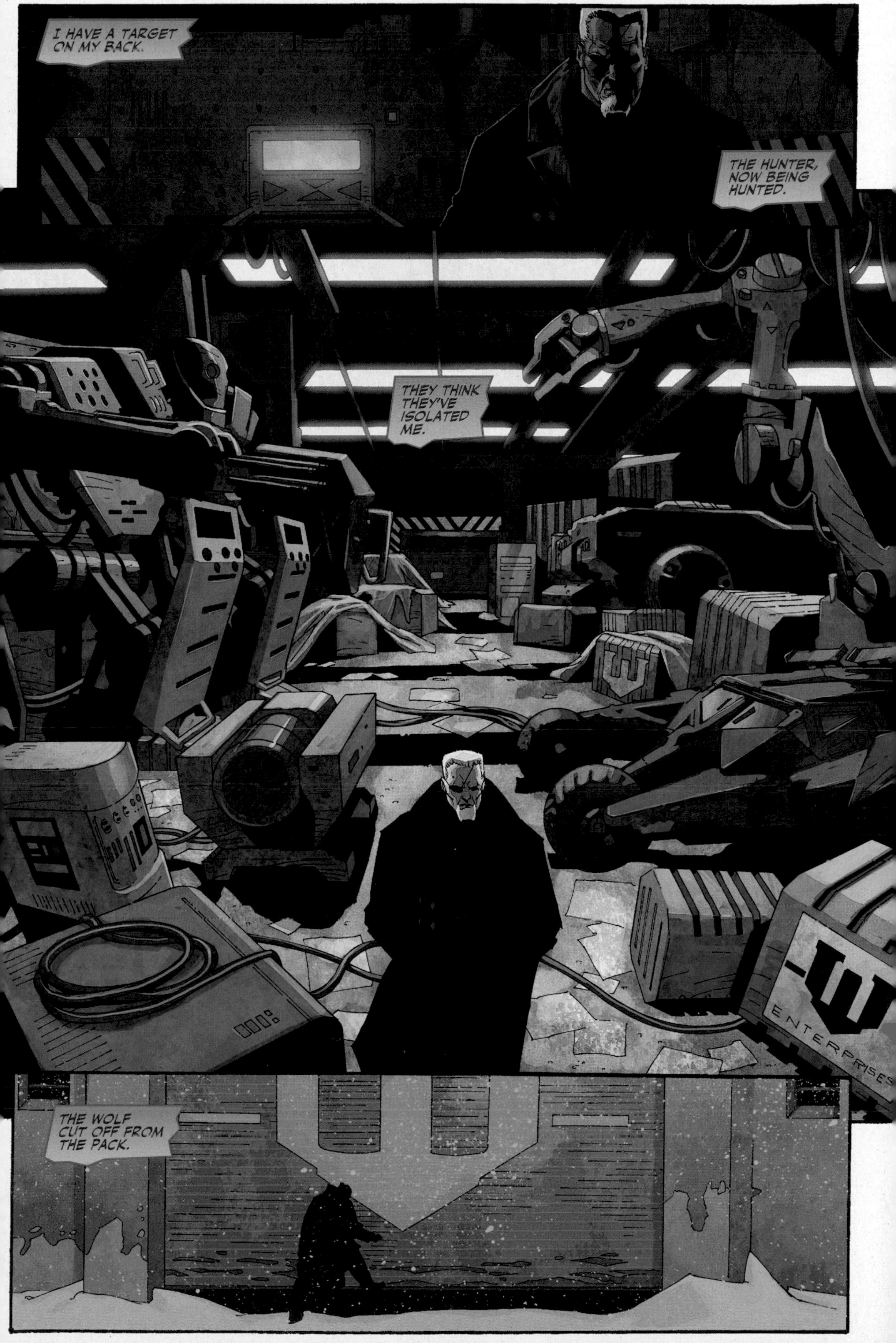
I HAVE A TARGET ON MY BACK.
THE HUNTER, NOW BEING HUNTED.
THEY THINK THEY'VE ISOLATED ME.
ENTERPRISES
THE WOLF CUT OFF FROM THE PACK.

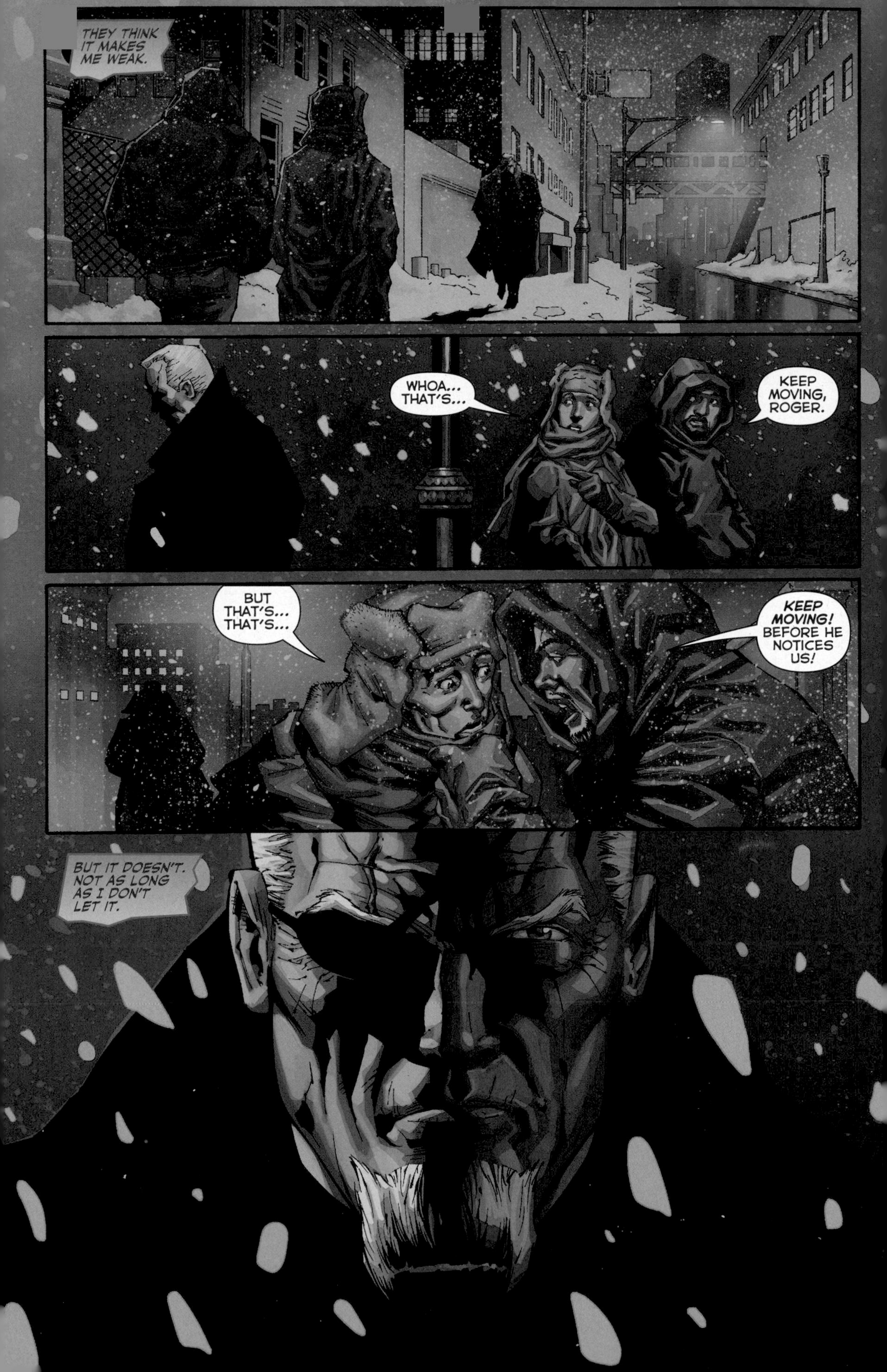
THEY THINK IT MAKES ME WEAK.
WHOA... THAT'S...
KEEP MOVING, ROGER.
BUT THAT'S... THAT'S...
KEEP MOVING! BEFORE HE NOTICES US!
BUT IT DOESN'T. NOT AS LONG AS I DON'T LET IT.

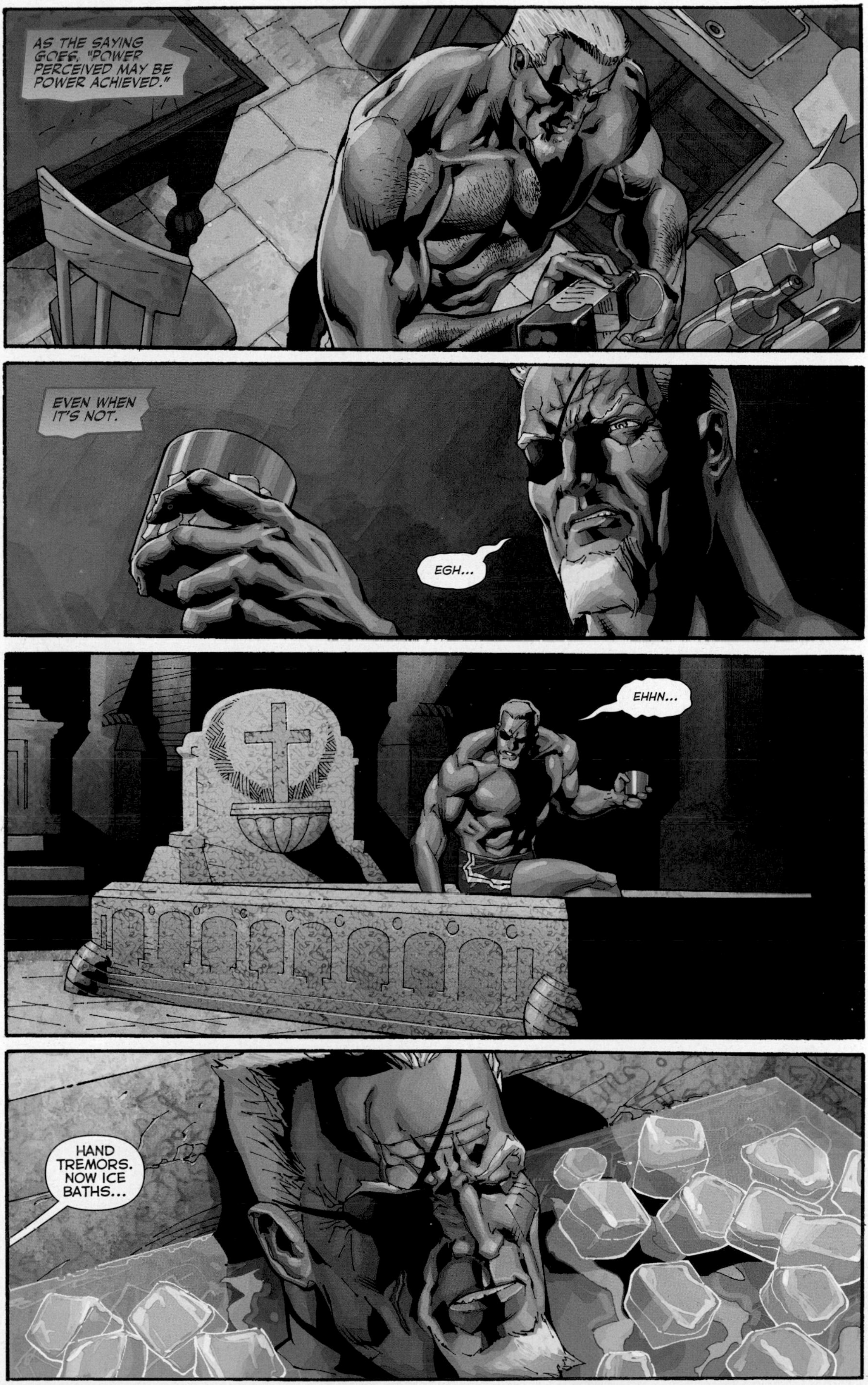
AS THE SAYING GOES, "POWER PERCEIVED MAY BE POWER ACHIEVED."
EVEN WHEN IT'S NOT.
EGH...
EHHN...
HAND TREMORS. NOW ICE BATHS...

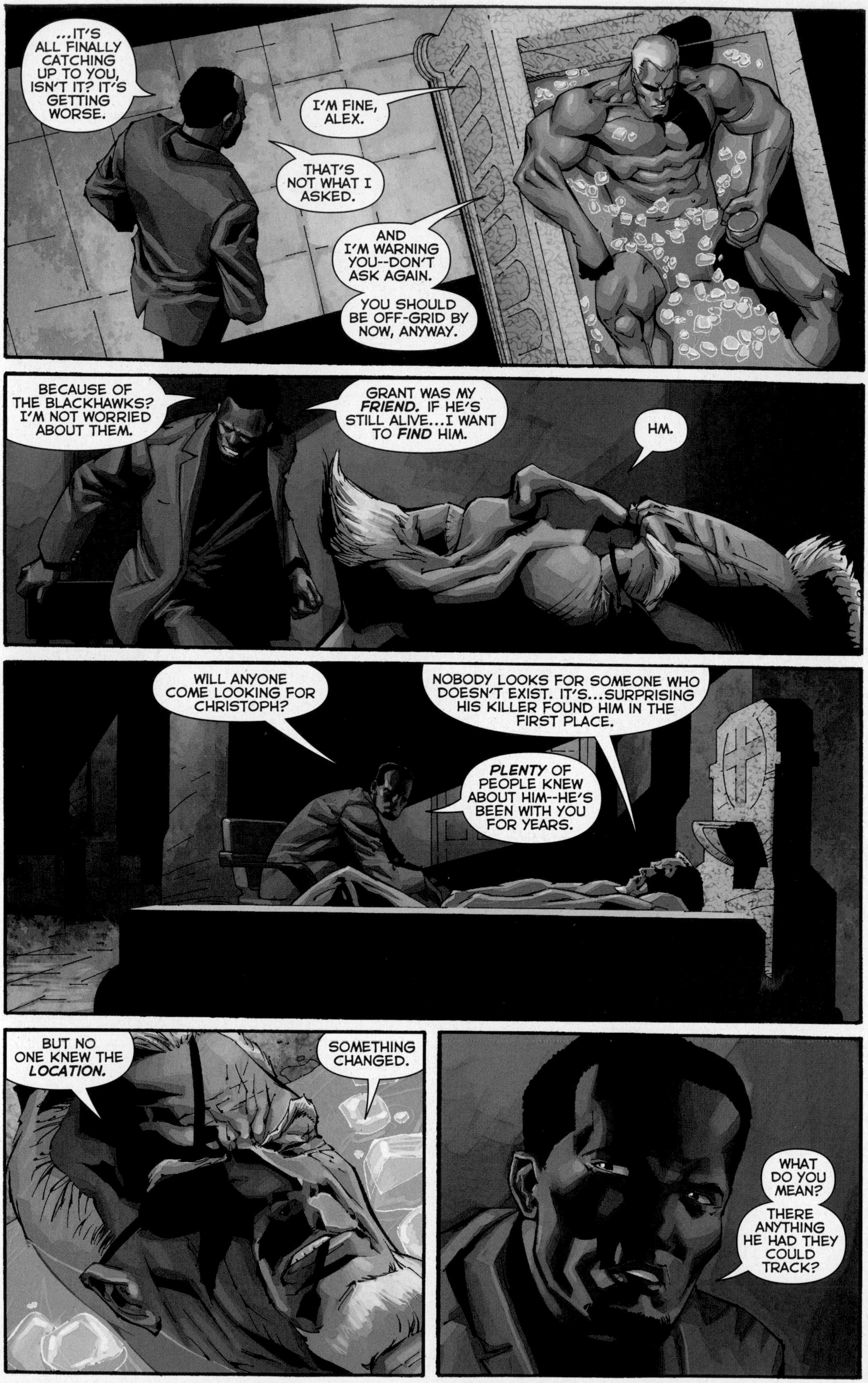
...IT'S ALL FINALLY CATCHING UP TO YOU, ISN'T IT? IT'S GETTING WORSE.
I'M FINE, ALEX.
THAT'S NOT WHAT I ASKED.
AND I'M WARNING YOU--DON'T ASK AGAIN.
YOU SHOULD BE OFF-GRID BY NOW, ANYWAY.
BECAUSE OF THE BLACKHAWKS? I'M NOT WORRIED ABOUT THEM.
GRANT WAS MY FRIEND. IF HE'S STILL ALIVE...I WANT TO FIND HIM.
HM.
WILL ANYONE COME LOOKING FOR CHRISTOPH?
NOBODY LOOKS FOR SOMEONE WHO DOESN'T EXIST. IT'S...SURPRISING HIS KILLER FOUND HIM IN THE FIRST PLACE.
PLENTY OF PEOPLE KNEW ABOUT HIM--HE'S BEEN WITH YOU FOR YEARS.
BUT NO ONE KNEW THE LOCATION.
SOMETHING CHANGED.
WHAT DO YOU MEAN?
THERE ANYTHING HE HAD THEY COULD TRACK?

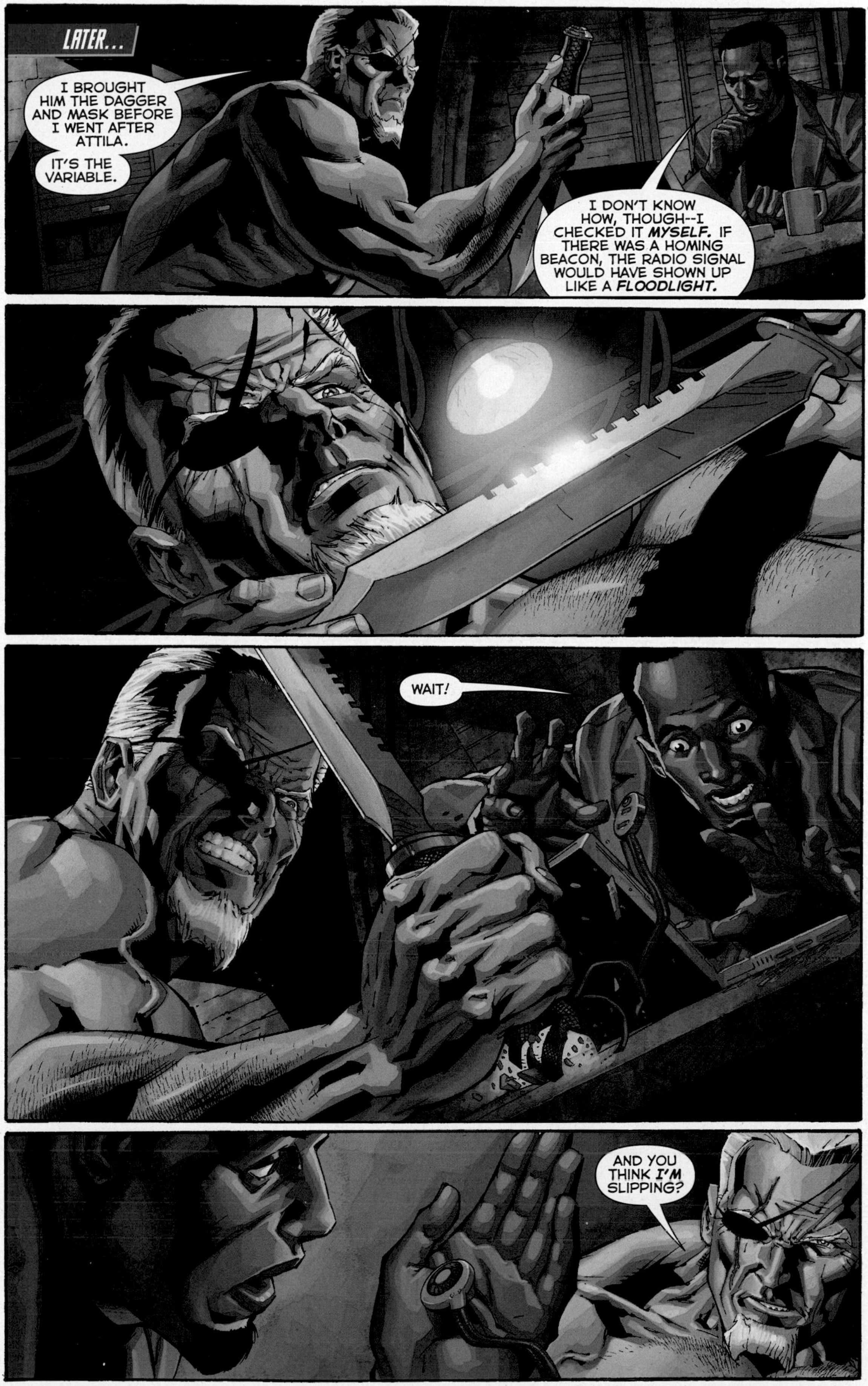
LATER...
I BROUGHT HIM THE DAGGER AND MASK BEFORE I WENT AFTER ATTILA.
IT'S THE VARIABLE.
I DON'T KNOW HOW, THOUGH--I CHECKED IT MYSELF. IF THERE WAS A HOMING BEACON, THE RADIO SIGNAL WOULD HAVE SHOWN UP LIKE A FLOODLIGHT.
WAIT!
AND YOU THINK I'M SLIPPING?

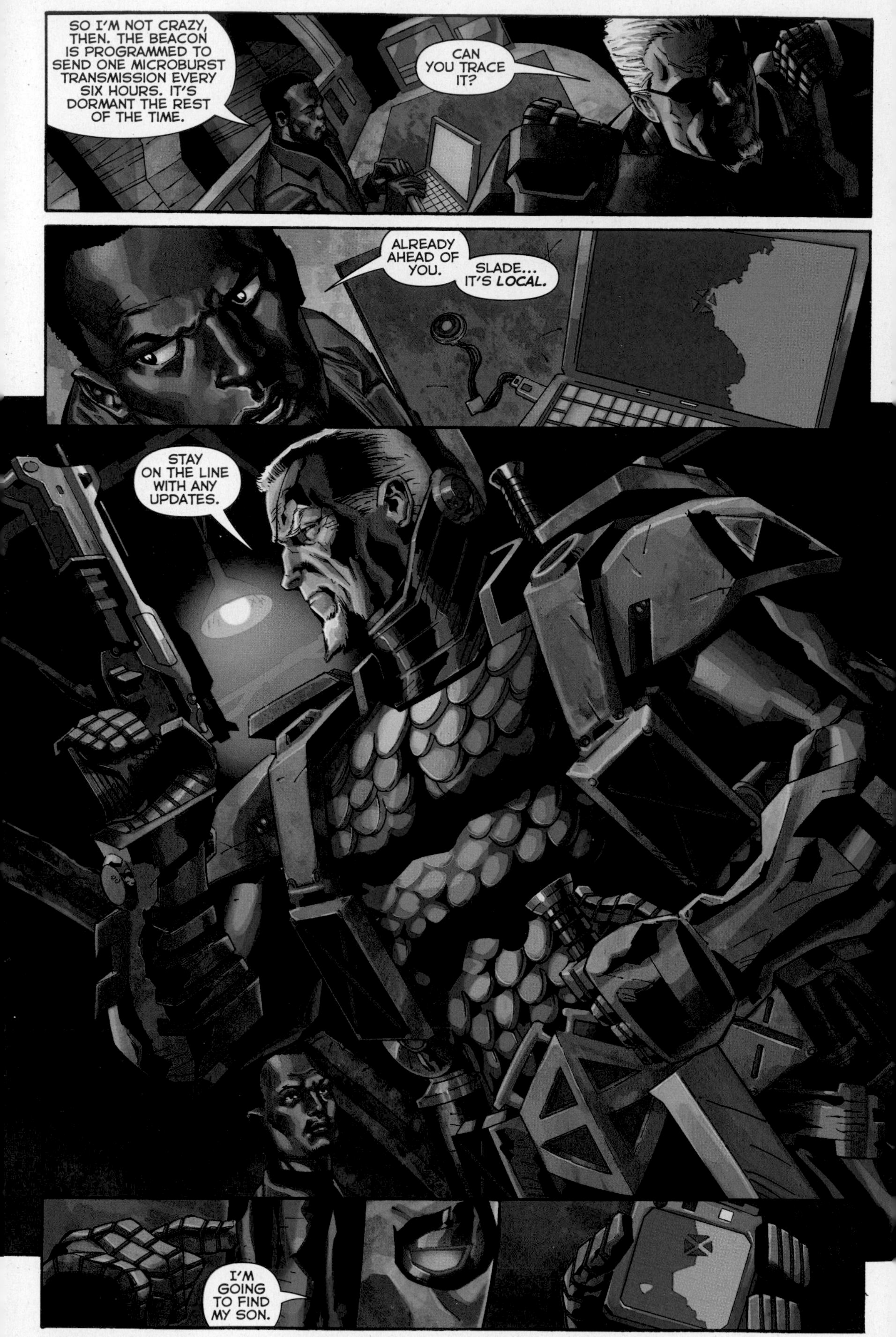
SO I'M NOT CRAZY, THEN. THE BEACON IS PROGRAMMED TO SEND ONE MICROBURST TRANSMISSION EVERY SIX HOURS. IT'S DORMANT THE REST OF THE TIME.
CAN YOU TRACE IT?
ALREADY AHEAD OF YOU.
SLADE... IT'S *LOCAL.*
STAY ON THE LINE WITH ANY UPDATES.
I'M GOING TO FIND MY SON.

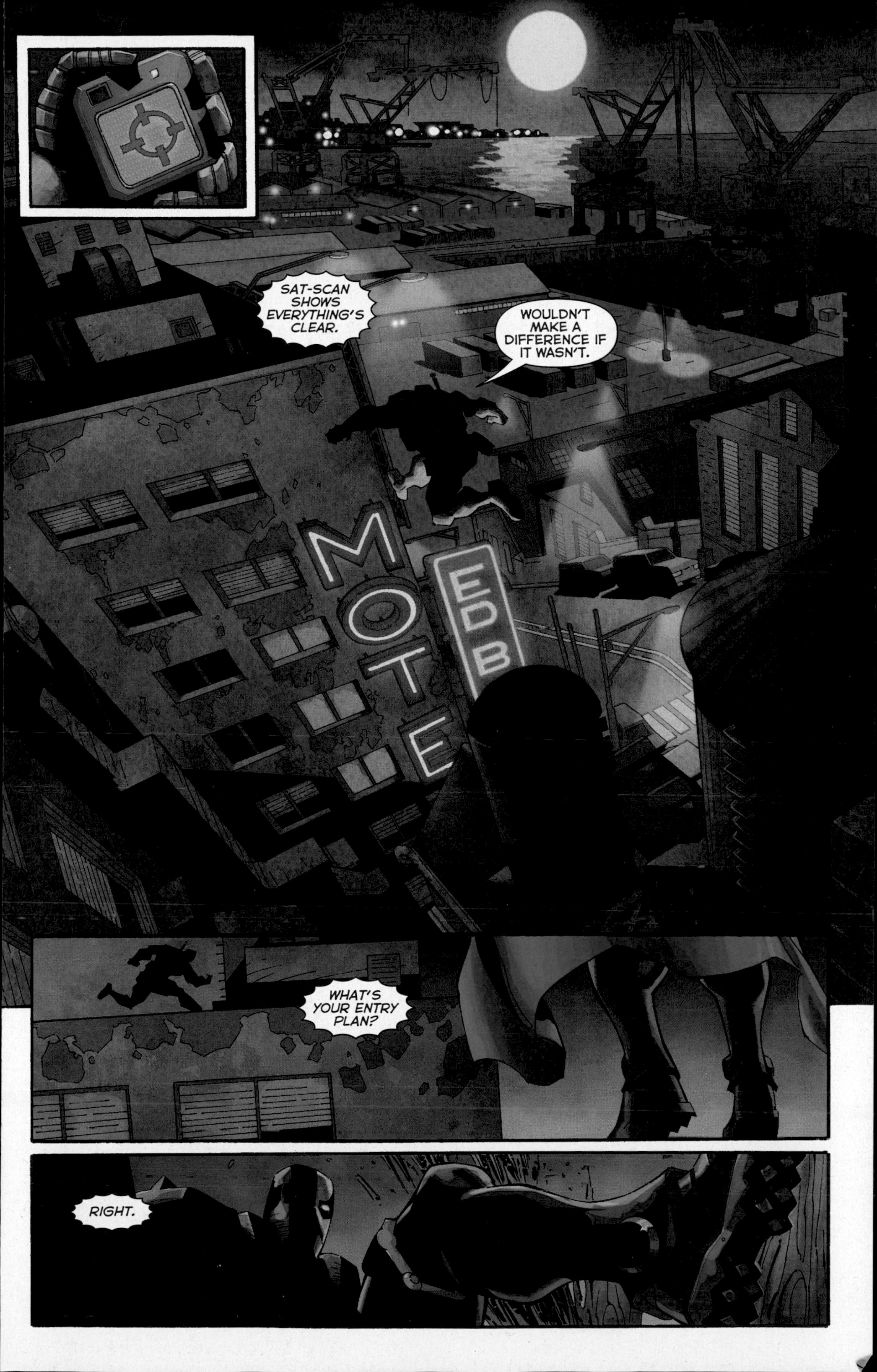
SAT-SCAN SHOWS EVERYTHING'S CLEAR.
WOULDN'T MAKE A DIFFERENCE IF IT WASN'T.
WHAT'S YOUR ENTRY PLAN?
RIGHT.

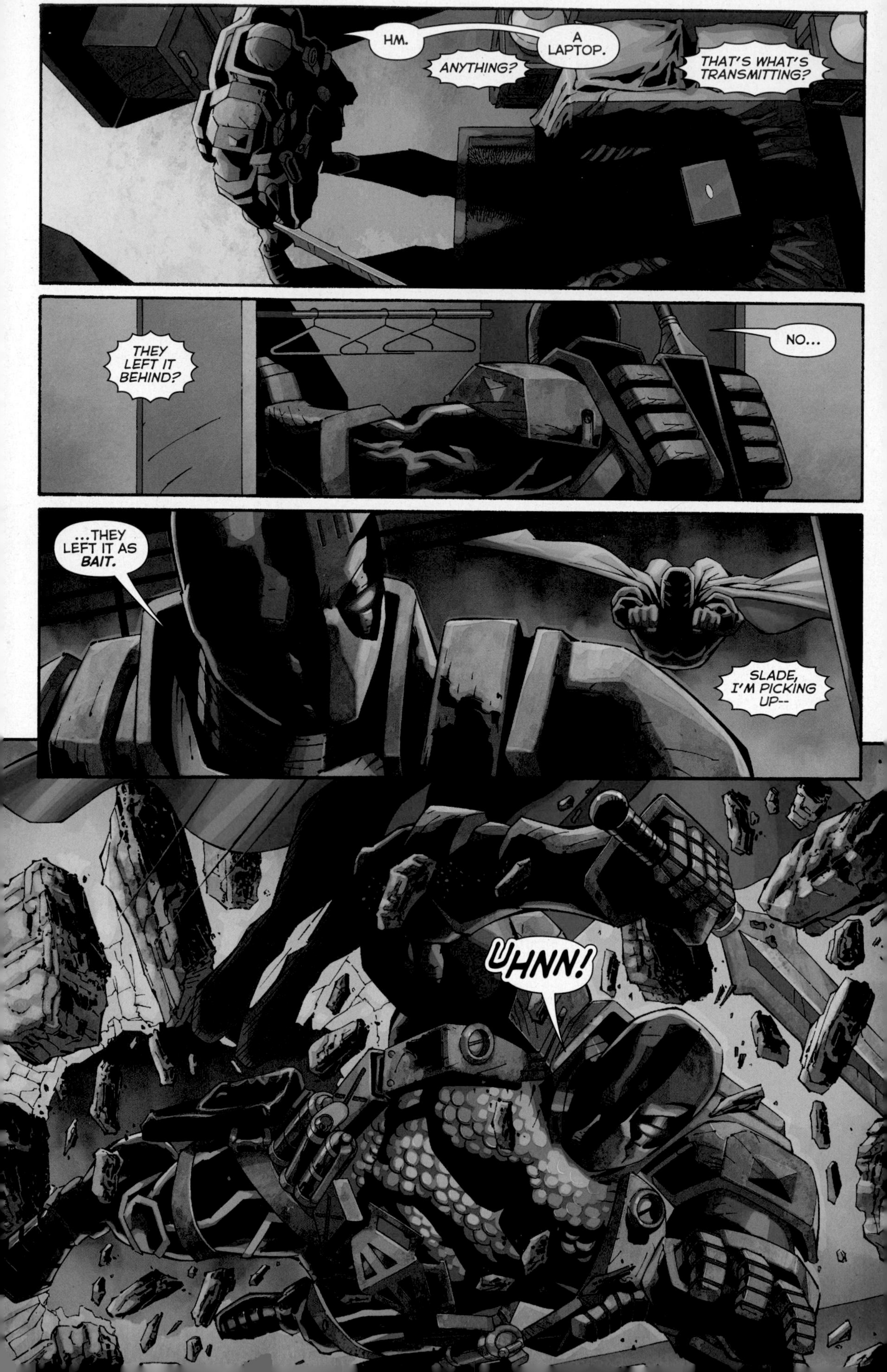
HM.
ANYTHING?
A LAPTOP.
THAT'S WHAT'S TRANSMITTING?
THEY LEFT IT BEHIND?
NO...
...THEY LEFT IT AS BAIT.
SLADE, I'M PICKING UP--
UHNN!

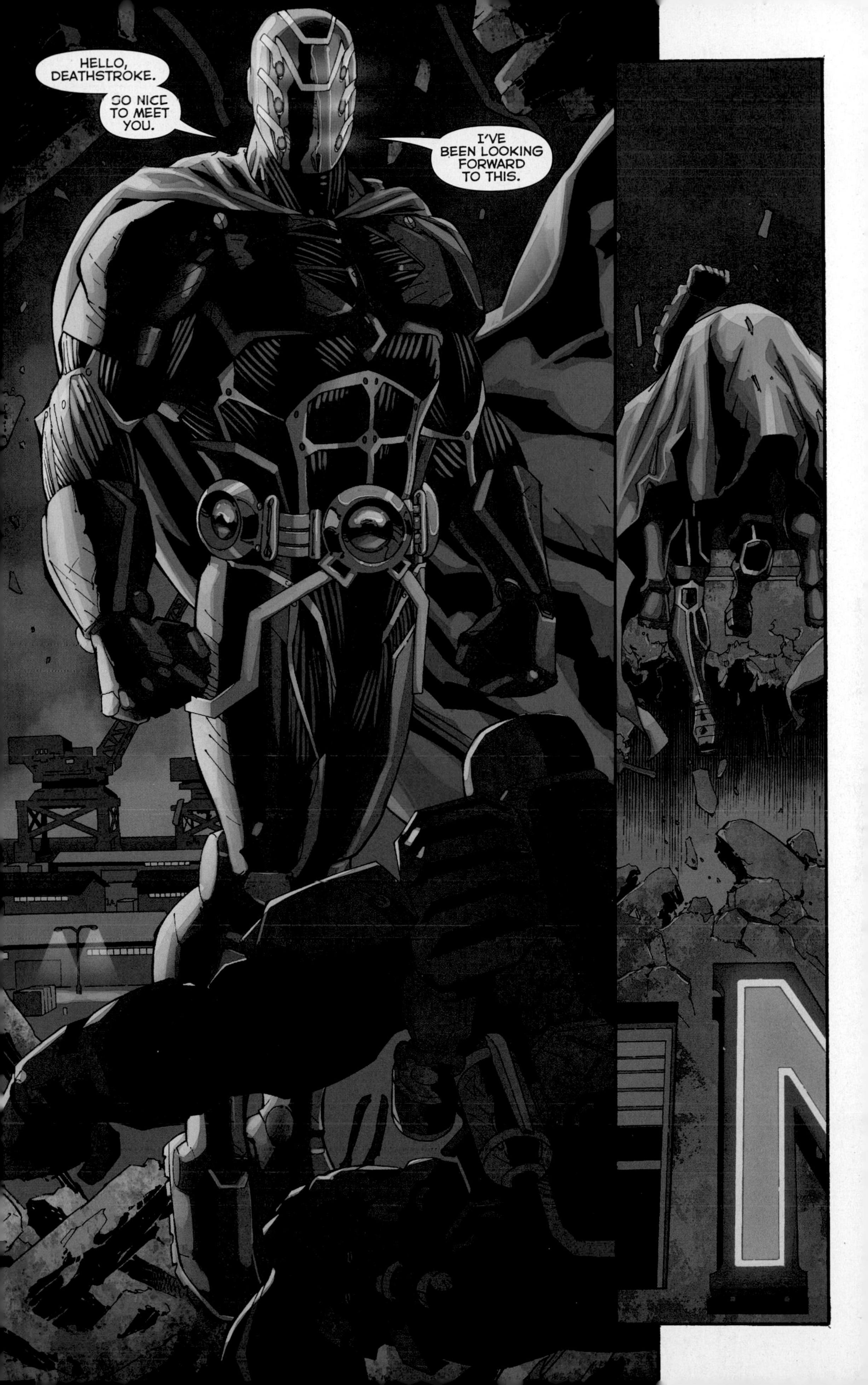
HELLO, DEATHSTROKE.
SO NICE TO MEET YOU.
I'VE BEEN LOOKING FORWARD TO THIS.

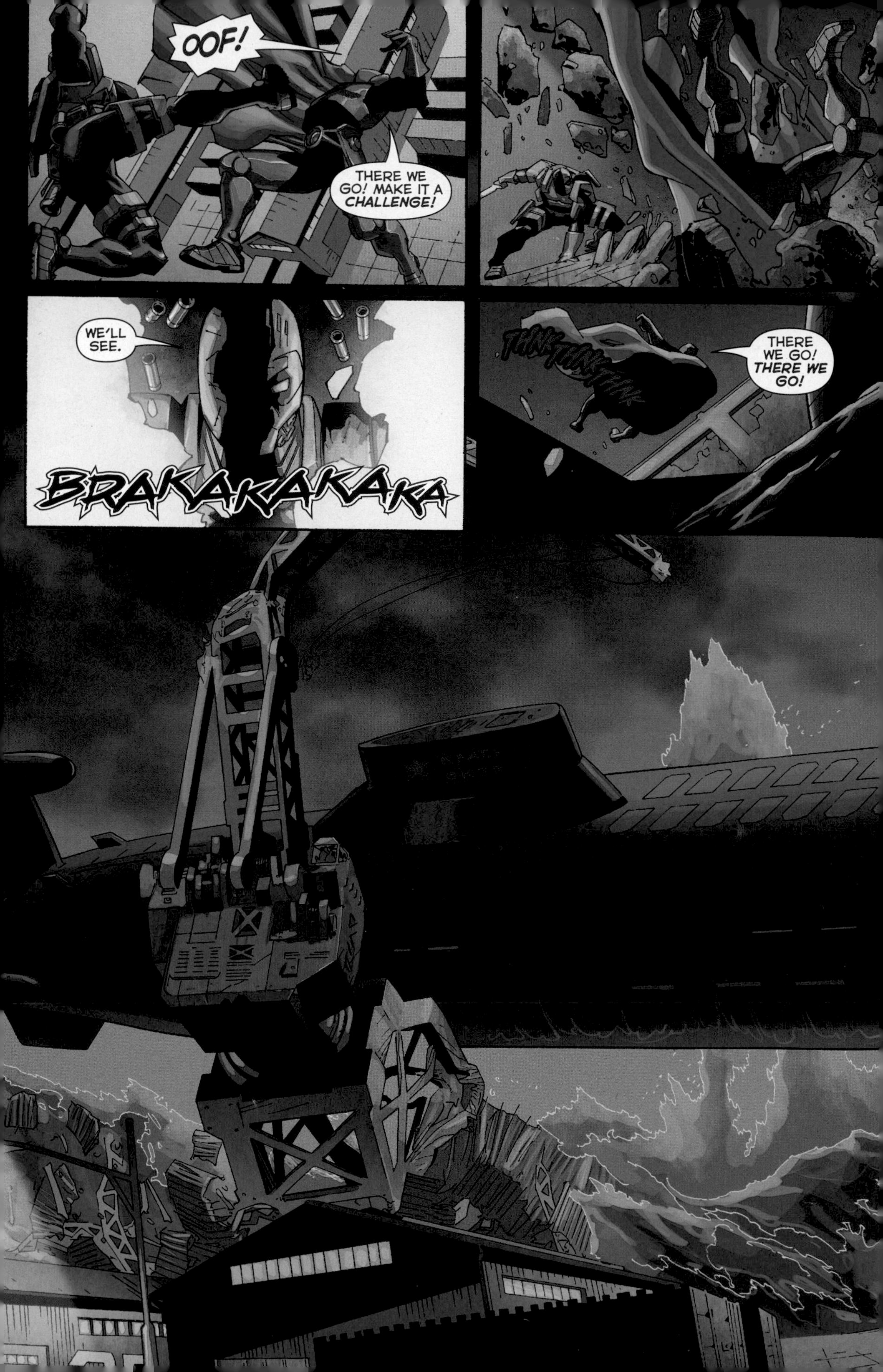
OOF!
THERE WE GO! MAKE IT A CHALLENGE!
WE'LL SEE.
BRAKAKAKAKA
THINK THINK THINK
THERE WE GO! THERE WE GO!

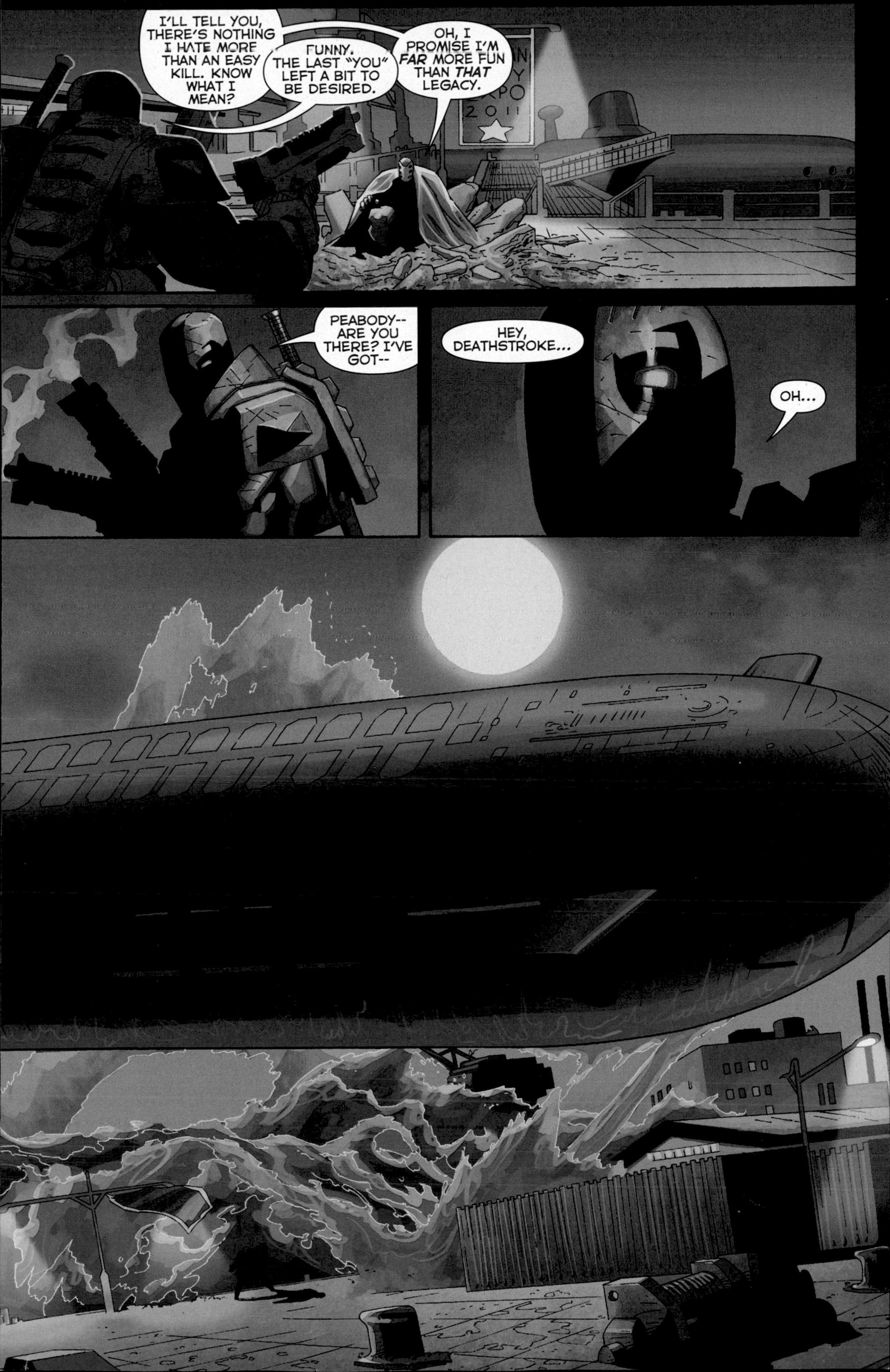
I'LL TELL YOU, THERE'S NOTHING I HATE MORE THAN AN EASY KILL. KNOW WHAT I MEAN?
FUNNY. THE LAST "YOU" LEFT A BIT TO BE DESIRED.
OH, I PROMISE I'M *FAR* MORE FUN THAN *THAT* LEGACY.
EXPO 2011
PEABODY-- ARE YOU THERE? I'VE GOT--
HEY, DEATHSTROKE...
OH...

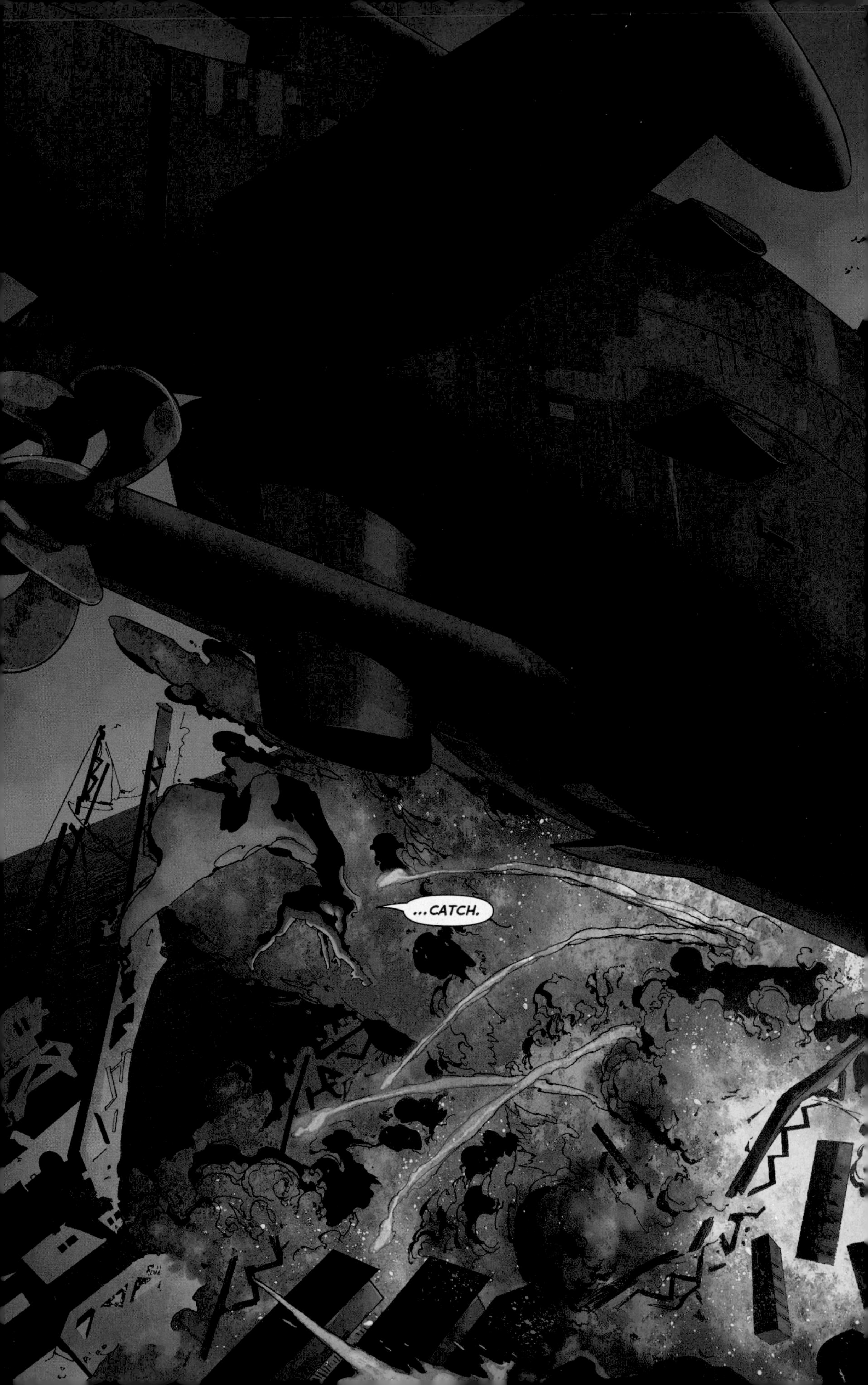
...CATCH.

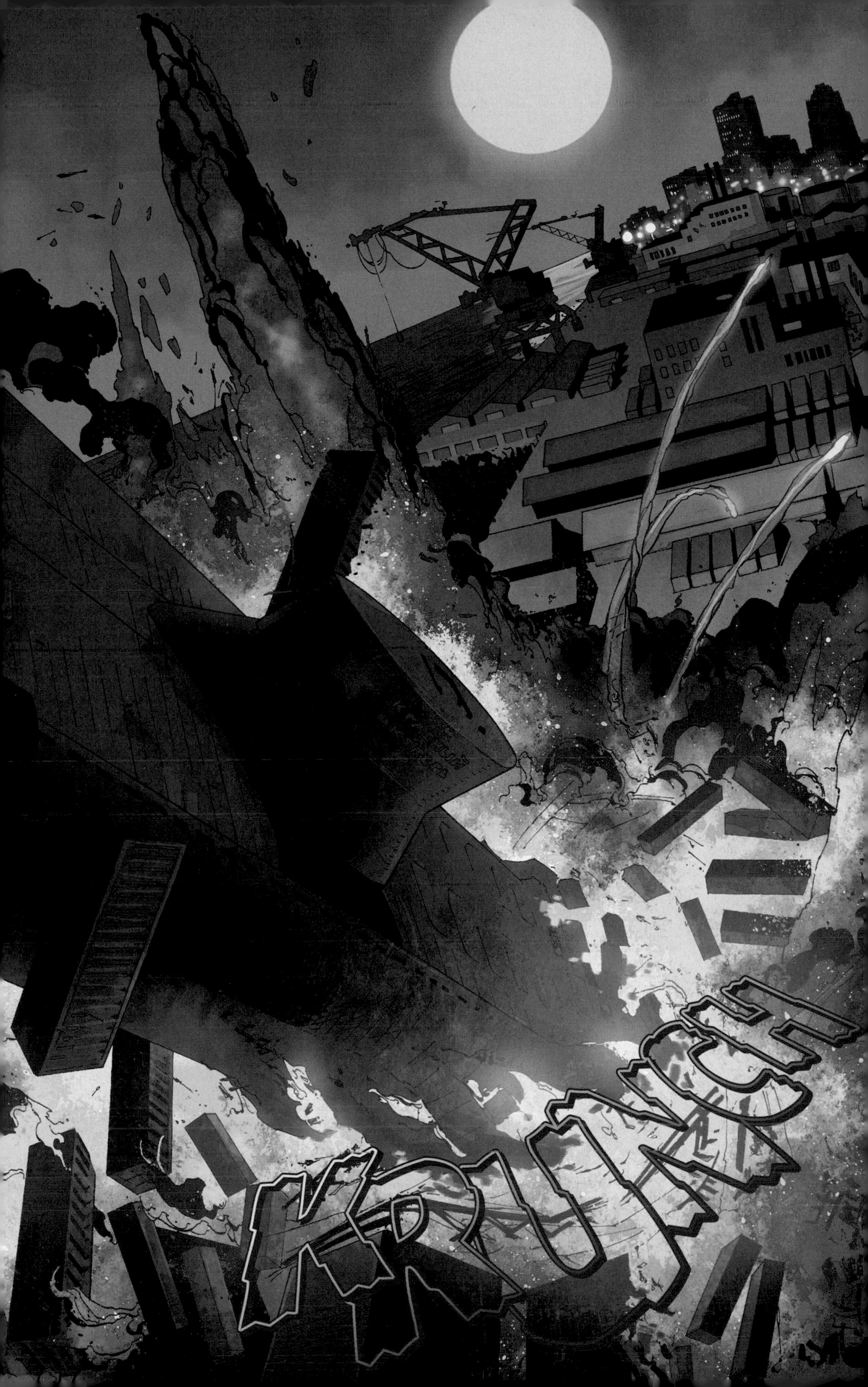
KRUNCH

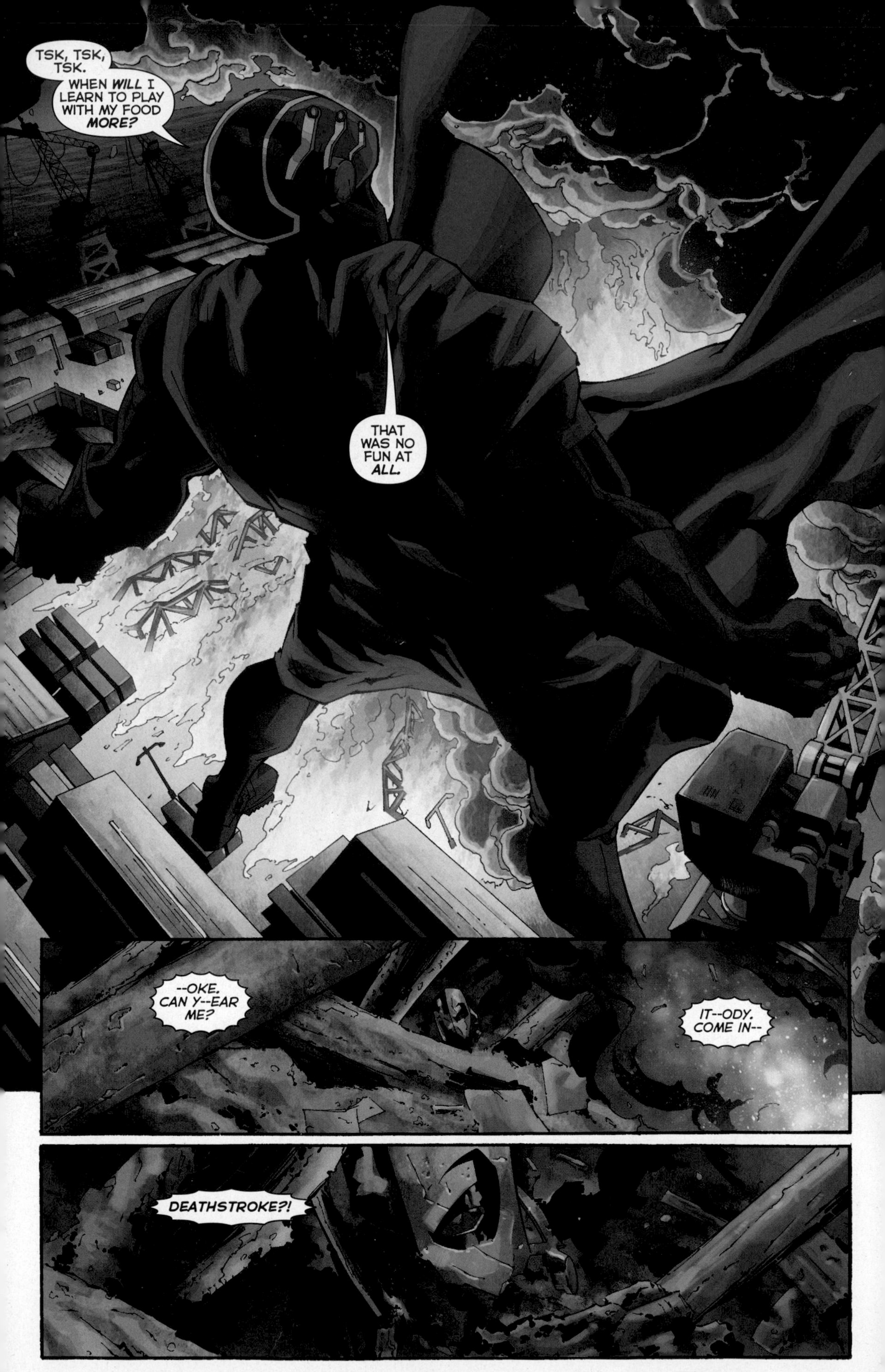
TSK, TSK, TSK. WHEN WILL I LEARN TO PLAY WITH MY FOOD MORE?
THAT WAS NO FUN AT ALL.
--OKE. CAN Y--EAR ME?
IT--ODY. COME IN--
DEATHSTROKE?!

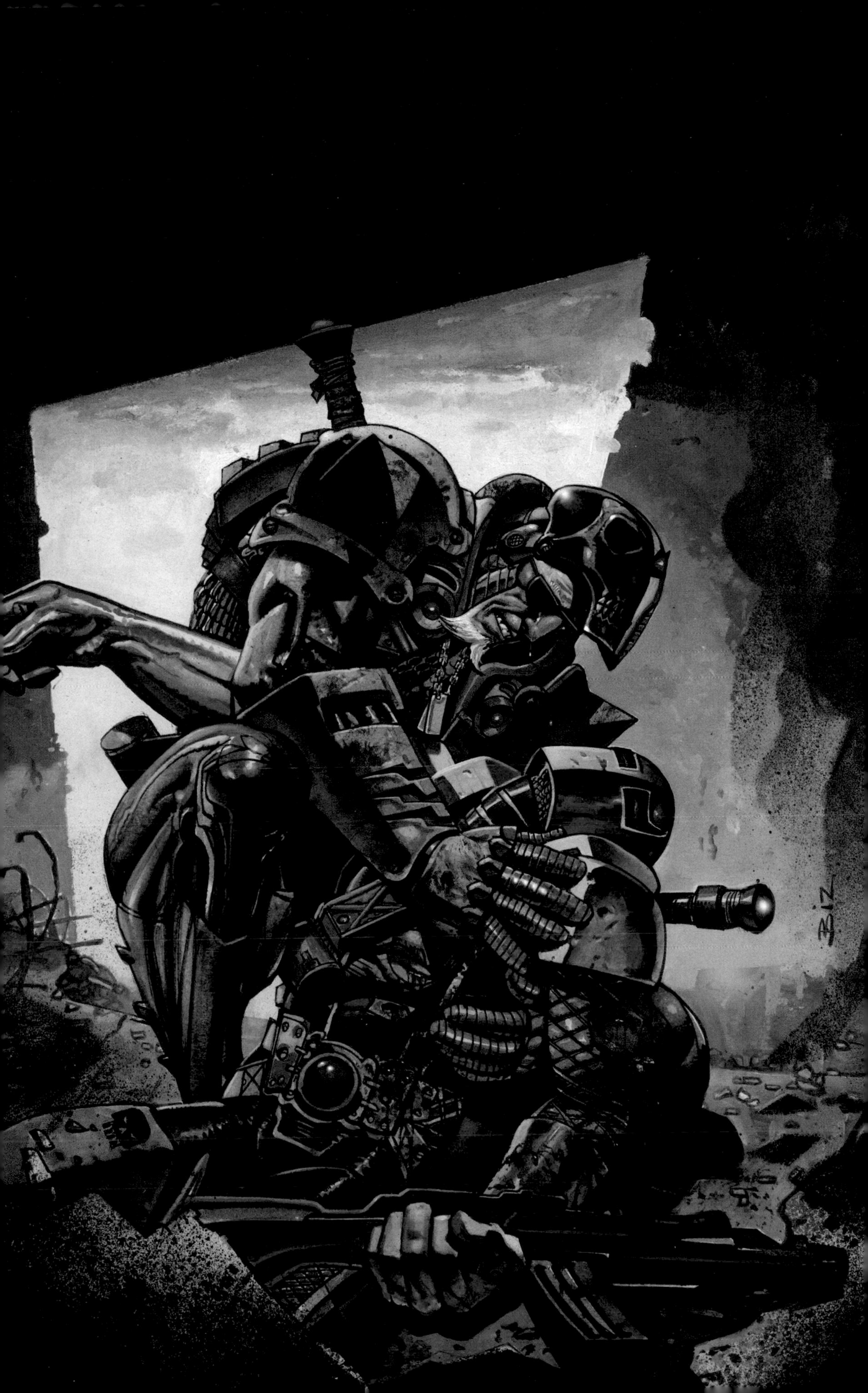
BIZ

ACHILLES HEEL

KYLE HIGGINS writer **JOE BENNETT** layouts **EDUARDO PANSICA** finishes **VICENTE CIFUENTES** inker cover by **SIMON BISLEY**

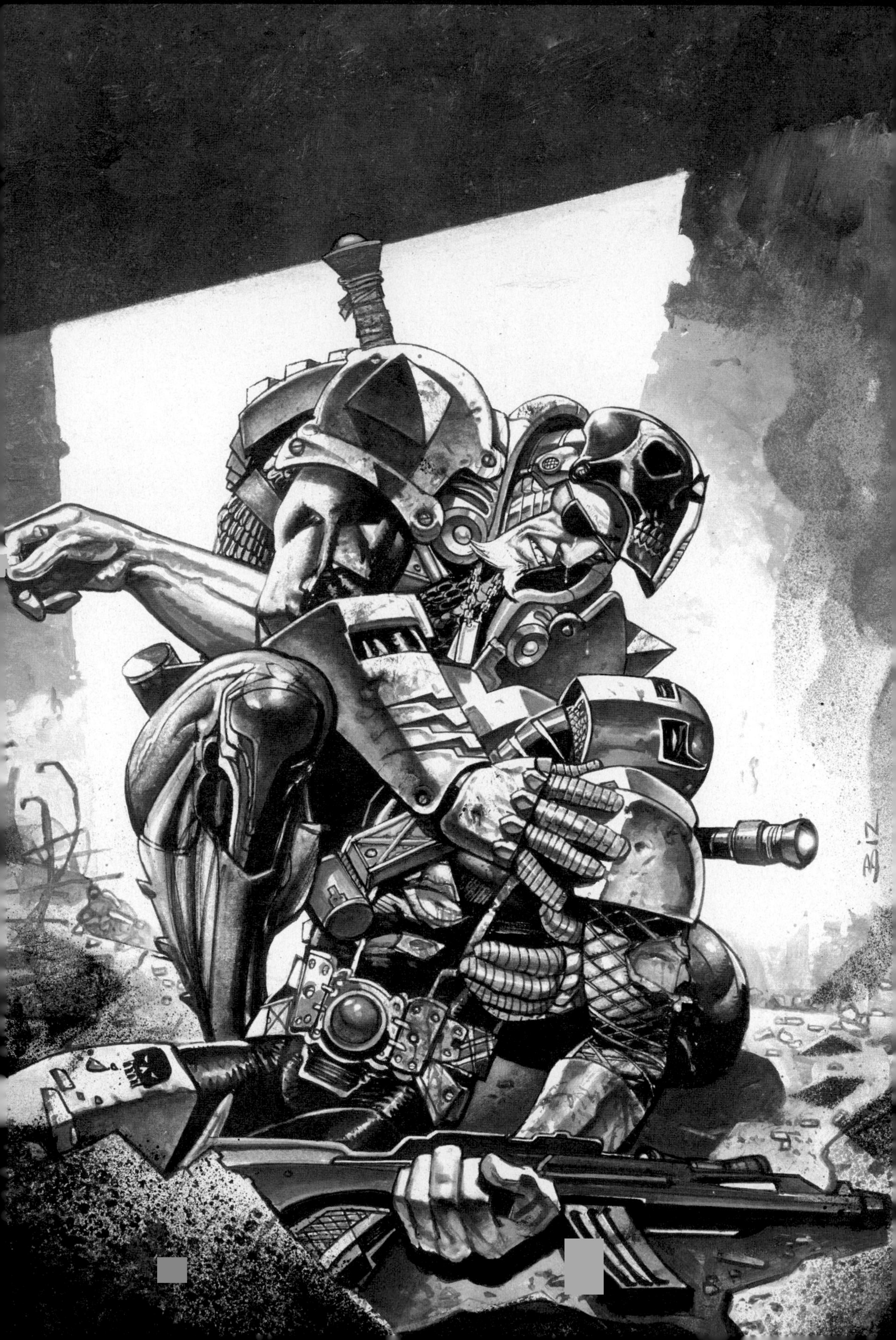
BIZ

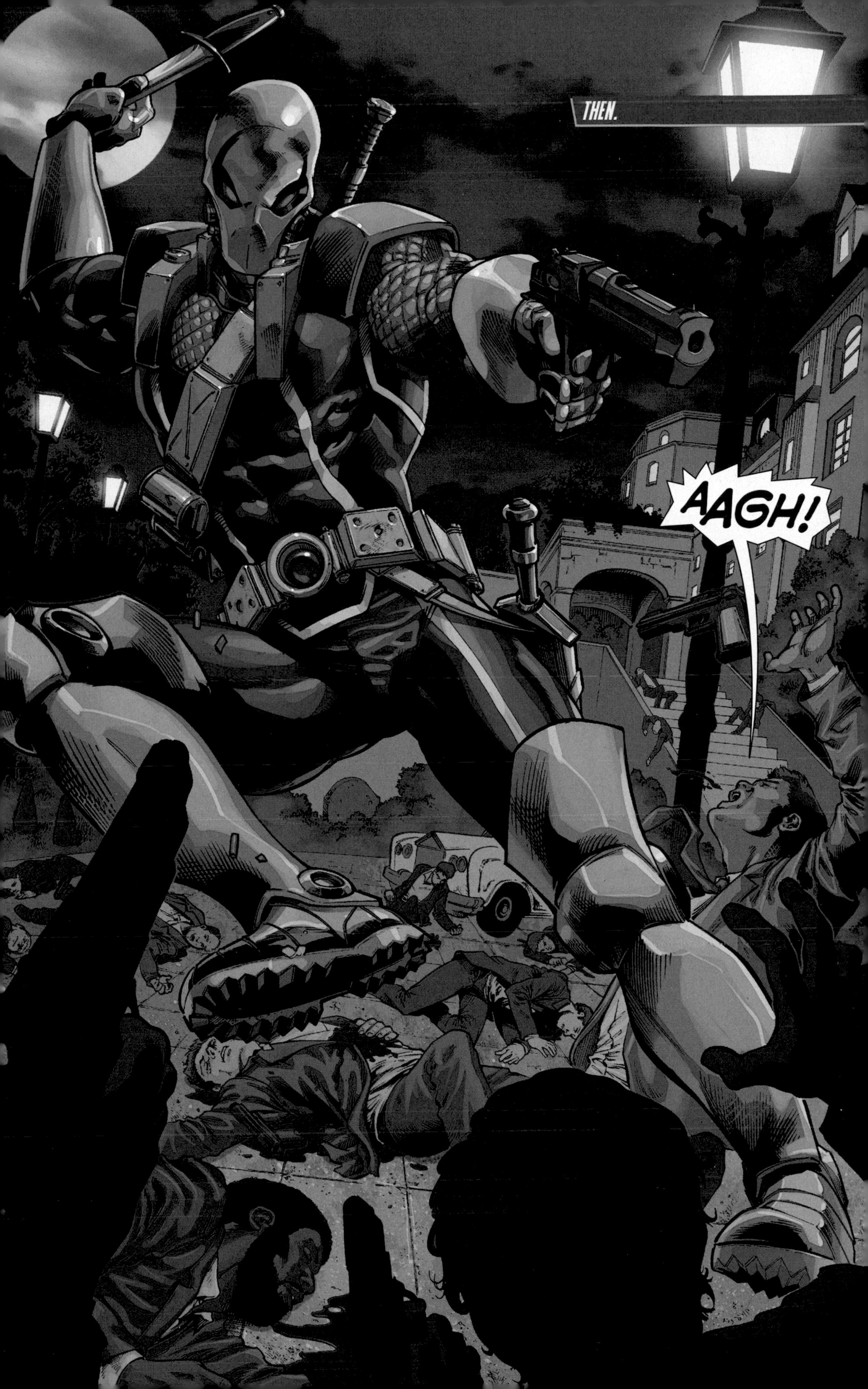
THEN.
AAGH!

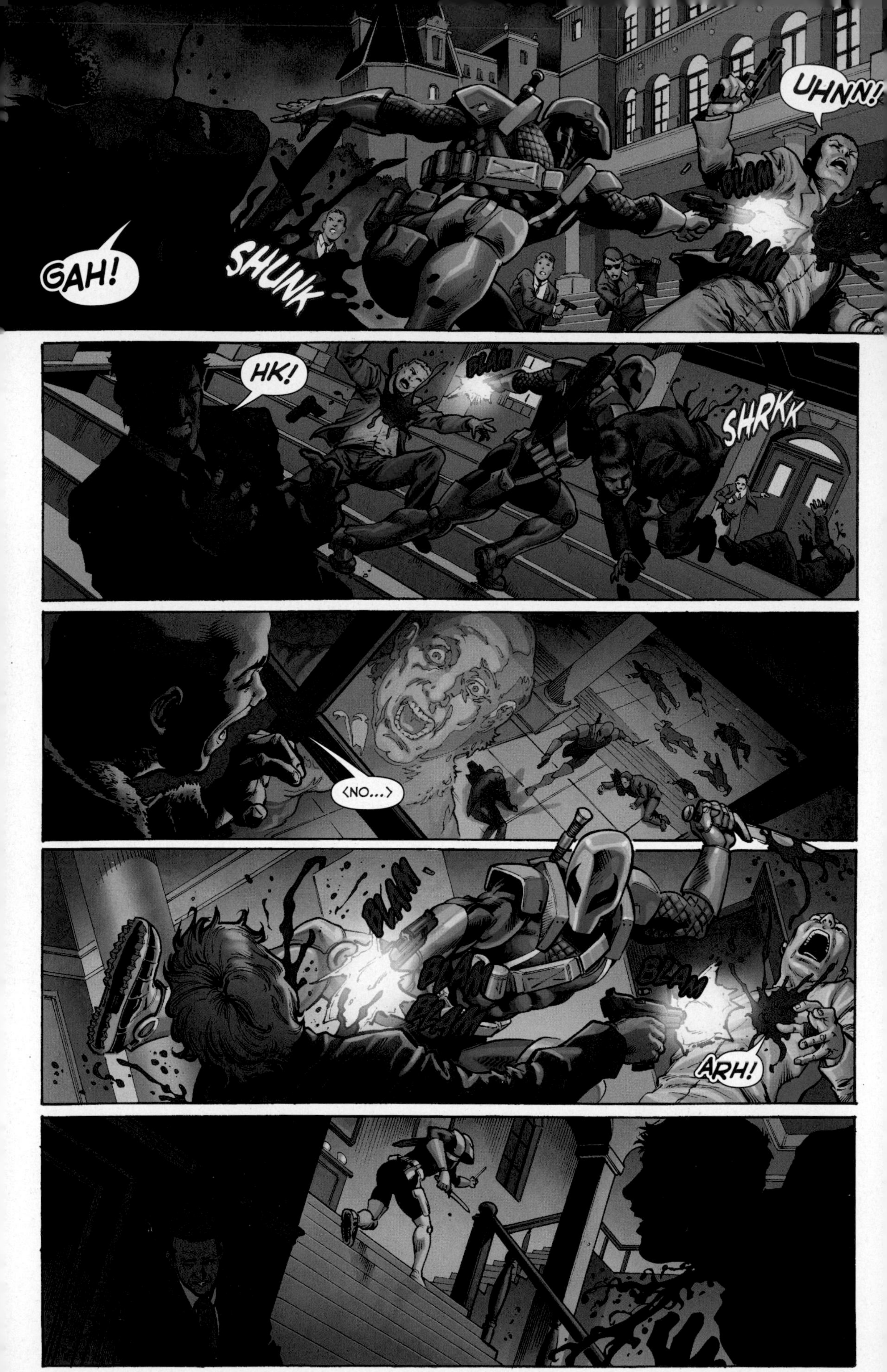

UHNN!
BLAM
BLAM
GAH!
SHUNK
HK!
BLAM
SHRKK
<NO...>
BLAM
BLAM
BLAM
BLAM
ARH!

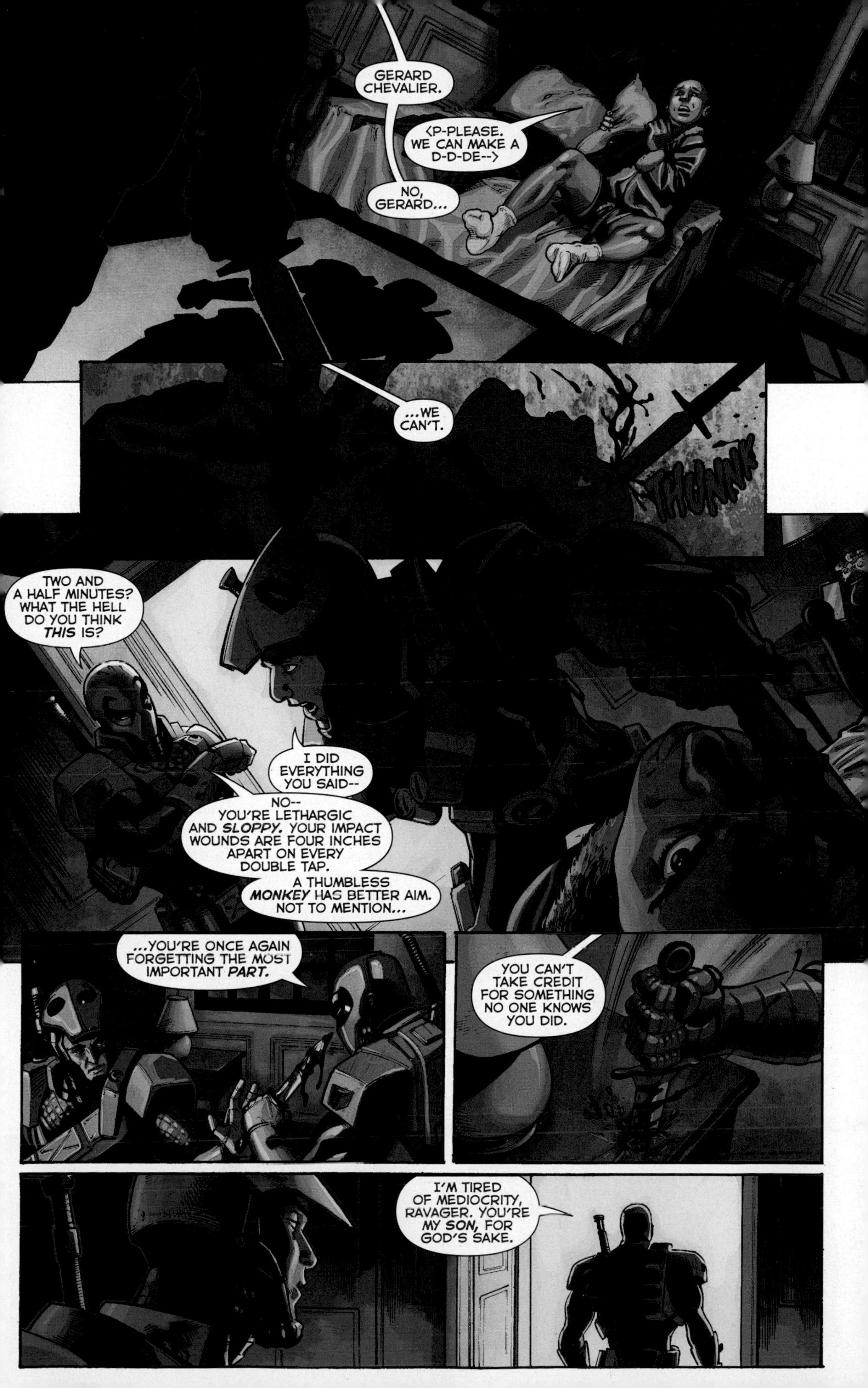
GERARD CHEVALIER.
<P-PLEASE. WE CAN MAKE A D-D-DE-->
NO, GERARD...
...WE CAN'T.
THUNK
TWO AND A HALF MINUTES? WHAT THE HELL DO YOU THINK THIS IS?
I DID EVERYTHING YOU SAID--
NO-- YOU'RE LETHARGIC AND SLOPPY. YOUR IMPACT WOUNDS ARE FOUR INCHES APART ON EVERY DOUBLE TAP.
A THUMBLESS MONKEY HAS BETTER AIM. NOT TO MENTION...
...YOU'RE ONCE AGAIN FORGETTING THE MOST IMPORTANT PART.
YOU CAN'T TAKE CREDIT FOR SOMETHING NO ONE KNOWS YOU DID.
I'M TIRED OF MEDIOCRITY, RAVAGER. YOU'RE MY SON, FOR GOD'S SAKE.

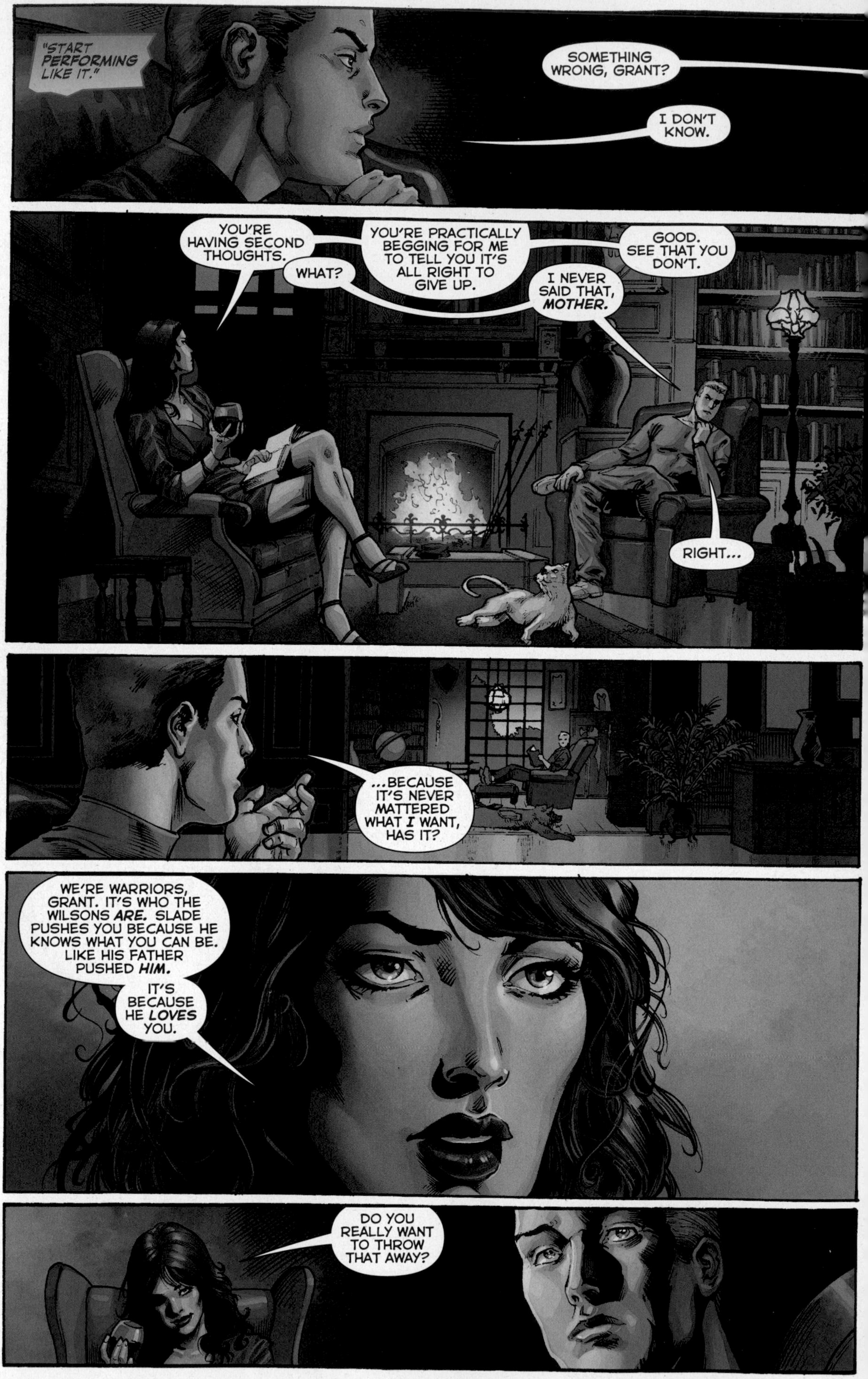
"START PERFORMING LIKE IT."
SOMETHING WRONG, GRANT?
I DON'T KNOW.
YOU'RE HAVING SECOND THOUGHTS.
WHAT?
YOU'RE PRACTICALLY BEGGING FOR ME TO TELL YOU IT'S ALL RIGHT TO GIVE UP.
I NEVER SAID THAT, MOTHER.
GOOD. SEE THAT YOU DON'T.
RIGHT...
...BECAUSE IT'S NEVER MATTERED WHAT I WANT, HAS IT?
WE'RE WARRIORS, GRANT. IT'S WHO THE WILSONS ARE. SLADE PUSHES YOU BECAUSE HE KNOWS WHAT YOU CAN BE. LIKE HIS FATHER PUSHED HIM.
IT'S BECAUSE HE LOVES YOU.
DO YOU REALLY WANT TO THROW THAT AWAY?

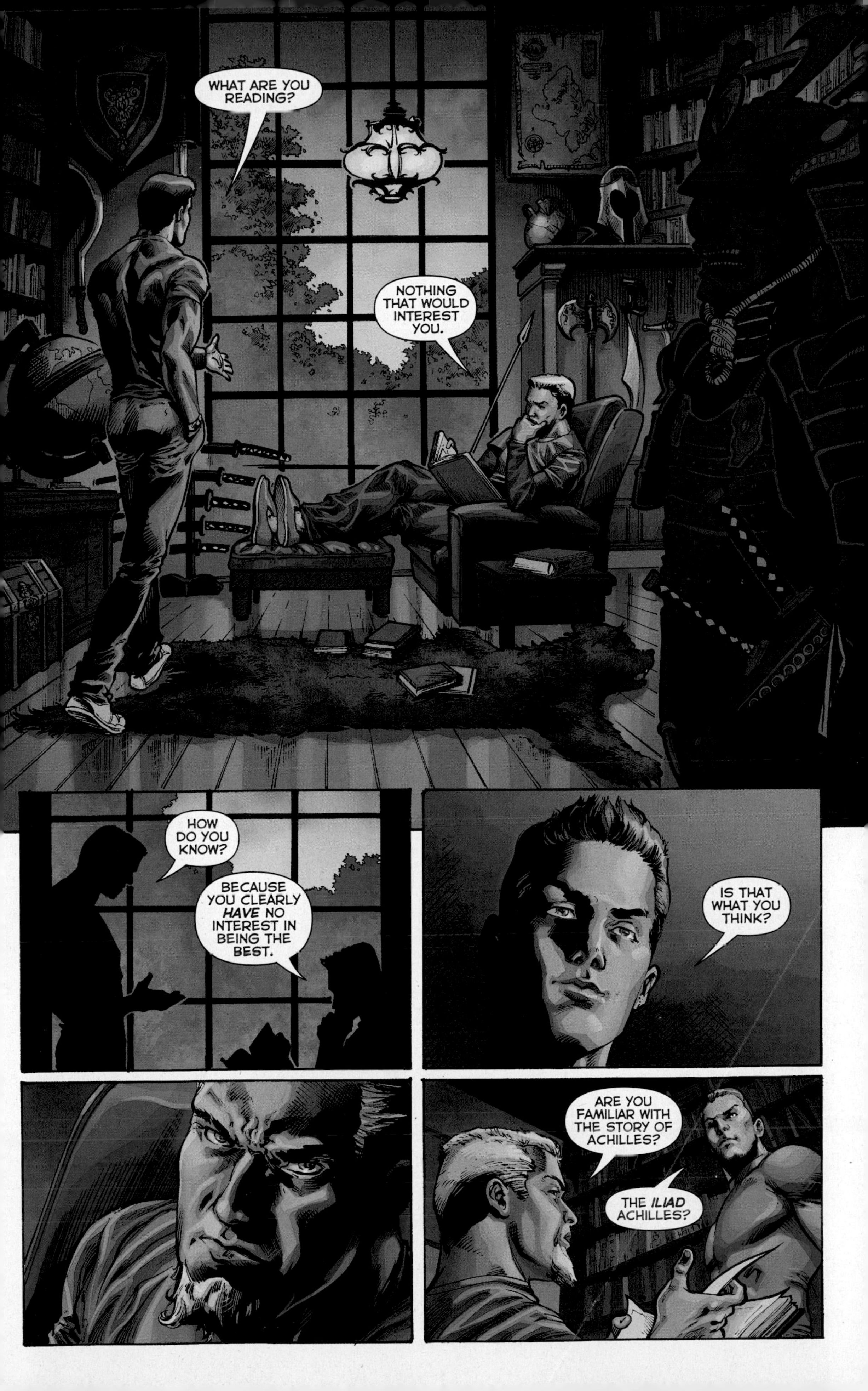
WHAT ARE YOU READING?
NOTHING THAT WOULD INTEREST YOU.
HOW DO YOU KNOW?
BECAUSE YOU CLEARLY *HAVE* NO INTEREST IN BEING THE BEST.
IS THAT WHAT YOU THINK?
ARE YOU FAMILIAR WITH THE STORY OF ACHILLES?
THE *ILIAD* ACHILLES?

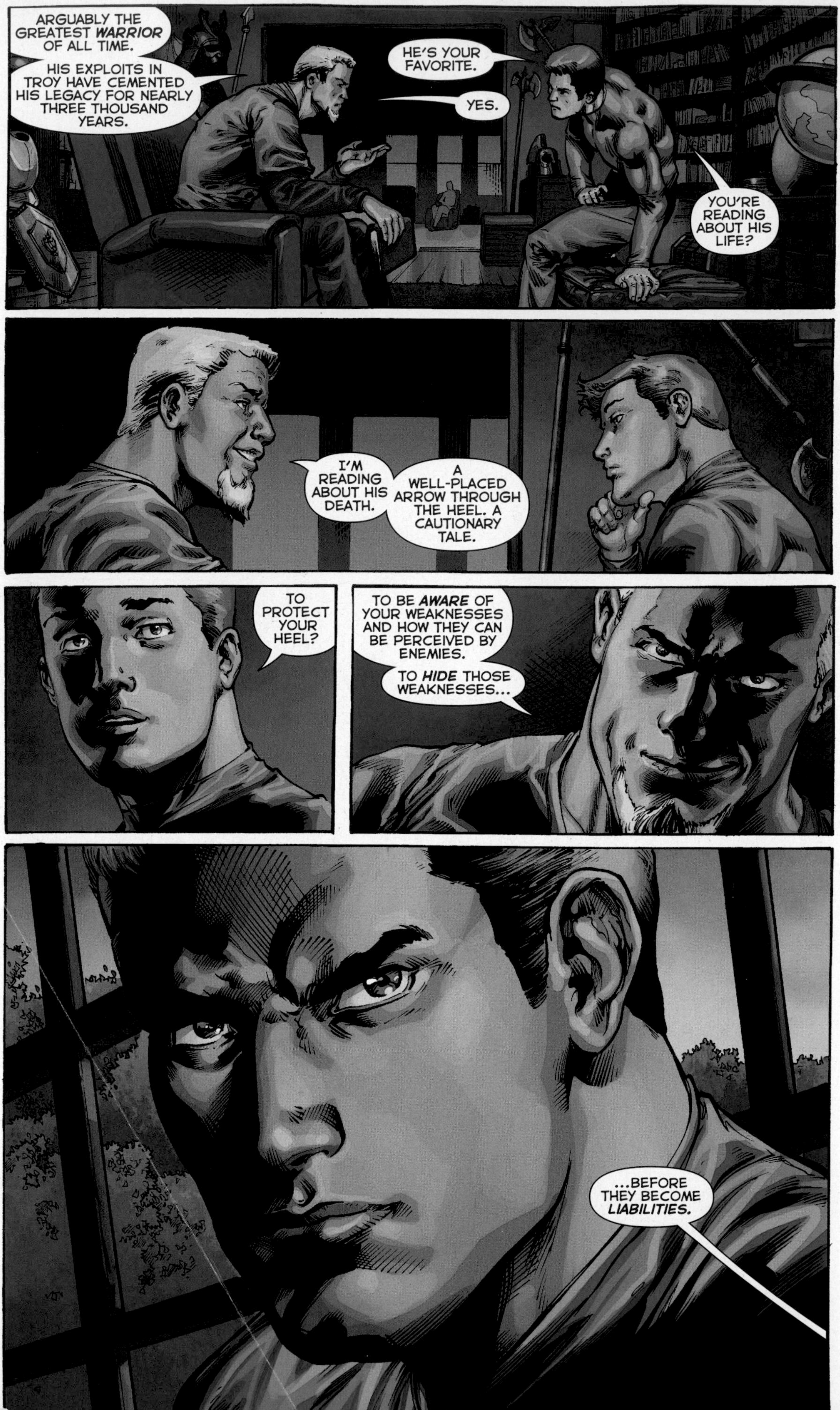
ARGUABLY THE GREATEST WARRIOR OF ALL TIME.
HIS EXPLOITS IN TROY HAVE CEMENTED HIS LEGACY FOR NEARLY THREE THOUSAND YEARS.
HE'S YOUR FAVORITE.
YES.
YOU'RE READING ABOUT HIS LIFE?
I'M READING ABOUT HIS DEATH.
A WELL-PLACED ARROW THROUGH THE HEEL. A CAUTIONARY TALE.
TO PROTECT YOUR HEEL?
TO BE AWARE OF YOUR WEAKNESSES AND HOW THEY CAN BE PERCEIVED BY ENEMIES.
TO HIDE THOSE WEAKNESSES...
...BEFORE THEY BECOME LIABILITIES.

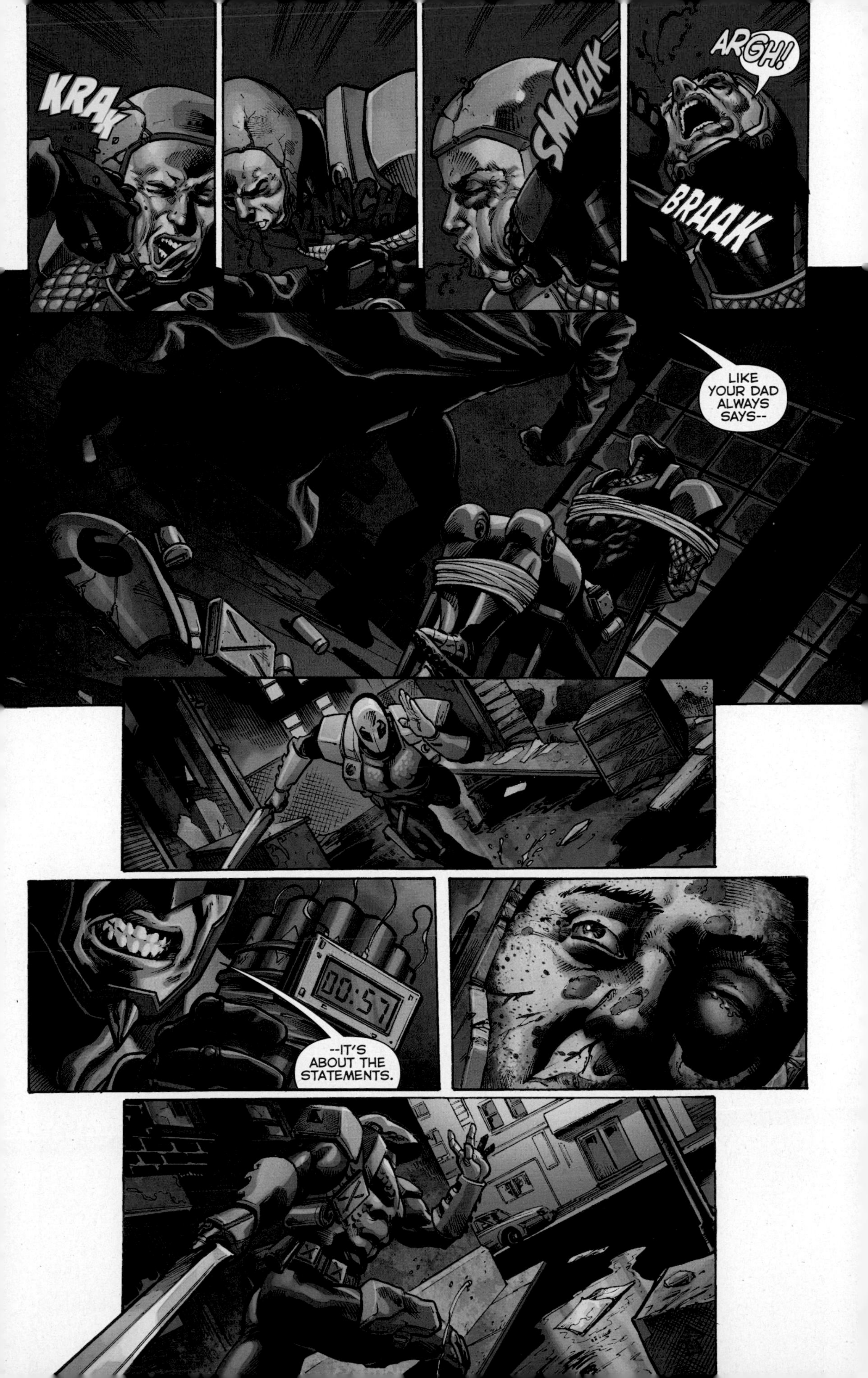
KRAK
SMAAK
ARGH!
BRAAK
LIKE YOUR DAD ALWAYS SAYS--
00:57
--IT'S ABOUT THE STATEMENTS.

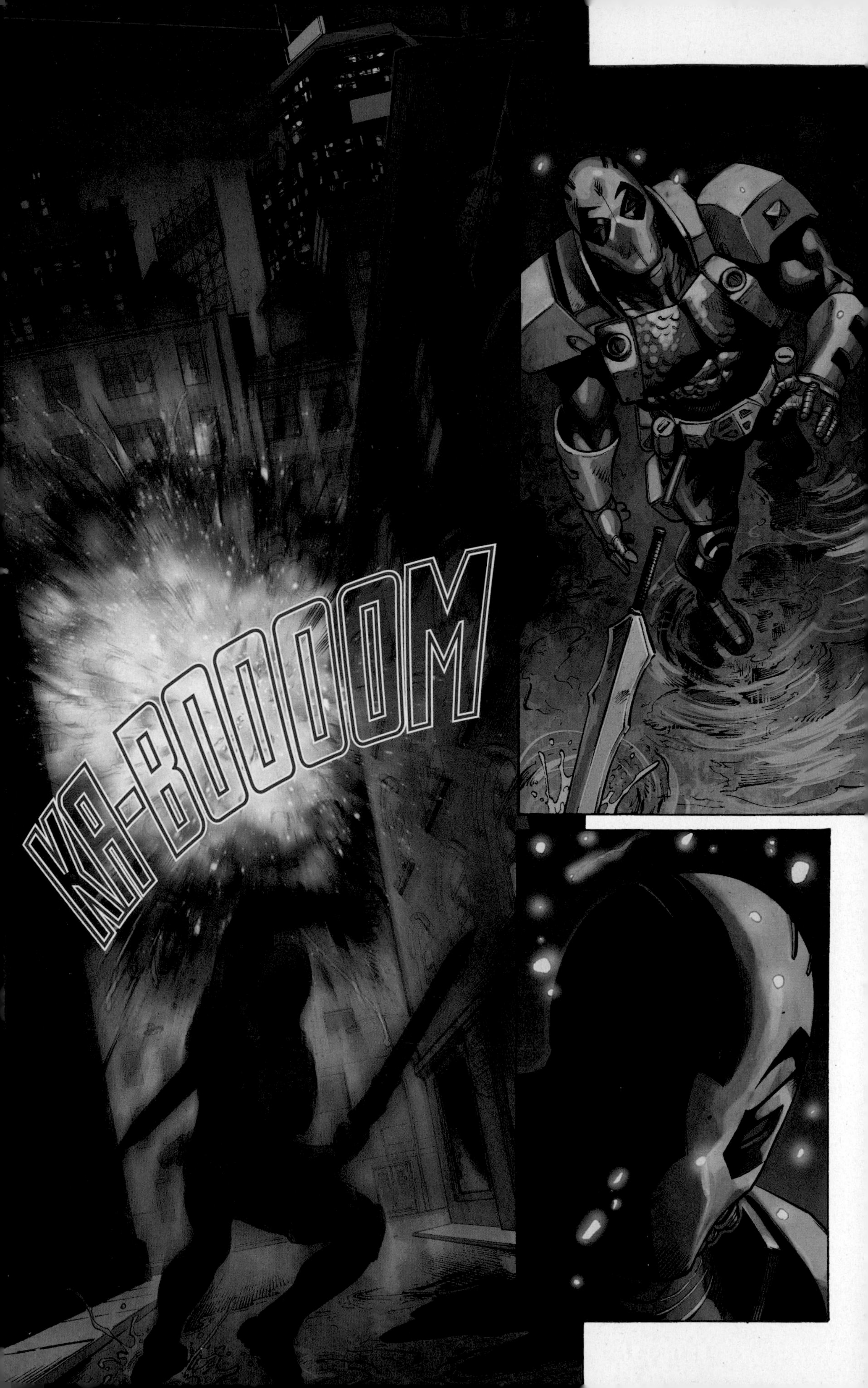
KA-BOOOOM

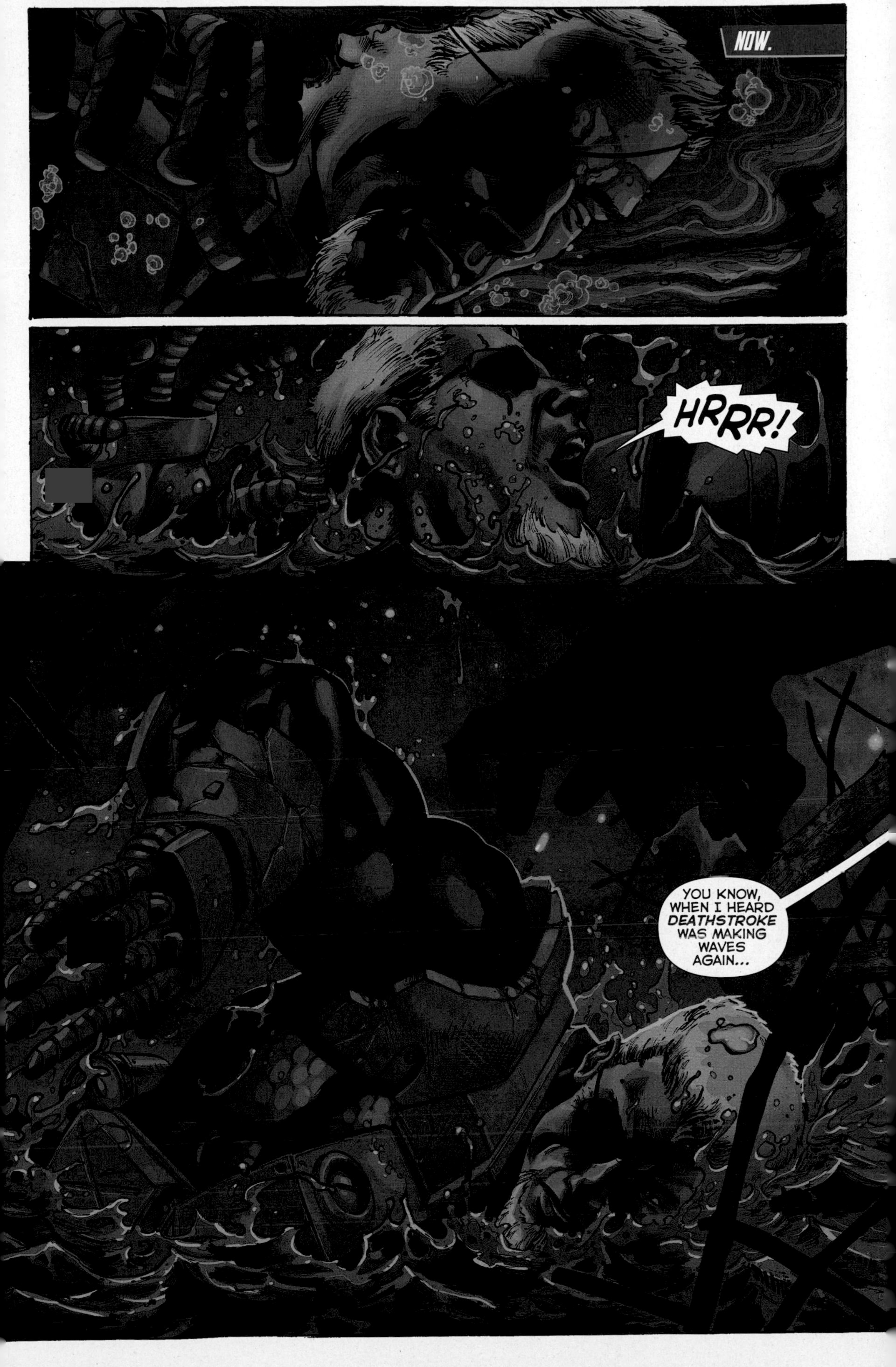
NOW.
HRRR!
YOU KNOW, WHEN I HEARD *DEATHSTROKE* WAS MAKING WAVES AGAIN...

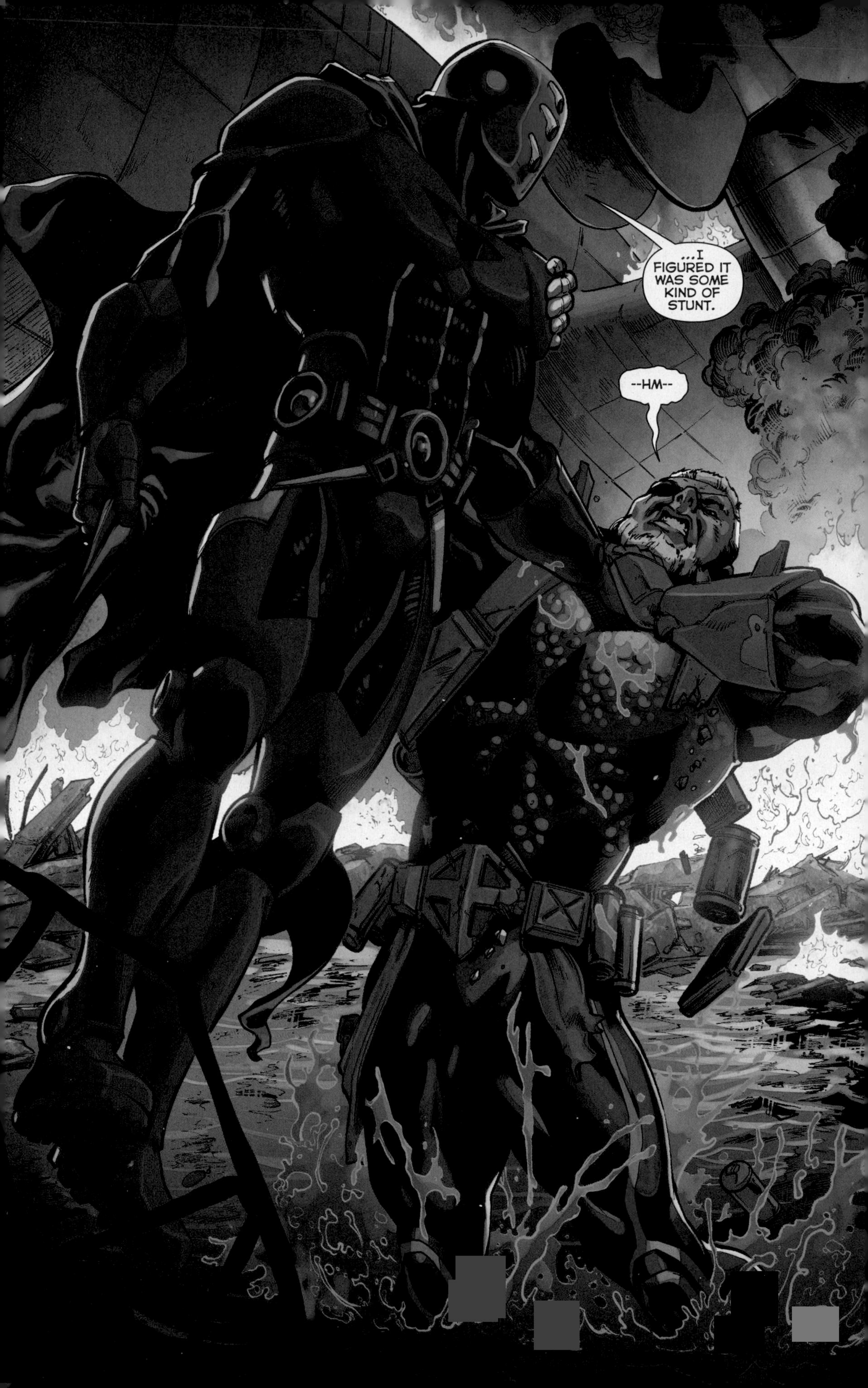
...I FIGURED IT WAS SOME KIND OF STUNT.
--HM--

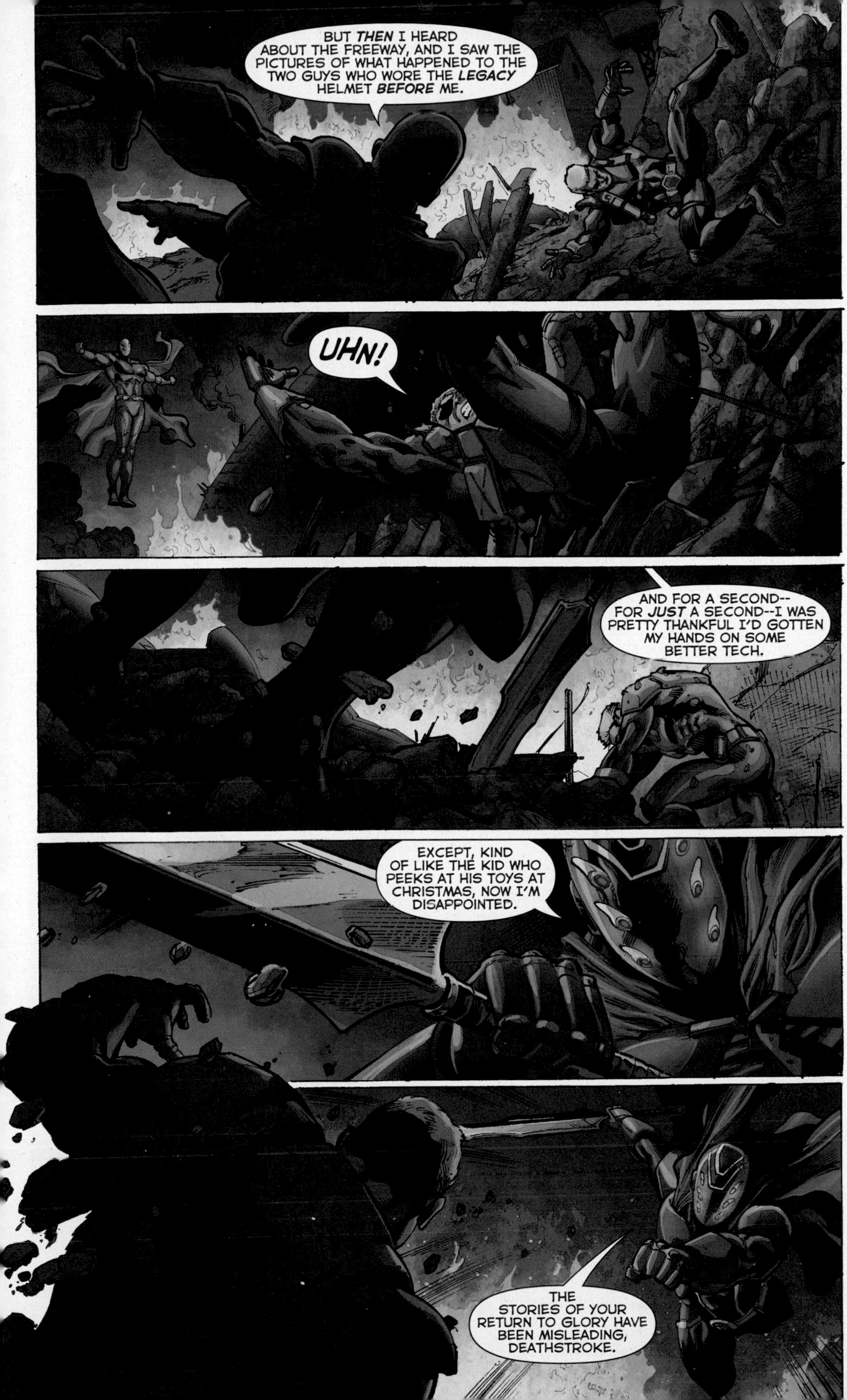

BUT *THEN* I HEARD ABOUT THE FREEWAY, AND I SAW THE PICTURES OF WHAT HAPPENED TO THE TWO GUYS WHO WORE THE *LEGACY* HELMET *BEFORE* ME.
UHN!
AND FOR A SECOND-- FOR *JUST* A SECOND--I WAS PRETTY THANKFUL I'D GOTTEN MY HANDS ON SOME BETTER TECH.
EXCEPT, KIND OF LIKE THE KID WHO PEEKS AT HIS TOYS AT CHRISTMAS, NOW I'M DISAPPOINTED.
THE STORIES OF YOUR RETURN TO GLORY HAVE BEEN MISLEADING, DEATHSTROKE.

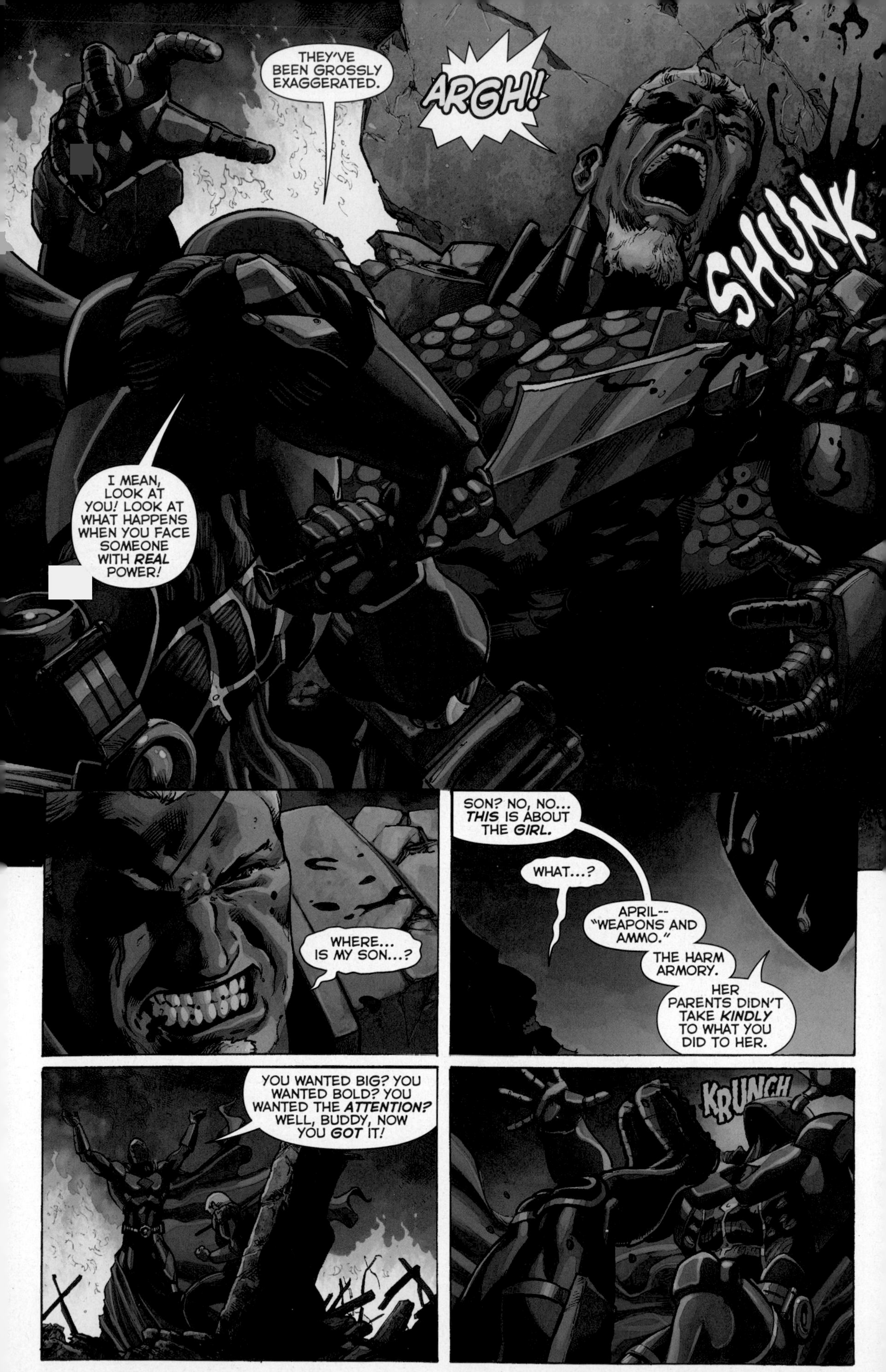
THEY'VE BEEN GROSSLY EXAGGERATED.
ARGH!
SHUNK
I MEAN, LOOK AT YOU! LOOK AT WHAT HAPPENS WHEN YOU FACE SOMEONE WITH REAL POWER!
WHERE... IS MY SON...?
SON? NO, NO... THIS IS ABOUT THE GIRL.
WHAT...?
APRIL-- "WEAPONS AND AMMO."
THE HARM ARMORY.
HER PARENTS DIDN'T TAKE KINDLY TO WHAT YOU DID TO HER.
YOU WANTED BIG? YOU WANTED BOLD? YOU WANTED THE ATTENTION? WELL, BUDDY, NOW YOU GOT IT!
KRUNCH

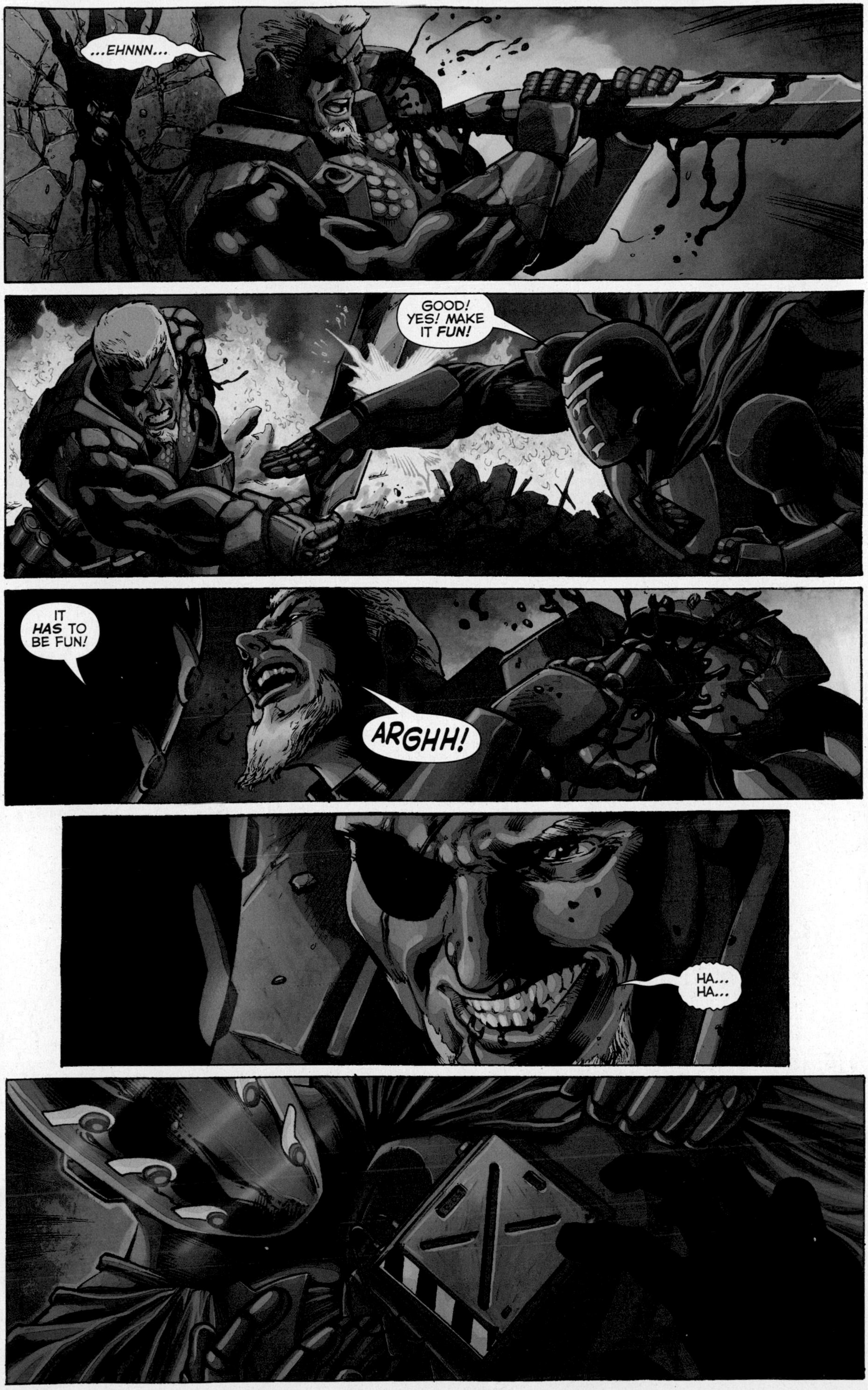
...EHNNN...
GOOD! YES! MAKE IT FUN!
IT HAS TO BE FUN!
ARGHH!
HA... HA...

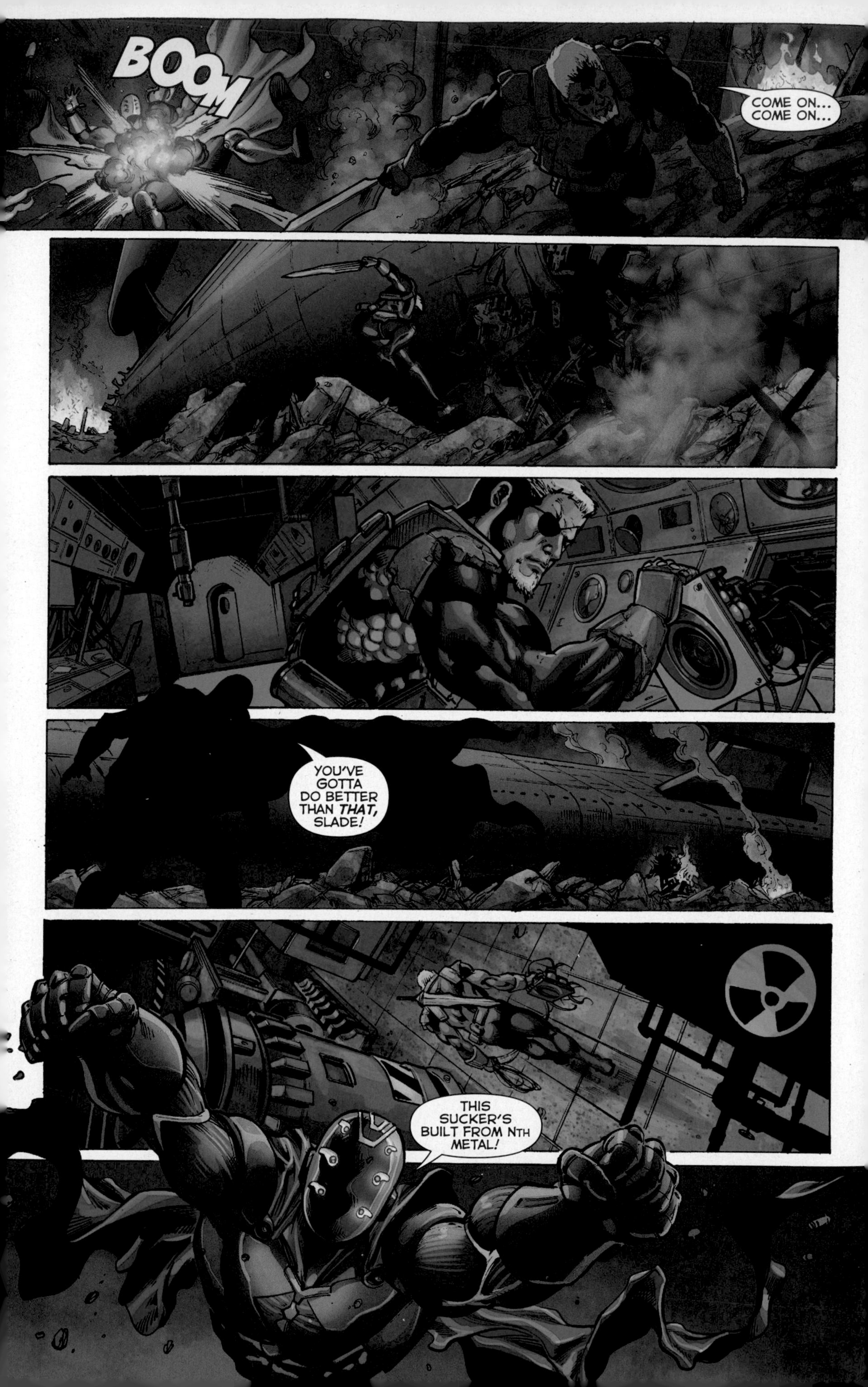
BOOM
COME ON... COME ON...
YOU'VE GOTTA DO BETTER THAN *THAT*, SLADE!
THIS SUCKER'S BUILT FROM NTH METAL!

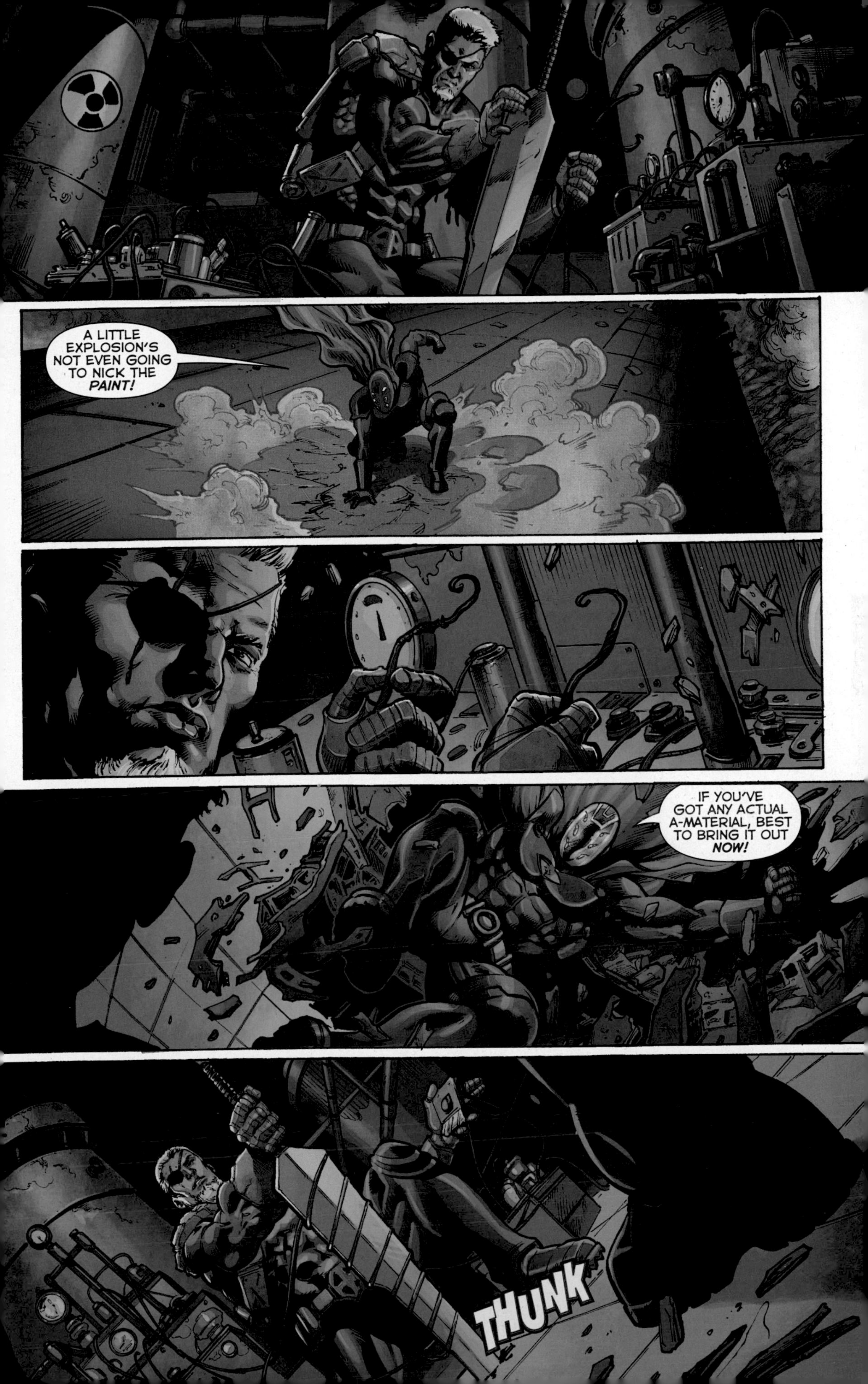
A LITTLE EXPLOSION'S NOT EVEN GOING TO NICK THE PAINT!
IF YOU'VE GOT ANY ACTUAL A-MATERIAL, BEST TO BRING IT OUT NOW!
THUNK

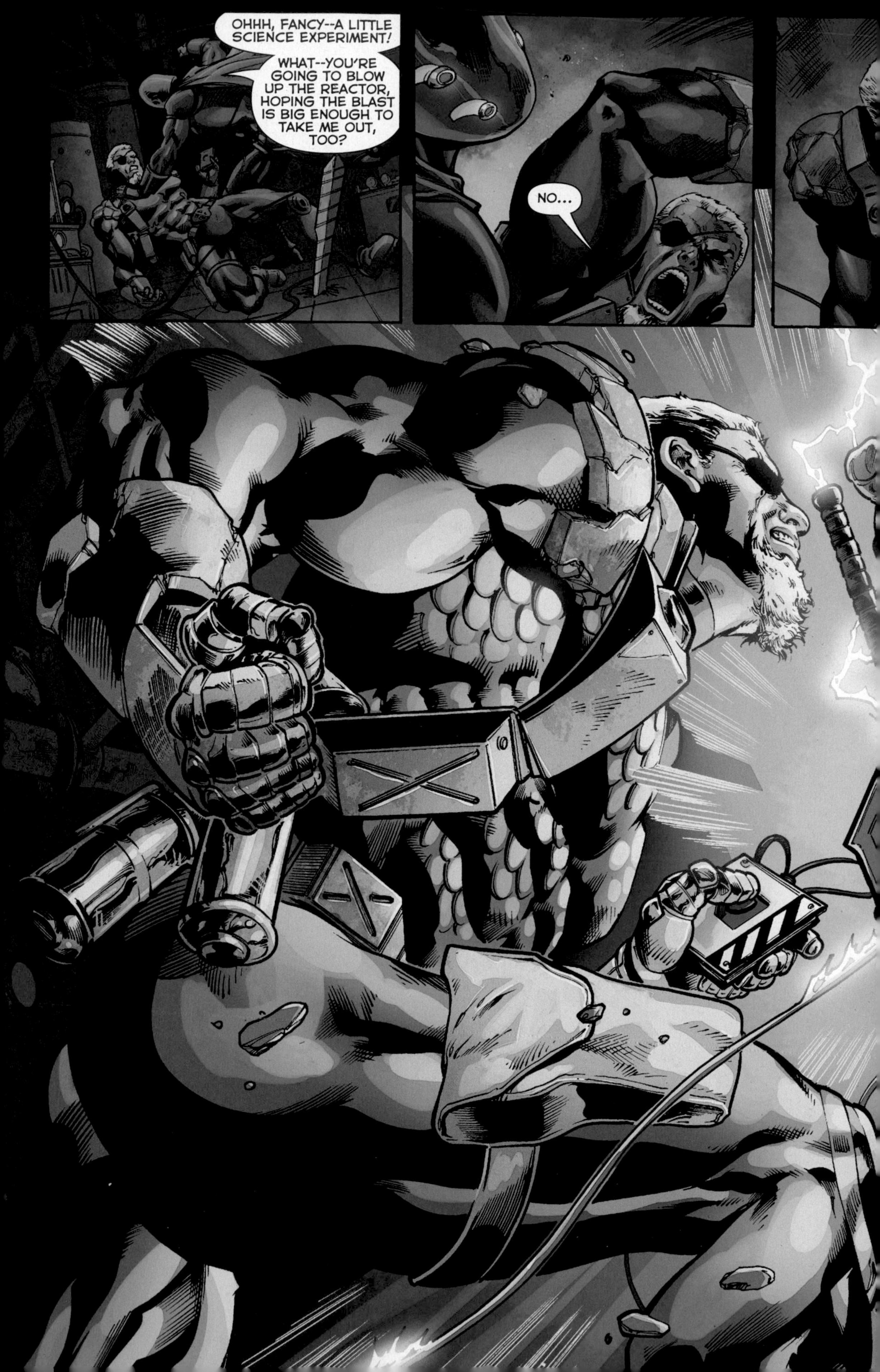
OHHH, FANCY--A LITTLE SCIENCE EXPERIMENT!
WHAT--YOU'RE GOING TO BLOW UP THE REACTOR, HOPING THE BLAST IS BIG ENOUGH TO TAKE ME OUT, TOO?
NO...

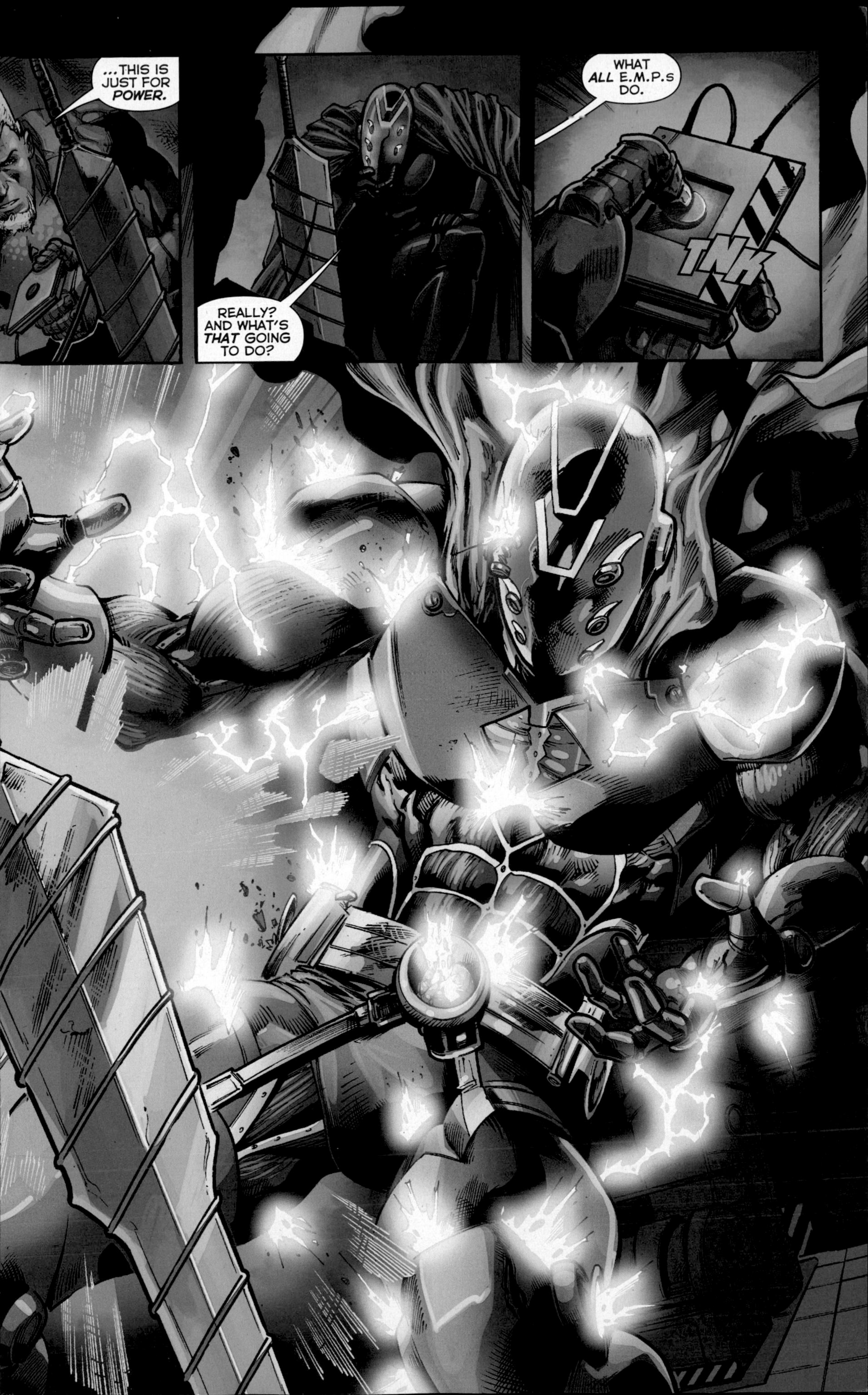
...THIS IS JUST FOR POWER.
REALLY? AND WHAT'S THAT GOING TO DO?
WHAT ALL E.M.P.s DO.
TNK

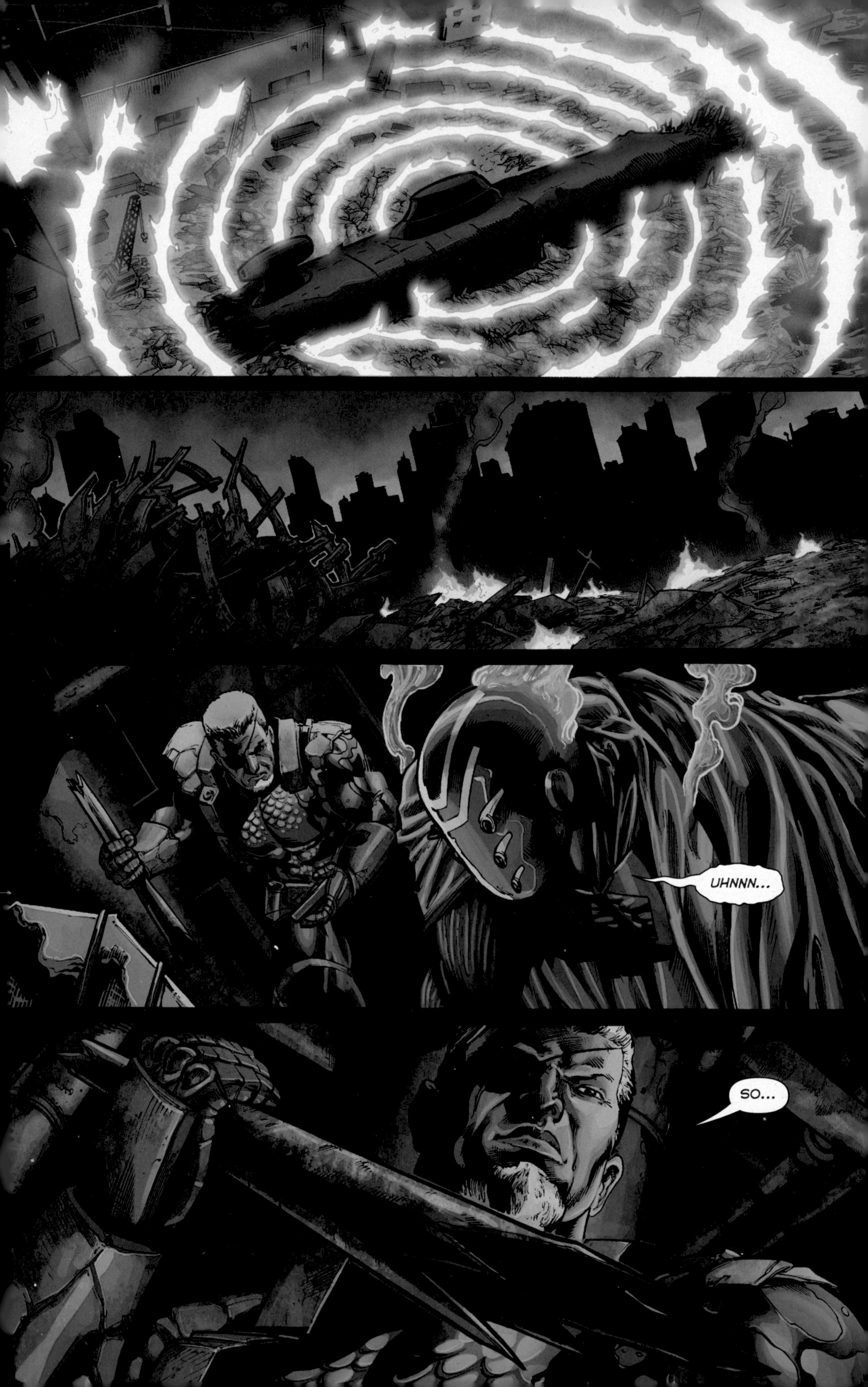
UHNNN...
SO...

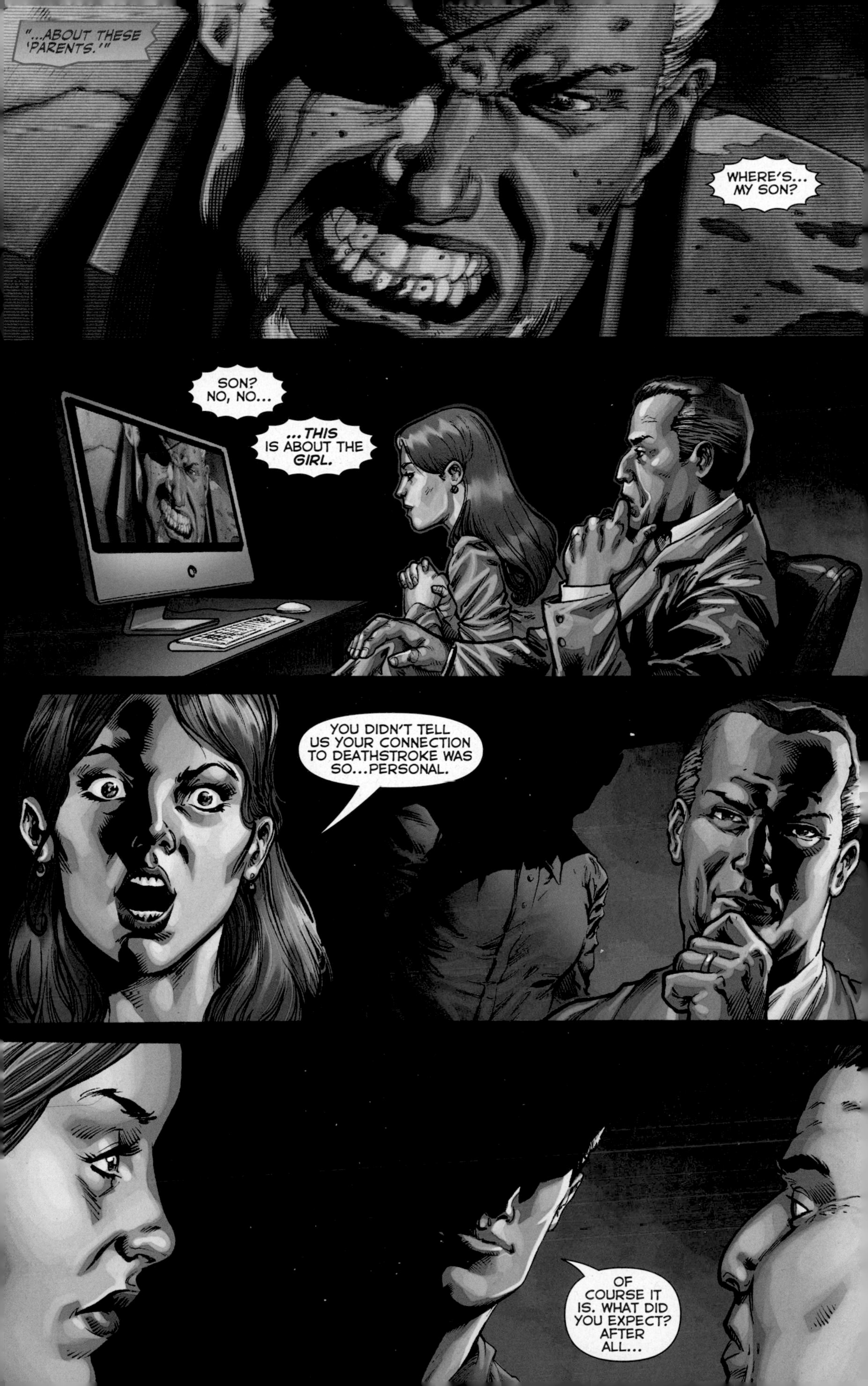
"...ABOUT THESE 'PARENTS.'"
WHERE'S... MY SON?
SON? NO, NO...
...THIS IS ABOUT THE GIRL.
YOU DIDN'T TELL US YOUR CONNECTION TO DEATHSTROKE WAS SO...PERSONAL.
OF COURSE IT IS. WHAT DID YOU EXPECT? AFTER ALL...

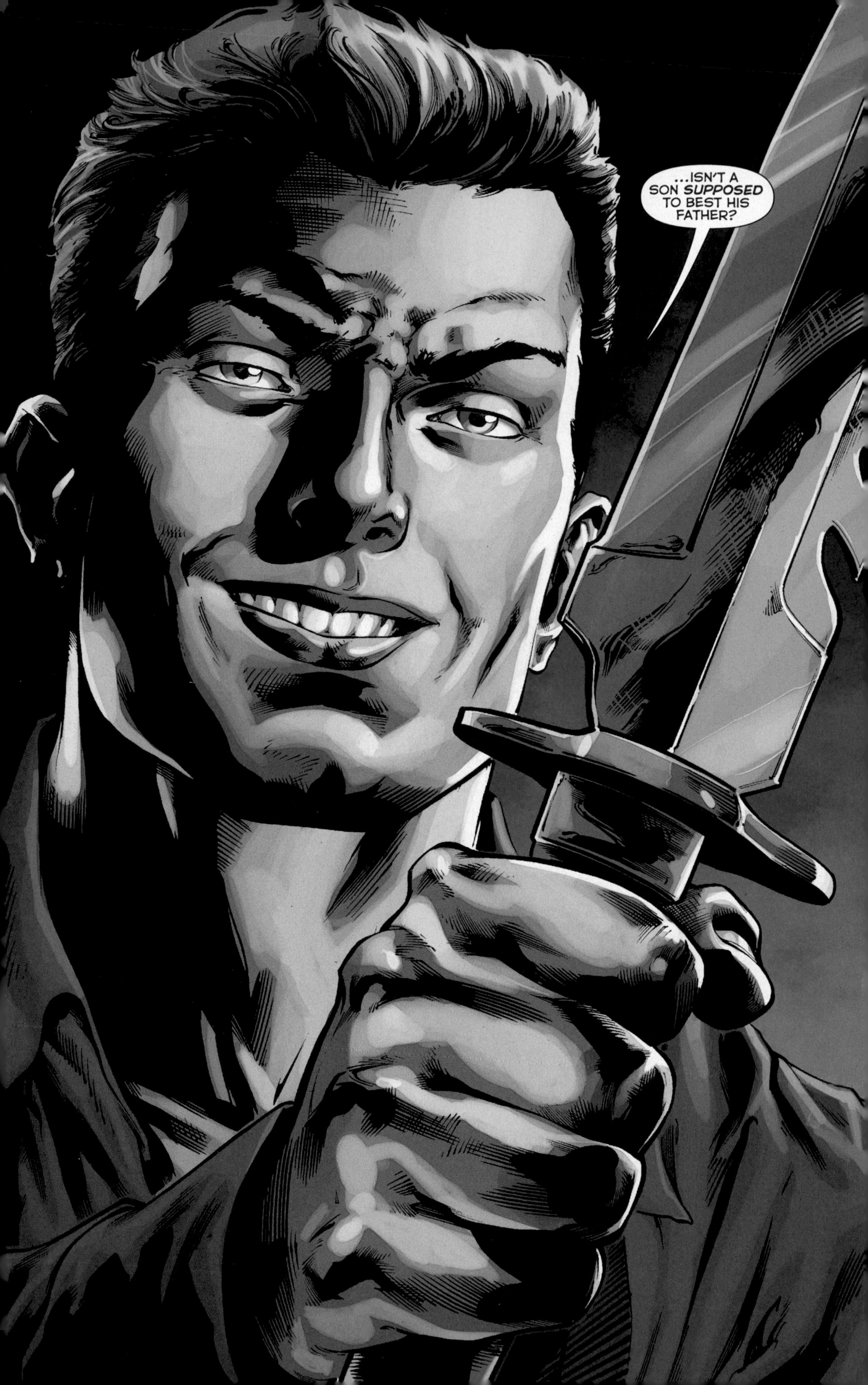
...ISN'T A SON SUPPOSED TO BEST HIS FATHER?

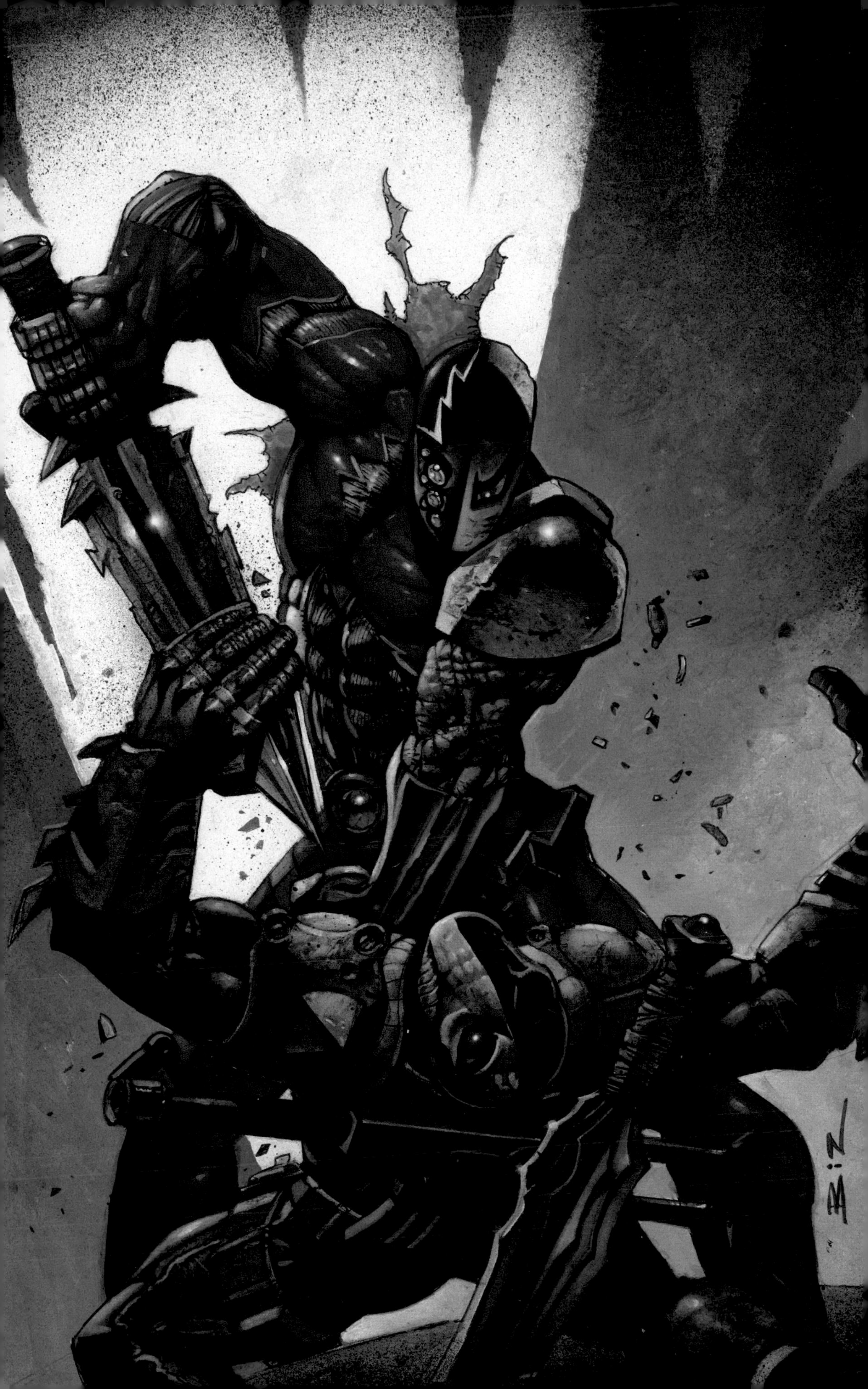

DEADLY REUNIONS

KYLE HIGGINS writer **JOE BENNETT** penciller **ART THIBERT** inker cover by **SIMON BISLEY**

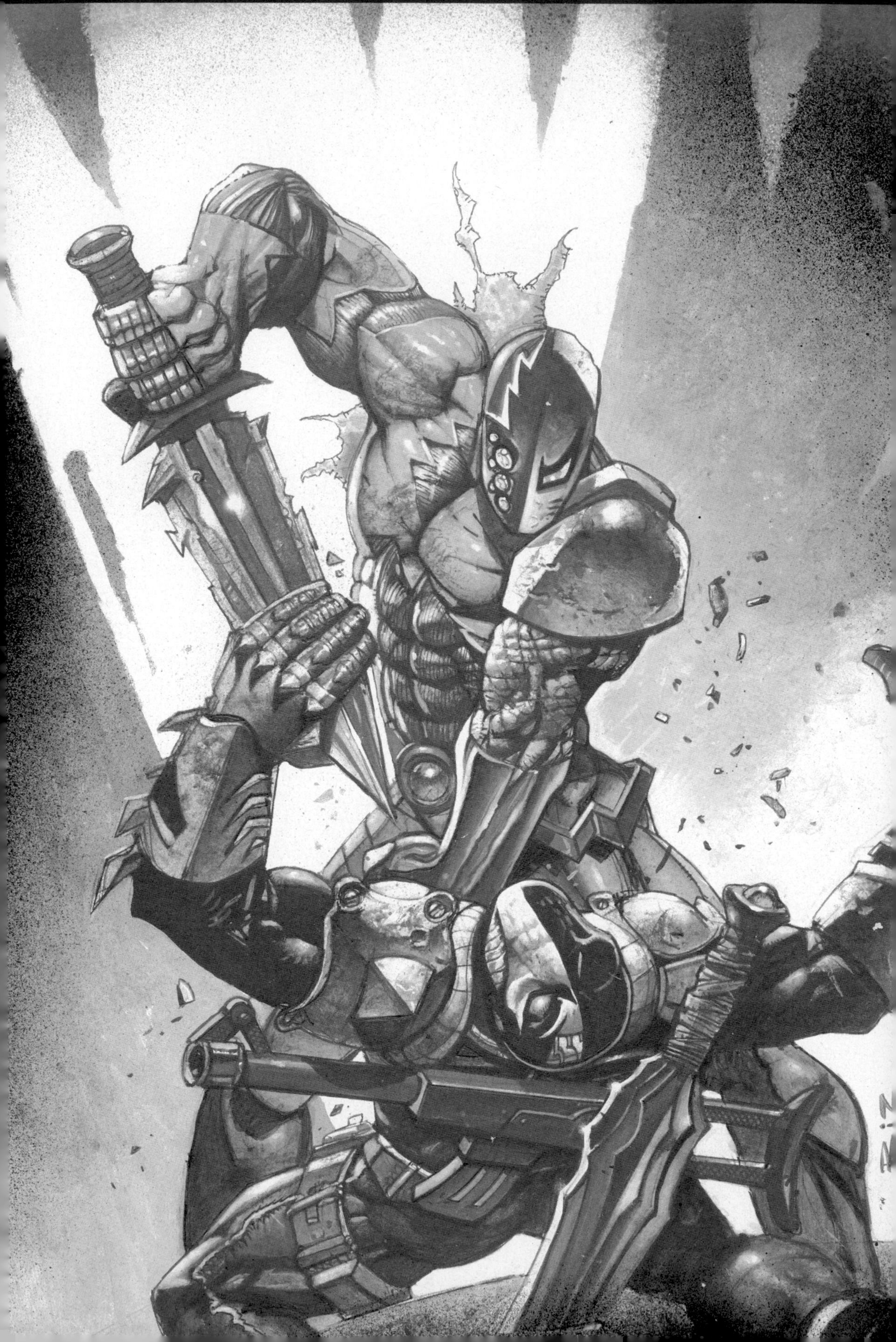

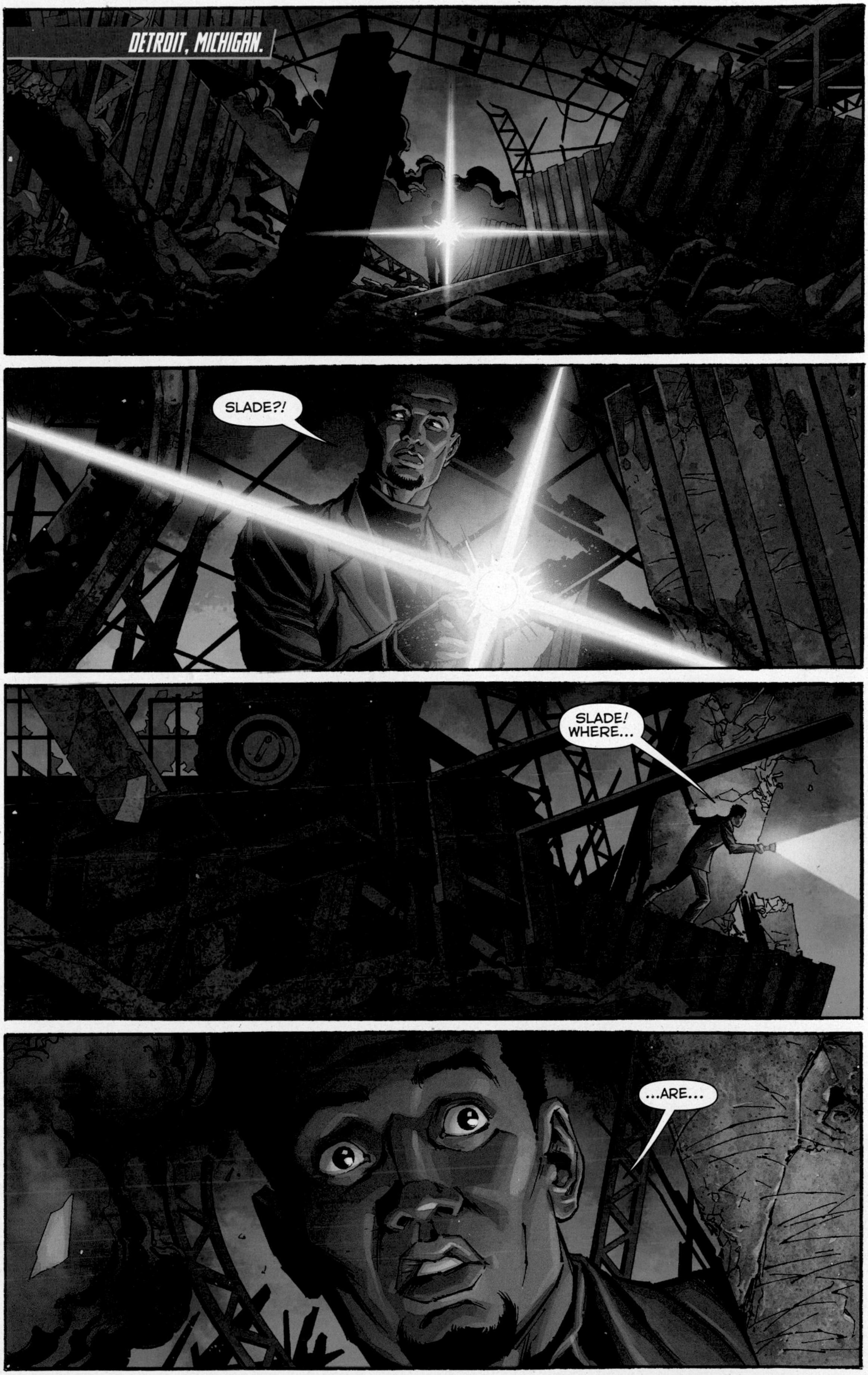
DETROIT, MICHIGAN.
SLADE?!
SLADE! WHERE...
...ARE...

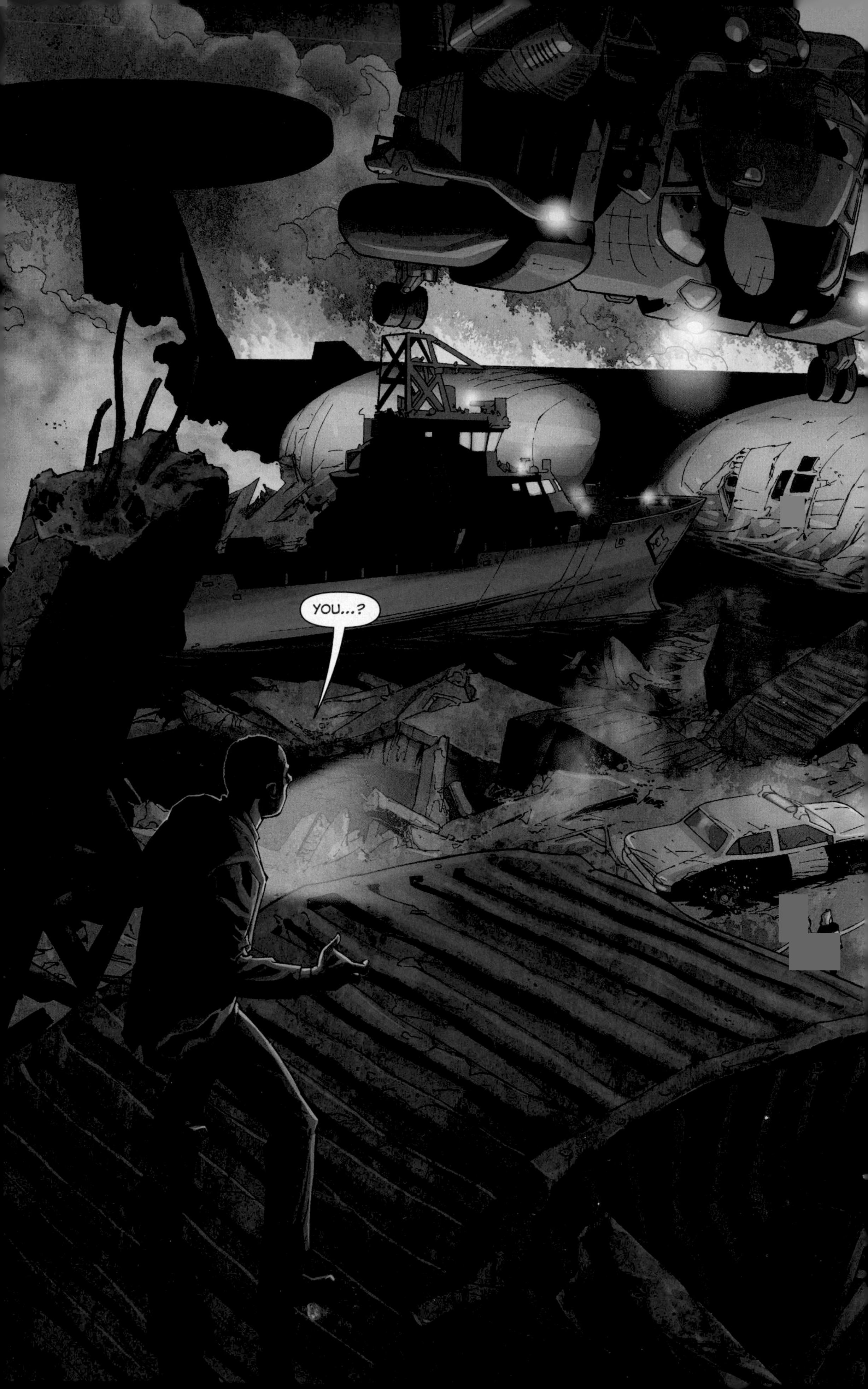
YOU...?

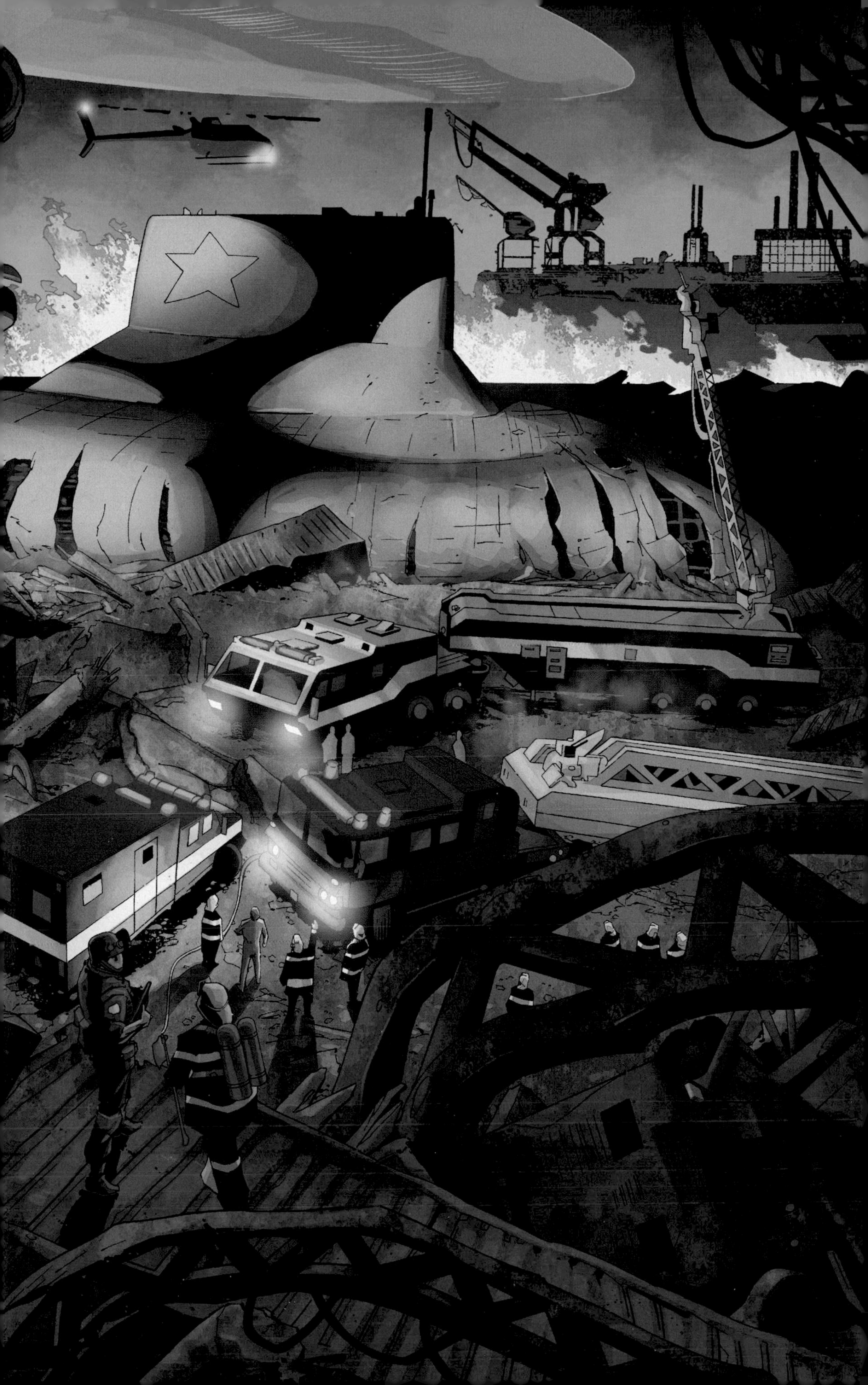

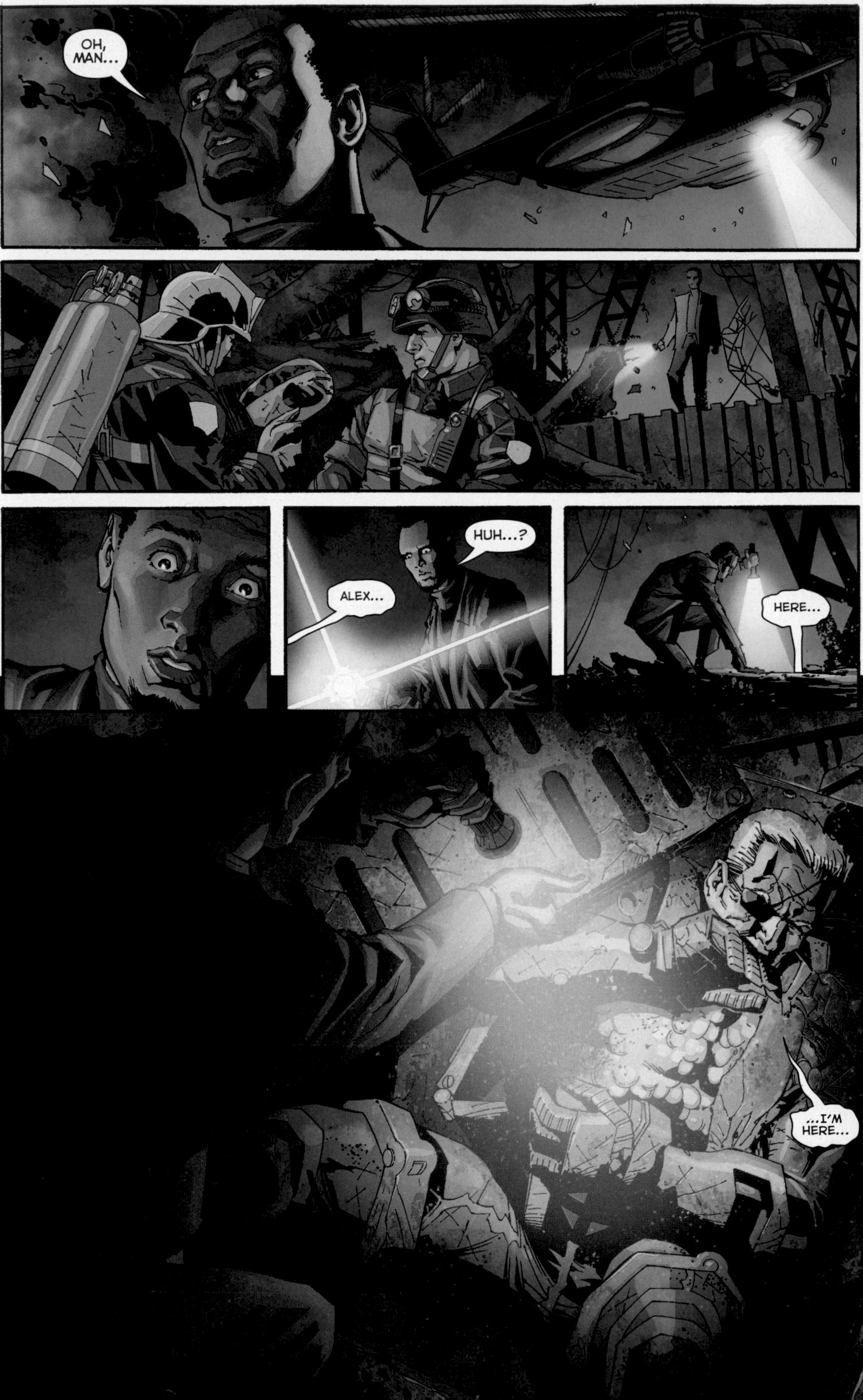
OH, MAN...
HUH...?
ALEX...
HERE...
...I'M HERE...

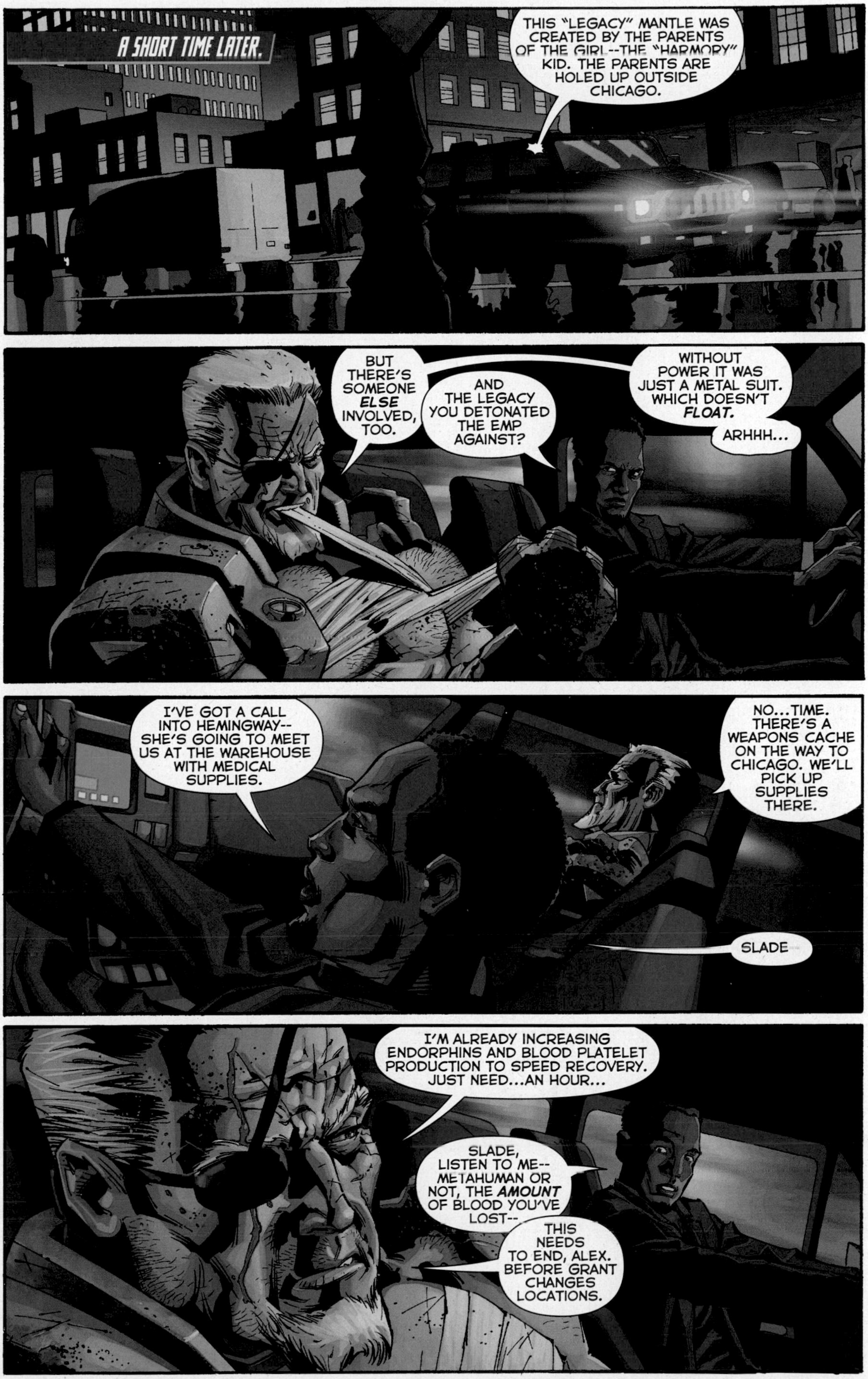
A SHORT TIME LATER.
THIS "LEGACY" MANTLE WAS CREATED BY THE PARENTS OF THE GIRL--THE "HARMORY" KID. THE PARENTS ARE HOLED UP OUTSIDE CHICAGO.
BUT THERE'S SOMEONE ELSE INVOLVED, TOO.
AND THE LEGACY YOU DETONATED THE EMP AGAINST?
WITHOUT POWER IT WAS JUST A METAL SUIT. WHICH DOESN'T FLOAT.
ARHHH...
I'VE GOT A CALL INTO HEMINGWAY--SHE'S GOING TO MEET US AT THE WAREHOUSE WITH MEDICAL SUPPLIES.
NO...TIME. THERE'S A WEAPONS CACHE ON THE WAY TO CHICAGO. WE'LL PICK UP SUPPLIES THERE.
SLADE
I'M ALREADY INCREASING ENDORPHINS AND BLOOD PLATELET PRODUCTION TO SPEED RECOVERY. JUST NEED...AN HOUR...
SLADE, LISTEN TO ME--METAHUMAN OR NOT, THE AMOUNT OF BLOOD YOU'VE LOST--
THIS NEEDS TO END, ALEX. BEFORE GRANT CHANGES LOCATIONS.

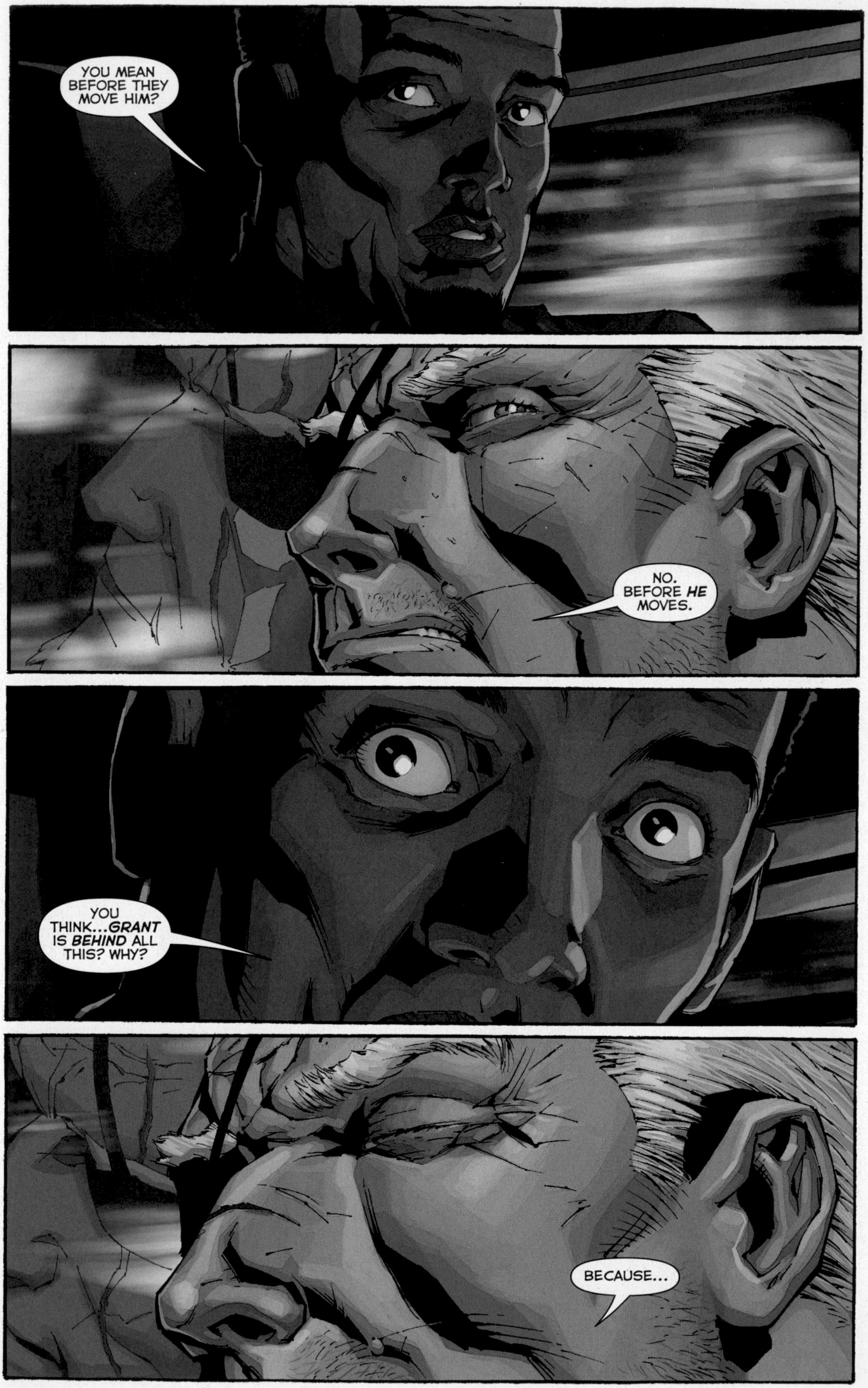
YOU MEAN BEFORE THEY MOVE HIM?
NO. BEFORE HE MOVES.
YOU THINK...GRANT IS BEHIND ALL THIS? WHY?
BECAUSE...

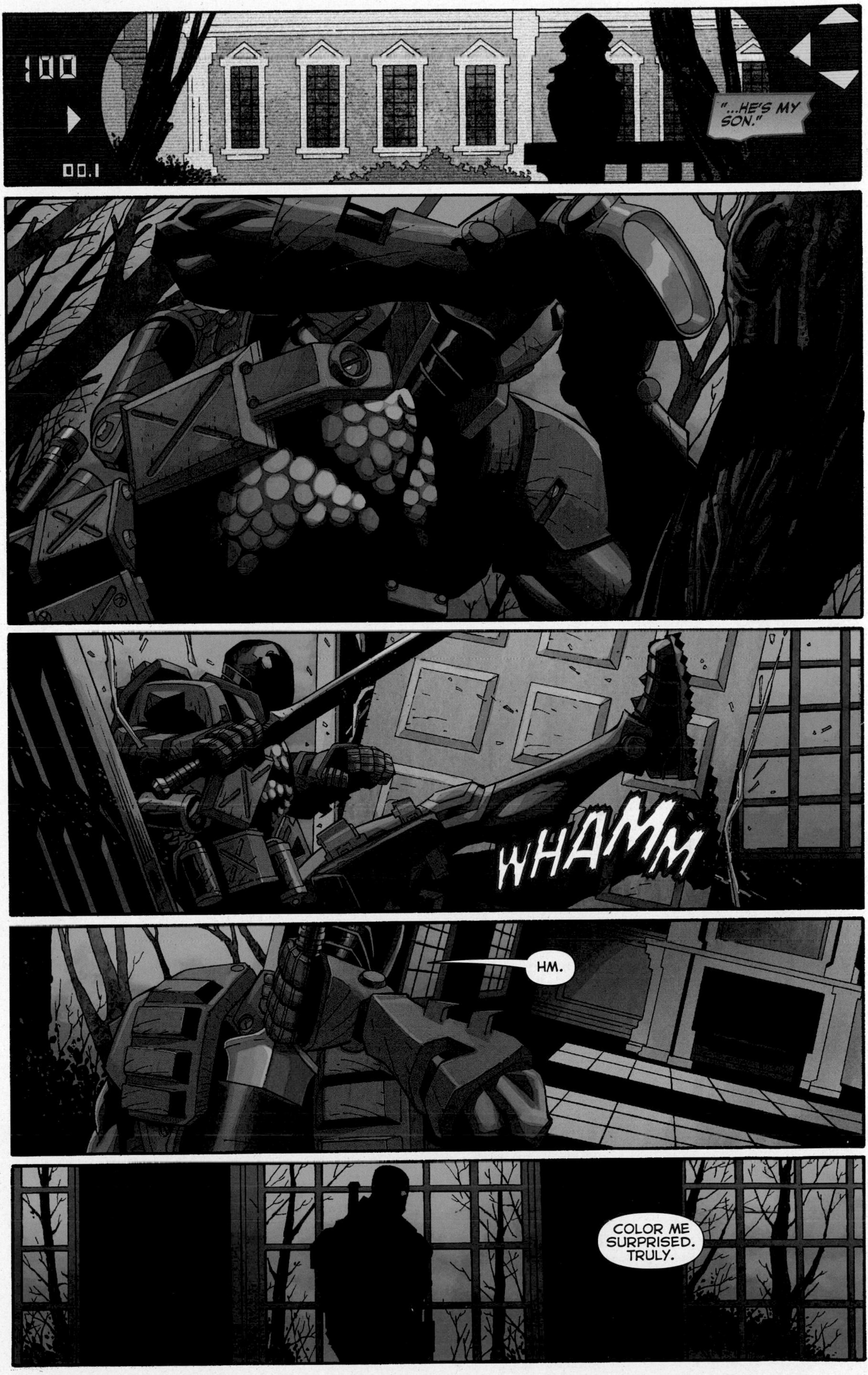
100
00.1
"...HE'S MY SON."
WHAMM
HM.
COLOR ME SURPRISED. TRULY.

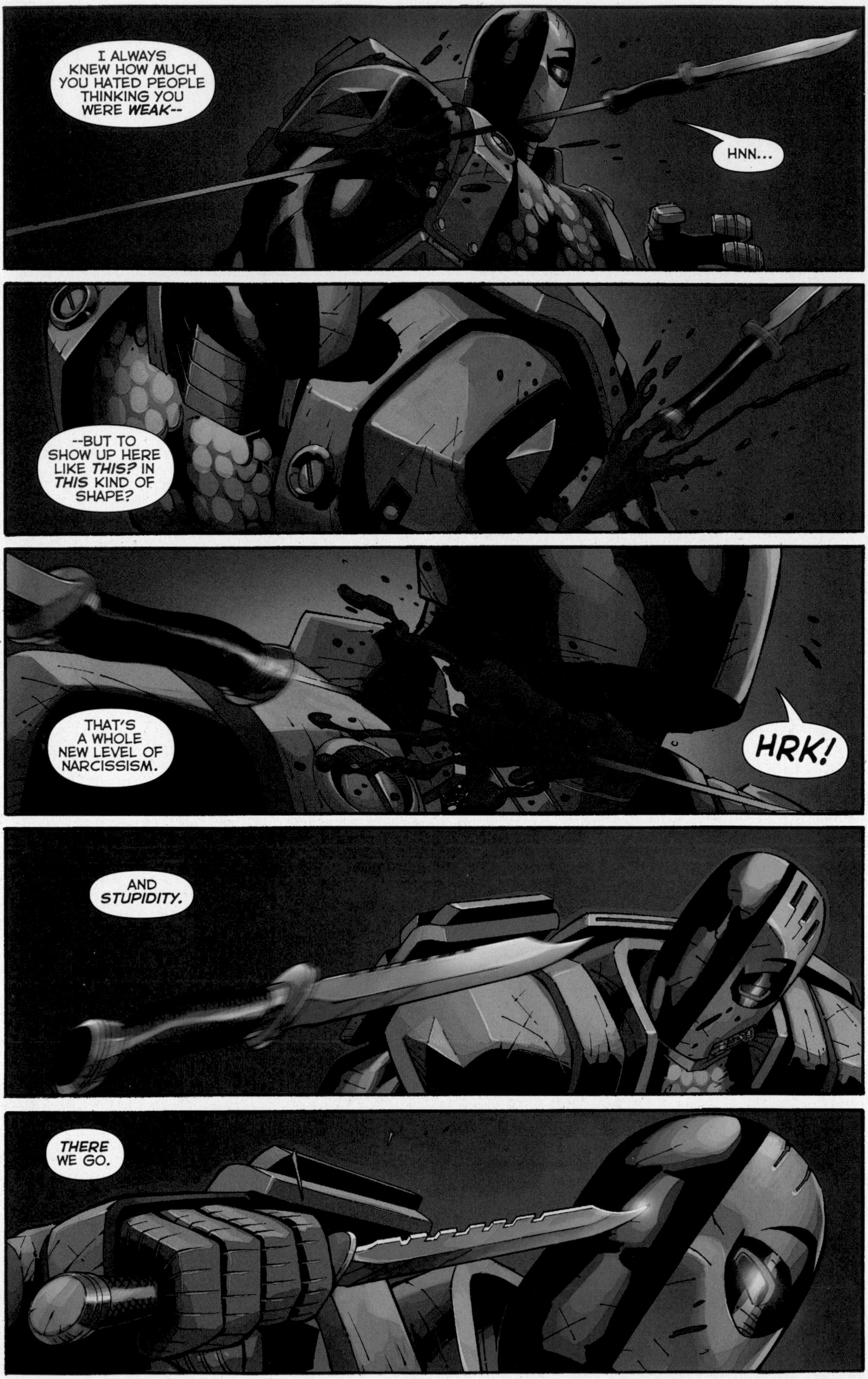
I ALWAYS KNEW HOW MUCH YOU HATED PEOPLE THINKING YOU WERE *WEAK*--
HNN...
--BUT TO SHOW UP HERE LIKE *THIS?* IN *THIS* KIND OF SHAPE?
THAT'S A WHOLE NEW LEVEL OF NARCISSISM.
HRK!
AND *STUPIDITY.*
THERE WE GO.

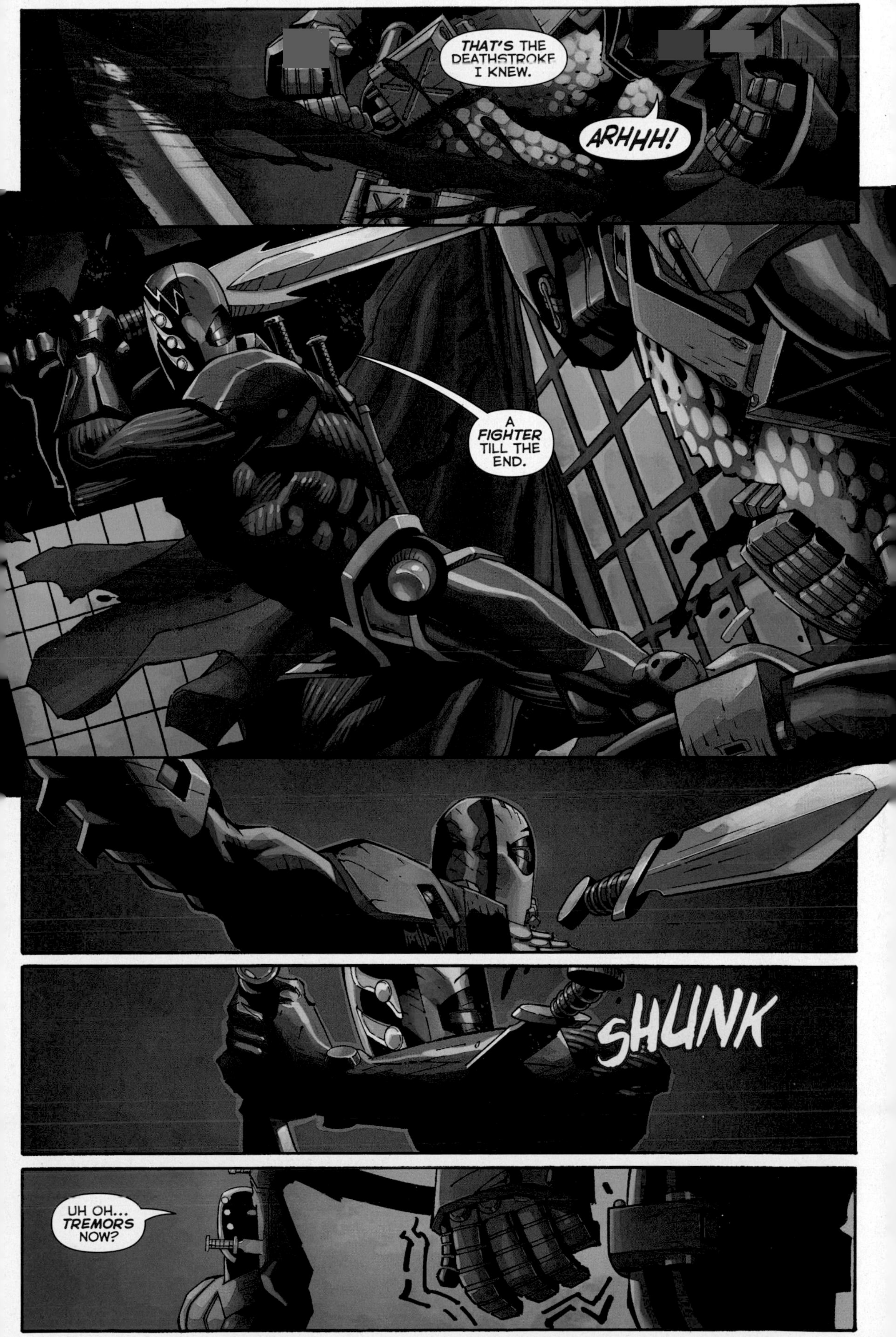
THAT'S THE DEATHSTROKE I KNEW.
ARHHH!
A FIGHTER TILL THE END.
SHUNK
UH OH... TREMORS NOW?

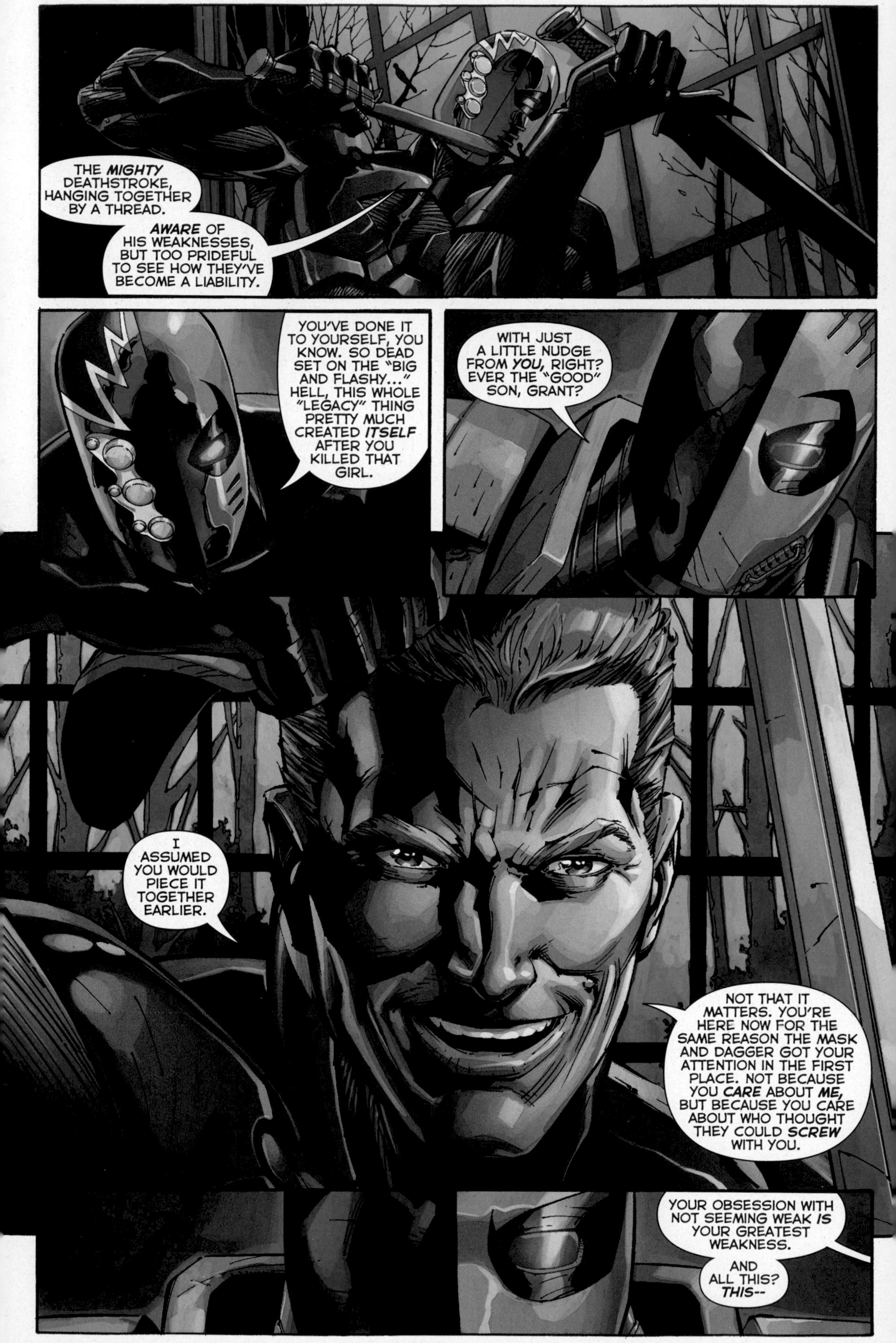
THE MIGHTY DEATHSTROKE, HANGING TOGETHER BY A THREAD.
AWARE OF HIS WEAKNESSES, BUT TOO PRIDEFUL TO SEE HOW THEY'VE BECOME A LIABILITY.
YOU'VE DONE IT TO YOURSELF, YOU KNOW. SO DEAD SET ON THE "BIG AND FLASHY..." HELL, THIS WHOLE "LEGACY" THING PRETTY MUCH CREATED ITSELF AFTER YOU KILLED THAT GIRL.
WITH JUST A LITTLE NUDGE FROM YOU, RIGHT? EVER THE "GOOD" SON, GRANT?
I ASSUMED YOU WOULD PIECE IT TOGETHER EARLIER.
NOT THAT IT MATTERS. YOU'RE HERE NOW FOR THE SAME REASON THE MASK AND DAGGER GOT YOUR ATTENTION IN THE FIRST PLACE. NOT BECAUSE YOU CARE ABOUT ME, BUT BECAUSE YOU CARE ABOUT WHO THOUGHT THEY COULD SCREW WITH YOU.
YOUR OBSESSION WITH NOT SEEMING WEAK IS YOUR GREATEST WEAKNESS.
AND ALL THIS? THIS--

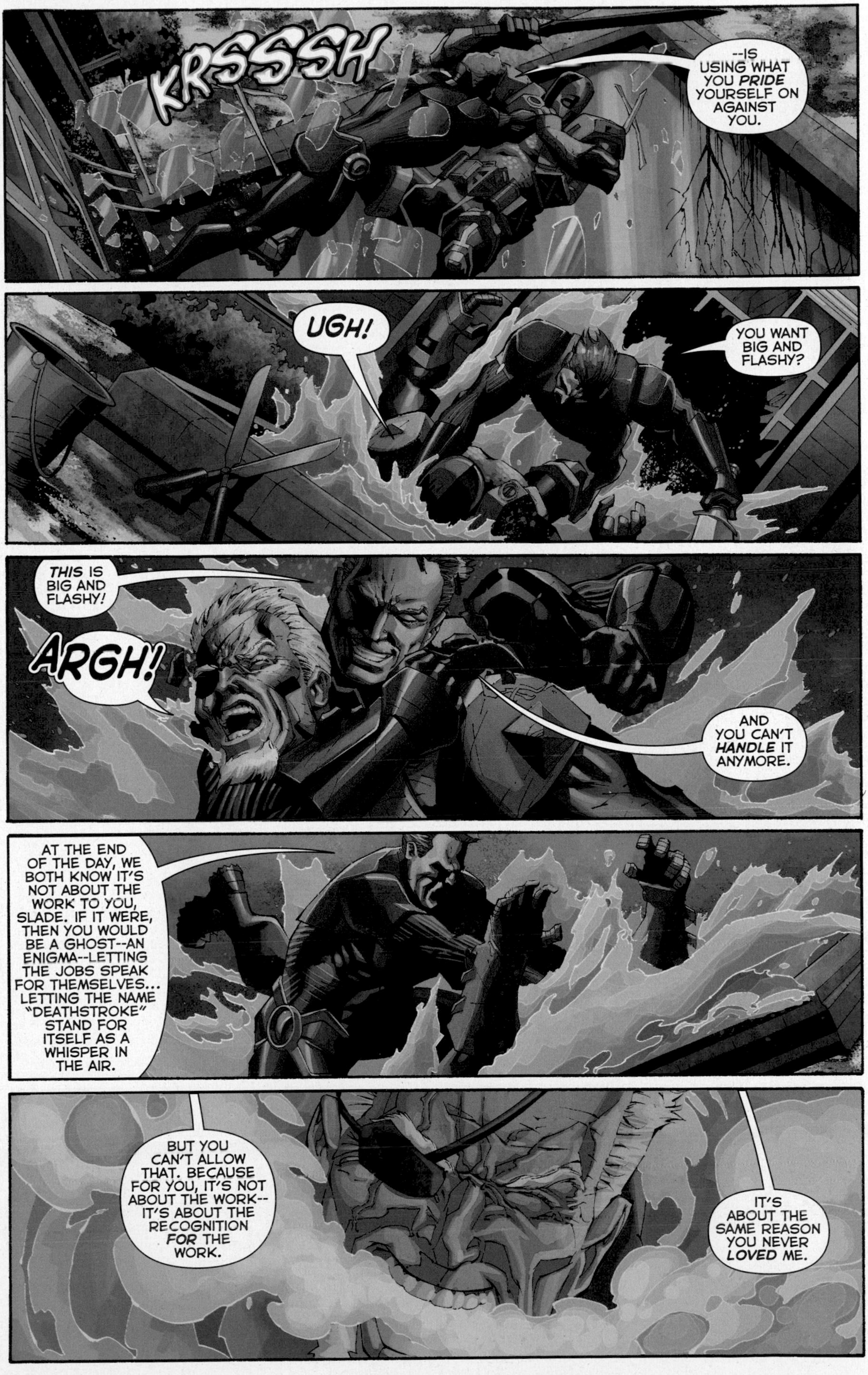
KRSSSH
--IS USING WHAT YOU PRIDE YOURSELF ON AGAINST YOU.
UGH!
YOU WANT BIG AND FLASHY?
THIS IS BIG AND FLASHY!
ARGH!
AND YOU CAN'T HANDLE IT ANYMORE.
AT THE END OF THE DAY, WE BOTH KNOW IT'S NOT ABOUT THE WORK TO YOU, SLADE. IF IT WERE, THEN YOU WOULD BE A GHOST--AN ENIGMA--LETTING THE JOBS SPEAK FOR THEMSELVES... LETTING THE NAME "DEATHSTROKE" STAND FOR ITSELF AS A WHISPER IN THE AIR.
BUT YOU CAN'T ALLOW THAT. BECAUSE FOR YOU, IT'S NOT ABOUT THE WORK--IT'S ABOUT THE RECOGNITION FOR THE WORK.
IT'S ABOUT THE SAME REASON YOU NEVER LOVED ME.

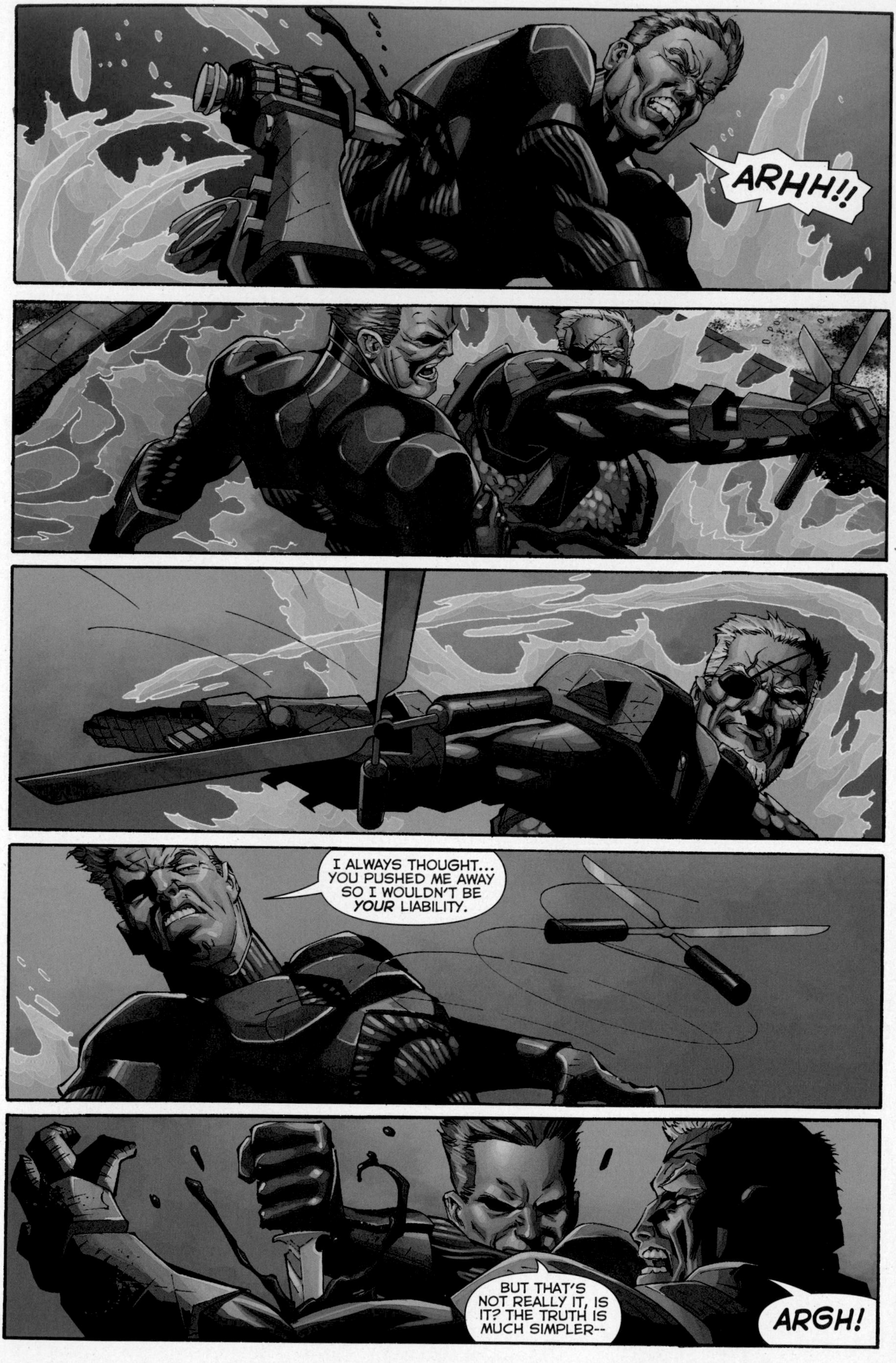
ARHH!!
I ALWAYS THOUGHT... YOU PUSHED ME AWAY SO I WOULDN'T BE YOUR LIABILITY.
BUT THAT'S NOT REALLY IT, IS IT? THE TRUTH IS MUCH SIMPLER--
ARGH!

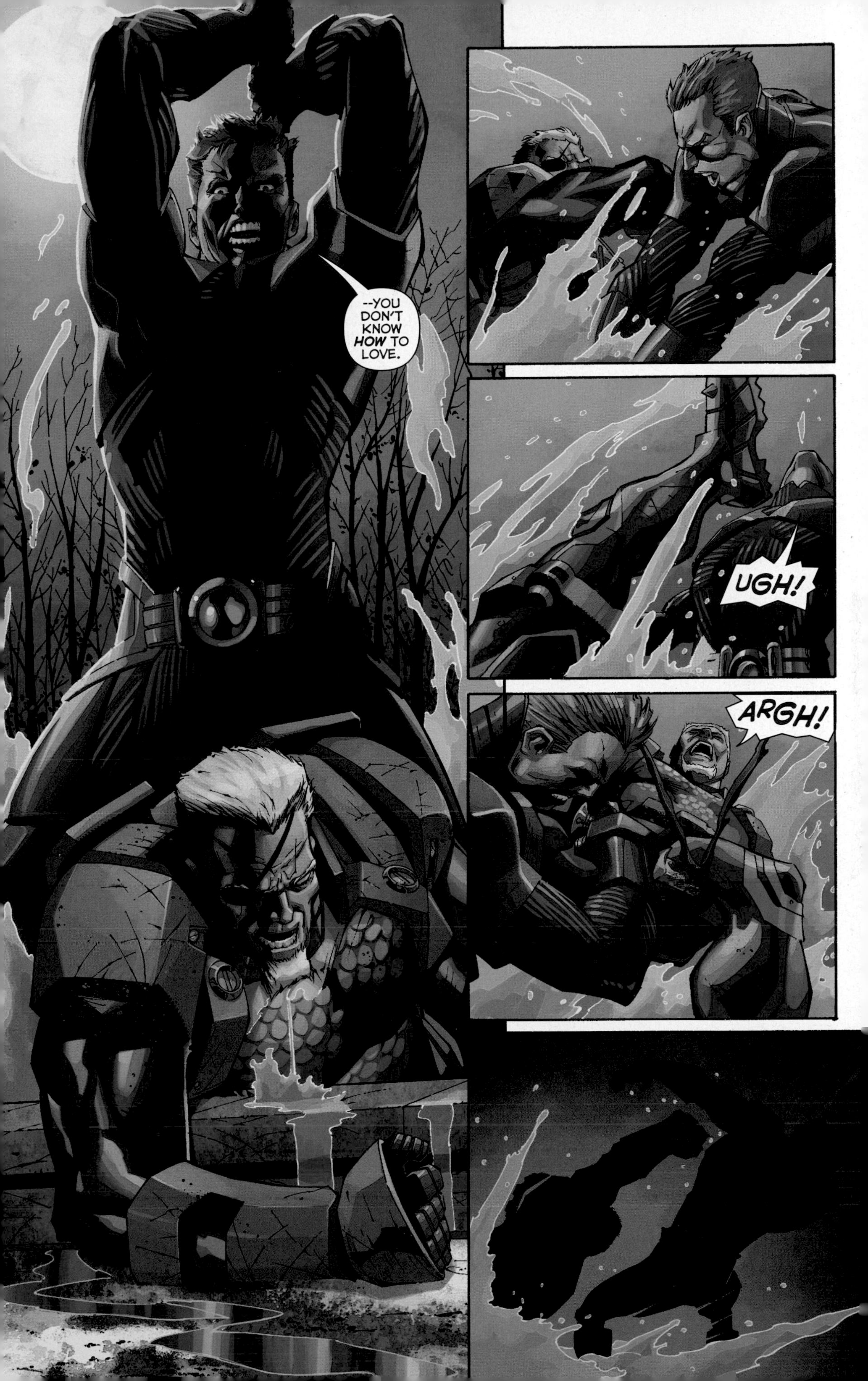
--YOU DON'T KNOW HOW TO LOVE.
UGH!
ARGH!

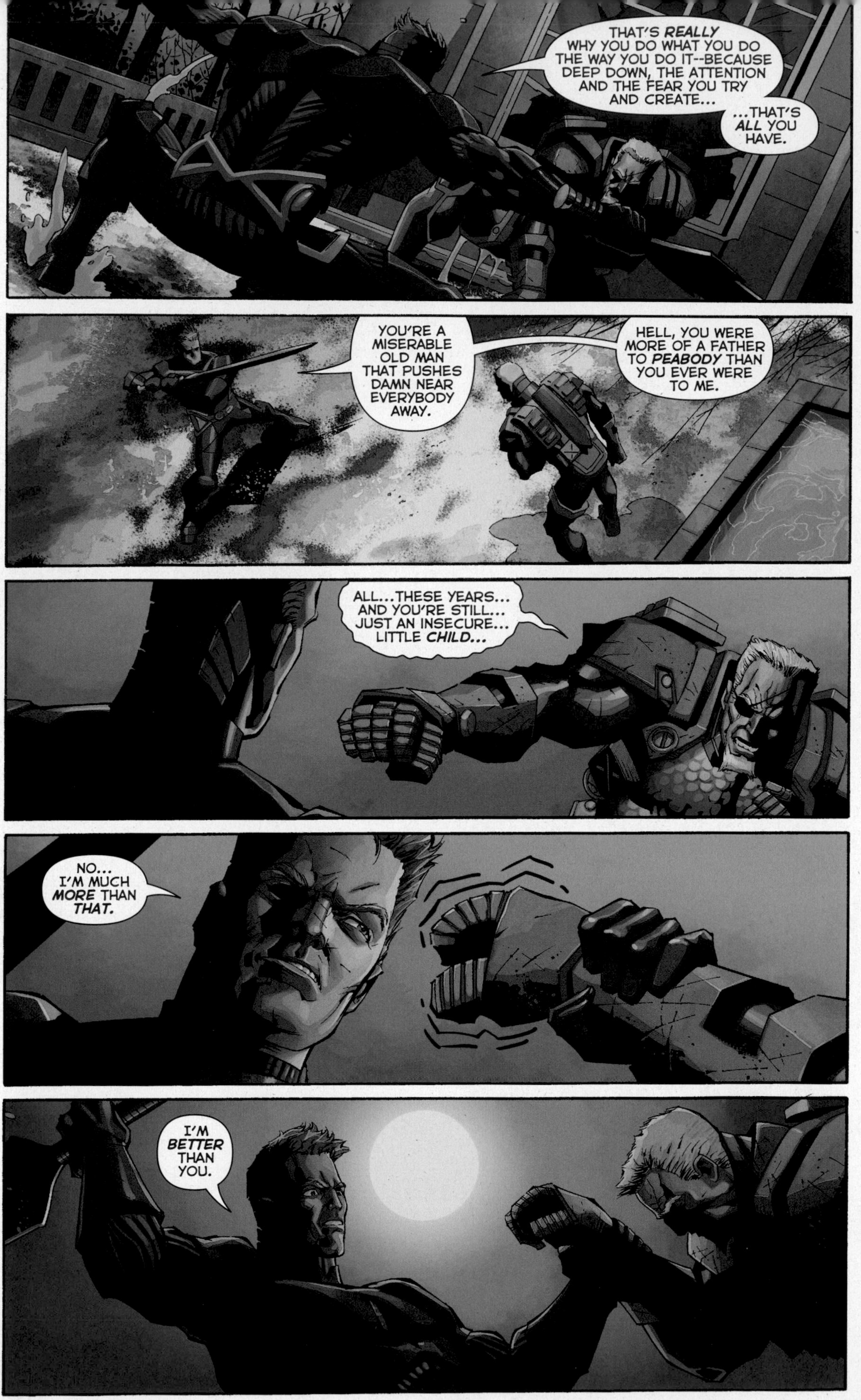
THAT'S REALLY WHY YOU DO WHAT YOU DO THE WAY YOU DO IT--BECAUSE DEEP DOWN, THE ATTENTION AND THE FEAR YOU TRY AND CREATE...
...THAT'S ALL YOU HAVE.
YOU'RE A MISERABLE OLD MAN THAT PUSHES DAMN NEAR EVERYBODY AWAY.
HELL, YOU WERE MORE OF A FATHER TO PEABODY THAN YOU EVER WERE TO ME.
ALL...THESE YEARS... AND YOU'RE STILL... JUST AN INSECURE... LITTLE CHILD...
NO... I'M MUCH MORE THAN THAT.
I'M BETTER THAN YOU.

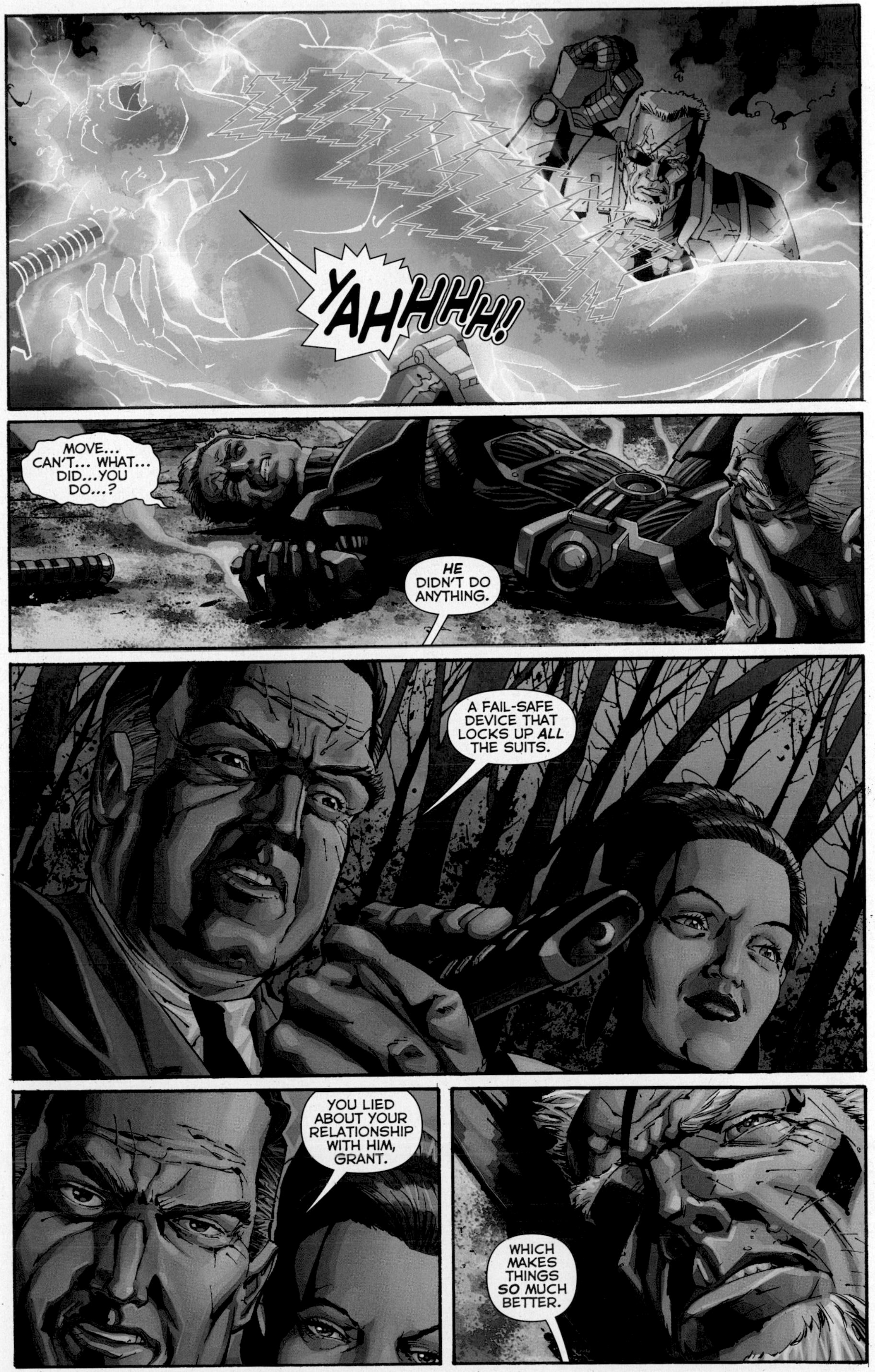
YAHHHH!
MOVE... CAN'T... WHAT... DID...YOU DO...?
HE DIDN'T DO ANYTHING.
A FAIL-SAFE DEVICE THAT LOCKS UP ALL THE SUITS.
YOU LIED ABOUT YOUR RELATIONSHIP WITH HIM, GRANT.
WHICH MAKES THINGS SO MUCH BETTER.

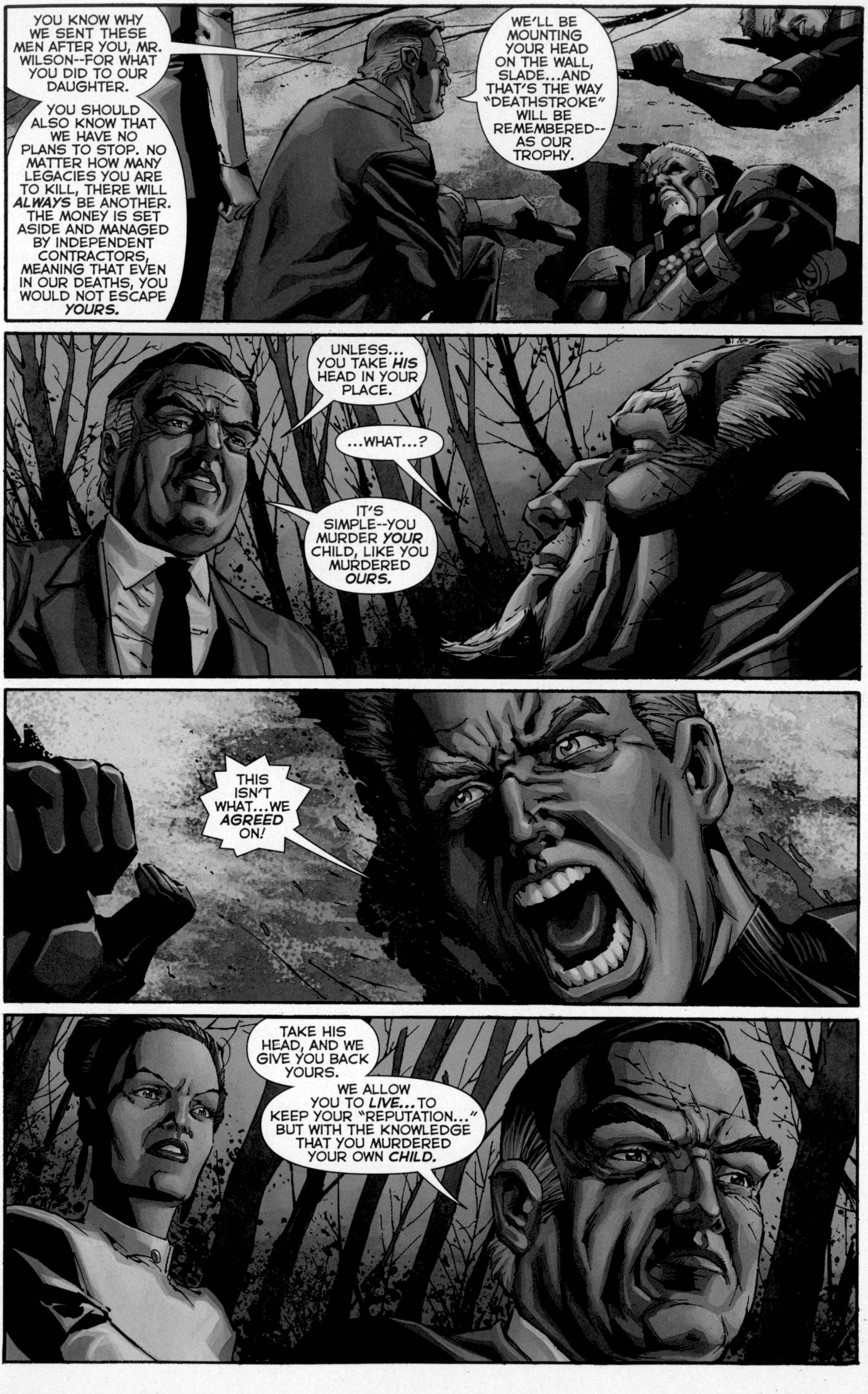

YOU KNOW WHY WE SENT THESE MEN AFTER YOU, MR. WILSON--FOR WHAT YOU DID TO OUR DAUGHTER.
YOU SHOULD ALSO KNOW THAT WE HAVE NO PLANS TO STOP. NO MATTER HOW MANY LEGACIES YOU ARE TO KILL, THERE WILL ALWAYS BE ANOTHER. THE MONEY IS SET ASIDE AND MANAGED BY INDEPENDENT CONTRACTORS, MEANING THAT EVEN IN OUR DEATHS, YOU WOULD NOT ESCAPE YOURS.
WE'LL BE MOUNTING YOUR HEAD ON THE WALL, SLADE...AND THAT'S THE WAY "DEATHSTROKE" WILL BE REMEMBERED--AS OUR TROPHY.
UNLESS... YOU TAKE HIS HEAD IN YOUR PLACE.
...WHAT...?
IT'S SIMPLE--YOU MURDER YOUR CHILD, LIKE YOU MURDERED OURS.
THIS ISN'T WHAT...WE AGREED ON!
TAKE HIS HEAD, AND WE GIVE YOU BACK YOURS.
WE ALLOW YOU TO LIVE...TO KEEP YOUR "REPUTATION..." BUT WITH THE KNOWLEDGE THAT YOU MURDERED YOUR OWN CHILD.

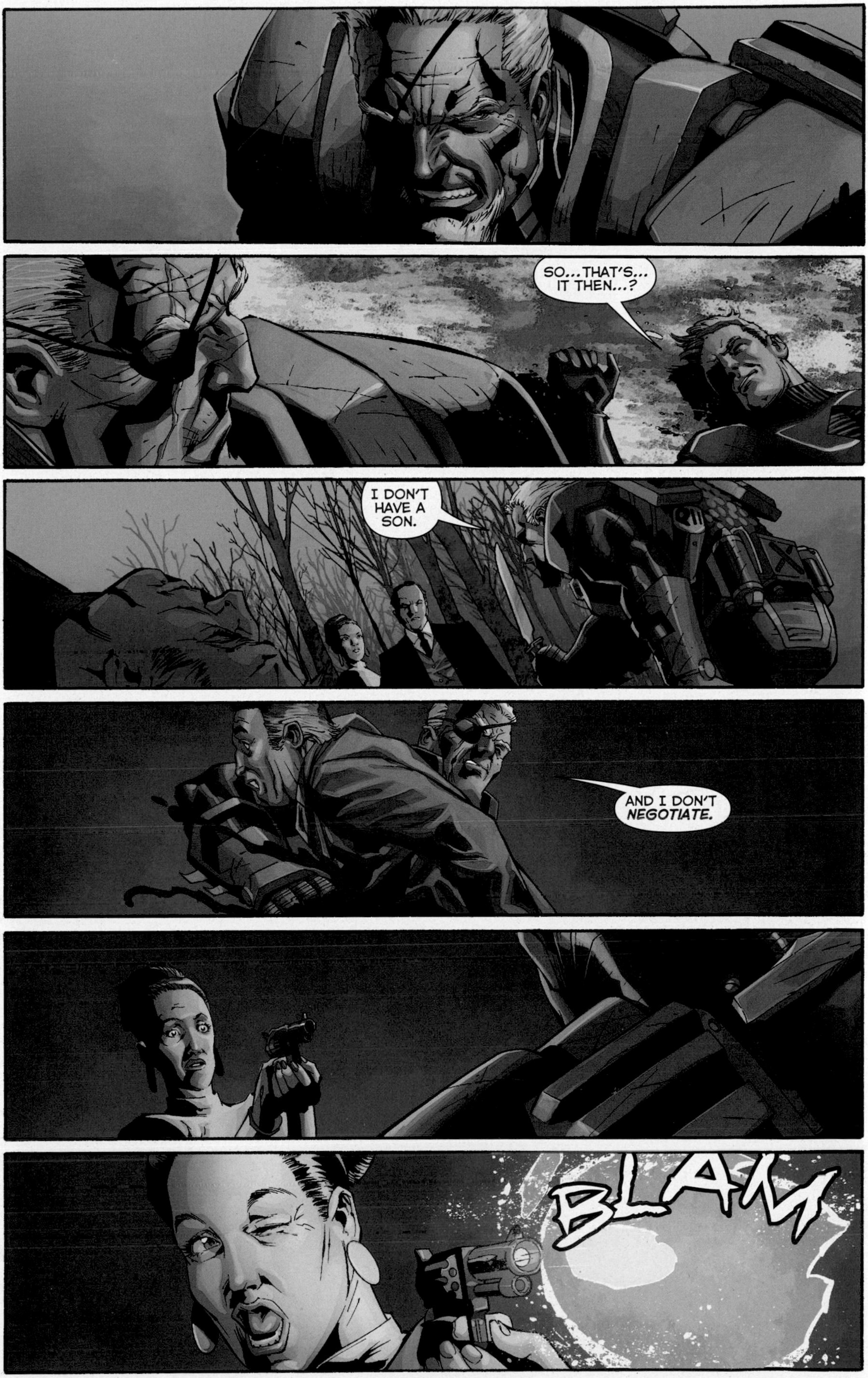
SO...THAT'S... IT THEN...?
I DON'T HAVE A SON.
AND I DON'T *NEGOTIATE.*
BLAM

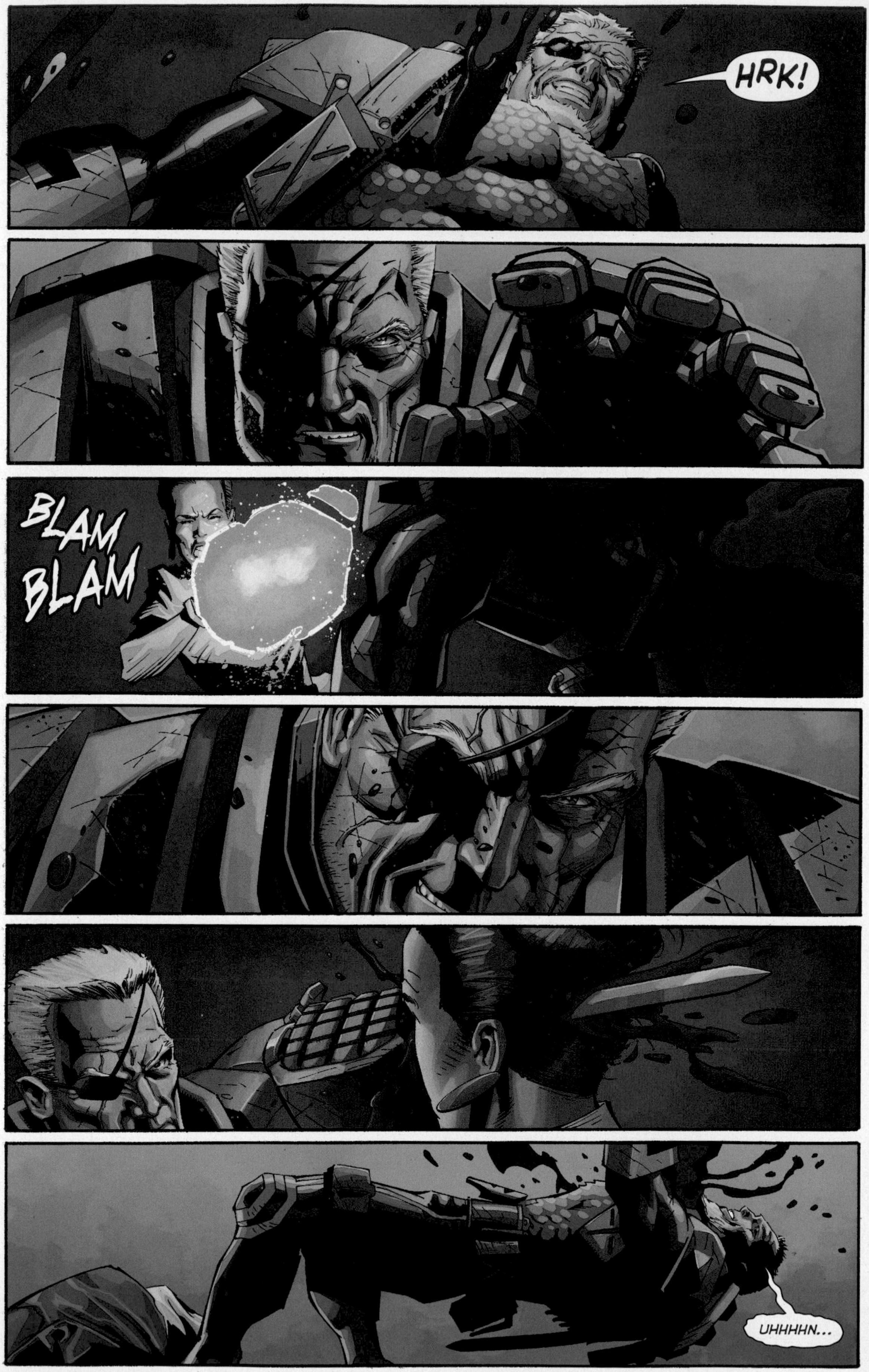
HRK!
BLAM
BLAM
UHHHHN...

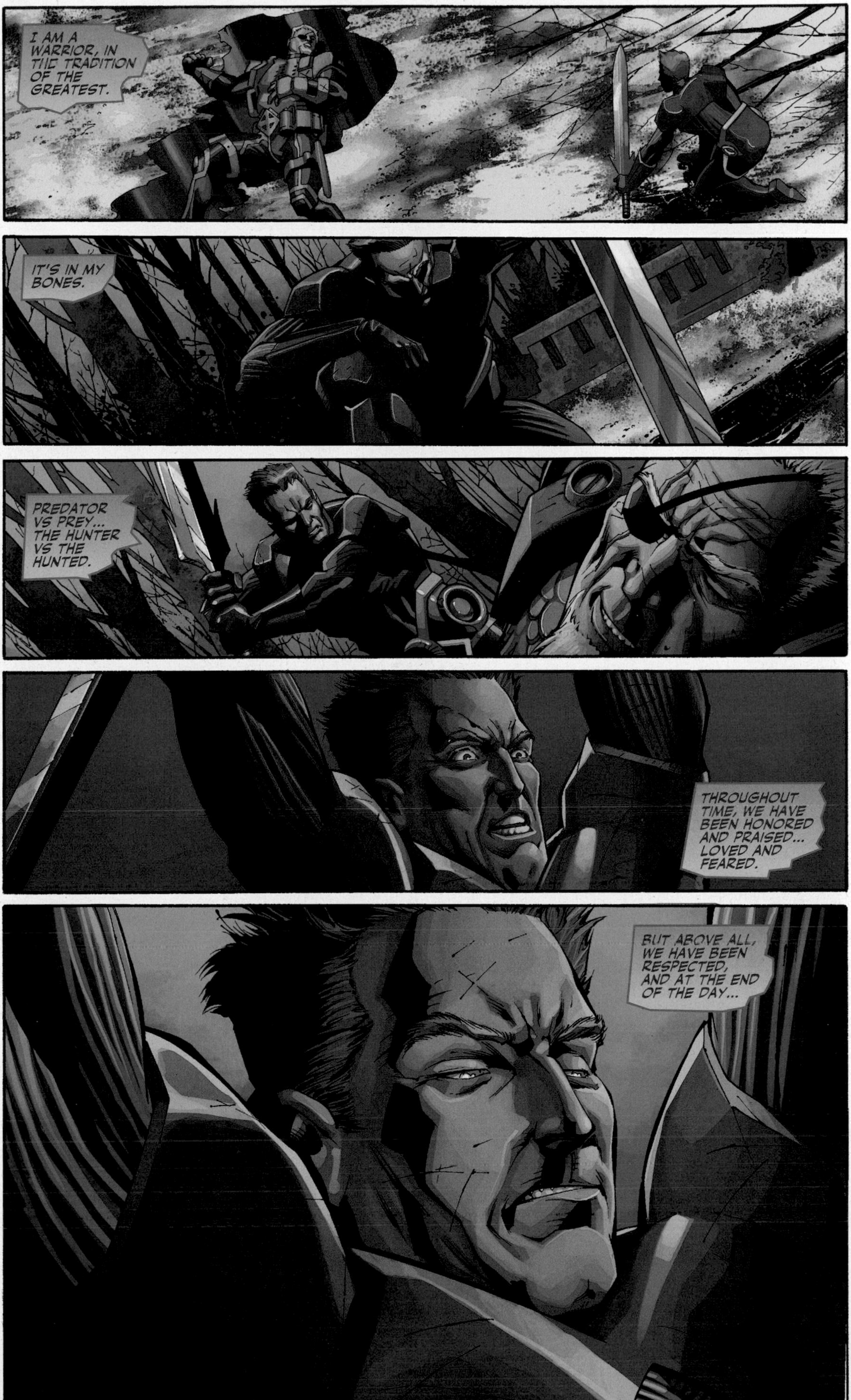
I AM A WARRIOR, IN THE TRADITION OF THE GREATEST.
IT'S IN MY BONES.
PREDATOR VS PREY... THE HUNTER VS THE HUNTED.
THROUGHOUT TIME, WE HAVE BEEN HONORED AND PRAISED... LOVED AND FEARED.
BUT ABOVE ALL, WE HAVE BEEN RESPECTED, AND AT THE END OF THE DAY...

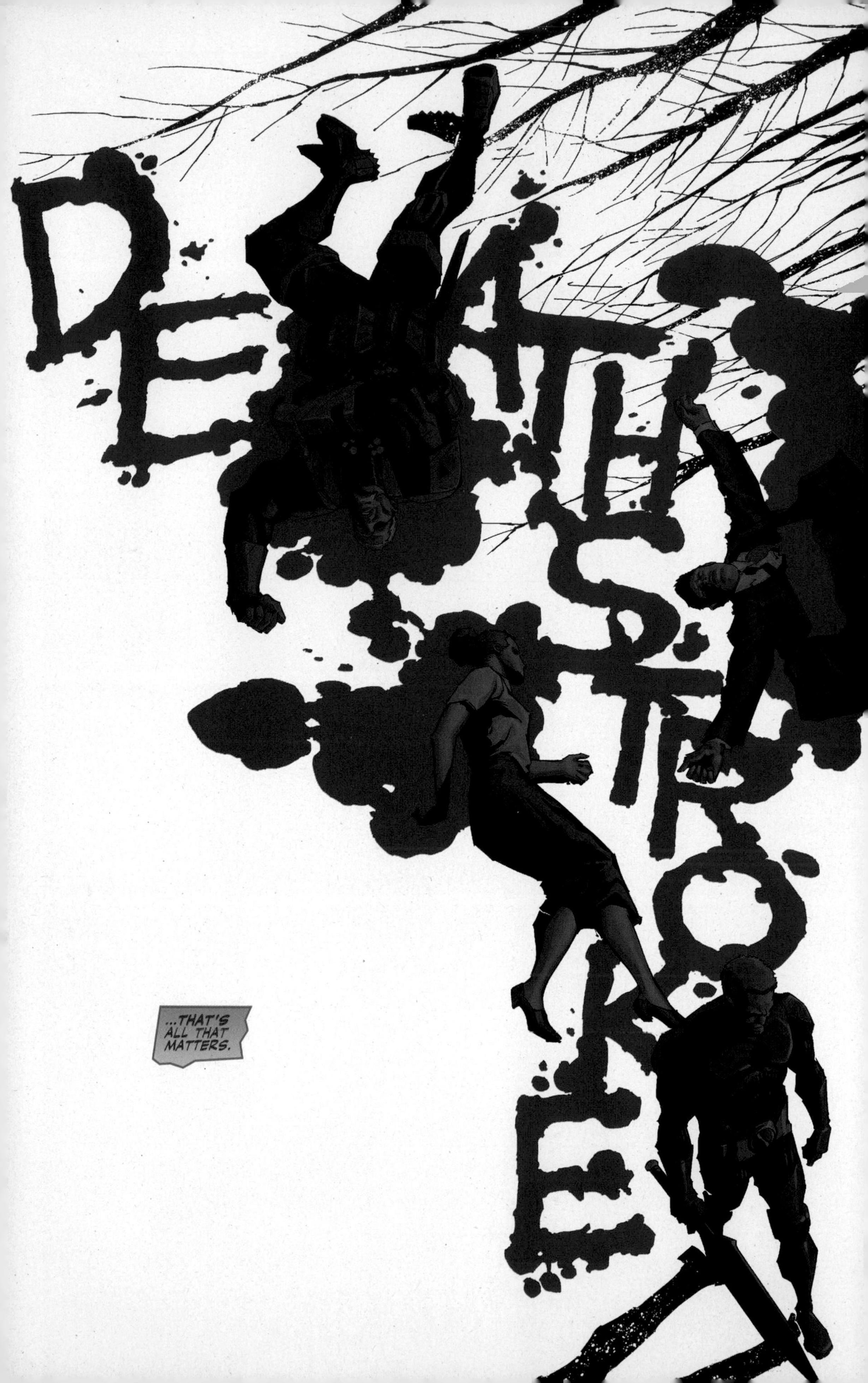
DEATHSTROKE
...THAT'S ALL THAT MATTERS.

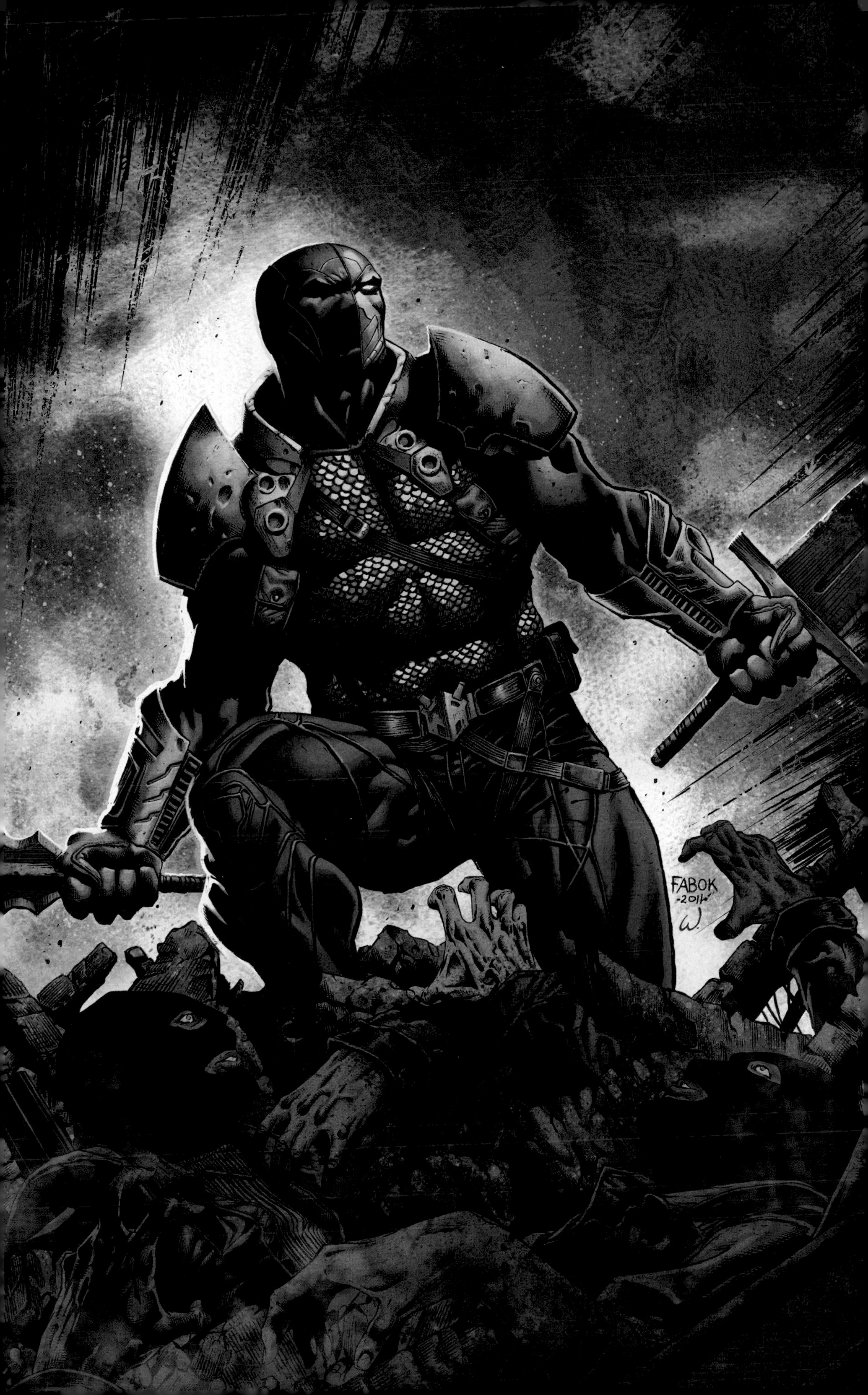
FABOK
-2011-
W.

CIRCLE OF LIFE

KYLE HIGGINS writer **EDUARDO PANSICA** penciller **ART THIBERT** inker cover by **JASON FABOK & JASON WRIGHT**

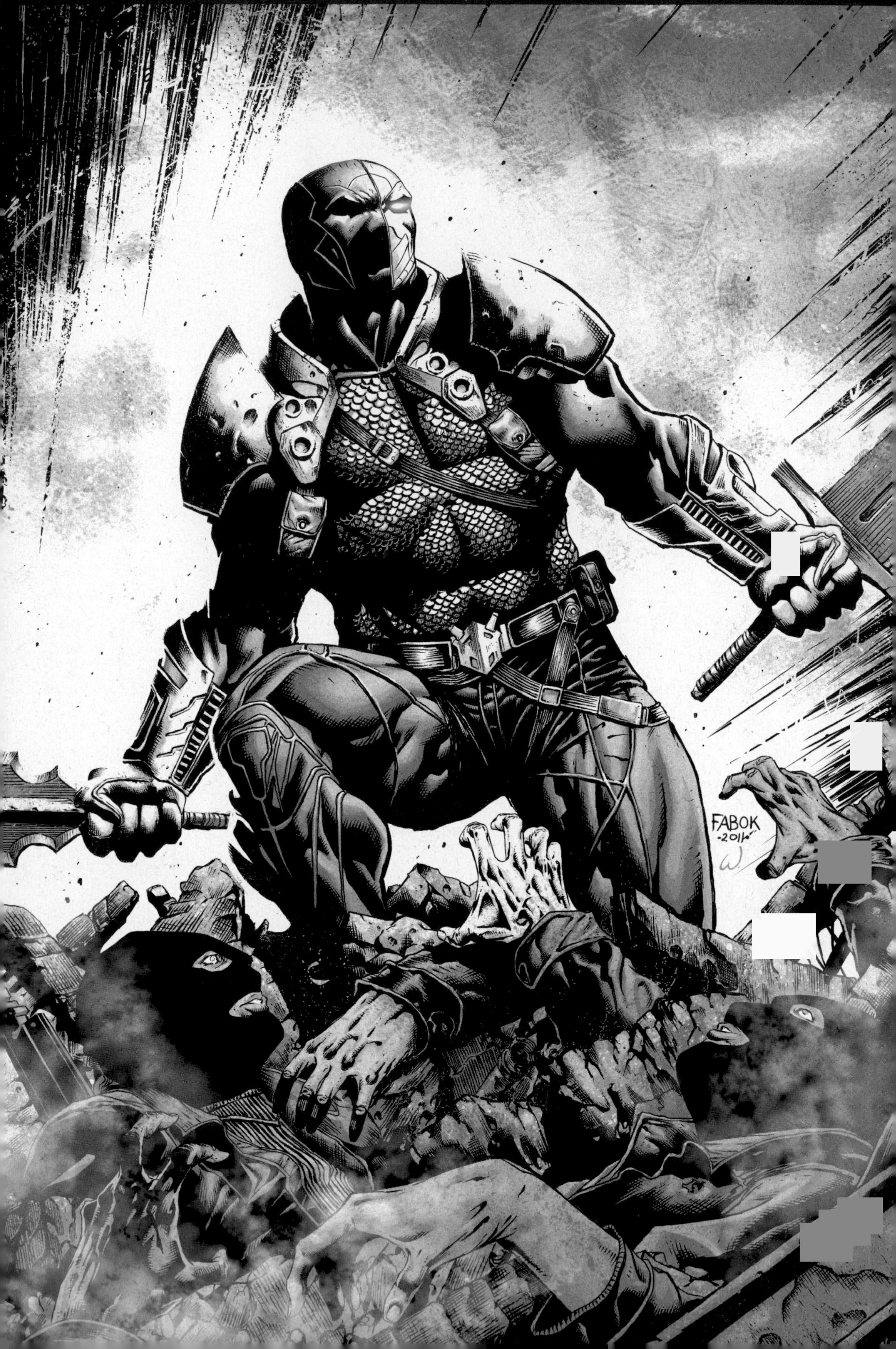
FABOK
-2011-

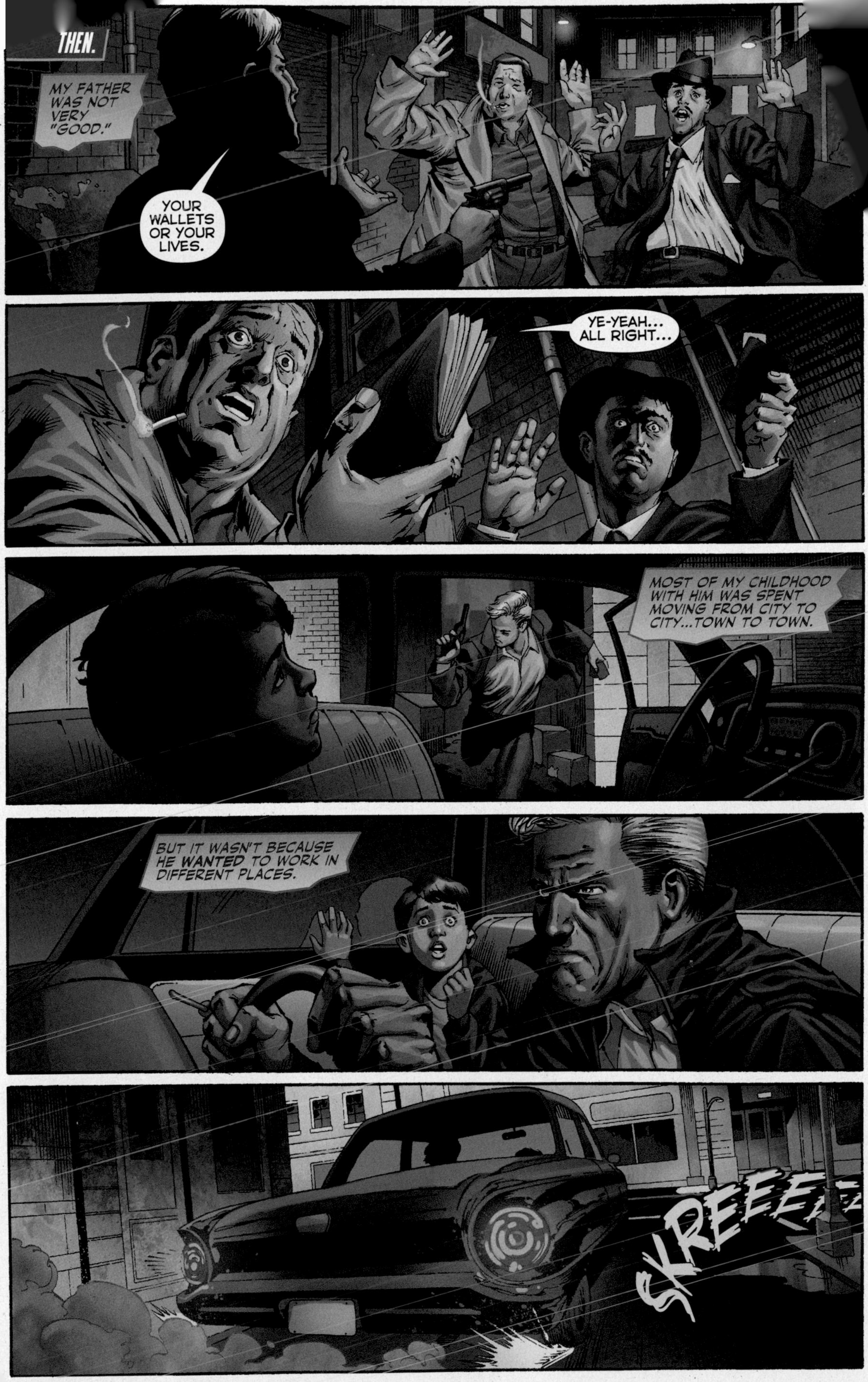
THEN.
MY FATHER WAS NOT VERY "GOOD."
YOUR WALLETS OR YOUR LIVES.
YE-YEAH... ALL RIGHT...
MOST OF MY CHILDHOOD WITH HIM WAS SPENT MOVING FROM CITY TO CITY...TOWN TO TOWN.
BUT IT WASN'T BECAUSE HE WANTED TO WORK IN DIFFERENT PLACES.
SKREEEE

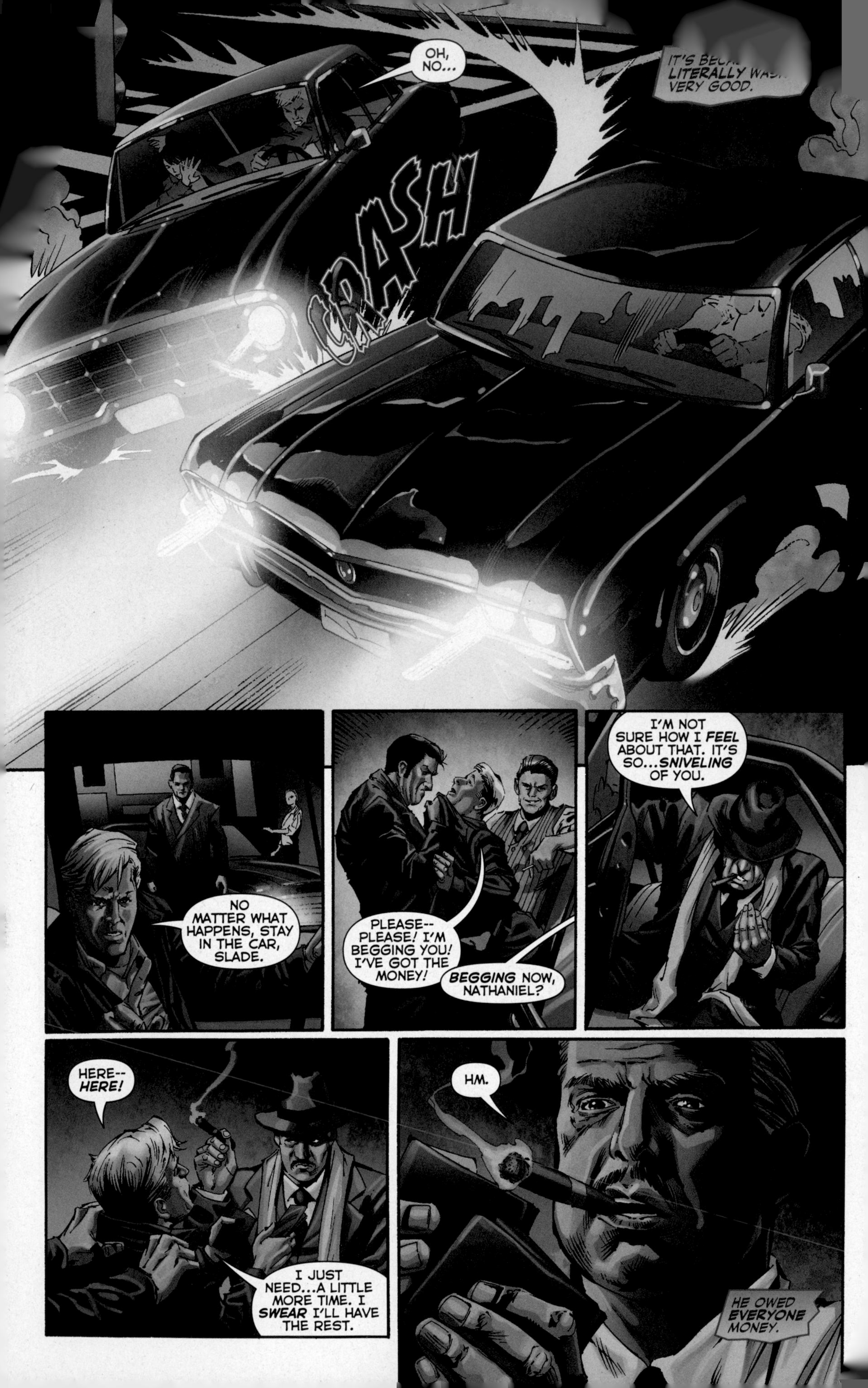
OH, NO...
IT'S BEC... LITERALLY WAS... VERY GOOD.
CRASH
NO MATTER WHAT HAPPENS, STAY IN THE CAR, SLADE.
PLEASE-- PLEASE! I'M BEGGING YOU! I'VE GOT THE MONEY!
BEGGING NOW, NATHANIEL?
I'M NOT SURE HOW I FEEL ABOUT THAT. IT'S SO...SNIVELING OF YOU.
HERE-- HERE!
I JUST NEED...A LITTLE MORE TIME. I SWEAR I'LL HAVE THE REST.
HM.
HE OWED EVERYONE MONEY.

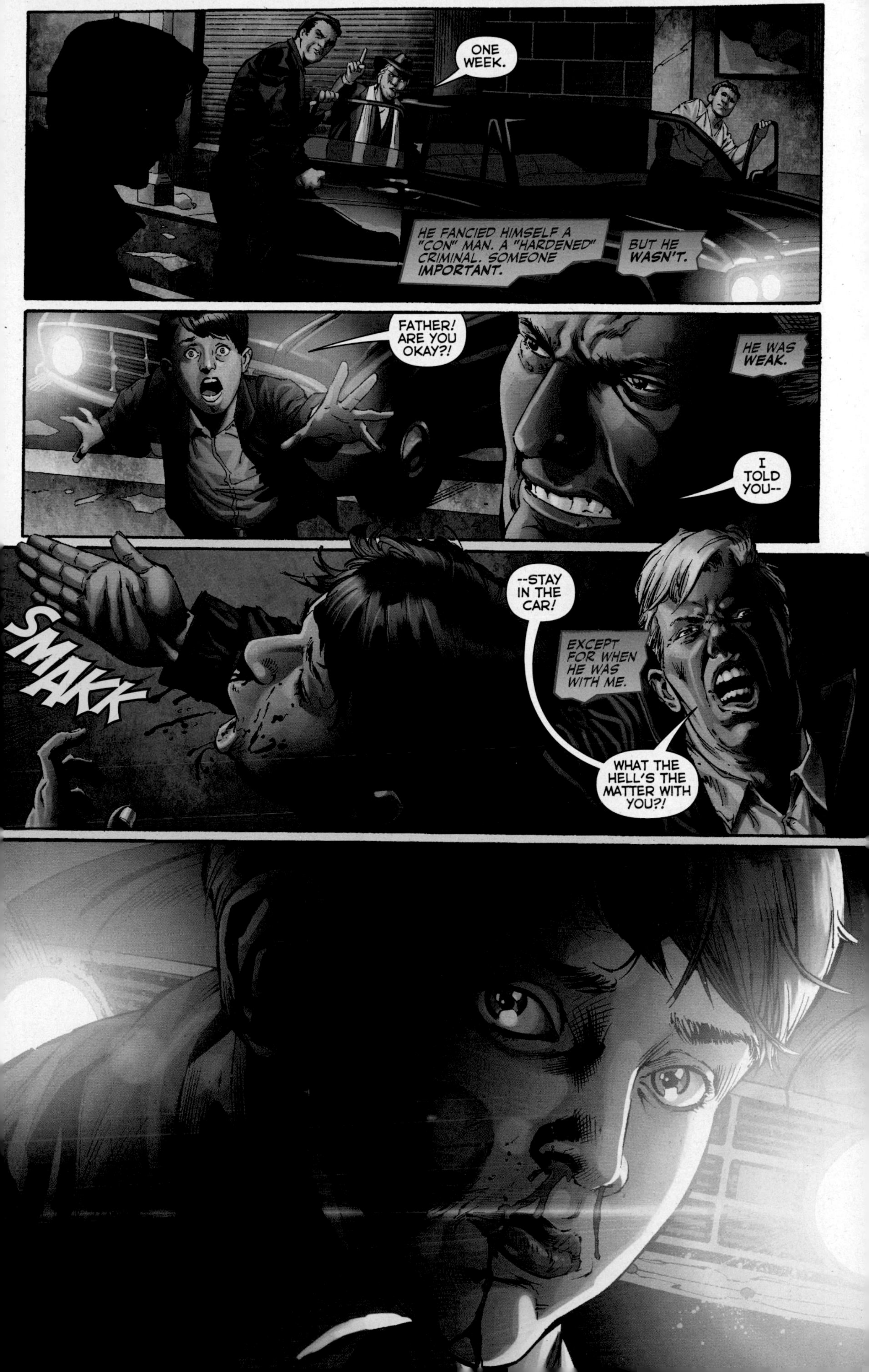
ONE WEEK.
HE FANCIED HIMSELF A "CON" MAN. A "HARDENED" CRIMINAL. SOMEONE IMPORTANT.
BUT HE WASN'T.
FATHER! ARE YOU OKAY?!
HE WAS WEAK.
I TOLD YOU--
SMAKK
--STAY IN THE CAR!
EXCEPT FOR WHEN HE WAS WITH ME.
WHAT THE HELL'S THE MATTER WITH YOU?!

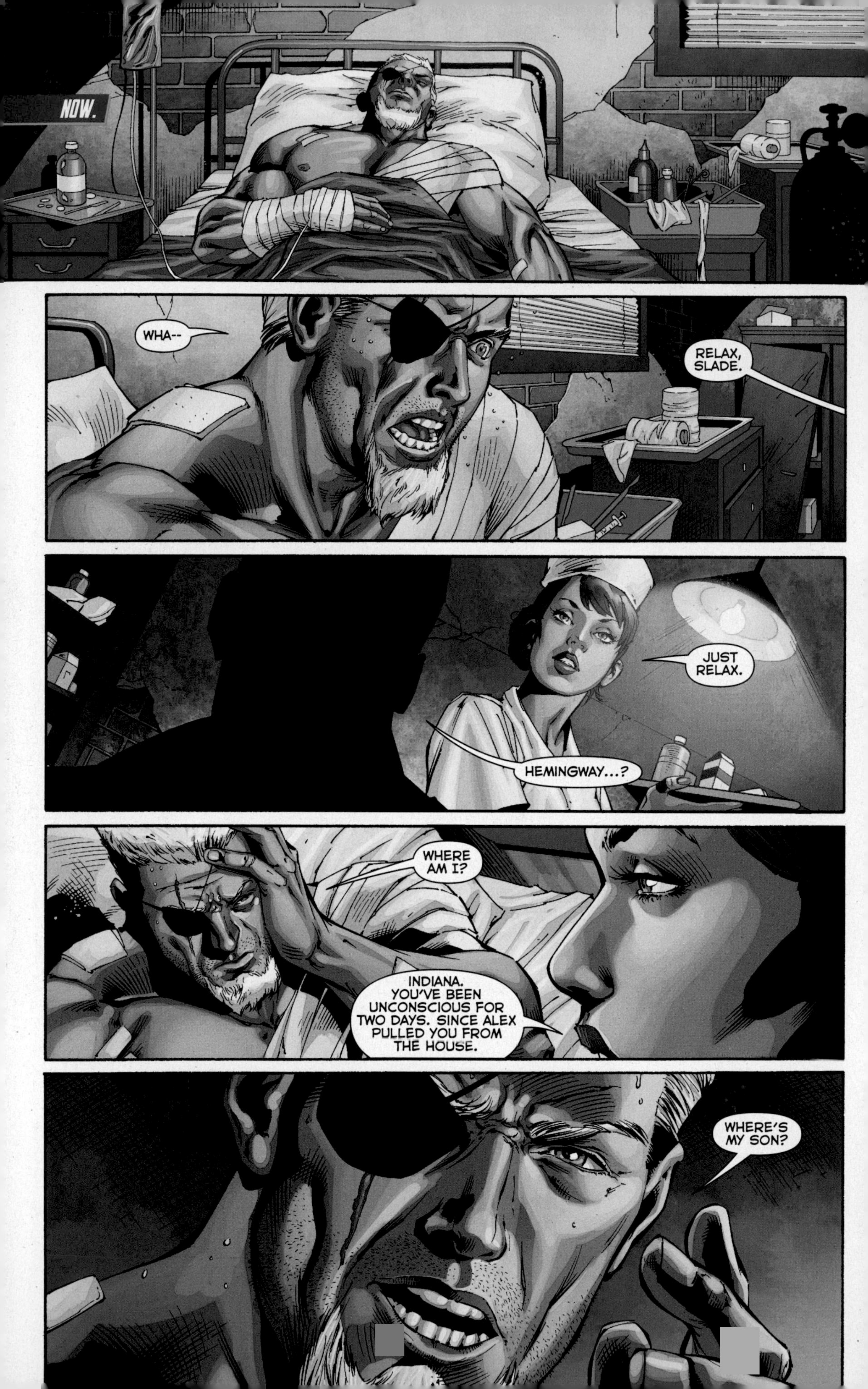
NOW.
WHA--
RELAX, SLADE.
JUST RELAX.
HEMINGWAY...?
WHERE AM I?
INDIANA. YOU'VE BEEN UNCONSCIOUS FOR TWO DAYS. SINCE ALEX PULLED YOU FROM THE HOUSE.
WHERE'S MY SON?

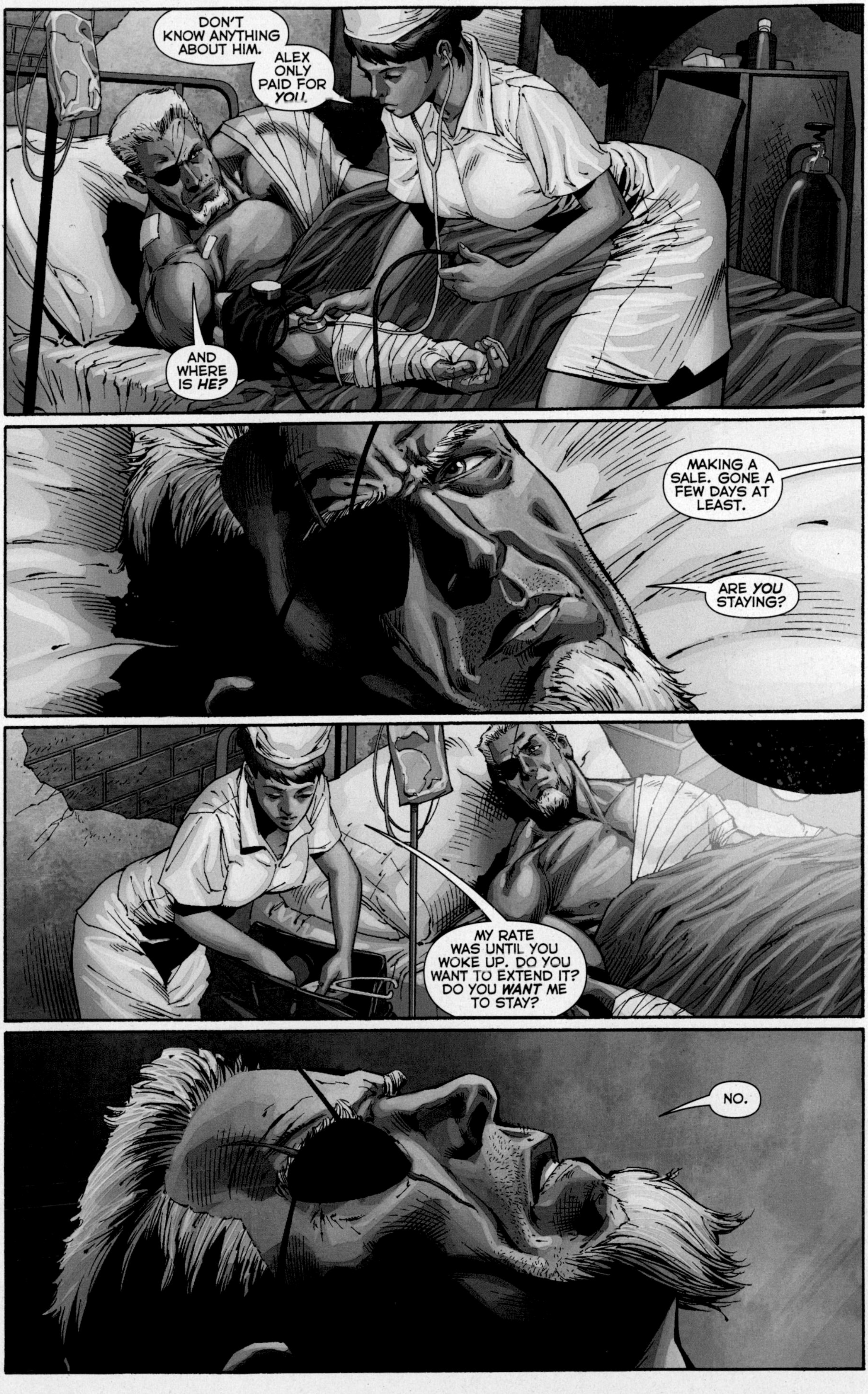
DON'T KNOW ANYTHING ABOUT HIM.
ALEX ONLY PAID FOR *YOU*.
AND WHERE IS *HE*?
MAKING A SALE. GONE A FEW DAYS AT LEAST.
ARE *YOU* STAYING?
MY RATE WAS UNTIL YOU WOKE UP. DO YOU WANT TO EXTEND IT? DO YOU *WANT* ME TO STAY?
NO.

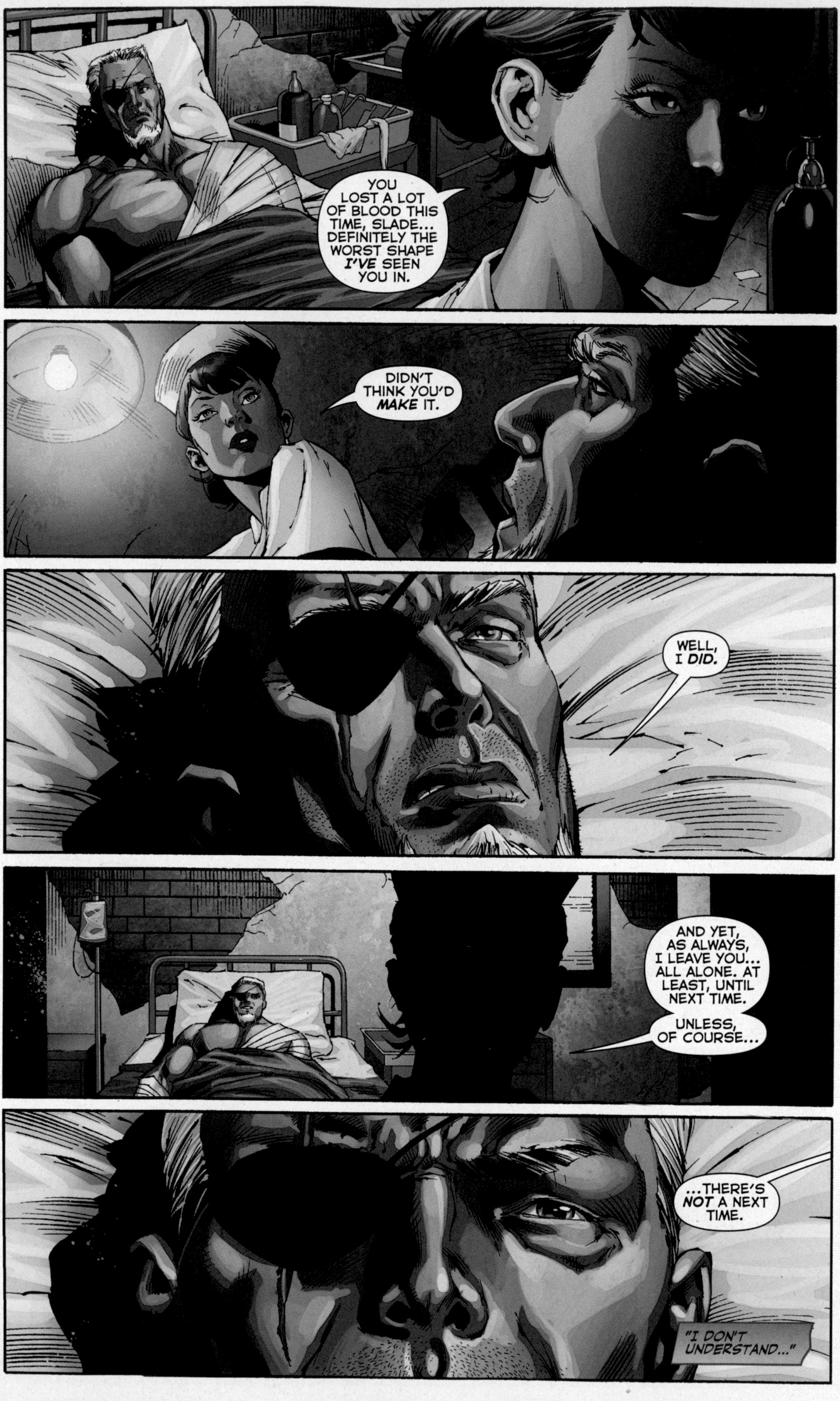
YOU LOST A LOT OF BLOOD THIS TIME, SLADE... DEFINITELY THE WORST SHAPE I'VE SEEN YOU IN.
DIDN'T THINK YOU'D MAKE IT.
WELL, I DID.
AND YET, AS ALWAYS, I LEAVE YOU... ALL ALONE. AT LEAST, UNTIL NEXT TIME.
UNLESS, OF COURSE...
...THERE'S NOT A NEXT TIME.
"I DON'T UNDERSTAND..."

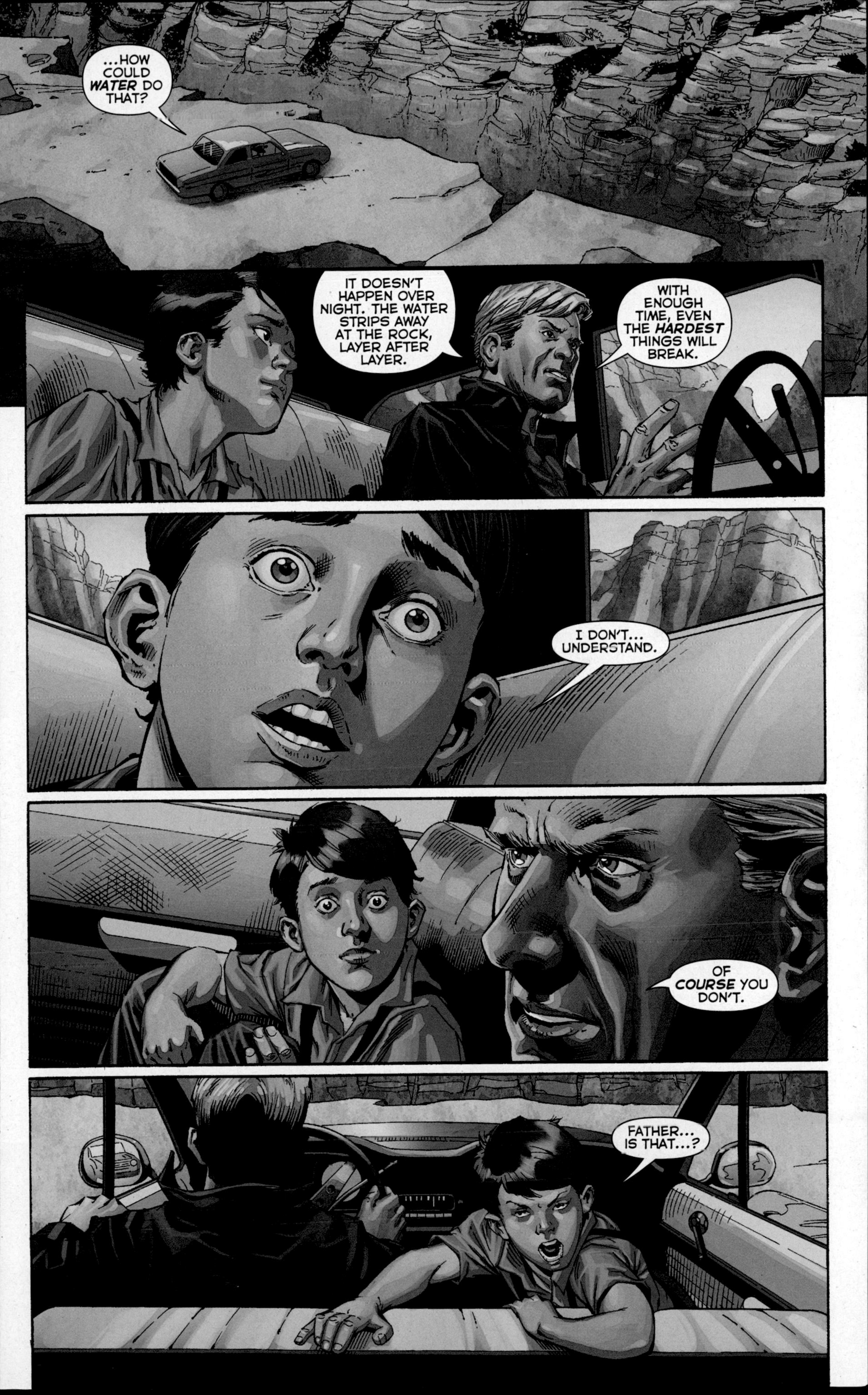
...HOW COULD WATER DO THAT?
IT DOESN'T HAPPEN OVER NIGHT. THE WATER STRIPS AWAY AT THE ROCK, LAYER AFTER LAYER.
WITH ENOUGH TIME, EVEN THE HARDEST THINGS WILL BREAK.
I DON'T... UNDERSTAND.
OF COURSE YOU DON'T.
FATHER... IS THAT...?

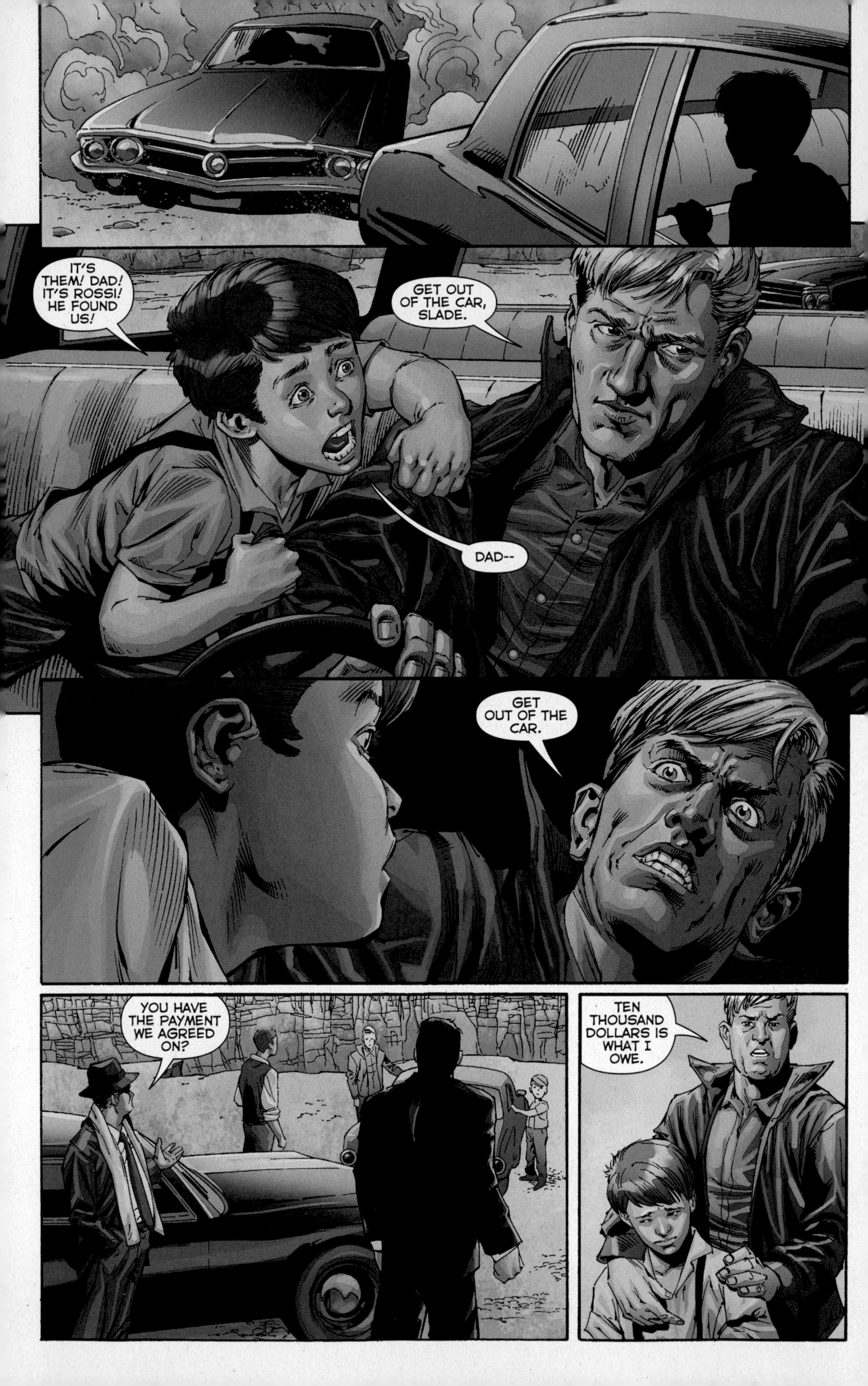
IT'S THEM! DAD! IT'S ROSSI! HE FOUND US!
GET OUT OF THE CAR, SLADE.
DAD--
GET OUT OF THE CAR.
YOU HAVE THE PAYMENT WE AGREED ON?
TEN THOUSAND DOLLARS IS WHAT I OWE.

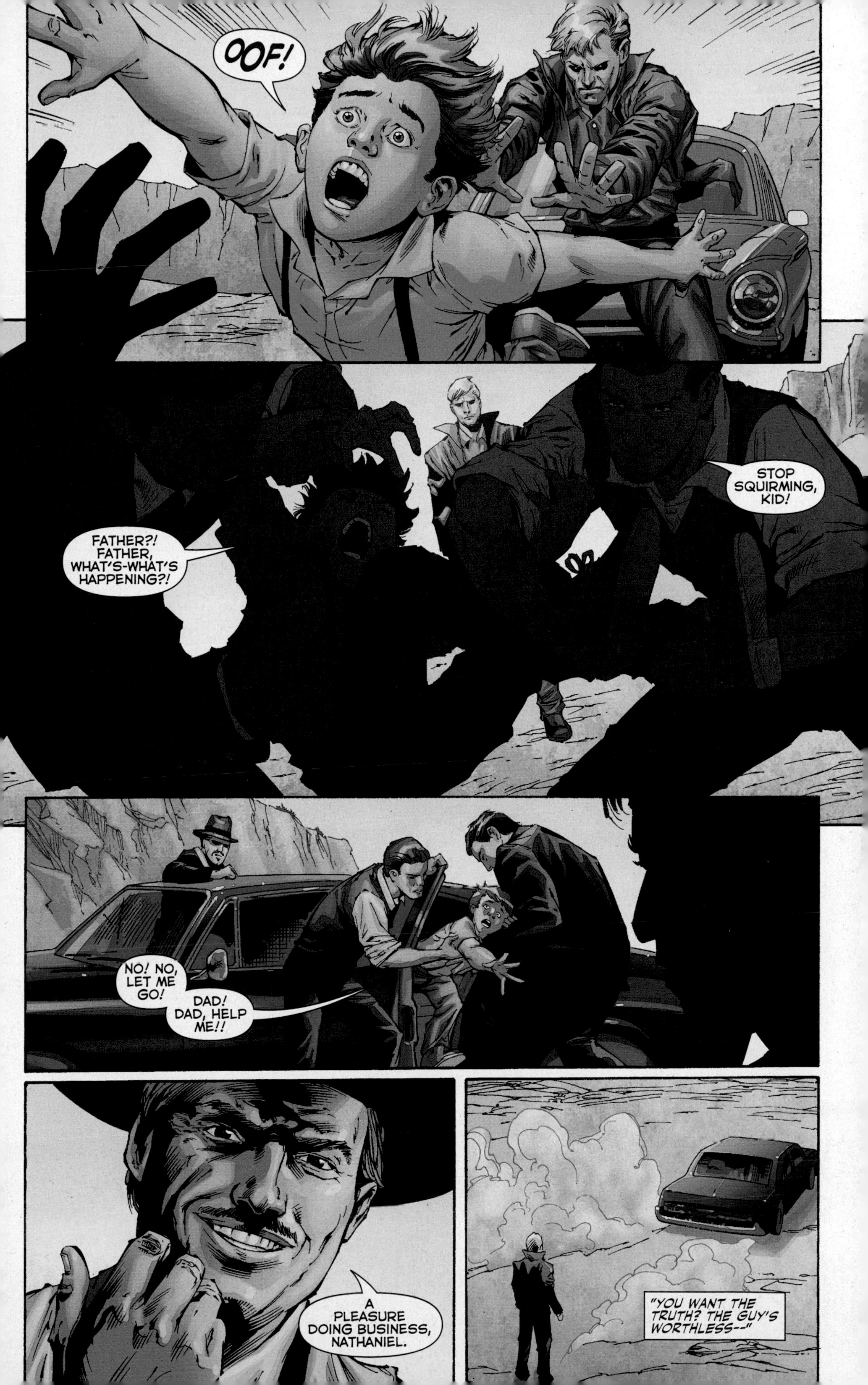
OOF!
STOP SQUIRMING, KID!
FATHER?! FATHER, WHAT'S-WHAT'S HAPPENING?!
NO! NO, LET ME GO!
DAD! DAD, HELP ME!!
A PLEASURE DOING BUSINESS, NATHANIEL.
"YOU WANT THE TRUTH? THE GUY'S WORTHLESS--"

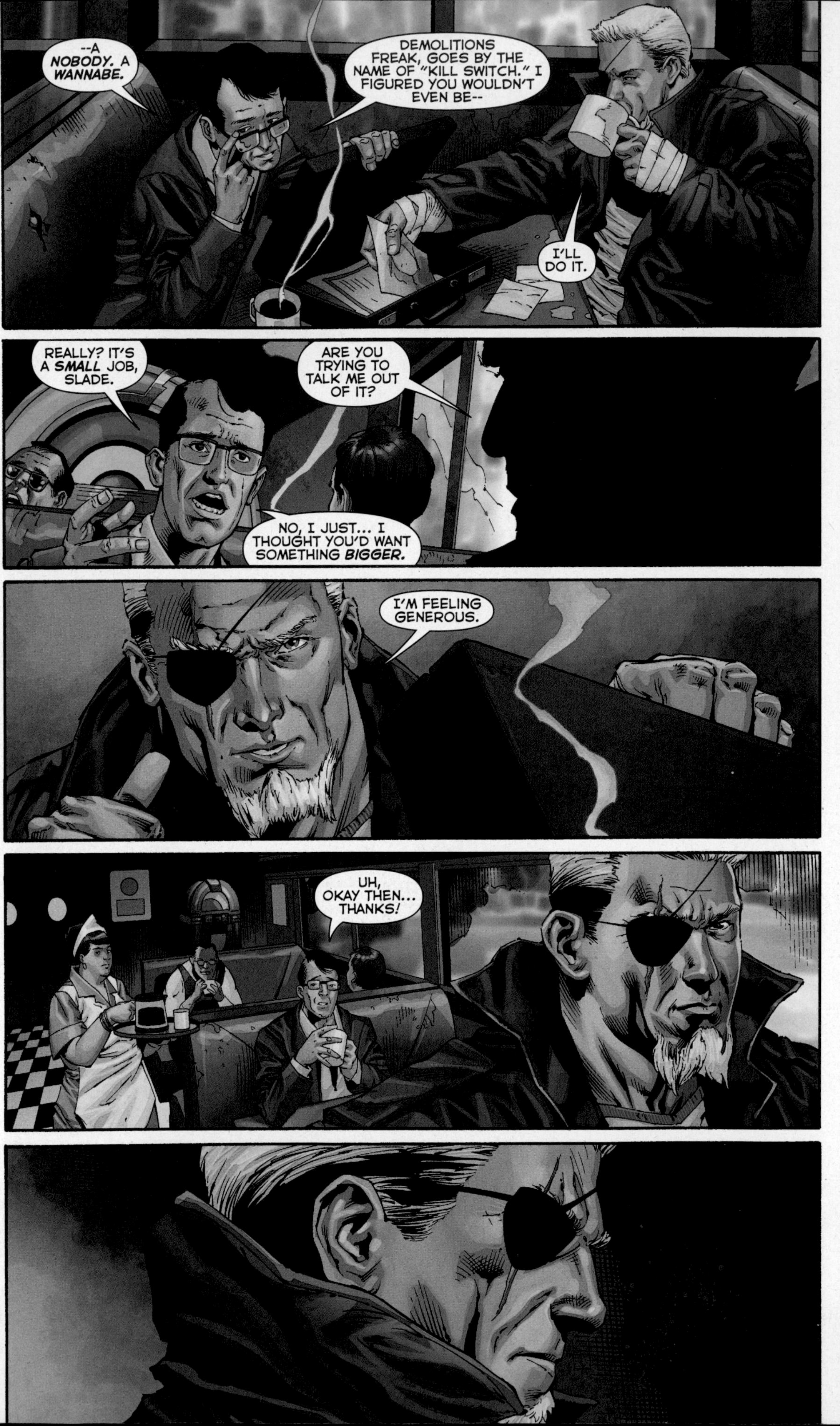
--A NOBODY. A WANNABE.
DEMOLITIONS FREAK, GOES BY THE NAME OF "KILL SWITCH." I FIGURED YOU WOULDN'T EVEN BE--
I'LL DO IT.
REALLY? IT'S A SMALL JOB, SLADE.
ARE YOU TRYING TO TALK ME OUT OF IT?
NO, I JUST... I THOUGHT YOU'D WANT SOMETHING BIGGER.
I'M FEELING GENEROUS.
UH, OKAY THEN... THANKS!

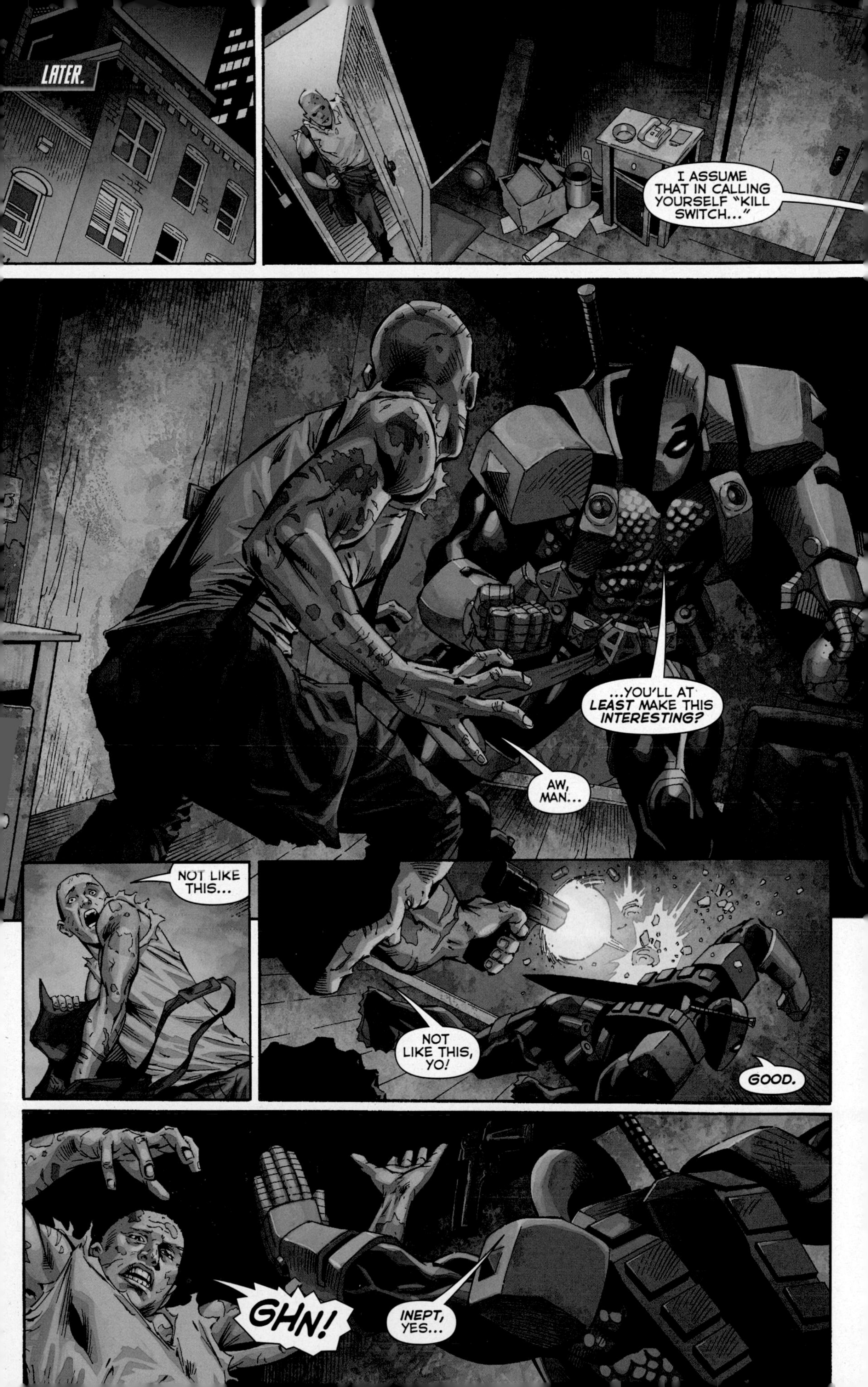
LATER.
I ASSUME THAT IN CALLING YOURSELF "KILL SWITCH..."
...YOU'LL AT LEAST MAKE THIS INTERESTING?
AW, MAN...
NOT LIKE THIS...
NOT LIKE THIS, YO!
GOOD.
GHN!
INEPT, YES...

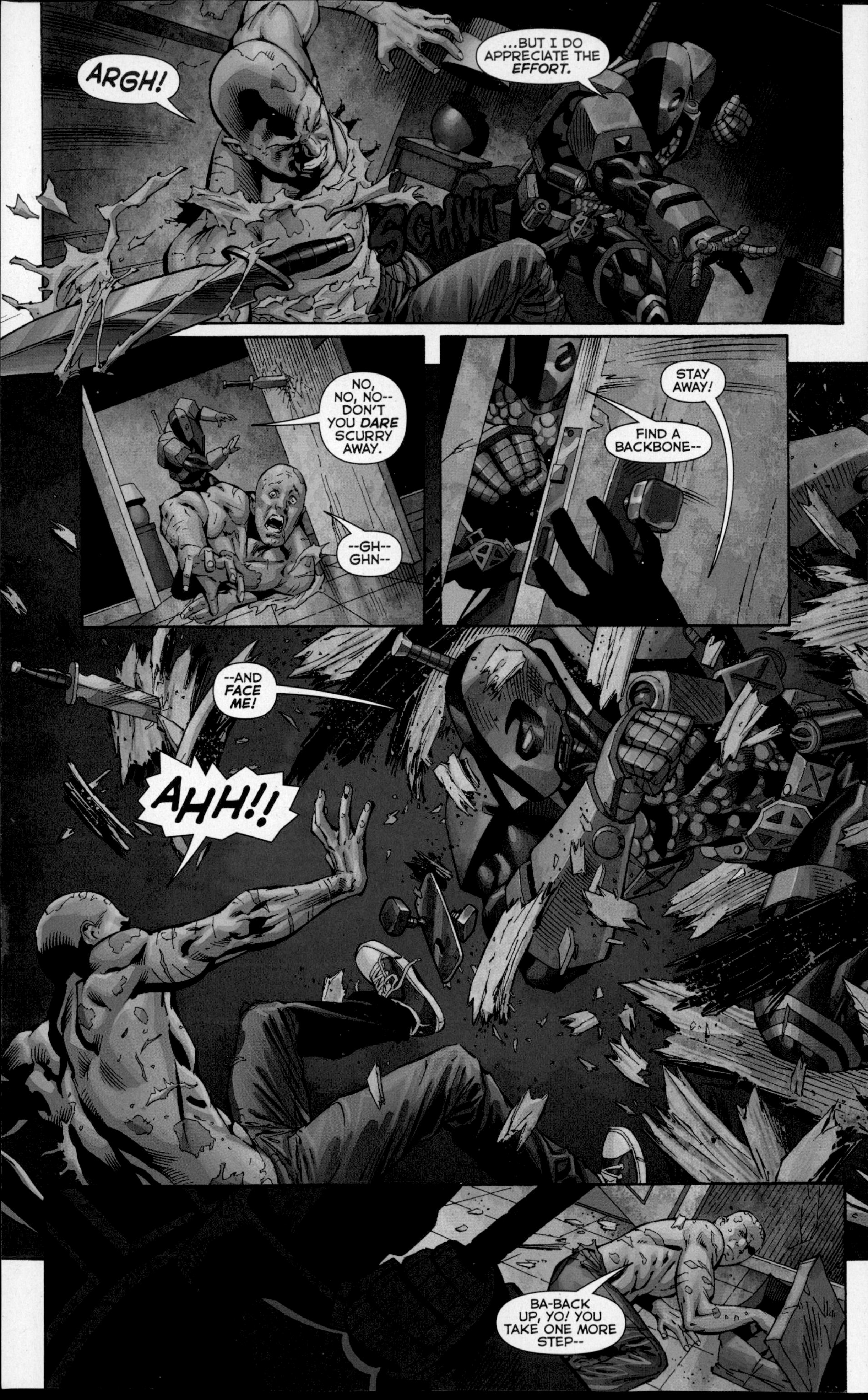
ARGH!
...BUT I DO APPRECIATE THE EFFORT.
SCHWT
NO, NO, NO-- DON'T YOU DARE SCURRY AWAY.
--GH-- GHN--
FIND A BACKBONE--
STAY AWAY!
--AND FACE ME!
AHH!!
BA-BACK UP, YO! YOU TAKE ONE MORE STEP--

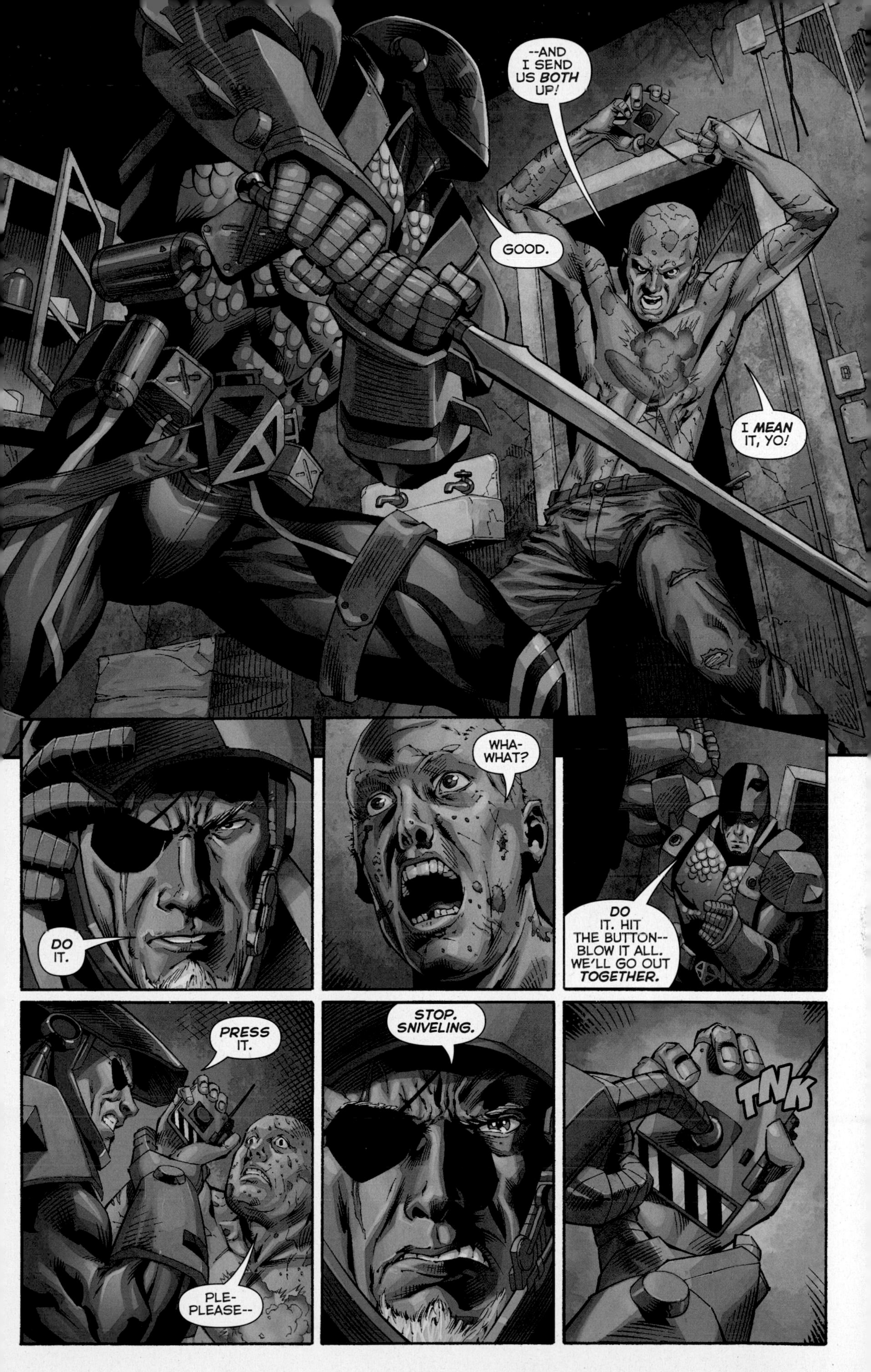
--AND I SEND US BOTH UP!
GOOD.
I MEAN IT, YO!
DO IT.
WHA-WHAT?
DO IT. HIT THE BUTTON-- BLOW IT ALL. WE'LL GO OUT TOGETHER.
PRESS IT.
PLE- PLEASE--
STOP. SNIVELING.
TNK

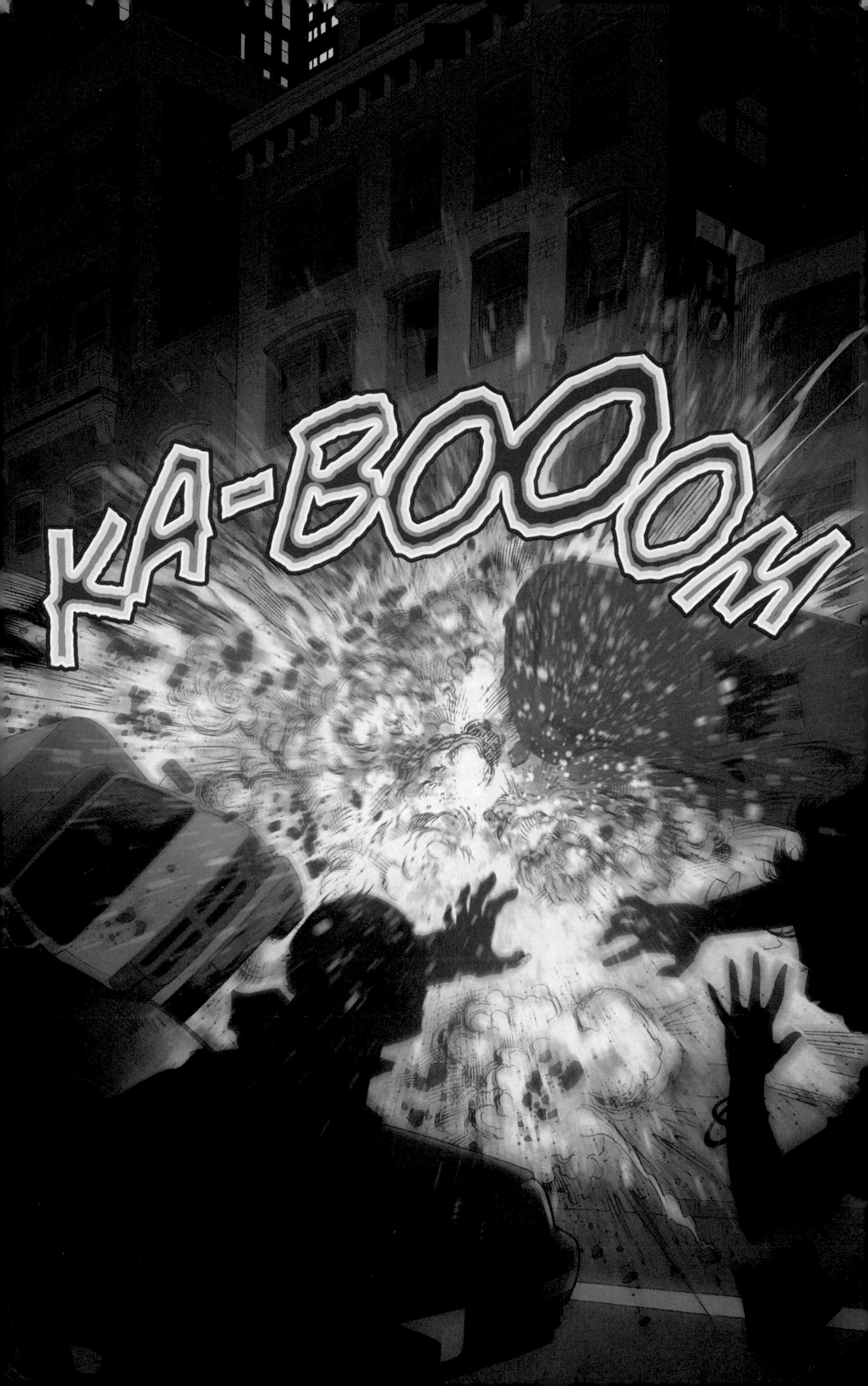
KA-BOOOM

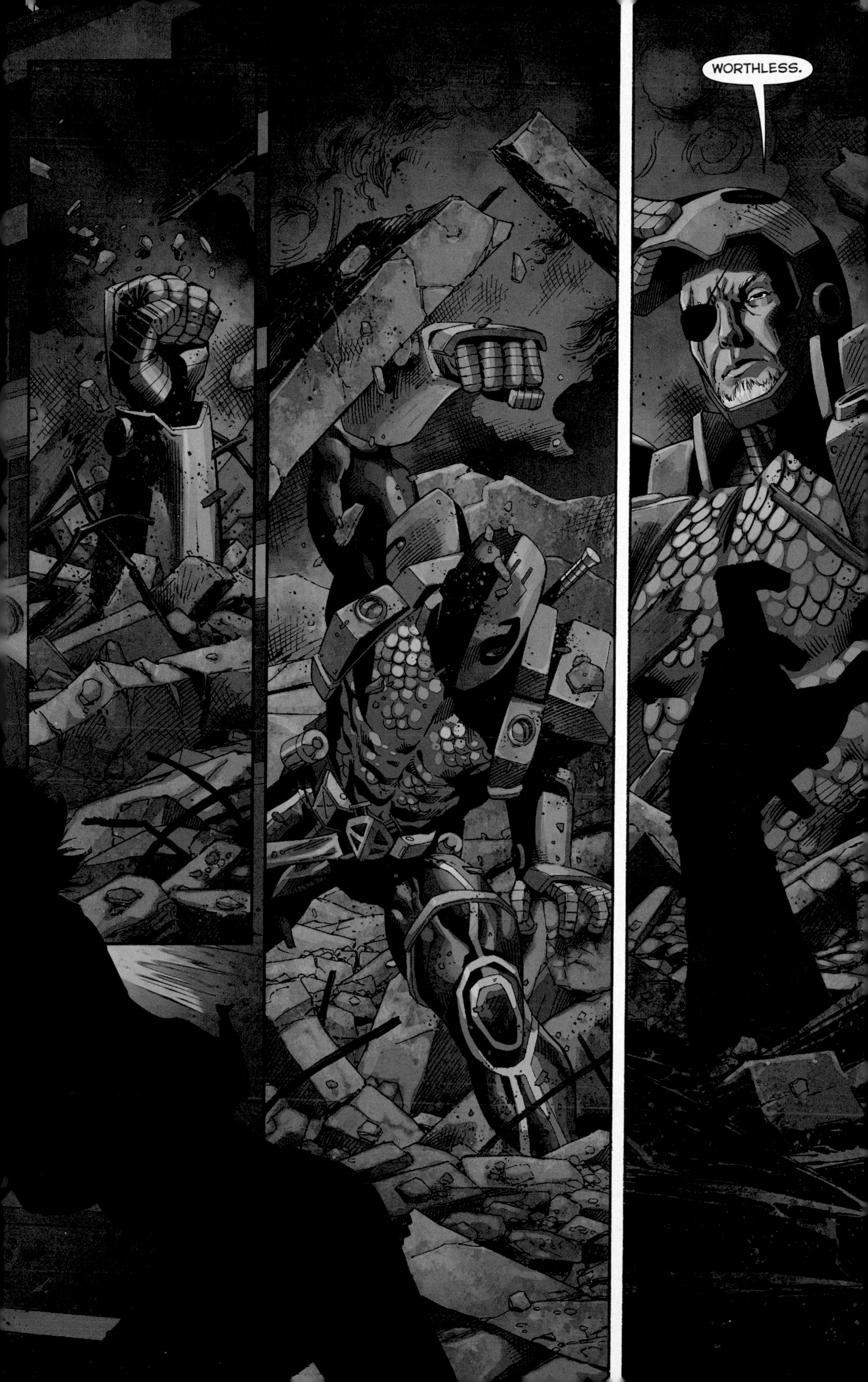
WORTHLESS.

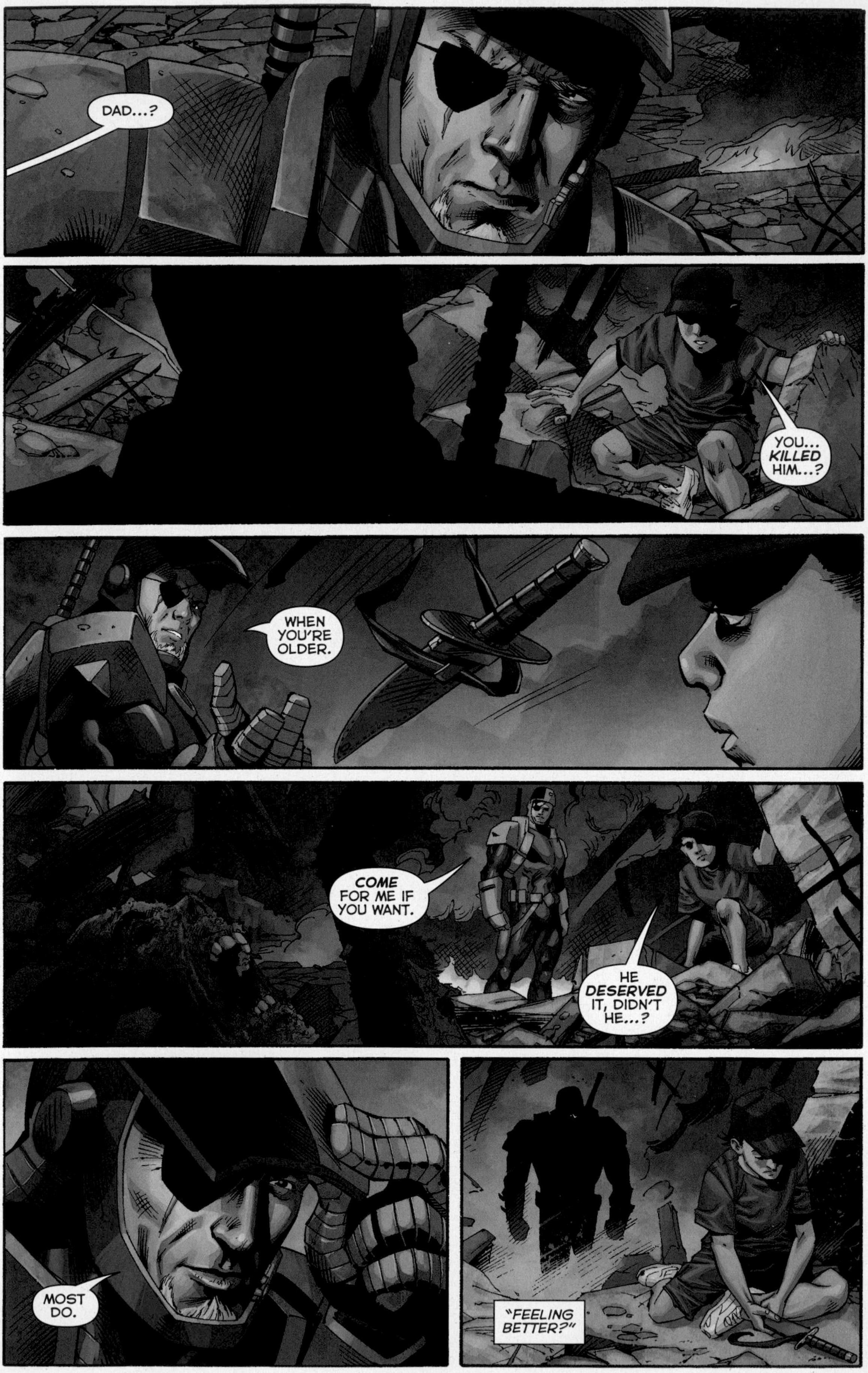
DAD...?
YOU... KILLED HIM...?
WHEN YOU'RE OLDER.
COME FOR ME IF YOU WANT.
HE DESERVED IT, DIDN'T HE...?
MOST DO.
"FEELING BETTER?"

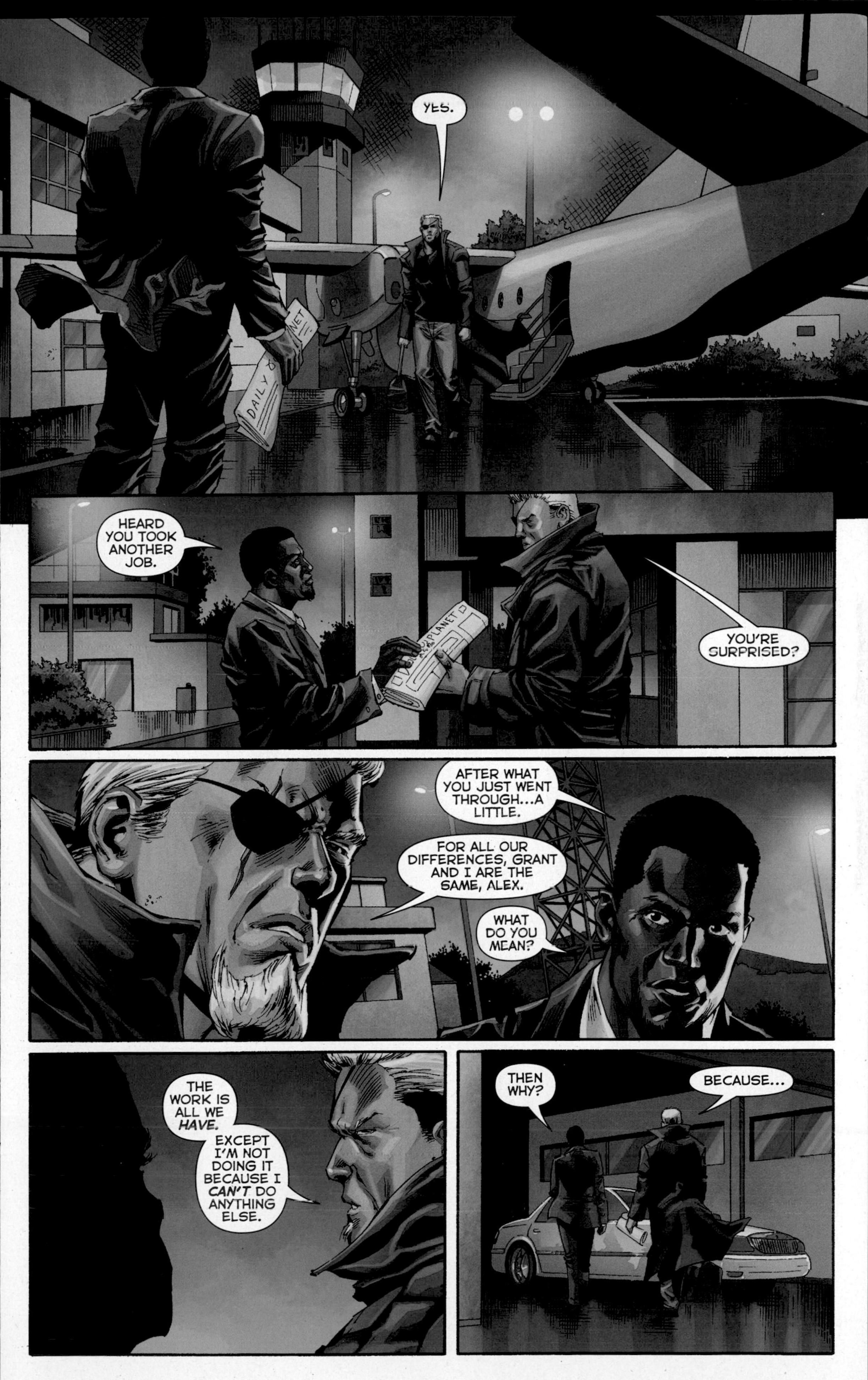
YES.
DAILY PLANET
HEARD YOU TOOK ANOTHER JOB.
YOU'RE SURPRISED?
AFTER WHAT YOU JUST WENT THROUGH...A LITTLE.
FOR ALL OUR DIFFERENCES, GRANT AND I ARE THE SAME, ALEX.
WHAT DO YOU MEAN?
THE WORK IS ALL WE *HAVE*.
EXCEPT I'M NOT DOING IT BECAUSE I *CAN'T* DO ANYTHING ELSE.
THEN WHY?
BECAUSE...

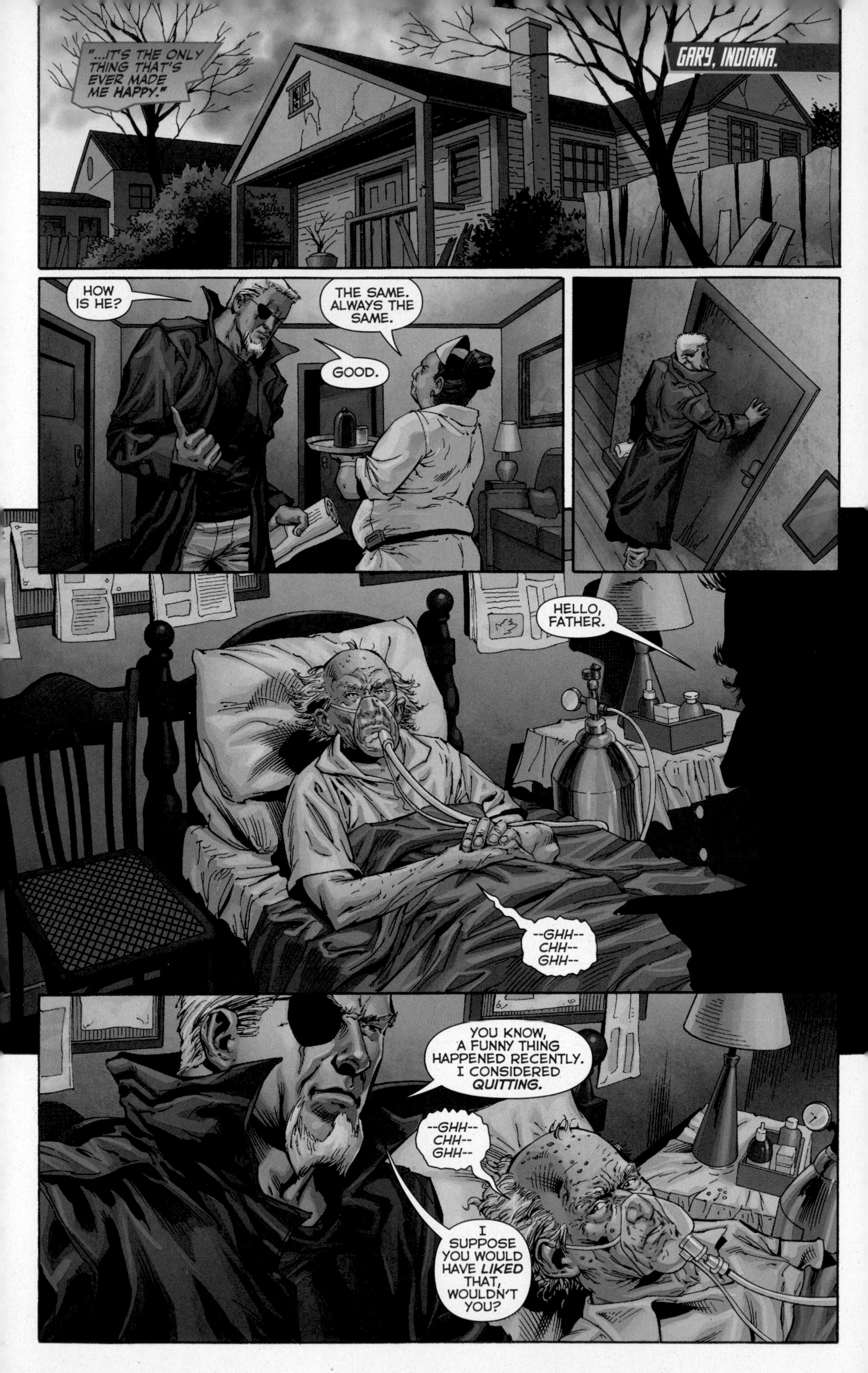
"...IT'S THE ONLY THING THAT'S EVER MADE ME HAPPY."
GARY, INDIANA.
HOW IS HE?
THE SAME. ALWAYS THE SAME.
GOOD.
HELLO, FATHER.
--GHH-- CHH-- GHH--
YOU KNOW, A FUNNY THING HAPPENED RECENTLY. I CONSIDERED QUITTING.
--GHH-- CHH-- GHH--
I SUPPOSE YOU WOULD HAVE LIKED THAT, WOULDN'T YOU?

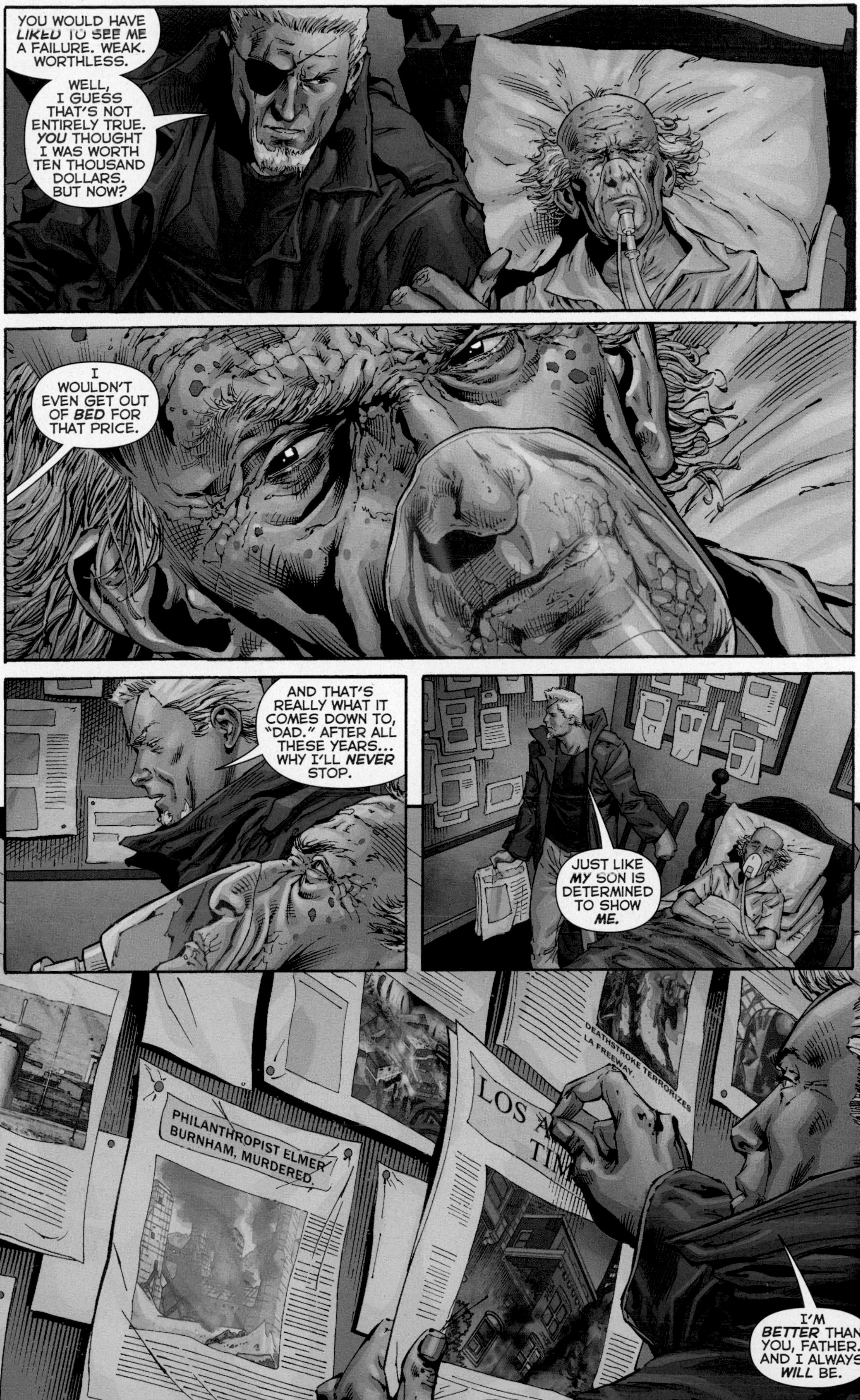
YOU WOULD HAVE LIKED TO SEE ME A FAILURE. WEAK. WORTHLESS.
WELL, I GUESS THAT'S NOT ENTIRELY TRUE. YOU THOUGHT I WAS WORTH TEN THOUSAND DOLLARS. BUT NOW?
I WOULDN'T EVEN GET OUT OF BED FOR THAT PRICE.
AND THAT'S REALLY WHAT IT COMES DOWN TO, "DAD." AFTER ALL THESE YEARS... WHY I'LL NEVER STOP.
JUST LIKE MY SON IS DETERMINED TO SHOW ME.
DEATHSTROKE TERRORIZES LA FREEWAY.
PHILANTHROPIST ELMER BURNHAM, MURDERED.
I'M BETTER THAN YOU, FATHER. AND I ALWAYS WILL BE.

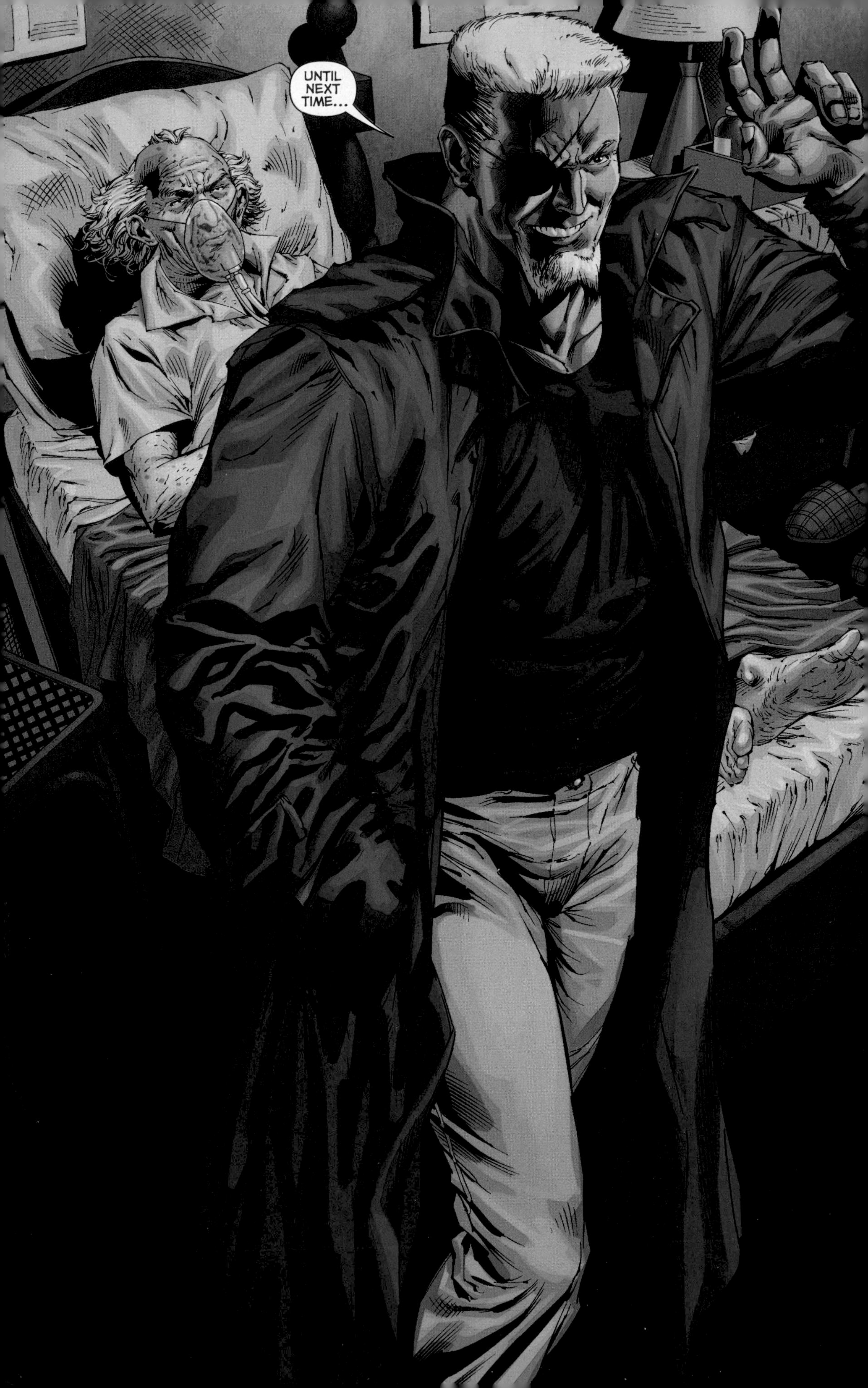
UNTIL NEXT TIME...

Design by Cully Hamner.

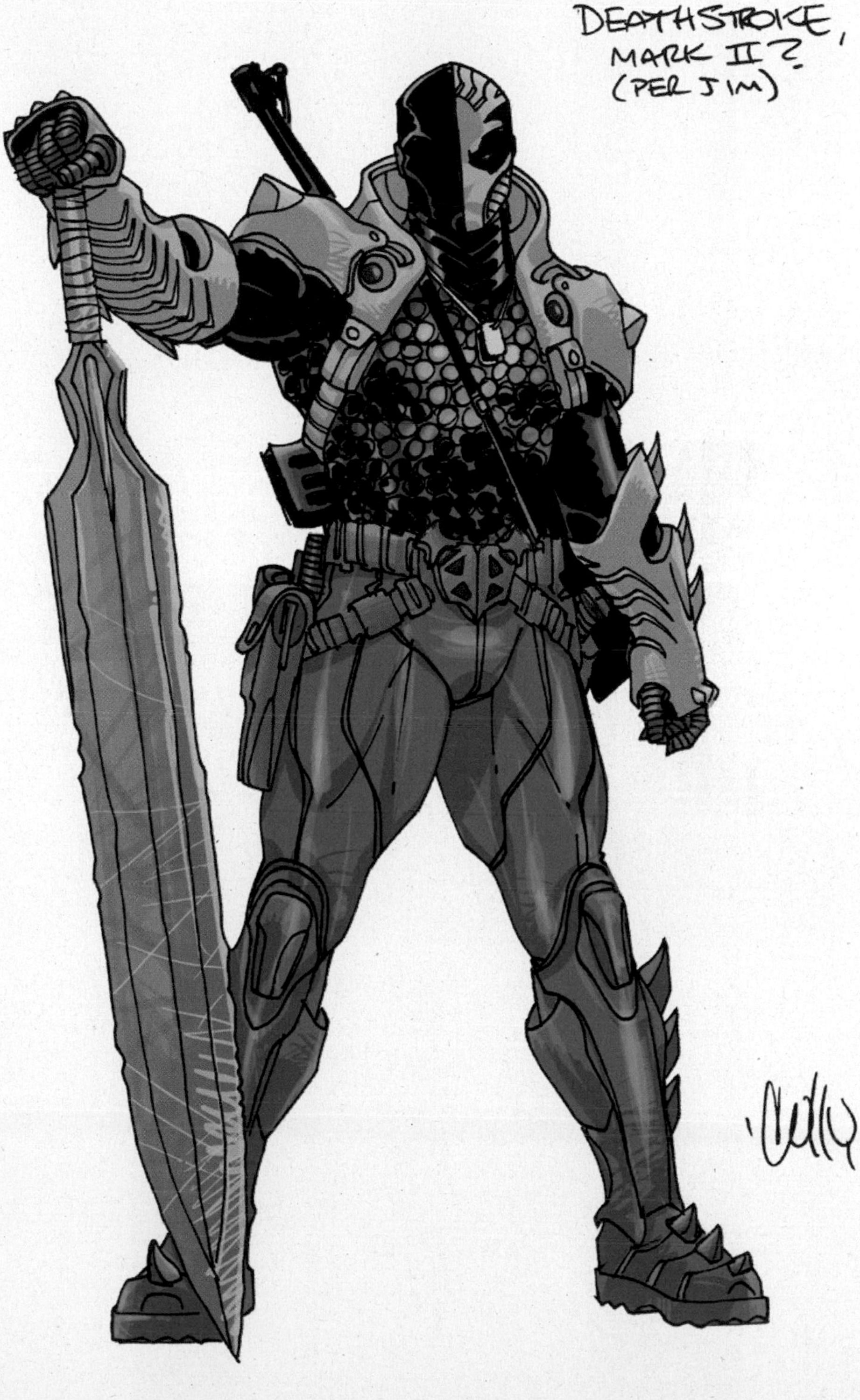
DEATHSTROKE,
MARK II?
(PER JIM)
CULLY

Designs by Jim Lee.

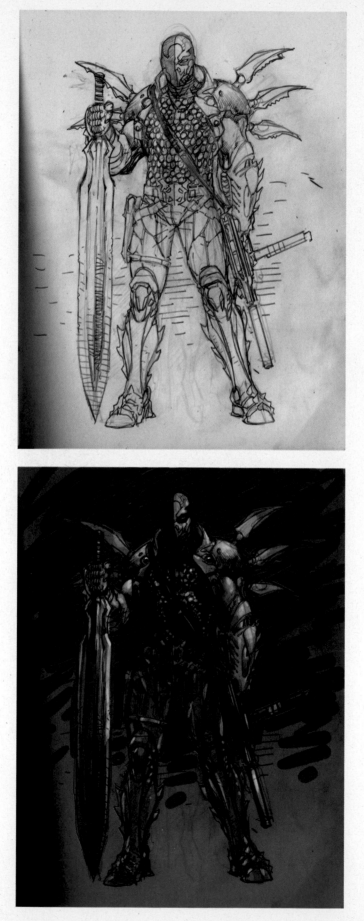

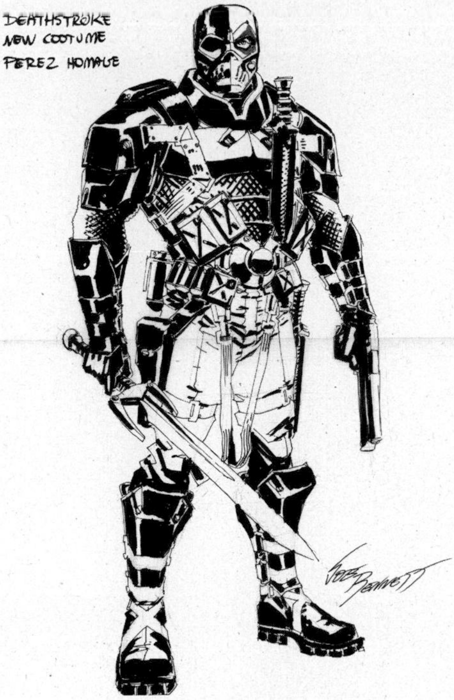
DEATHSTROKE
NEW COSTUME
PEREZ HOMAGE
JOE BENNETT

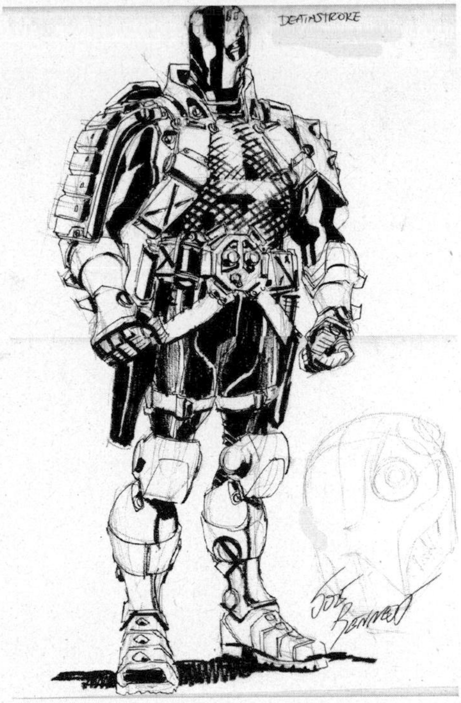
DEATHSTROKE
JOE BENNETT

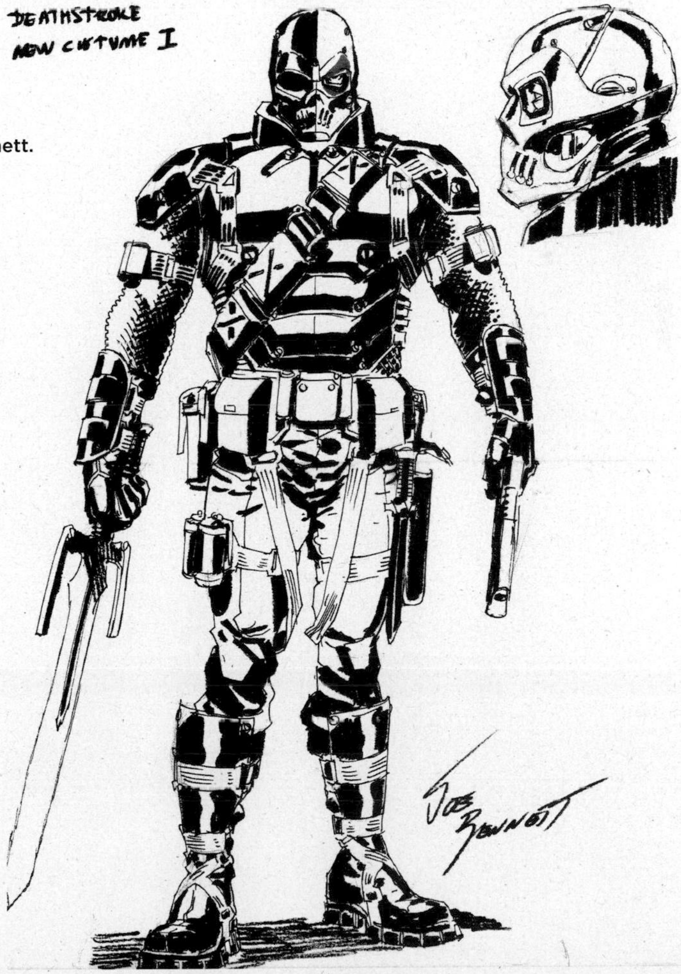
DEATHSTROKE
NEW COSTUME I
JOE BENNETT

Designs by Joe Bennett.

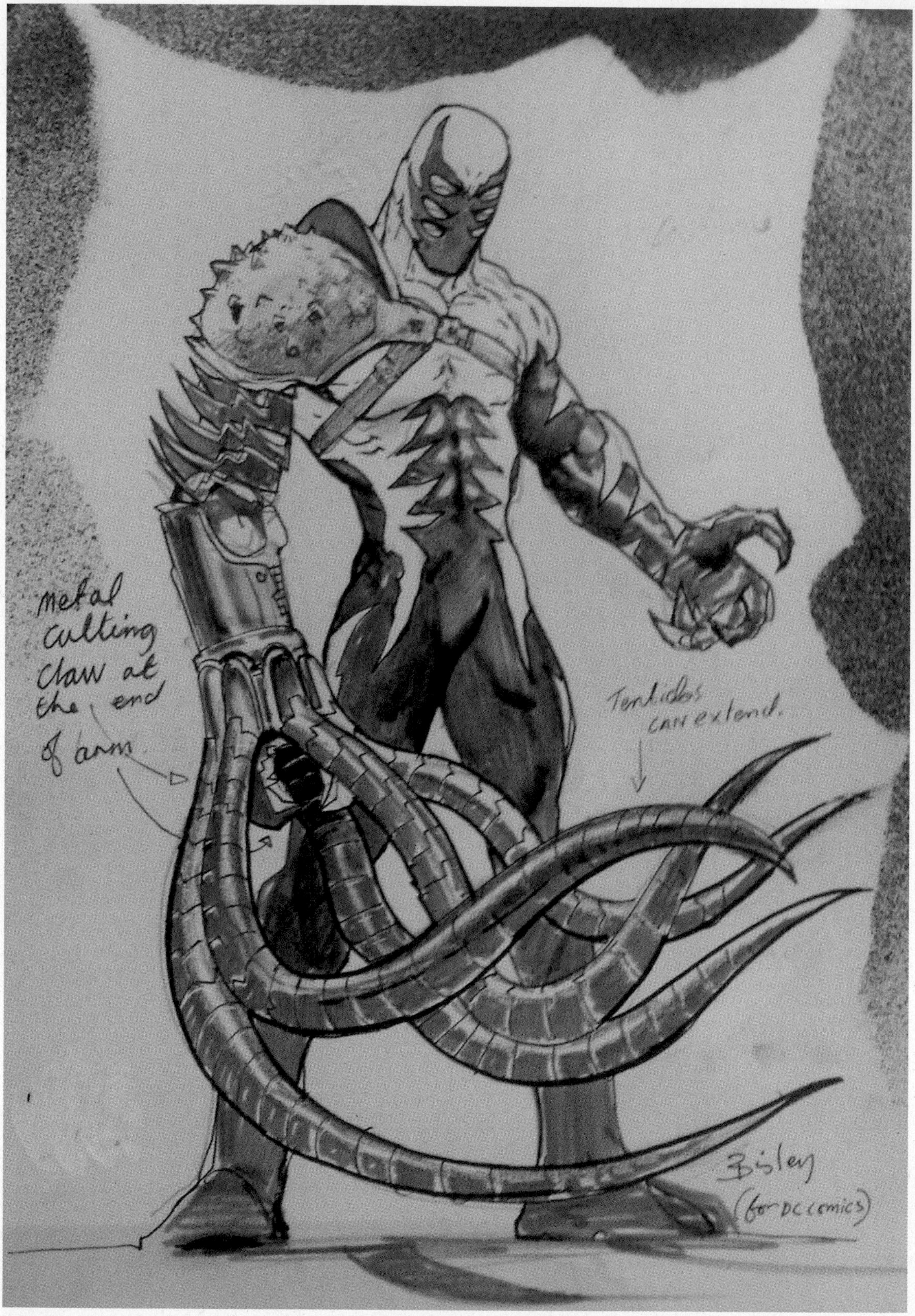
metal cutting claw at the end of arm
Tenticles can extend.
Bisley
(for DC comics)

Design by Simon Bisley.

DEATHSTROKE
COVER SKETCHES BY SIMON BISLEY

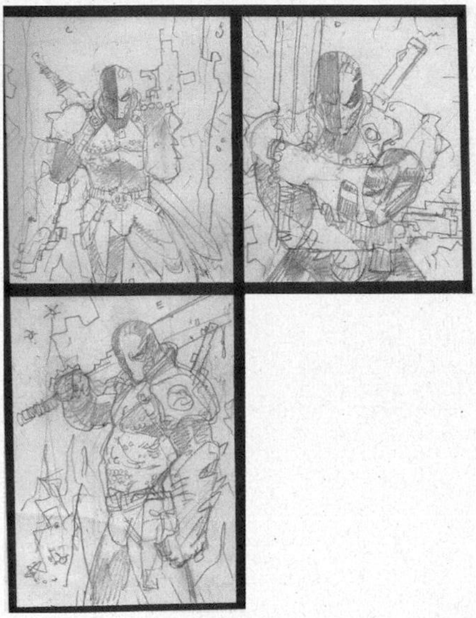

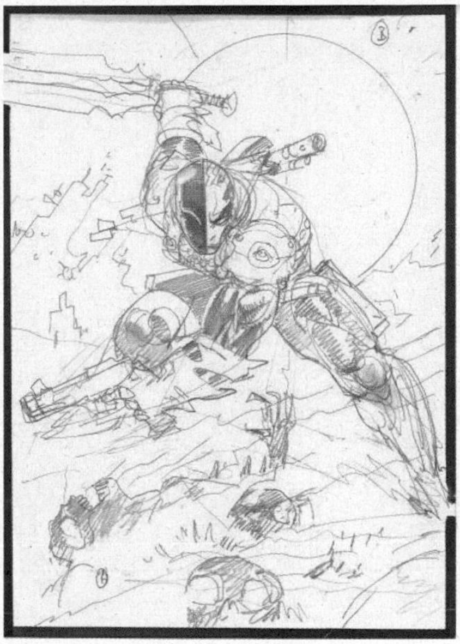

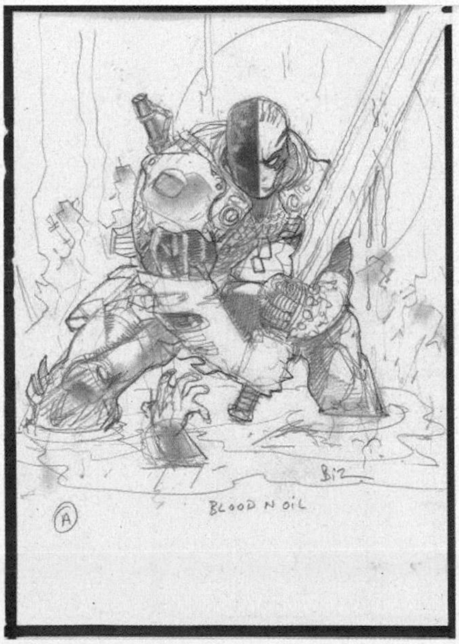
BIZ
BLOOD N OIL

RoadRage
BIZ

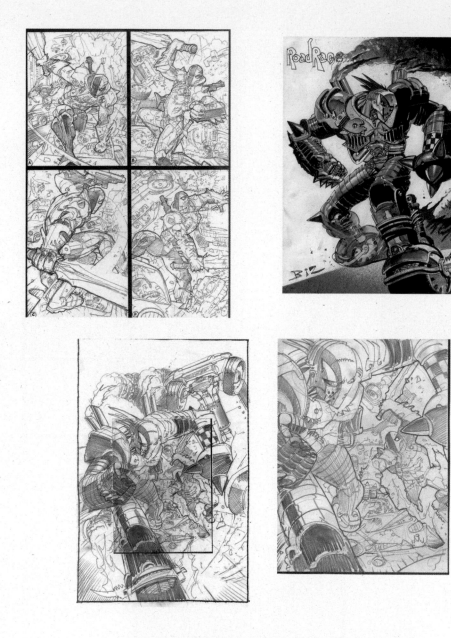

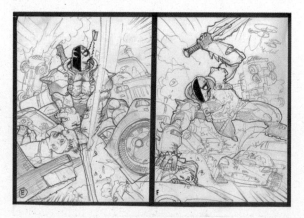

B
A
STRAIGHT JACKET
DS STRAPPED TO DEVICE

KINDA COOL
C
RIOT
POLICE
LOOKS MUCH COOLER IN MASK!!
D
Really like this one..
POLI
RIOT SQUAD

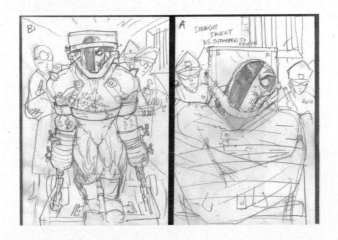

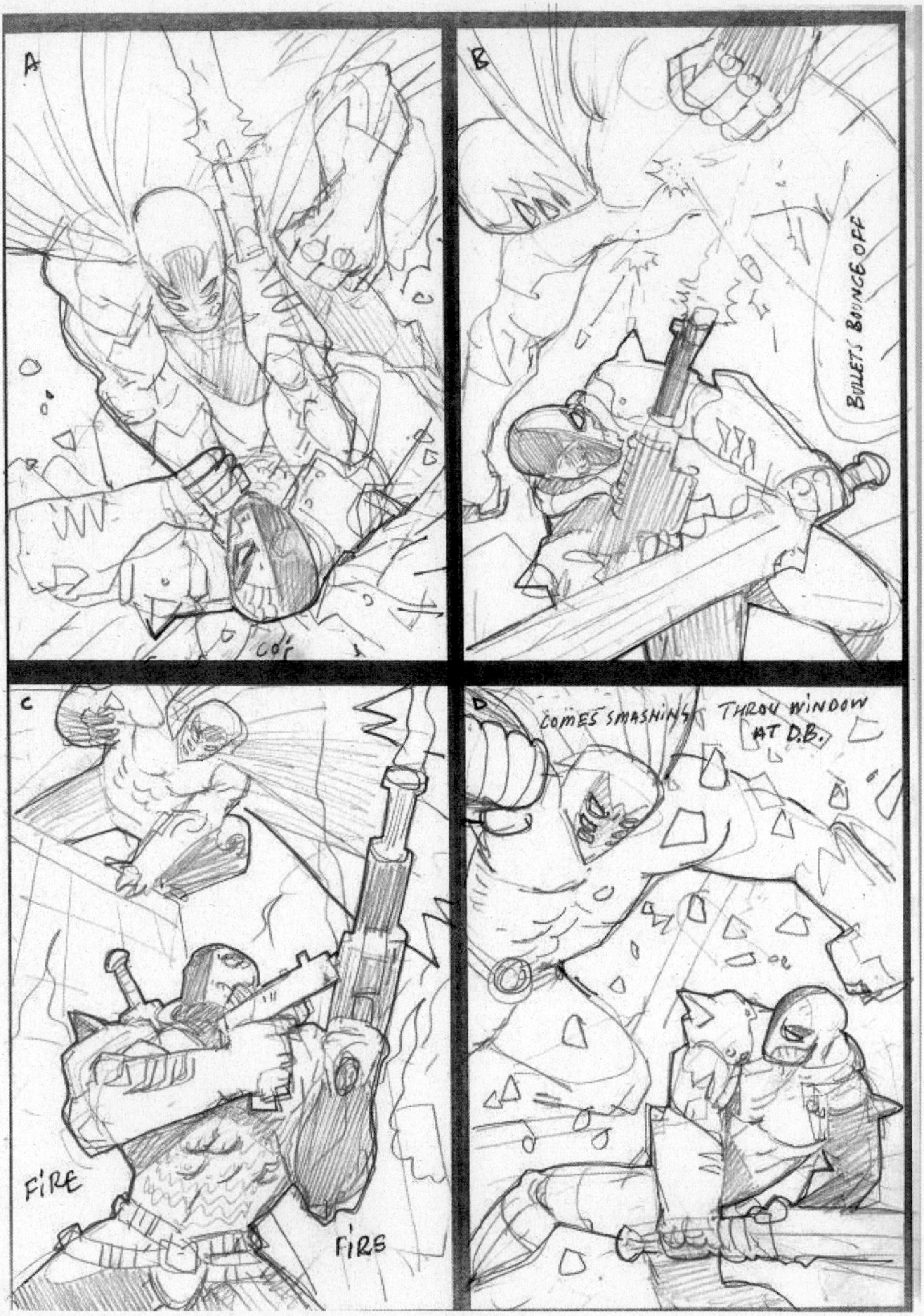
A
B
BULLETS BOUNCE OFF
C
FIRE
FIRE
D
COMES SMASHING THROU WINDOW AT D.B.

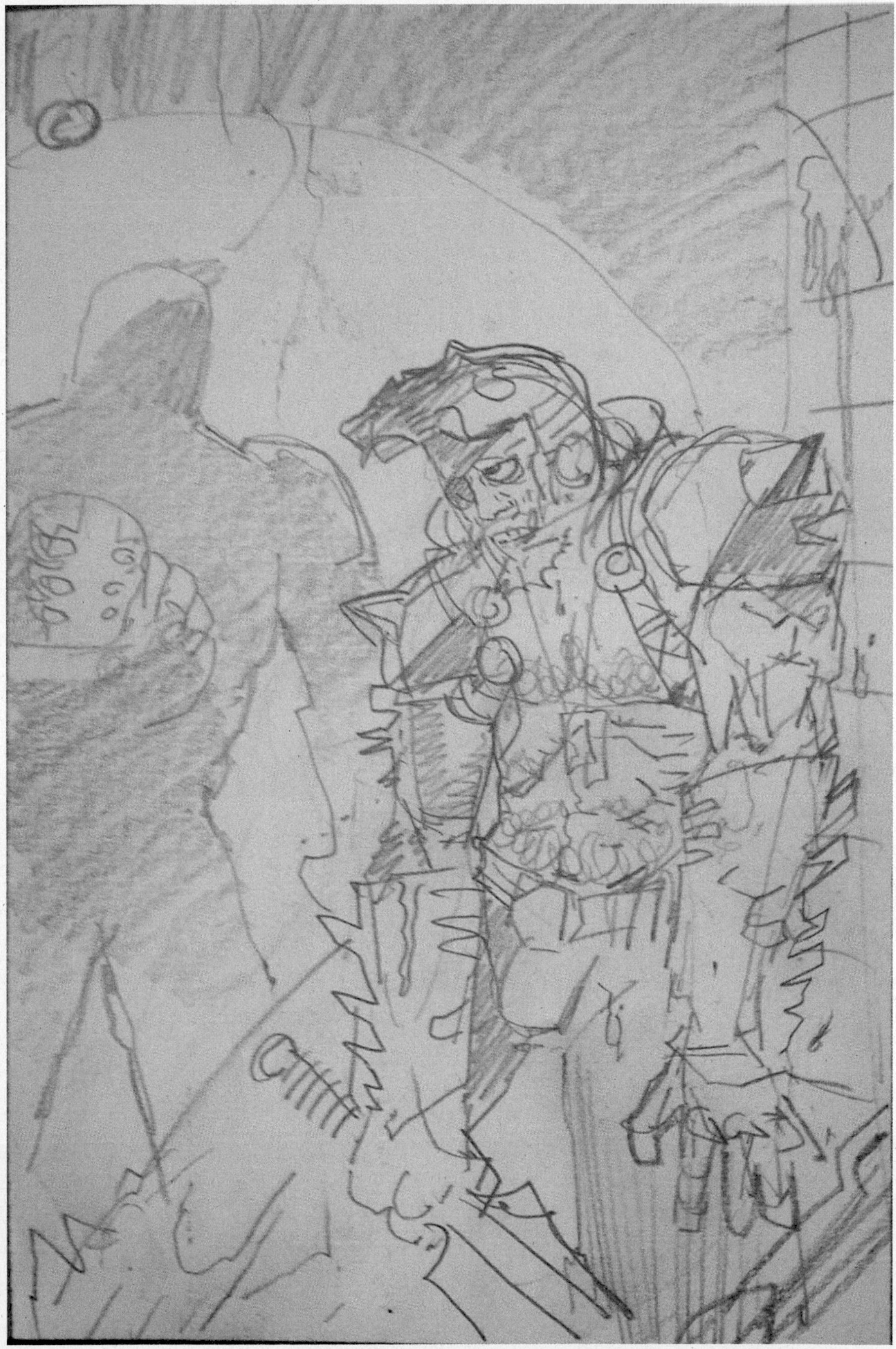

DC COMICS™

"A pretty irresistible hook. What if the good guys assembled a bunch of bad guys to work as a Dirty Dozen-like superteam and do the dirty work traditional heroes would never touch (or want to know about)?"—THE ONION/AV CLUB

START AT THE BEGINNING!

SUICIDE SQUAD
VOLUME 1: KICKED IN THE TEETH

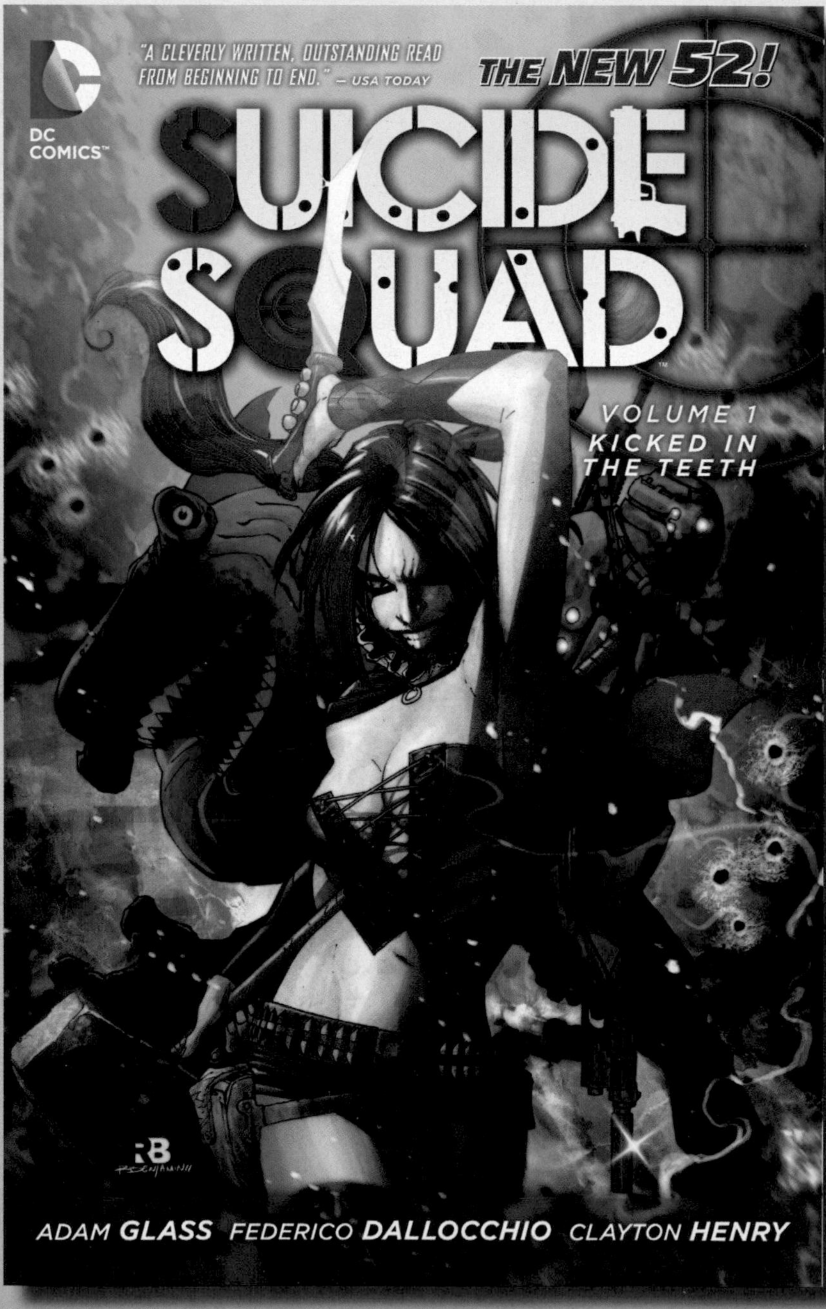
"A CLEVERLY WRITTEN, OUTSTANDING READ FROM BEGINNING TO END." – USA TODAY
THE NEW 52!
DC COMICS™
SUICIDE SQUAD
VOLUME 1 KICKED IN THE TEETH
ADAM GLASS FEDERICO DALLOCCHIO CLAYTON HENRY

SUICIDE SQUAD VOL. 2: BASILISK RISING

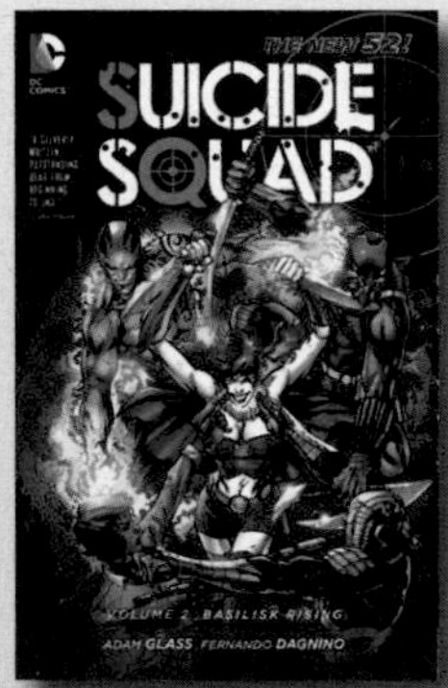
THE NEW 52!
SUICIDE SQUAD
VOLUME 2 BASILISK RISING
ADAM GLASS FERNANDO DAGNINO

SUICIDE SQUAD VOL. 3: DEATH IS FOR SUCKERS

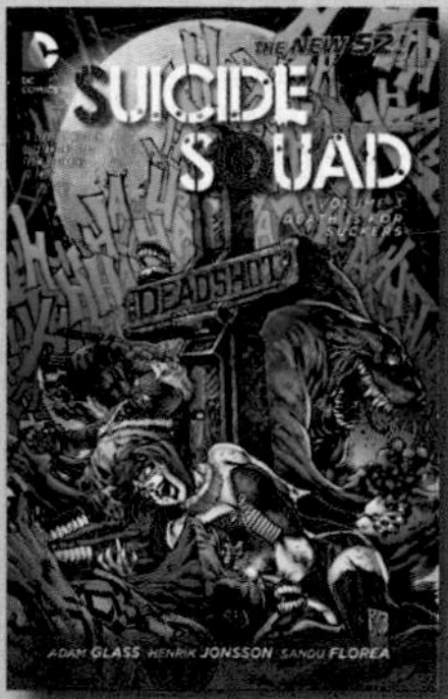
THE NEW 52!
SUICIDE SQUAD
DEADSHOT
ADAM GLASS HENRIK JONSSON SANDU FLOREA

DEATHSTROKE VOL. 1: LEGACY

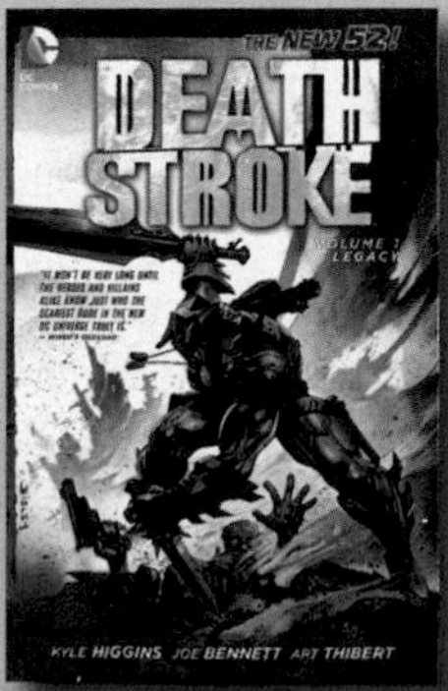
THE NEW 52!
DEATHSTROKE
VOLUME 1 LEGACY
KYLE HIGGINS JOE BENNETT ART THIBERT

HARLEY QUINN
VOLUME 1: HOT IN THE CITY

AMANDA **CONNER** · Jimmy **PALMIOTTI** · Chad **HARDIN**
STEPHANE **ROUX** · Alex **SINCLAIR** · Paul **MOUNTS**

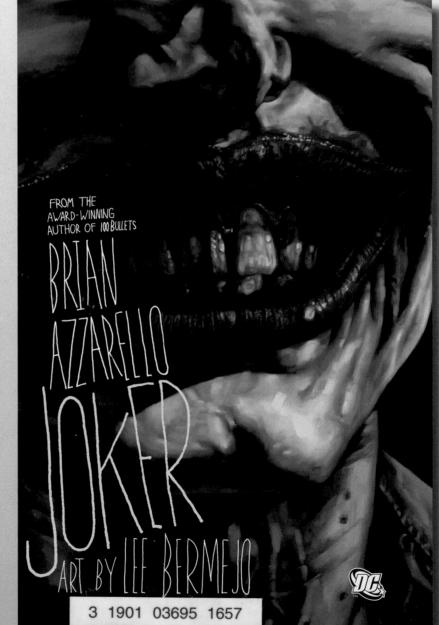